1942

1942

WINSTON CHURCHILL AND
BRITAIN'S DARKEST HOUR

TAYLOR DOWNING

PEGASUS BOOKS
NEW YORK LONDON

1942

Pegasus Books, Ltd.
148 West 37th Street, 13th Floor
New York, NY 10018

First Pegasus Books cloth edition October 2022

ISBN: 978-1-63936-232-5

10 9 8 7 6 5 4 3 2 1

Printed in the United States of America
Distributed by Simon & Schuster
www.pegasusbooks.com

Contents

List of Maps   vii

Prologue   1

1   'The Sleep of the Saved'   19

2   Happy New Year, 1942   38

3   Confidence   57

4   The Channel Dash   75

5   Imperial Collapse   92

6   'Hard Adverse War'   111

7   Shipping Perils   127

8   Grave Deterioration   140

9   Arctic Convoys   156

10   Bombing   175

11   Island Fortress   193

12   The Desert War   211

13 Global Battles 229

14 Disgrace 250

15 Censure 268

16 'Have You Not Got a Single General
Who Can Win Battles?' 284

17 From the Pyramids to the Ogre's Den 303

18 'Extreme Tension' 321

19 'The End of the Beginning' 339

Epilogue 355

Acknowledgements 371

Bibliography 375

Notes 385

Index 409

List of Maps

1:   The Arctic Convoys   162

2:   The Desert War   213

3:   The Middle East Command   237

4:   The Pacific War   240

Prologue

Just before the declaration of war in September 1939, the government introduced a host of regulations in the Emergency Powers Act that began to affect almost every aspect of the lives of the British people. Normal life was effectively closed down for the duration of the war. The economy came under centralised governmental control which covered everything from determining the output of Rolls-Royce manufacturing plants to the management of ports and harbours, from dictating what farmers grew and produced to what was supplied to the corner shop in every high street or village (self-service supermarkets were unknown in the war years and most food shopping was done by women in their local butcher's and grocery store). Companies were told what they could produce, what price they could sell their products for, and how much profit they could make.

At the beginning of the war there was panic buying on a grand scale. Anyone who could afford to hoard tinned goods, sugar or candles did so. There were stories of wealthy folk turning up in their cars and buying up almost the entire stock of small grocery shops. All of this of course hastened the introduction of food rationing, although the government hesitated at first fearing that the public would not accept centralised control and restrictions on the liberty of the individual. Every person was provided with a national identity card and a vast register was made of every street in the land listing exactly who lived where, even down to the pets people owned, so that in the event of their home being bombed rescuers would know how many people and animals they were looking for. Hospitals were emptied so that beds, even in maternity wards, could be kept free for the anticipated rush of air raid casualties. But these did not come for months. Travel was severely curtailed. Petrol was rationed at the beginning of the war but was still difficult to find for a private motorist without an official pass. Travel by railways, although theoretically possible, came to be immensely difficult as the need to move military personnel, goods and equipment became the first priority of the railway companies, causing regular cancellations and the revision of timetables. If you had to set out on a long-distance rail journey you had very little idea of how long it would take and when you would arrive. On the other hand, pubs and cinemas were open and unrationed. Pamphlets and posters everywhere told people what they could and could not do and tried to stiffen resolve and encourage cheerfulness. The whole system of do's and don'ts was policed by a vast bureaucracy of petty officials and local busybodies.

A Mass Observation diarist perfectly described one official who luxuriated in the importance of his work in the Food Office in Whitchurch, Hampshire. The diarist had to register her hens with the office on a form specially designed for this purpose, in order to obtain feed. 'His ruling principle,' she wrote of the clerk, 'seemed to be "You cannot be too careful". He would not allow us to help by filling in our own names, etc.' So the official carefully wrote out the name and address several times as required by different pages of the hen form, each time checking it with the preceding name and address to ensure correctness. 'Eventually he was satisfied with his copying and put down his pen and picked up a red pencil.'

He then marked in red every page that needed to be approved. 'Putting down his pencil, he picked up a rubber stamp and pressed it on the egg page.' He then produced a razor blade and slowly cut out the counterfoils that needed removing. Only then did he seem happy with his important work. All of this should have taken just a couple of minutes. But 'each applicant was waiting with more or less patience for about 20 minutes for his work to be finished to his satisfaction'. The diarist concluded: 'I waited in all about one and a half hours. I am told that afternoon callers who arrived at 2 or after were not seen at all as the office closed at 3 p.m. punctually.'[1] Sadly there were no doubt thousands of such self-important officials across the land. But, broadly speaking, Britons accepted the need for regulations and controls, and adhered to them.

In the early stages of the war, the government was criticised firstly for not making sufficient preparations beforehand to supply all that would be necessary for, for instance, blackout curtains, sandbags and gas mask containers. Secondly, the government was criticised for its dithering. It would announce a new restriction and then when it proved unpopular it would withdraw or amend the restriction. Cinemas and sports venues were closed at the start of the war and then reopened again after a couple of weeks when it was realised what a disastrous effect this had on morale. Shops were ordered to shut well before the blackout and then it was announced they could stay open later. Hotels were commandeered for government departments to evacuate to and long-term residents were thrown out. Then the government officials moved somewhere else and the residents were allowed to return. The beginning of a national emergency was going to be a difficult time for any government, but it seemed particularly problematic for Neville Chamberlain's administration.[2]

Food rationing was not introduced until January 1940 but immediately it helped stabilise the process of shopping which in the first months of the war had been chaotic. Everyone was issued with a ration book and had to register with local retailers. Shop owners could then calculate how much of every rationed product they needed and everyone was assured of the supply of basics. According to the polls carried out at the time, most people thought the system, which supposedly applied equally to dukes and to dockers, was fair and reasonable.

In addition to the ration, people were encouraged to grow whatever they could for themselves. Gardens and parks across the country sprouted potato plants, cabbages, frames for runner beans and a variety of other fruit and vegetables. The number of allotments soared. Pig clubs were started up wherever there was an opportunity to keep a pig. And of course a black market soon developed, usually on a modest local scale although some big city networks were run by criminal gangs. Rogue traders and 'spivs' could supply almost anything, at a price. And favouritism among shop owners led to the phrase 'under the counter' becoming regularly used both as a term of endearment and gratitude, for those who benefited from something special being kept for them, and an expression of anger and resentment, for those who did not profit from such favours.[3]

During the 1930s planners had become terrified by the prospect of the bombing of civilian centres. Prime Minister Stanley Baldwin had used the phrase 'the bomber will always get through', and there was universal fear that bombing would cause a massive loss of life and a likely collapse in civilian morale. To try to mitigate this, a nationwide blackout was ordered from the first day of war. At sunset the entire country was plunged into darkness, or at least that was the idea. Lights, it was believed, could help guide enemy bombers to their targets. So, no light was to leak out from any home, office or shop. Householders and shopkeepers had to go around their property every evening putting up specially made blackout curtains over every window, a laborious ritual. In some large offices this chore had to start mid-afternoon to be ready for the blackout. All street lights and illuminated signs were to be extinguished. Cars, buses, trains and trams had to mask their headlights and cover any interior lights. All of this was enforced by an army of local air raid precaution (ARP) wardens. The admonition shouted by an enraged warden, 'Put that light out!', was heard in every town and city of Britain. Some of these wardens were volunteers, genuinely fired up by the desire to do their bit for the community. Others were officious, bullying jobsworths who enjoyed exercising their authority over neighbours. Anyone in breach of the regulations could be fined by the police. Tens of thousands were.

As a blanket of blackness descended across the country from sunset to dawn, people fell down their stairs, walked into street lights or pillar-boxes, and were hit by cars and buses. Over 4,000 people were killed in road accidents in the first four months of war. Deaths on the road doubled in 1940. For the first six months of war it was more dangerous to be on the roads of Britain than in the armed forces.[4] Hundreds of thousands were injured in domestic accidents. Life in cities was transformed. As one observer noted, 'when the bright lights of a city are turned off, bright life is turned off too'. People were reluctant to go out of an evening. Those living alone, a smaller proportion of the population in the 1940s than today, were particularly affected. Many people reported feeling lonely, tired, and said they were suffering from low spirits. The war brought a fear of random death, terrible injury or the destruction of one's home and possessions from aerial bombing. The blackout seemed to emphasise this. There was then no way of measuring the impact of the blackout and the uncertainty that came with war on mental health, but there were many reports of people feeling depressed. The word 'blackout' almost became synonymous with 'shut down'.[5]

Those who faithfully conformed to all the regulations were deeply resentful of those who seemed to be lax in letting a chink of light escape, thus invalidating all their efforts. The consequence of an enemy bomber identifying a target through lights from the ground was potentially a stick of bombs on your street. One correspondent to *The Times* complained that from the roof garden of his West End house he could look over the suburbs of London and spot top-floor lights, difficult to detect from the ground, which 'could be seen for miles from an approaching aeroplane and would therefore nullify the effect of the blackout'.[6]

The irony of all the dislocation caused by the blackout was that during the Blitz the Luftwaffe bomber crews, often flying at between 15,000 and 20,000 feet, never bothered to look down for stray lights. Instead they were guided straight to their objectives by sophisticated networks of high-frequency, short-wavelength beams with names like Knickebein and X-Geraet. These were transmitted from their bases in northern France forming a grid that helped the aircraft locate their targets precisely, sometimes to within 100 yards. The way to prevent them finding their targets was not by blacking out the countryside below but for scientists to discover ways of jamming or distorting the signals in a struggle that became known as the 'Battle of the Beams'.[7]

Most middle-class homes in 1930s Britain had access to some form of domestic labour, although the numbers in full-time service had declined markedly since the First World War. Nevertheless, most domestic servants soon went into war work and many wealthy Britons had to learn to live with the new realities of war. The ladies of the house had to discover how to cook meals for their families, to wash their clothes and answer their own front doors. Evenings for many women were taken up with knitting, darning or repairing worn clothing. For many working-class men, the pub was still a haven. Sitting at home reading books or newspapers, or doing the football pools, also become commonplace. Listening to BBC radio was by far the biggest form of domestic entertainment. Nine out of ten households possessed what was still commonly called a 'wireless' set. The middle classes preferred the Home Service, primarily a speech-based station. Younger people, those living away from home in hostels or in barracks, preferred the lighter and more music-based Forces Programme. This had been created specifically to entertain those in the military but was soon popular across the nation. For whole families, listening to BBC radio and especially to the *Nine O'Clock News* on the Home Service became an essential ritual. About two out of every three adults in the country, approximately 23 million people, listened to the BBC news every evening.[8]

From 1940 the Limitation of Supplies Order banned the manufacture of all 'non-essential' items. Factories turned over from producing prams to trucks, from electric radios to radar, from cars to military aircraft. Products like cooking pans, crockery, glass dishes and pottery, and white goods such as refrigerators, vacuum cleaners and washing machines, remained almost impossible to get hold of as industry was mobilised for the production of goods needed to fight the war. In one typical cartoon, a woman asks a shopgirl standing before a row of empty shelves, 'Is this haberdashery?' The girl answers, 'No, it's over there,' and points to another completely bare counter.[9]

With a Conservative majority of 213 seats, Chamberlain was almost unassailable as Prime Minister. But there was growing hostility to his lacklustre pursuit of the war. Hundreds of thousands of children had been urgently evacuated at the beginning of September 1939 but when the predicted Nazi bombs failed to fall most of them had been brought home by anxious parents. The spring of 1940 was unusually warm, and as people took holidays or relaxed at home, life seemed to carry on as normal regardless of what was then called the Bore War, but later came to be remembered as the Phoney War. The Cabinet decided not to seize the offensive by bombing German industry or military installations, in case it provoked Hitler into reprisal raids on Britain. And the Secretary for the Air Sir Kingsley Wood pointed out that bombing the Ruhr industrial zone would involve bombing private property, and that would never do.[10] In a statement full of complacency and misunderstanding, Chamberlain told the House on 4 April that time was on Britain's side and he was now ten times more confident of victory than he had been at the start of the war. In a disastrous phrase, he claimed that Hitler had 'missed the bus' in failing to pursue the war against Britain and France.

The following week, Hitler invaded Norway. A defence was mounted by the British and French which turned into a fiasco. British troops were landed without artillery, anti-aircraft weapons and essential supplies. The Royal Navy failed to coordinate with the RAF and suffered severe losses including that of the aircraft carrier HMS *Glorious*. The Chief of the Imperial General Staff General Edmund Ironside chafed at the lack of clear direction of the campaign by his political masters. 'Always too late. Changing plans and nobody directing,' he complained in his diary. 'Very upset at the thought of our incompetence.'[11] This was clearly no way to run a war.

In early May, the Commons Vote of Adjournment for the Whitsun recess became the opportunity to mobilise opposition to the government's handling of the war. There were various groups of Tory rebels who had decided change was needed at the top. One group led by the Tory grandee Lord Salisbury decided Chamberlain had to go and that a truly national coalition government was needed. Another group of backbenchers led by Leo Amery had also decided by early May that Chamberlain had to be removed. And a separate group made up of younger members of the party such as

Harold Macmillan and Bob Boothby, known as the 'Glamour Boys', had also decided that change was essential and must start at the top. But none of these groups had a coordinated view on who should replace Chamberlain. Some members thought that Churchill was the obvious candidate. He had been famously and consistently opposed to appeasement. He had a passion for military affairs and had spent years writing military history, and in many people's minds was associated with pursuing a more rigorous war policy. But others were hostile to Churchill and saw him as an opportunist and a warmonger. His selection was far from inevitable.

The adjournment vote effectively became a motion of no-confidence in Chamberlain's government. Everywhere the Prime Minister's support seemed to be crumbling, and when on 8 May the tellers read out the results, thirty-three Conservatives had voted against their government and sixty had abstained. Chamberlain's majority was reduced from well over 200 to just eighty-one. It was a major humiliation. The formation of a national coalition to take over the running of the war seemed inevitable. The following day, the Labour Party confirmed that they would not support a coalition led by Chamberlain. It was the fatal blow. At a meeting in the Cabinet Room that afternoon Chamberlain agreed to stand down and suggested that Lord Halifax, the Foreign Secretary, should replace him. He was urbane, aristocratic, a great Yorkshire landowner, known for his sound judgement, a natural leader. The other candidate, Winston Churchill, was impetuous, unpredictable and difficult. In his diary, Halifax describes how a terrible pain grew in the pit of his stomach. He was literally almost sick with fear at the thought of taking over leadership of the nation at this critical juncture. Halifax had no real knowledge of military affairs and knew he was not the right man for the daunting task now on offer. He certainly realised that he would soon be overshadowed by Churchill. It was, in his mind, an impossible situation. Halifax agreed to stand aside. It would have to be Churchill.[12]

Still Chamberlain hesitated and did not go to the Palace to resign that evening. Churchill had a quiet dinner with friends and when his son, Randolph, called him for an update, Winston replied, 'I think I shall be Prime Minister tomorrow.'[13]

The following morning, 10 May, Hitler launched his invasion of Belgium and the Netherlands. Airborne troops seized key sites and within hours the German advance was rolling rapidly forward. The Phoney War was over. The battle for survival had begun. Although Chamberlain now argued that it was not the time to change the nation's leadership, and the Conservative government should continue, wiser counsels advised that he had to stand down. At a time of major crisis a National Government, a coalition, was needed. In accordance with tradition, Chamberlain went to the Palace to resign. King George VI, like most of the Establishment – that is, the Conservative Party, the senior figures in the civil service and *The Times* newspaper – thought Halifax was the 'obvious man' to replace Chamberlain. But Chamberlain said Halifax had ruled himself out. The King was disappointed but later noted in his diary that only 'one person' was left who would have the confidence of the country 'and that was Winston'.[14] Churchill was called to the Palace and soon after six o'clock that evening was appointed Prime Minister. At that moment, two million German, French, Belgian, Dutch and British troops were fighting for the future of western Europe. Most men would have been daunted or overwhelmed by the task ahead of them. But Churchill later wrote that he felt a profound sense of relief that at last he had the authority to direct the war effort. He wrote momentously that he felt his entire past life had been 'a preparation for this hour and for this trial'. He felt, in his famous phrase, that he was now 'walking with destiny'.[15]

Churchill gives his famous V-for-Victory sign in Downing Street.
As an optimist, Churchill always believed in victory, especially
so after Pearl Harbor brought America into the war.

Churchill began to bring about a revolution in government. At the centre of his new administration was the War Cabinet that initially consisted of only five members (although later in the war it grew in size). Churchill as Prime Minister also appointed himself Minister of Defence. There was no precedent for this. It gave him unique authority to oversee all matters of military policy. His joint role put him in total control of Britain's military effort. There was virtually no aspect of war administration he could not influence. And this would be a vital feature of his leadership.

Showing no malice, Churchill appointed his predecessor, Neville Chamberlain, as Lord President of the Council – even though for years Chamberlain had derided his warnings of the threat posed by Hitler and had tried everything he could to keep him out of Downing Street. But this was not just an act of perverse generosity. Chamberlain was still leader of the Conservative Party and Churchill at this point in time was an unpopular figure in the party. He was thought to be reckless, irresponsible and ambitious. Although he had opposed appeasement for years, he had lost a lot of support in the party by favouring Edward VIII at the time of his abdication and as a result of his campaign against the India bill, which offered Indians a limited amount of self-government. Churchill knew that he could not govern without Chamberlain's support. It was an astute political appointment. On 13 May, when Churchill made his first speech in the Commons as PM proclaiming 'I have nothing to offer but blood, toil, tears and sweat', the only cheering was from the Labour members. The Conservative benches remained silent.

As this was a national *coalition*, the leader of the Labour Party Clement Attlee was appointed Lord Privy Seal. Lord Halifax as Foreign Secretary was included, and the fifth member was Arthur Greenwood, the deputy Labour leader.

The War Cabinet met every day for the first months of Churchill's premiership. Usually in attendance too were the three service chiefs, the men who ran the Royal Navy, the British Army and the Royal Air Force. The chiefs of staff formed a sort of war room headquarters. They met every morning, and at times of extreme crisis often more than once a day. Around the chiefs were a variety of committees who fed them all the information they needed on matters of intelligence, on strategic planning, and on the logistics needed to achieve war aims. Everything was streamlined to focus information and detail so that the chiefs of staff and the War Cabinet could concentrate on making the key strategic decisions and those lower down the chain could devote themselves to achieving the tactical tasks necessary. The man who acted as liaison between Churchill and the chiefs of staff was Major-General Sir Hastings Ismay. He and Churchill met daily, and Ismay nearly always travelled with the Prime Minister when he was abroad. Churchill called Ismay his *éminence khaki*. He became a faithful supporter and confidant of Churchill and was one of the few who came into post in May 1940 and stayed with Churchill for five long and immensely challenging years. They had a good relationship, sometimes strained, but enduring. Churchill's affectionate nickname for Ismay was 'Pug'.

Churchill brought an immense, restless energy to the top of government that it had definitely lacked under Chamberlain. As all management training makes clear today, change needs to start at the top. The chief executive has to be the model and to set the pace. From Churchill's desk flowed a stream of minutes, instructions, requests, exhortations and diktats unprecedented in the government of Britain. At no point in the Second World War was there anything comparable – from Stalin in the Kremlin, or from Roosevelt in the White House. Over the next few weeks and months Churchill was to enquire about and instruct on an enormously wide range of issues. What progress is being made with rockets? with the development of sensitive fuses? with bombsights and with radio detection finding? Can Turin and Milan be bombed from England? Can more trees be felled to reduce the reliance on imports and to save shipping? Can regular troops be moved from India? Can a better reserve be built up in the Middle East? How are the coastal watches and coastal batteries being organised? How are harbour defences being

built up? Sometimes he would attach a red sticker to a memo
marked 'Action This Day'. And with Churchill's personal style
of leadership, no detail was too small to escape his attention
or interest. Observers reported seeing staid civil servants *running* from office to office in their hurry to answer questions.
Another described a searchlight roaming across government,
at any one moment likely to stop on your desk and bring you
under the spotlight. Many people claimed that the whole pace
of government speeded up under Churchill's leadership.[16]

On the other hand, there was much criticism of Churchill
for generating an excessive amount of extra work for busy
officials. One senior figure in the War Office said he needed
two separate staffs, 'one to deal with the Prime Minister, the
other with the war'.[17] Additionally, Churchill was not popular
for calling meetings of the chiefs of staff late at night, often
at 11 p.m. The Prime Minister enjoyed a few hours of sleep
most afternoons. He was fresh come the evening. His military
chiefs did not enjoy such luxury and were often exhausted
before being called on to make crucial strategic decisions. It
was Churchill's way of turning the war from a 9-to-5 affair
into a 24/7 operation. But whether he got the best out of his
generals, admirals and air marshals at this late hour is doubtful. After one particularly tense and difficult meeting, at
2 a.m. Churchill offered his First Sea Lord a whisky and soda.
'I never drink spirits in the morning,' said Dudley Pound, 'I'll
have a glass of port.'[18]

The pace of events over the next few weeks and the collapse of France astonished everyone. France had stood up to
German invasion and occupation of part of its territory for
nearly four and a half years from 1914 to 1918. But six weeks
after the invasion in 1940 it surrendered and signed a treaty
with Hitler. Britons then saw themselves as standing alone
against the might of a determined and ferocious foe who in a
matter of months had defeated and occupied Poland, Norway,

Denmark, Belgium, Luxembourg, the Netherlands and France. Of course Britain had its vast empire behind it, with considerable support from Canada, India, Australia, New Zealand and South Africa. But to many it felt like the nation was indeed standing alone on the edge of Europe.

This story and the impact of Churchill's great speeches at the time are well known. After the Battle of France had been lost and the Battle of Britain was about to begin, Churchill told the British people that we would 'fight them on the beaches' and 'never surrender'. As the RAF battled it out with the Luftwaffe in the skies above southern England, Churchill claimed, 'Never in the field of human conflict was so much owed by so many to so few.' The words stuck as a permanent tribute to the Spitfire and Hurricane pilots of Fighter Command. Churchill framed the conflict in epic terms as one between good and evil, light and darkness, civilisation and barbarism. He had a strong sense of England's history and of what he saw as its destiny to come to the aid of Europe when a tyrant threatened to overwhelm the continent – whether it was Louis XIV, Napoleon or Hitler. Without doubt, these speeches helped to inspire the nation to fight on, when invasion seemed certain and defeat looked highly likely.[19]

The Prime Minister had to provide leadership, guidance and encouragement and ensure that the people of Britain never lost the will to fight on. This he did in magnificent form, and several commentators said that each of his major speeches was akin to adding another battleship to the British arsenal. The great American journalist Ed Murrow, who reported from London at the time, summed it up when he said that Churchill 'mobilized the English language and sent it into battle'.[20] A September 1940 Gallup poll reported an extraordinarily high 88 per cent approval rating.[21]

All of this helped create several myths about the year of national crisis. The traditional view was that the nation came

together in the face of the emergency and the threat of invasion, that divisions of class, status and region were all put
on one side in a magnificent display of national solidarity.
'We was all one' as the phrase had it. The people endured the
strains of bombing, civilian deaths and physical destruction
of vast stretches of many cities with fortitude, resolution and
cheerfulness. This was the version the government wanted
people to believe at the time and it was repeated in some of
the official histories of the war soon after it was over.[22] This
interpretation of events was repeated right down to the
mid-1960s when A. J. P. Taylor wrote in *The Oxford History
of England* that the bombing of Britain 'cemented national
unity' and the English people believed that 'by showing they
"could take it", they were already on the way to winning
the war'.[23]

A few years later a new warts-and-all, revisionist interpretation began to emerge to challenge this comforting view of
Britain in 1940–1. It picked out other features that character-
ised the year, like the panic that followed major bombing raids
and the total collapse of local authorities and their inability
to manage the human problems they faced; the looting of
bombed homes; the strikes and absenteeism in vital war factories; crime and the black market. For some years this new
view gained momentum in a variety of publications about the
'People's War'.[24]

More recently, the barometer has swung back again, as it
often does, to a more nuanced view that accepts the bravery
of the few and the determination of the many, that acknowl-
edges the inspiration provided by a determined leadership
but also recognises that the morale of the people was several
times severely shaken but never completely broken. It recognises that while not everyone was a hero and that defeatism
was not uncommon, that while a few people did not cheer
Churchill's speeches and were critical of his leadership,

something tangible did exist in Britain in these months that could realistically be called the 'Blitz spirit'.[25]

Most studies of the impact of the war on the Home Front in Britain have concentrated on the period from May 1940 to June 1941, from Hitler's invasion of France, Belgium and the Netherlands to the moment when Nazi Germany widened the conflict with its invasion of the Soviet Union. In Churchill's own phrase, this has come to be known as Britain's 'finest hour'. This is probably the best-known chapter in the story of Britain's war and a period that has become indelibly marked in the national memory. It is the period for which the Home Front and the People's War are best remembered. It is repeatedly assumed that this crisis represented the biggest threat to the morale of the people and from mid-1941 onwards, with a few minor wobbles, it was plain sailing on to victory. This book fundamentally challenges that notion by telling the story of a year in which military disasters led to political crises and the near collapse of public morale.

It is usually taken as read that if morale survived the onslaught of the Battle of Britain and the Blitz, it somehow survived intact for the rest of the war. Everyone knows that we went on to win the war and it is difficult to view the events that followed other than with the wisdom of this hindsight. Popular historians tend to gloss over events on the Home Front after the year of crisis and pick up after the tide had turned at El Alamein and Stalingrad at the end of 1942.[26]

The point of this book is to challenge that timeline. In 1942 a series of military disasters created a political crisis in Westminster. This prompted and was further fuelled by a domestic crisis across Britain. Public morale nearly collapsed and there was a widespread feeling that Winston Churchill was no longer the right man to lead the nation. Churchill remains a controversial figure: some see him as a racist, but for many people he is a national hero and the 'Greatest Briton'.[27]

In the course of the crisis, two motions attacking Churchill's leadership were debated in Parliament. A credible rival for Prime Minister emerged. Meanwhile, as the people of Britain began a major national debate about what British society would be like after the war (in December, William Beveridge published his report calling for a new, fairer society post-war), Churchill adamantly refused any discussion about future conditions fearing it would alienate America. Instead his focus remained fixed entirely on military matters.

If the ability and willingness of the British people to carry on fighting the war had collapsed, Britain would have had to negotiate a truce with Hitler. The consequences of this would have been catastrophic for the Allied cause as America had not yet fully entered the European war. Having lost Britain as a base, it would have been almost impossible for the US to fight back in Europe. The survival of fascism in Europe, the outcome of the titanic battles on the Eastern Front and the ultimate result of the war could all have been very different. People think that 1940 was Churchill's toughest year. But it was not. It was his finest hour. 1942 was his most difficult time, his darkest hour.

In July 1942, the novelist and journalist Mollie Panter-Downes looked back on the emotional journey ordinary people had made in the first six months of that year, writing, 'What they have been through in the last six months has been less noisy, perhaps, but no less wearing to the spirit and nerves than were the bad times of 1940, when the bombs were falling.'[28]

1942: Britain at the Brink will tell the story of this precarious moment when the British people nearly lost it.

1

'The Sleep of the Saved'

Unusually, on this particular evening the serving of dinner did not cheer up the Prime Minister. Dinner was a major feature in Winston Churchill's daily routine. It was always four courses, beginning with a traditional English soup. Often the meal was accompanied by reasonable quantities of wine, sometimes with Pol Roger, Churchill's favourite champagne. After hard, stressful days the serving of soup alone could be a restorative for the Prime Minister. He would immediately brighten up and start to become more animated. The ritual of dinner was an occasion for lively, amusing conversation across a wide range of subjects. New ideas and suggestions for solving the challenges of the day were exchanged and dinner guests were invited to contribute their thoughts, when they could get a word in. Frequently, by dessert, dinner had developed into a monologue in which Churchill, with many witticisms and one-liners, would regale his companions with his ideas on military strategy, on history or on current events.[1]

On Sunday 7 December 1941, however, this was not the case. Churchill was at the Prime Minister's country residence, Chequers, an impressive pile dating back to the Tudor era set in the beautiful southern Chilterns in rolling

Buckinghamshire countryside. He had been cheered the previous Friday by the surprising news that his hard-pressed Soviet allies had launched a counter-attack outside Moscow. The German Army had advanced 500 miles since invading the Soviet Union and forward patrols had reached the outskirts of the capital, able to see the towers of the Kremlin in their binoculars.[2] But then the winter snows had set in. Not expecting a long campaign, the German Army had failed to equip its soldiers with adequate winter clothing. And the Soviets brought in fresh troops from eastern Asia, fully trained and equipped for winter warfare. Their assault threw back the German forces. Moscow, Stalin and, for this winter at least, the Soviet Union had been saved. But this positive news was soon overtaken by anxious threats coming out of Japan against British and Dutch territories in south-east Asia and against the independent state of Siam (today Thailand). Communication with Washington had produced a joint Anglo-American agreement that an attack on Siam would be regarded as an attack upon themselves. President Roosevelt was due to announce this publicly in a few days.

On the Sunday evening, Churchill had dinner with Ismay, his secretary John Martin and two American guests, the US ambassador to the UK John G. Winant, and a visiting diplomat, Averell Harriman. Dinner did not shift Churchill's glum mood. Harriman found the PM 'tired and depressed' that evening. 'He didn't have much to say throughout dinner and was immersed in his thoughts, with his head in his hands part of the time.'[3] This was rare behaviour for Britain's usually ebullient and ever optimistic Prime Minister. Britain had been at war for two years and three months. Churchill, now aged sixty-seven, had led Britain as it stood isolated, albeit supported by its vast empire, against the threat of invasion during the 'Spitfire Summer' of 1940. His speeches in Parliament and on the radio and his visits to bombed cities had rallied a battered nation. But the continuing strain was beginning to tell. Now he was not even able to amuse his important American guests with his wit or repartee.

After dinner a small radio set was brought to the Chequers dining room. The BBC's *Nine O'Clock News* was full of stories about fighting on the Russian front and in North Africa but ended with a short flash that the Japanese had launched an air attack on the US Navy in Hawaii. Churchill barely registered the news but Harriman was immediately alerted by the report. Churchill's valet, Frank Sawyers, who was acting as butler at dinner, came into the room and confirmed what they had just heard on the news in the kitchens, saying, 'It's quite true. We heard it ourselves outside. The Japanese have attacked the Americans.'

There was a short silence.

After a few moments, Churchill got up from the table and walked hurriedly across the hall to the communications office and asked for a call to be put through to President Roosevelt in the White House. Two or three minutes later, the President came on the line.

'Mr President, what's this about Japan?' asked the Prime Minister.

'It's quite true,' Roosevelt replied. 'They have attacked us at Pearl Harbor. We are all in the same boat now.'

The American ambassador had followed him into the office, and Churchill put him on the line and he spoke with the President for a few minutes. Then Churchill finished off the quick call by saying to President Roosevelt, 'This certainly simplifies things. God be with you.'[4]

The three men stood in the hallway stunned, trying to take on board the immense significance of the news they had just heard. At this point they had no idea of the terrible losses suffered by the US Pacific Fleet as it lay at anchor in Pearl Harbor. The facts that four battleships had been sunk and more than 2,000 American sailors had lost their lives did not come through until much later. At this point Churchill's two American guests seemed to feel relief, as though a long period of pain or anxiety had come to an end. The Prime Minister was rapidly engulfed in a whirlwind of activity. He had said that if the Japanese attacked America then he would declare war on Japan 'within an hour'. He called the Foreign Office to prepare to implement a declaration of war. He sent messages to the members of the War Cabinet, the chiefs of staff and the service ministers. He told his office to call the Speaker of the House of Commons and the chief whips and to instruct them to recall Parliament for an urgent session the following afternoon.

More than anything, Churchill immediately grasped the huge geopolitical significance of having America in the war on Britain's side. It was an outcome for which he had been striving for months, almost since he had first become Prime Minister. When he dictated this section of his memoirs five years later, Churchill wrote of his instant realisation of what the events of this day meant. He recalled the phrase he had been told in the First World War, that America was like 'a gigantic boiler. Once the fire is lighted under it there is no limit to the power it can generate.' Churchill knew that America's entry to the war was the culmination of his dreams and aspirations. 'We had won after all!' he wrote. After all the setbacks and struggles of the last two and a half years 'England would live; Britain would live; the Commonwealth of Nations and the Empire would live ... Once again in our long island history we should emerge, however mauled or mutilated, safe and victorious.' With officials rushing about and calls coming in and going out, Churchill retired, elated. He later wrote, 'Being saturated and satiated with emotion and sensation, I went to bed and slept the sleep of the saved and thankful.' In the first draft of his memoirs he added a sentence: 'One hopes that eternal sleep will be like that.' But this was dropped in the final published edition.[5]

The next few days and weeks brought great highs and terrible lows for Winston Churchill. The following morning he resolved that an immediate trip to Washington to confer with the President would be essential. Now that their two nations were at last fighting together, priorities needed to be set and strategies agreed. He knew that American supplies to Britain, already vital for its war effort, would probably be diverted to America's own war machine and this needed to be addressed. Roosevelt was initially not keen. He had other pressing concerns, and even after Congress rushed to declare war on Japan there were a host of major issues to attend to. On the pretext that he thought the Prime Minister's journey across the Atlantic would be too dangerous, he suggested delaying meeting for a month and to convene instead in Bermuda where they could talk in secret. But Churchill was insistent, saying that only immediate discussion at the highest executive level could resolve the issues. 'I never felt so sure about final victory,' Churchill added in his telegram to the President, 'but only concerted action will achieve it.'[6]

Not for the last time, Roosevelt yielded to Churchillian pressure and went one step further, inviting the Prime Minister to stay in the White House if he could arrive just before Christmas. Churchill had expected to stay at the home of the British ambassador in Washington. But this was the warmest possible invitation and a clear display of the unity of the Allied leaders, demonstrating their joint resolve to the rest of the world.

However, on the morning of 10 December, Churchill was sitting in bed in his favourite green and gold dressing gown, going through his boxes with a female typist present to take his dictation, as was his custom, when a call came through on his bedside telephone. It was the First Sea Lord, Sir Dudley

Pound. His voice was strained. He gave a cough and a gulp. Churchill could not hear him clearly. But Pound told him of the loss of two British warships in the sea off Malaya, the battleship HMS *Prince of Wales* and the battlecruiser HMS *Repulse*. Churchill was completely shattered by the news. He had sailed across the ocean to meet Roosevelt and sign the Atlantic Charter only four months before on the *Prince of Wales*. He knew its captain, Admiral Tom Phillips, and many of the crew well. It was reported they had all gone down with their ship. Churchill dismissed the typist. He turned and twisted in bed. Although he did not openly admit it, it had been his decision to send the *Prince of Wales* and *Repulse* to the Far East as a sign of British naval might and as a deterrent to the Japanese. Moreover, he had insisted they go ahead of their air cover, and now Japanese torpedo bombers flying out of Saigon (today Ho Chi Minh City) had struck and sunk the undefended warships. Churchill was always deeply moved by losses at sea and this news hit him hard. 'In all the war I never received a more direct shock,' he later wrote. His mind leapt to the thought that with these two battleships at the bottom of the sea and the US Pacific Fleet out of action after Pearl Harbor, the Japanese Navy had mastery of both the Indian and Pacific Oceans. Britannia no longer ruled the waves in the Far East. Churchill concluded that, 'Over all this vast expanse of waters Japan was supreme, and we everywhere were weak and naked.'[7]

The following day, in an extraordinary upturn of fortune for Britain, Hitler declared war on the United States. He wanted to show support for his Japanese allies in their conflict with America. This has often been presented as one of the most remarkable decisions of the war. In reality, Hitler felt that the US was so committed to Britain that it was already effectively at war but wanted to get in first with a declaration made in front of the sycophantic Reichstag, which cheered wildly. He also assumed the Japanese would be indomitable in the Pacific and that America would not be able to fight a war on two fronts. He saw great opportunity for his U-boats in the Atlantic. Some have seen Hitler's declaration as the ultimate act of folly of a crazed dictator. Others have seen it as an acceptance of the inevitable, that America would soon be at war in Europe as well as in Asia. Hitler, all powerful having occupied much of Europe and with his armies close to the Russian capital, certainly felt supreme in the west and wanted to lead events rather than follow them. Mussolini went along with the Führer in declaring war on the United States on the same day. For Churchill, having led Britain and its empire alone for so long in its conflict with Nazi Germany, the widening of the war was a 'miracle of deliverance'. His telegram to Roosevelt that evening was simple: 'I am enormously relieved at the turn world events have taken.'[8] The principal British strategic mission was now to ensure that America would confirm previous guarantees that if, or when, at war, Germany would be its first and principal enemy.

With the war now a global conflict, on the following evening Churchill left London by night train for Scotland to begin his journey to Washington. He was accompanied by a complete signals unit of nearly thirty men to keep him in regular, hourly contact with London and with his field commander in North Africa, General Claude Auchinleck, who was leading an offensive in Libya. The Foreign Secretary, Anthony Eden, was already en route to Moscow and Churchill was determined to maintain close contact with him as he reported on his meeting with Stalin. As issues of supply and distribution would dominate the meeting with the President, Churchill also took with him Lord Beaverbrook, the Minister of Supply and a close friend whom he could freely bounce ideas off. The chiefs of staff also accompanied the Prime

Minister: Admiral Sir Dudley Pound, head of the Royal Navy, and Air Marshal Sir Charles Portal, Chief of the Air Staff. Lieutenant-General Alan Brooke, the newly appointed Chief of the Imperial General Staff (CIGS), did not join the party: Churchill instructed him to remain in London to grapple with his new duties at the War Office. Instead, Field Marshal Sir John Dill, his predecessor, went. Also with the Prime Minister was a support staff of trusted and loyal assistants, including his map officer, a shorthand dictation taker and his personal doctor, Sir Charles Wilson, all of whom would cater to his daily needs.

On 13 December, Churchill and his substantial entourage boarded HMS *Duke of York*, the sister ship to the *Prince of Wales*, on Clydeside. The fast-moving battleship immediately set sail and headed west into the stormy Atlantic. A journey that usually took only five days was extended by the dreadful winter weather to twice that. Despite the frustrations of the slow pace and the heaving motion of the ocean, Churchill loved the voyage and was one of the few civilians who did not suffer from seasickness. From the luxury of the admiral's cabin near the bridge he read extensively, including a book about Napoleon and Josephine, slept well and went to the ship's cinema each evening. He enjoyed dining with his party and senior members of the crew. More importantly, he kept up a regular communication with the War Cabinet. As bad news arrived of Japanese landings in north Borneo and on Hong Kong island, Churchill minuted the chiefs of staff about the need to hold Singapore and not to tie up troops in the defence of the Malayan peninsula. 'Nothing compares with the importance of the fortress [of Singapore],' he wrote. 'Are you sure we shall have enough troops for the prolonged defence?'[9]

After several days of pitching and rolling in the heavy seas, the *Duke of York* moved ahead of its slower-moving escorts to try to speed up its crossing. The captain decided to maintain radio silence and so, cut off from communication with London, Churchill spent these days dictating memos on strategy and the future conduct of the war. These opinion papers typed up and circulated by his team were discussed at length with the military chiefs who also wrote papers on the technical details of the strategies to be pursued. So, although the warship zig-zagged through wild seas to avoid U-boats and for many the journey proved long, tiresome and sickening, by the time of their arrival the British delegation had rehearsed all their arguments and arrived at commonly agreed positions.

The plan had been to sail majestically into Washington up the Potomac, but by the time the *Duke of York* reached Hampton Roads, Virginia, everyone had had enough of their never-ending sea voyage. They went ashore and took a short flight to Washington. President Roosevelt was waiting at the airport in a presidential limousine to meet the Prime Minister, a unique honour. They drove to the White House where Churchill was to live in a suite of rooms on the second floor of the mansion. Churchill remained in North America for the next three weeks – an unheard-of length of time for a modern politician to spend on an official visit. But Churchill believed there was much work to be done that was of supreme importance and that the length of the arduous journey justified the time spent in the American capital.

From the very first meetings, President Roosevelt, General George Marshall, his chief of staff, and Harry Hopkins, a sort of prototype national security adviser, all assured the Prime Minister and the British chiefs of staff that their 'Germany first' policy still stood. Despite having been so brazenly attacked by the Japanese, the US leaders agreed that the Atlantic and the European theatre of war was to be 'decisive'. They made it clear 'that Germany is still the key to victory' and that having crushed Hitler, 'the collapse of Italy and the defeat of Japan must follow'.[10] The British, concerned that public outrage over Pearl Harbor would drive the Americans to concentrate on prioritising battle in the Pacific, heaved a huge sigh of relief. Moreover, British plans for continuing the war in North Africa rather than accepting the American demand to launch an invasion of northern Europe were somewhat reluctantly accepted by the American military chiefs. The British had prepared their arguments well on the long sea crossing and the American planners were comprehensively out-argued. But with the massive lack of landing craft and with so few American troops projected to be in the UK for some time, it was not just British urgings but good sense that prevailed. The Americans were after all joining a war that was already being fought and had little opportunity to alter its strategy before becoming the major military partner in the alliance. Roosevelt went further and surprised his staff by agreeing to a combined Anglo-American landing in French-occupied North Africa later in the year. And it was also agreed that the first American troops to be sent to the UK would go to Northern Ireland, to relieve British troops garrisoned there and as a show to impress the neighbouring Irish Free State.[11]

The Washington conference was given a codename, as were all later summits, appropriately named 'Arcadia'. After twelve meetings between the American and British chiefs of staff it was decided to set up a new body called the Combined Chiefs of Staff that would implement the broad programme of requirements to meet the strategies agreed between the President and Prime Minister. In addition, a Combined Raw Materials Board would form a common pool for all the resources of the US and the UK and allocate the raw materials necessary for the Allied nations to accomplish their strategic objectives. Even at a time of national emergency this was an unprecedented step for allies to take, effectively to share resources and the planning for war; it was the beginning of what would be known as the 'special relationship'. It was also agreed that each theatre of war should have an integrated command structure. American, British, Australian, Canadian, Indian, New Zealand, French, Polish and other servicemen would all serve in their own units but under a unified Allied command. The British delegation could not have been more pleased with the outcome of the talks. The agreement reached in Washington at this first Allied summit would shape the organisation of the Allied war effort for the next four years.

Following the principle of unity of command, the chiefs decided to appoint a Supreme Commander for the entire south-west Pacific battle zone. He would have command of all the Allied naval, land and air forces across a huge area, from Burma (Myanmar), down through Malaya, including the naval fortress of Singapore, along what were then known as the Dutch East Indies to New Guinea to the north of Australia, a line three times the length of the entire Eastern Front. General Marshall felt that only by coordinating all the forces in this region could an effective defence against the Japanese advance be mounted. The British chiefs of staff were more sceptical, especially when Marshall proposed that Archibald Wavell, the British general, should be put in command. They thought the Americans were looking for a 'fall guy' and wanted blame for future defeats to land on British and not American shoulders. But Roosevelt was convinced and persuaded Churchill, who in turn pressed the British chiefs to agree. Wavell, who was commander-in-chief of the British forces in India, returned from a day's pig-sticking in Kadir (a traditional British pursuit in imperial India) to find a telegram from the Prime Minister telling him of his surprise appointment. As a good and trustworthy imperial servant, Wavell accepted the post and took command of that vast area of 12 million square miles in an arc of some 5,000 miles from Burma to Australia. With Japanese troops surging forward and with only scattered and limited numbers of defenders, his role as Supreme Commander would indeed become something of a poisoned chalice.[12] For the Anglo-American relationship it was the first of many appointments of senior commanders who would have unprecedented authority over the forces of several Allied nations.

The Arcadia conference also addressed issues of industrial output. After discussions with Beaverbrook, the President was persuaded to accept a more ambitious programme and agreed to dramatically increase the objectives for America's war factories. A new 'Victory Program' was announced and targets for 1942 were reset at 45,000 combat aircraft, 45,000 tanks, 14,000 anti-tank guns, half a million machine guns and 8 million tons of merchant shipping. For the following year these targets were increased to 100,000 aircraft, 75,000 tanks and 10 million tons of shipping. All other war supplies were to be increased in similar proportions.[13] These colossal targets would never be met but they helped to focus hearts and minds. American industry was to be mobilised for war from the shipyards of the east and west coasts to the huge motor factories of Detroit and the iron and steel mills of the Midwest. America was set on the path to become the arsenal of the Allied nations.

Of equal importance for the next phase of running the war, the President and the Prime Minister forged a close personal bond during the three weeks of Arcadia. Historians have argued for decades over whether the two men simply developed a good working relationship or formed a genuine mutual friendship. Certainly, at this stage of the war, a real warmth seems to have developed between the two leaders. Roosevelt not only invited Churchill into his office but also into his home. Eleanor Roosevelt, the First Lady, not known for being a great hostess, did everything on this occasion to make Churchill welcome. For the duration of his visit he had lunch together with the President almost every day, often alone or with only Harry Hopkins present. Dinner was a bigger affair with other department leaders and military top brass joining them. Churchill described how the President would mix the cocktails before dinner (even though Churchill preferred whisky and soda to Roosevelt's mild version of a dry martini) and he would push Roosevelt from the drawing room to the lift in his wheelchair. He described how the two men saw many issues in the same way, later writing, 'his heart seemed to respond to many of the impulses that stirred my own'.[14] Roosevelt had a tendency to retire early to bed but when Churchill visited he would stay up late, talking on a variety of subjects ranging from wartime strategy to American history. One observer wrote, 'Churchill was one of the few people to whom Roosevelt cared to listen, and vice versa.'[15] Churchill spent Christmas Day with the Roosevelts and they sang hymns together in church. They often visited each other in their living quarters. One report that circulated among officials at the time was that the President was wheeled into Churchill's suite one morning just as he was emerging stark naked from the bath. The President immediately withdrew but Churchill called him back, proclaiming, 'The Prime Minister of Great Britain has nothing to hide from the President of the United States!'[16] In early January, Churchill described the atmosphere in the White House during his stay to the Labour leader Clement Attlee. 'We live here as a big family,' he reported, 'in the greatest intimacy and informality, and I have formed the very highest regard and admiration for the President.'[17] Several later US presidents and British prime ministers have got along well, most especially Ronald Reagan and Margaret Thatcher, and Bill Clinton and Tony Blair. But few have shared the closeness Roosevelt and Churchill enjoyed at this point of the war.

However, there is no avoiding the many differences that existed between the outlooks of the President and the Prime

Minister. Roosevelt was a patrician Democrat who had led the United States out of the greatest economic depression in its history by funding public works and generating employment. He was a reformer, at times a radical one. Churchill was a staunch imperialist many of whose beliefs had been formed in the Victorian era. He was conservative through and through. Roosevelt grew deeply suspicious of Britain's claim to be fighting for democracy and freedom while Churchill refused to consider any form of independence for its Indian and other imperial subjects. While Churchill felt Britain had stored up two years' worth of credit while fighting alone against the dictators, enduring aerial bombardment and struggling against the might of the German armies, Roosevelt had little time for claims of special privilege. Britain was now mortgaged up to the hilt to the US and the President would have no hesitation over calling in the debt when needed.[18]

And the two men had very different personalities. Churchill was extrovert, emotional, eloquent and full of energy. Roosevelt was a smooth talker, controlled, much more difficult to read and far less open than the PM. Both men were interested in shaping military strategy but Roosevelt left the implementation to his generals and admirals. Churchill, on the other hand, had a great love of military detail and was regarded as an impossible interferer or micromanager by his military chiefs. However, there is no doubting that at this point Roosevelt needed an easy relationship with Churchill and wanted to promote a close alliance with Britain. The RAF had fought the Luftwaffe to a standstill in the summer of 1940. The British Army was fighting German and Italian divisions in North Africa. The Royal Navy had won the first round of the Battle of the Atlantic against the U-boats. Roosevelt had few other military options but to go along with British military requests. But he remained suspicious of British ambitions, as did many senior American politicians and military men. General Marshall most clearly of all came to believe that the whole Mediterranean theatre was a sideshow and repeatedly argued that the only plausible way to defeat Nazi Germany was to invade northern Europe in order to draw the Wehrmacht into a full-scale European battle.

Later in the war the relationship between Roosevelt and Churchill fundamentally changed, but in December 1941, Britain was militarily the most significant partner. As this was transformed as Britain became the junior partner in the alliance and Roosevelt became the dominant force in the partnership, the President's relationship with Stalin became in some ways more important to him than his friendship with Churchill. And on a personal level he grew tired of the Prime Minister's overbearing presence and long monologues. Even Eleanor Roosevelt came to see Churchill's presence as a bad influence on her husband, and not just because he encouraged the President to stay up late and drink more than he usually would. But all that lay in the future. For now, Churchill lapped up the welcome he received in Washington and poured praise on the President whom he rightly saw as not just the commander-in-chief of American military forces but also as the coordinator of American industrial might. His visit made him supremely confident of ultimate victory in Europe and Asia. And he believed himself to be the key link in forging what he called the 'grand alliance'. When he reported back to the King he told him that after many months of 'walking out' Britain and America were 'now married'.[19]

The public highlight of the visit was unquestionably Churchill's address to a Joint Session of Congress on 26 December. The speech was broadcast live on the radio and was sent around the world. Parts of it were filmed for the newsreels. Its reach was truly global. Churchill felt a strong bond with the American people as his mother was

American and through her he could trace this line of his ancestry back to an officer in George Washington's army. This gave him the opportunity to get the speech off to a brilliant start when he told the Senators and Representatives, 'I cannot help reflecting that if my father had been American and my mother British, instead of the other way round, I might have got here on my own. In that case this would not have been the first time you would have heard my voice!' The Congressmen loved that. For the next twenty minutes, Churchill's rhetoric rose and fell as he described the cruelty of their foes in Europe and Asia and the folly of taking on the might of America, the power of the British empire and the huge resources of Soviet Russia and China. He still predicted a long, hard struggle ahead but his voice rose in a dramatic crescendo when he spoke of the Japanese and demanded of the assembled Senators and Representatives, 'What kind of people do they think we are? Is it possible they do not realise that we shall never cease to persevere against them until they have been taught a lesson which they and the world will never forget?' He concluded with a rallying cry that rang out across the two English-speaking nations: 'I avow my hope and faith, sure and inviolate, that in the days to come the British and American peoples will for their own safety and for the good of all walk together side by side in majesty, in justice and in peace.'[20]

Congress erupted into cheering. When he turned and made his V for victory sign, 'The cheers swelled into a roar,' according to the Washington Post, 'and fingers spread in the victory sign were raised in scores of places throughout the chamber.'[21] The members of Congress crowded around him in congratulation. If he could have been held aloft he would have been. His son Randolph, who heard the speech on the radio in Cairo, wrote, 'It was the best you have ever done, particularly the delivery which was wonderfully confident and clear.'[22]

*Churchill addresses Congress, 26 December 1941, providing
a rallying cry for the English-speaking nations.*

Eventually the secret service men shuffled the Prime Minister
away and took him back to the White House.

That night as he lay in bed he felt hot and the room seemed
stuffy. He tried to open his bedroom window but it proved
stiff and required a lot of effort. As he struggled he realised
he was short of breath. He felt a dull pain in his chest that
ran down his left arm. The following morning he called in
his doctor to discover what it could have been. 'Did I pull
a muscle?' he asked Sir Charles Wilson. The doctor put a
stethoscope to his chest. He could detect what he described
as a 'coronary insufficiency', today better known as angina
pectoris. This was usually a sign of an inadequate flow of
blood to the heart. It could be an early symptom or a warning

of either angina or, worst of all, a coronary thrombosis, a fatal heart attack. While he paused to examine the Prime Minister, Wilson had to think fast. The normal response to this at the time in a man of Churchill's age would be to demand six weeks in bed and total rest. But at this crucial moment, with America having just joined Britain at war, nothing like that could be possible. The press would have portrayed the Prime Minister as an invalid with a dicky heart and a troubled future. On the other hand, if he said nothing and another perhaps fatal incident followed then, as his doctor, he would be blamed for not insisting on rest. It was an extraordinary dilemma the doctor faced.

After the brief examination, Churchill asked, 'Well, is my heart all right?'

'There is nothing serious,' Wilson replied, 'you've been overdoing things.'

'Now Charles,' said the Prime Minister, 'you're not going to tell me to rest. I can't. I won't. No one else can do this job. I must.'

Wilson told the PM it was not serious, that his circulation was sluggish and that he must otherwise avoid physical exertion. This was what Churchill wanted to hear. At that moment Harry Hopkins came into the room. Wilson slipped away, relieved not to come under more pressure from the Prime Minister. And Churchill would carry on, business as usual. The Cabinet in London was not told.[23]

Churchill continued with his tour. He visited Ottawa and addressed the Canadian Parliament. In this speech he came up with another memorable phrase when he mocked the French generals who when he had announced that Britain would fight on alone if France withdrew in 1940 had said Britain would have its neck wrung like a chicken. In Ottawa, Churchill exclaimed: 'Some chicken – some neck.' The Parliament, like Congress, loved his grit, determination and humour. After Canada, he managed to slip a few days' rest into his schedule by spending a short while at a villa on the beach in Florida. There he bathed in the sea and enjoyed the temperate weather. Then he returned to Washington to wrap up his business with a series of Anglo-American agreements, and he instructed Field Marshal Dill to remain in Washington as British liaison with the new Combined Chiefs of Staff Committee. Dill established a good relationship with the American military leaders, especially Marshall. It was an excellent appointment and seemed a good omen for future relations.

On 16 January 1942, Churchill finally left Washington to begin his return to London. This time he avoided the long sea journey by crossing the ocean in a luxury flying boat – the first time he had flown across the Atlantic. While outwardly his sojourn in North America had been a great success, Winston Churchill had indeed suffered a minor heart attack. Although this was kept from the public in America, Britain and elsewhere, the Prime Minister had received a powerful reminder of his own mortality. And it was not just his physical health that was to come under immense strain. Over the coming months until almost the end of 1942, Churchill would be reminded repeatedly that he was not immune from the slings and arrows of bad news, military disasters and political crises. The calamities that followed in 1942 would require immense reserves of strength to withstand.

2

Happy New Year, 1942

By early January 1942, Britain had been at war for two years and four months. For the first part of the conflict, until September 1941, there were more deaths among civilians in the UK than there were among British armed forces.[1] This extraordinary fact, unique in the history of British warfare, reveals the extent to which civilians were in the front line in the war. It illustrates the true meaning of total warfare, where a telegram of condolence was just as likely to be sent from a soldier's home town to the unit with which he was serving in the forces, as the other way around.

When the main Blitz came to an end in May 1941, the British people felt as though they were emerging into the light after the horror of night bombing for nearly a year. From 7 September 1940, London had been bombed every night with one exception until 2 November. Then the Luftwaffe turned its attention to the other industrial cities of Britain. The last major raid took place on 16 May 1941 on Birmingham. The fear generated by regular heavy bombing slowly began to lift. And with its end so the threat of invasion seemed less acute. In June 1941, Hitler's attack upon the Soviet Union also made Britons feel they were no longer standing alone against Hitler. But six months of hefty defeats, desperate withdrawals and immense losses on the Russian Front soon revived a fear that if Hitler defeated the Soviet Union he would turn again, this time even more powerfully, against Britain. Then in December came Pearl Harbor and Hitler's declaration of war on the United States. Once again, people dared to hope that the war might end in victory. It had been a crazy year.

Christmas 1941 was not an easy time. It was difficult to find in the shops the things that people wanted to give as presents. Everyone was used to queuing but for this third Christmas of the war the queues were longer than usual and in the department stores shoppers found it hard to lay their hands on anything special. A young woman behind a cosmetics counter in Woolworths observed, 'Everybody seems to have plenty of money to spend but they grumble because we haven't got the stuff they want. They want perfumes and make-up and powder of all sorts, but we haven't got any.' People tried to buy toys for their children but complained about the cost; board games, dolls, outfits for dressing up, even toy guns had all increased considerably in price. One mother moaned, 'I was trying to get something for my little boy, he's eight, and there was nothing but a football, 15/6d, and they used to be 3/6d!' But most people accepted that a wartime Christmas was going to be very different from one in peacetime and there was a tendency to make the best one could of what limited facilities were available. There was a quiet resignation about it all. So many families were separated that it was impossible to forget the war. A fifty-five-year-old man looked back a few days after Christmas and concluded, 'We made the best of a bad job, the son being away in the army. But we managed quietly round the fire.'[2]

On New Year's Eve people looked ahead to the coming year. Mass Observation noted that 60 per cent of the people they interviewed were optimistic that 1942 would see if not the end of the war then at least 'the beginning of the end'.

'There's a good chance things'll be better this time next year. Many sticky corners to turn though,' a forty-five-year-old man predicted. A young female remarked, 'If it's as bad as 1941 it'll be pretty awful.' A seventy-year-old man said he was 'almost certain that the war will be over by this time next year. The Russians are giving him [Hitler] a big hiding.'[3]

By 1942, Britons had grown weary of the food restrictions that the war had brought but still largely supported the system of rationing. The quantity of products 'on the ration' varied throughout the war but by the beginning of 1942 everyone was able to buy each week 4oz butter, 8oz sugar, 4oz bacon and ham, 2oz cooking fats, 8oz cheese and just 2oz of tea. Meat was limited by price at one shilling per person per week – roughly the equivalent of a pound of meat. Eggs were not rationed but were often difficult to find. A cartoon showed a woman calling to her husband, 'How would you like your egg done this month, dear?'[4] From the middle of 1942 dried egg powder became available from America. One tin (equivalent to about twelve eggs) was allowed to each person every eight weeks, provoking a host of jokes about the largely flavourless concoctions that could be produced. Another American import was tinned Supply Pressed American Meat (Spam).

The milk allowance had been cut to three pints per person per week by early 1942 although more was allowed for young children and pregnant women. Other items like vegetables, bread, tinned food, breakfast cereals and biscuits were never rationed, but were subject to local availability or, more frequently, the lack of. In December 1941 a new points system was introduced in which everyone was allocated initially sixteen points per month to spend on whatever they chose. As tinned foods from America started to become available these could be bought 'on points': two points for a tin of baked beans or pilchards, a few more points depending upon availability for a tin of fruit, right up to a whopping thirty-two points for a tin of red salmon. In the same month the Vitamin Welfare Scheme was launched with cheap or free orange juice and cod liver oil for young children and pregnant women. To a twenty-first-century consumer these rations sound puny and to middle-class Britons in 1942 they represented a substantial cutback from what they had been used to. But they kept the nation fed with a decent balance of protein and vitamins.

A Mass Observation report into rationing in February 1942 concluded that it 'forces everyone to think intelligently about what food they are getting and why' and that 'the result may in the end actually benefit our national diet'. It found that there was overwhelming support for rationing which was thought by housewives to be fair and honest. The principal area of criticism was that those at home could get to the shops in the morning and were able to buy the best of what was available, whereas workers in the war factories could only get there later in the day and buy what was left over. However,

The look of rationing in Britain, 1942. Although most housewives
thought the system was fair, the endless queuing got everyone down.

only one woman in fourteen expressed dissatisfaction with rationing.[5] Overall, by the end of the war many people were healthier than they had been before the war when there had been huge variations between the diet of the rich and the poor and one survey had estimated that at least one quarter of the population were undernourished. It was not for nothing that the pre-war decade had been called 'the Hungry Thirties'.[6]

By the beginning of 1942, the number of accidents caused by the blackout had mercifully reduced and most people had got used to the restrictions and darkness. Double summer time had been introduced in the spring of 1941 meaning that it got dark later than usual, reducing electricity consumption as well as accidents. Although petrol rationing ended in July 1942 it was impossible to obtain petrol except for certain professionals such as farmers, doctors or those who needed vehicles for the Home Guard. Consequently and rather bizarrely, Dad's Army became the centre for the illicit supply of fuel, spare parts and tyres on the black market. But most of the two million car owners chose to remove the wheels from their cars, take them off the road and 'brick them up' for the duration, so road accidents were far fewer.[7] And limited amounts of light were permitted from cinemas and shops, although it was 'lights off' as soon as the first air raid warning sounded. Altogether, it was an admirable display of how the vast majority of Britons would accept government restrictions, no matter how irksome.

Still, people moaned and complained incessantly, at the shortage of goods and the need for endless queuing; at the lack of meat, as for many male workers an evening meal of 'meat and two veg' was a symbol of their masculinity; at the National Loaf, which in order to save on wheat was no longer made as traditional white bread but was what today we would call wholemeal; and at the dramatic increase in prices of items on and, even more so, off the ration. Food prices had gone up by nearly 50 per cent between 1939 and the end of 1941, although the rise in the cost of living was only partly down to the scarcity of goods: it was also a consequence of full employment and the increase in average earnings.

From the middle of 1941 clothes had been rationed. Again, every adult was given a set of coupons, initially sixty-six per year, although this was reduced later in the war. Each garment required a number of coupons: a man's suit needed twenty-five, a shirt five, trousers eight, vests and pants eight; a woman's dress needed eleven if made of wool or seven for cotton or rayon, blouses and jumpers five, vests and knickers three, bras and suspender belts one each. Children, pregnant women and manual workers were given additional allocations of coupons. From later in 1942 Utility clothing was introduced. Plain and relatively simple but well-designed outfits were produced for men and women – no more turn-ups on trousers, fewer pleats, pockets and trimmings on skirts and dresses. With timber in short supply (it was used extensively in aircraft manufacturing), Utility furniture with simple, practical styles was also introduced in 1942. Fussy ornamentations were out (too much labour needed to produce them) and standardised designs were in. It all looked simple and austere to most people but it anticipated by a generation the Habitat design of basic, functional shapes. It was not available to all, just to those who could prove they needed new furniture, such as newly-weds or those who had been bombed out.

By 1942, the conflict was regularly being called a 'People's War' and the morale of the people would become a decisive factor in shaping the course of events. That the Home Front was inextricably tied up with progress on the fighting front was taken as given. But quite how the link worked and what would influence opinion at home was a complex business. At its heart was the challenge of maintaining public morale. And this meant controlling or influencing the information people received in order to sustain their support for the war.

The British government had learned a lot about the management of information in the First World War. At the start of that war the official view was that journalists were a nuisance and all they should do was rehash communiqués that were handed down to them by the War Office. Reporters were banned from visiting the front. Photographers and film cameramen were warned that they would be arrested as spies if they were discovered within 30 miles of the front line. And the punishment for spying was execution. Lord Kitchener, Secretary of War in 1914, defended that view in the House of Lords: 'It's not always easy to decide what information may or may not be dangerous, and whenever there is any doubt we do not hesitate to prevent publication.' Such an attitude clearly could not prevail for long in a twentieth-century confrontation.[8]

Before long, as the concept of 'total war' became more widespread so awareness grew of the concept of a Home Front. In this, industrial workers, women taking on the roles that men had performed before joining up and almost everyone putting up with shortages at home would play a role in supporting the fighting front. By the end of the war there had been a total revolution in news management. In 1917, a Department of Information was set up with the popular novelist John Buchan in charge. Then in 1918 came a Ministry of Information with the great newspaper barons running policy. Lord Beaverbrook, who owned the *Daily Express*, the *Sunday Express* and the *Evening Standard*, was made minister and given a seat in Cabinet. Lord Northcliffe, who owned the *Daily Mail*, the *Daily Mirror*, the *Observer* and *The Times*, was put in charge of propaganda aimed at winning the support of neutral countries. Such appointments were of course not without controversy, just as they would be today if press magnates were brought into central government. But it marked a full circle in terms of policy. On the Home Front there were posters, speakers, pamphlets and an increasing number of films intended to encourage healthier eating, to avoid waste, and to promote the range of new jobs that women had taken over.[9] By 1918, the government realised that to win a total war they needed the complete support of civilians and workers at home. And the conflict had become the first ever mass media war.[10]

However, by 1939 many of the lessons learned had been forgotten. Four years before war was declared, a Whitehall committee was set up to make plans for how to cajole, persuade and motivate civilian workers and families in the event of war, with the establishment of a new Ministry of Information (MoI).[11] In September 1939 the ministry sprang into existence overnight in the brutalist setting of London University's Senate House in the heart of Bloomsbury. But initially, the MoI became the home not of skilled and experienced news managers or publicists, nor of behavioural scientists, but of a group of worthies and retired public figures eager to do their bit but who couldn't be found jobs elsewhere. In one early discussion about how to avoid panic resulting from an air raid it was suggested 'that the most comforting thing ... was to have a cup of tea'.[12] The ministry rapidly acquired a reputation for its amateur approach, for being remote from the public, for blundering and getting things wrong most of the time. It became the butt of many popular jokes and was nicknamed the 'Ministry of Muddle'.

In the early stages of the war the MoI was led by middle- and upper-class men who totally failed to understand the style or approach that was needed to reach out to working people. In August and September 1939 householders were bombarded by a barrage of leaflets that came through their letterbox. They often featured language or phrases that were difficult for many people to understand. In one survey in the early weeks of war only one person in three admitted to having read any of the leaflets and only one person in seven could correctly identify the sound of an air raid warning. For some time many people failed to carry gas masks with them as they were supposed to do. What finally brought widespread acceptance of the need to carry a gas mask was not official directives but the example set by the Queen and other leading figures who were always seen carrying masks with them.[13]

This arrogant, patronising, from-the-top-down attitude was best symbolised by the poster cheerfully proclaiming 'Your Courage, Your Cheerfulness, Your Resolution Will Bring Us Victory'. Large versions of this poster were put up on hoardings in every town and village in the country; smaller versions went up at railway stations, on buses and in shop windows. A survey discovered that many working people found the poster silly or irritating, although upper-class members of the public liked it. Many people believed they were being asked to make sacrifices so the ruling elite could benefit. The poster was widely mocked, never more pointedly than by the brewers Courage who, after the duty on beer had gone up, put up their own poster which read 'Your cheerfulness, Your resolution, Your courage will add one penny per pint to the Exchequer. Strength and Quality maintained.'[14]

The first head of the MoI was a Scottish lawyer, Lord Hugh Pattison Macmillan, a lord of appeal known even in his day for being rather dull. He had no feel whatsoever for what moved or impressed the common man or woman. It was written that 'this precise peer and Scottish jurist lives in another (and older) world from the world of vulgar life, the world which calls a cigarette a fag'.[15] He was replaced in January 1940 by Lord Reith who had been the founder and first Director General of the BBC. He was initially welcomed as someone 'steeped in the process of disseminating information'.[16] But he, too, struggled with the vast responsibility of trying to control public morale. A tall, haughty individual, Reith was unpopular with Churchill (who called him 'Old Wuthering Heights') as he had kept him off the airwaves in the late 1930s because the politician's stand on rearmament did not fit with official government policy.[17] He was replaced when Churchill became Prime Minister in May 1940 by Alfred Duff Cooper, a supporter of the new PM who had resigned from government at the time of the Munich agreement. But by this point the MoI had grown to the extent that Cooper found it 'a monster ... so large, so voluminous, so amorphous that no single man could cope with it'.[18]

Cooper resigned in June 1941 and only then did the right man for the job appear in the form of Brendan Bracken, an ex-journalist who understood the world of news making and who later founded the modern version of the *Financial Times*. He was a close member of Churchill's pre-war set and a confidant of the PM. He demanded that the MoI tone down its hectoring style, which treated the public like naughty children and the press as its enemy, and instead take a more positive line, to encourage and inspire the British people to support the war effort. He remained minister until 1945.

The ministry consisted of various divisions. The Press and Censorship section looked after censorship of the press and of BBC radio broadcasting. In the first months of the war its chief censor was a rear admiral who struggled with his task. He was warned before arriving 'they're a bit of a mess in there. No one really knows what he's doing.'[19] In reality, it was only military information that was supposed to be censored in order to prevent valuable details from coming into the hands of the enemy. But this could be interpreted in a broad way. And, indeed, it was. In only the second week of the war, the ministry late one night demanded that all editions of the next day's papers be withdrawn because they reported the fact that the British Army was deploying in France. Within months every journalist had stories of arbitrary, petty and bizarre acts of censorship. One journalist called the ministry and asked for the text of a leaflet, millions of which had been dropped over Germany, but was told, 'We are not allowed to disclose information which might be of value to the enemy.'[20] The fact that the workers at Battersea Power Station had a football team was censored in case it gave information to the enemy about the location of the giant power station that was in reality obvious to every Luftwaffe pilot flying up the Thames. The press were soon uttering howls of outrage against the men from what journalists called the 'Ministry of *Dis*information'.

Radio censorship was another task of this MoI division. It was done discreetly to ensure that people still believed that the BBC was independent from government control. It was realised that if the people lost confidence in the independence and veracity of the news, they would cease to trust it. But, for instance, the script of every BBC radio news bulletin and feature on the war had to be submitted for approval in advance, and in the BBC archives it is still possible to see the pencilled alterations made by the censor on the scripts read by news-readers to ensure that the BBC broadcast the correct message.[21]

Other divisions of the MoI were responsible for disseminating the government's message through different media. In addition to the poster campaigns and the leaflets dropped through everyone's door, there was a Films Division that, after the successes in the Great War, commissioned documentaries for screening in every cinema. There was an immense range in both the content and quality of the films produced. Some, particularly at the beginning of the war, were crude, lecturing and in many cases risible. Others, usually from later in the war, show extraordinary creativity, humour and sophistication in how they address their subject matter.

In the 1930s a powerful documentary film movement had developed in Britain made up of a group of liberal film makers who were committed to using film to help build a fairer and socially progressive society. Much of this creative and original film making was produced for the Post Office in what became known as the GPO Film Unit. When war was declared these documentary film makers imagined they would soon be called upon to help motivate and inspire the civilian population. They were rapidly disappointed.

At the beginning of the war, the head of films at the MoI was Sir Joseph Ball, who had been in charge of the Conservative Party research department and was a close ally of Neville Chamberlain. He was implacably hostile to the documentary film movement whose members he saw as a bunch of left-wing radicals. Many of the early films produced by the MoI were patronising and poorly made, male narrators with middle-class plummy voices telling on-screen working women how to prepare porridge or make a 'proper' cup of tea in a canteen urn.[22]

Ball did not last long and was replaced by Kenneth Clark, who had been a great success as the young director of the National Gallery. Clark was urbane, cultured, charming and well connected. But he knew nothing whatsoever about film. He later speculated that he had been appointed because he was an authority on 'pictures' and the directors of the MoI thought that would be good enough. Again, he was only in post for a few months.[23]

Change finally came when Jack Beddington, the imaginative director of Shell's pre-war publicity and advertising, took over as head of the Films Division in April 1940. He had the ability to combine quality of content with mass popular appeal. He requisitioned the GPO Film Unit for the war effort and changed its name to the Crown Film Unit. It was based at Pinewood, a well-equipped studio complex taken over by the government which also became home to the Army Film and Photographic Unit. When Bracken took over as minister he insisted that the role of MoI films should be to encourage people to think in different ways when it came to issues like reducing waste and growing their own vegetables. 'Dig for Victory' became a common wartime slogan and several films were made to promote the idea. Another wartime theme, 'Make Do and Mend', gave birth to many imaginative films which explained in a witty way how old bones, wastepaper and scrap iron could all be of value to the war effort. In these films it is only the unthinking and flighty who want to use up scarce resources by buying new clothes when old ones will do.[24]

It's difficult to know how effective these short films were. Cinema attendances rose during the war as people no doubt sought an escape from their daily grind. At the start of the war about 20 million people went to the cinema every week. This was equivalent to nearly half the population going to 'the pictures' weekly. By the end of the war this had increased to around 30 million people per week.[25] A cinema programme then consisted of a main feature, often American, the principal attraction; a shorter 'B feature', sometimes British; and a newsreel in between. The government information films were shown alongside the newsreel but many cinema managers reported that audiences flocked out to the toilets or to buy sweets when the official films came on. No doubt audiences found some films laughable or they were simply ignored at the time.

During the war years the MoI commissioned a series of what today are called drama-documentaries, films based on fact using reconstructions often with ordinary people playing themselves, rather than with actors playing parts. From 1941, these films went up a gear with *Target for Tonight* (dir. Harry Watt), showing all the stages of planning and carrying out a bombing raid over Germany. Humphrey Jennings, the poet of the documentary movement, also directed several very

moving films including *Words for Battle* (1941) and the elabo-
rate drama-documentary *Fires Were Started* (1943).[26] The MoI
also assisted in the making of feature films, either by raising
initial cash or in helping to release 'stars' from military duties.
Many of these feature films beautifully capture the spirit of
Britons at war. For instance, the brilliantly funny and deeply
moving *Millions Like Us* (Sidney Gilliat and Frank Launder,
1943) shows the war from the point of view of a group of
'mobile' young women who are sent to work in a war factory. Where it felt that commercial funding might be difficult
to raise, the MoI also stepped in to help, as with Laurence
Olivier's *Henry V* (1944), which it saw as a huge morale booster
after the Normandy landings by invoking the spirit of an earlier English invasion of France.

In 1940 another section called 'Home Intelligence' was set
up at the MoI with the task of reporting back on the mood,
attitudes and behaviour of the British public at war. Unusually
for the Establishment of the time, a woman was put in charge
of this unit. Mary Adams had been the first ever female producer in the young BBC Television Service before the war.
She was an excellent administrator and a formidable creative
spirit who 'made people sit up, with ideas that were daring, in
support of what was new, often with a strong feminist slant,
and expressed with animation even provocation'.[27] The Home
Intelligence Unit employed the Wartime Social Survey to
carry out market research-style investigations into the public
mood with researchers asking people questions in face-to-face
surveys. Initially the idea was to produce a monthly survey
of public attitudes but from May 1940 onwards there was an
urgent need for more regular information about the state of
public opinion. The Home Intelligence Unit began producing a daily summary of popular attitudes paying particular
attention to morale, rumours and the popular reception of
ministerial broadcasts.[28]

The other principal source for the MoI's Home Intelligence Unit was Mass Observation (MO). This radical and unusual organisation had been set up in 1937 by Tom Harrison, a social anthropologist, Charles Madge, a poet, and Humphrey Jennings, the documentary film maker. Harrison had taken part in four scientific expeditions to Borneo and the Pacific and felt that he knew more about the behaviour and attitudes of so-called 'native' peoples around the world than he did about his own compatriots. He co-founded Mass Observation to record what people really felt about the coronation of George VI. It used a variety of unorthodox techniques to eavesdrop on people and record their words and behaviour. Its mission was to study 'the everyday lives and feelings of ordinary people' in what it called 'the Science of Ourselves'.[29] Some of the techniques used by MO were rather crude but filled a gap in trying to find out what people thought about a variety of issues. Observers would visit shops, cafés or canteens and write down verbatim what people were saying. Some would get jobs in factories and record word-for-word what people talked about on the shop floor and in the pub. Or they would join cinema queues and again note down the topics people were discussing. To analyse how effective a poster campaign was, an observer would stand by a hoarding, count each passer-by and note whether they looked at the poster. To gauge the reaction to certain films, observers would sit in the cinema and carefully record how the audience responded to certain scenes, noting reactions like cheers when Churchill came on in a newsreel, or boos when Hitler appeared. These surveys would be followed up by more conventional door-to-door questioning about the impact of a poster, leaflet or film.

Before the war, MO carried out in-depth studies into life in a working-class community in the Lancashire town of Bolton. The observers studied the politics of non-voters, how working people spent their leisure time, attitudes to religion, and produced a detailed study called 'The Pub and the People'. In London a great deal of research was focused on the then working-class borough of Fulham. In both places there were a series of full-time observers. In the first four months of the war MO observers recorded 3,000 overheard conversations and carried out 7,000 interviews. In addition, there was a national panel of some 1,500 voluntary observers around the country who were sent questions at least once a month and filled in their own thoughts and the reactions of those around them to issues such as what is the attitude where you live to rationing, how do people around you feel about prospects for the year ahead, and what is the effect of the war on sex life in your area? About 200 members of the national panel also agreed to keep daily diaries which were sent in to the MO office once a month. The panel were not a statistically selected cross-section of the British people but they included professionals (vicars, solicitors, teachers), a large number of housewives, many Oxbridge graduates, and some working people. By these techniques, MO hoped to get to the bottom of not only *what* was happening to public morale but *why* it was happening.

During the Phoney War of 1939–40, MO reported on what it observed to be an immense gulf of culture and understanding between politicians and civil servants in the Establishment on the one hand and the mass of the British people on the other.[30] As the war progressed and more official commissions came in, Mass Observation began to produce regular reports for the MoI Home Intelligence Unit and it would continue to build a vast archive reflecting the views of the diarists and the work of the observers. The organisation repeatedly claimed to be politically independent and certainly did not have an overt party political stance, but there is no doubt that the founders and many of the observers were broadly left-wing in their attitudes and this always needs to be taken into account when analysing the results of a MO study.

The key issue in 1940 when the Home Intelligence Unit began, and again in 1942, was that of morale. Almost everyone agreed that maintaining morale was going to be vital. Many in government came to realise that national defeat could follow not only a collapse on the battlefield but also the breakdown of morale at home. A pre-war assessment of the role of the BBC concluded that 'The maintenance of public morale should be the principal aim of war-time programmes.'[31] But it is notoriously difficult to define the morale of a people, especially of a nation of some 46 million (in 1940–2). It has been called 'the woolliest and most muddled concept of the war', exceptionally difficult to define, influence or measure.[32] Nella Last, a housewife in Barrow-in-Furness who kept a diary for Mass Observation, asked very pertinently in one entry, 'What *is* "morale" – and have I got any, or how much more could I call on in need, and where does it come from, and what is it composed of?'[33] Yet everyone knew it was supremely important, and trying to understand what affected it became an important part of government strategy.

Stephen Taylor, who took over from Mary Adams as head of the Home Intelligence Unit in 1941, a doctor by training and profession, tried at a more scientific explanation. Morale, he wrote, must be 'ultimately measured not by what a person thinks or says, but by what he does and how he does it'. He defined low morale as including 'panic, hysteria, grumbling about those in authority, scapegoating, absenteeism'. Whereas good or high morale was likely to encompass 'cheerfulness, cooperation, high productivity, volunteering'.[34] The issue of public morale would be centre stage in the crises that ensued in 1942.

So, by the beginning of 1942, the state was regulating nearly every aspect of public and private life. The British people had been through the Blitz, some 45,000 civilians had been killed in the bombing and about two million homes had been damaged, one tenth of which were completely uninhabitable.[35]

Many acres of housing, warehouses and factories in the East End of London and in many city centres such as Coventry, Bristol, Plymouth, Portsmouth, Hull and Liverpool had been devastated. Although it seemed as though the immediate threat of invasion had passed, the coasts around the nation were still lined with barbed wire and guarded by thousands of pill-boxes. Many Britons were cheered by having the Soviet Union as an ally, relieved that Britain was off the hook, and were moved by the resilience of the Russian and Ukrainian people. Anglo-Soviet Friendship Weeks were held in most British towns and cities. But people were less enthusiastic, at this stage anyway, with having America on their side. Britons sympathised with the dreadful plight of the Russian people under the Nazi onslaught but felt the Americans had had it too good up to now.

By the beginning of 1942, three and a half million men and over 200,000 women were serving in the armed forces. Another three and a half million were involved in various part-time activities like the Home Guard and the Women's Voluntary Service. War industries or factories turned over to war production employed four and a quarter million people, a million and a half more than in 1939. About one third of these were women.[36] Average weekly earnings were 46 per cent higher for civilian men working in war production than they had been before the war. But income tax had gone up to ten shillings in the pound, 50 per cent of income, and the lowering of thresholds had made some four million workers eligible for tax who had never paid before.[37]

People were weary of the war and felt they had suffered enough. With the massive losses of shipping in the Atlantic (412 British and neutral vessels had been sunk in May 1941 alone), rations fell to their lowest level in the war. People were fed up with making substitute coffee out of acorns, with eating fatless pastry, sugarless puddings, eggless cakes and meatless pies made out of oatmeal, suet and a single vegetable. And with the Japanese advances in the Pacific at the end of the year, supplies of rice, sugar and tea that had come from the Far East ceased. But nowhere in the UK experienced starvation or famine. Although most people felt that Britain would win in the end, many were generally 'browned off' by the war. Growing numbers of people wanted to look ahead and plan for a new order, a new type of society, after the war was over to justify the pain they had endured so far.

This was the general state and mood of Britain and its people when Churchill returned after a month away from his long trip to the United States and Canada on 17 January 1942.

3

Confidence

When the House of Commons reconvened on 8 January 1942, while Churchill was still in America, there was a debate on the progress of the war. Several Conservative MPs were openly critical of the Prime Minister. There were accusations that too little had been done to prepare to resist the Japanese in the Far East, and that naval warships had foolishly and tragically been put in harm's way by sending them out without air protection. Underlying it all was the feeling that Churchill had gathered too much authority around himself and that at the very least a Minister of Production was needed to smooth over problems of supply. In the evening after the debate, Conservative MP Henry 'Chips' Channon, who had been an appeaser before the war and was not friendly towards Churchill, wrote in his diary that 'Seventeen members dined at the Dorchester [Hotel] collected by [Alexander] Erskine-Hill [Conservative MP and chairman of the backbench 1922 Committee] ... Anthony Eden was present and seemed upset when every MP present told him that the Government was doomed. It was no use, they said, the PM coming back and making one of his magical speeches. This time, it would serve no purpose. The Government must be reformed, and that soon.'[1]

Churchill had had a long and difficult relationship with

the Conservative Party. He had been initially elected as a Conservative MP in 1900 but had crossed the floor of the House to join the Liberals in 1904. Two years later they were elected to government. As a Liberal he had been a senior member of the great reforming administration of Herbert Asquith before the First World War and had helped introduce unemployment benefits and old age pensions funded by a tax on the rich. He returned to the Conservative benches in the 1920s and Stanley Baldwin appointed him Chancellor of the Exchequer. After the Conservatives were defeated in 1929 Churchill found himself out of office for a decade, what he called his 'wilderness years'. Throughout the inter-war years many Tories still distrusted him for his defection which they regarded as an opportunistic venture simply to attain office, and they saw him as a class traitor because of his support for social reforms and the redistribution of wealth by taxing the wealthy to help the less well off.

While out of office, Churchill earned considerable sums from his writing, a stream of books and a torrent of newspaper articles, but he became increasingly isolated from the Conservative Party. His passionate belief in the virtues of the British empire meant that for five years he opposed a moderate form of devolution for India in what finally became the India Act of 1935. His belief in monarchy led him to support Edward VIII in the abdication crisis the following year, and he so misjudged parliamentary opinion that he was shouted down in the Commons. Many Tories thought his career was over.

From the mid-1930s onwards, however, he increasingly spoke with alarm about the growth of the Nazi Party, outraged at their thuggish and murderous behaviour towards their opponents and predicting that Nazi Germany would become a military threat to Britain because of its rearmament, against the terms of the Versailles Treaty. But the Conservative Party was committed to peace, as were the vast majority of

British people. War memorials with long lists of the dead had gone up in almost every town and village in the country as a reminder of the great sacrifice of 1914–18. There were millions of maimed and wounded veterans struggling to make a living, many with the loss of arms or legs as visible evidence of their wounds. Others had invisible psychological scars that provoked periods of erratic or violent behaviour. The Great War, as it was called, had been the war 'to end all wars'. Millions favoured international disarmament and tens of thousands joined groups like the Peace Pledge Union to ensure Britain would not go to war again.[2] The appeasement of Hitler was a genuinely popular policy and by sounding his alarms Churchill seemed like an old warlord banging his drum and calling for bellicose action.

But Churchill continued to predict the likelihood of war and the futility of appeasing a man like Hitler whom he asserted would simply be encouraged by the weakness of his enemies to come back with even greater demands. By the summer of 1939, as his predictions seemed to be coming true, his popularity had revived, at least in much of the popular press if not within his party. Chamberlain invited him back into the Cabinet on the declaration of war as First Lord of the Admiralty, the position he had held in 1914. By May 1940, with Chamberlain discredited and Halifax ruling himself out as PM, the only real choice as successor had to be Churchill.

By November he had become an acclaimed war leader and saviour of the nation and so in that month, after the death of Chamberlain, Churchill was elected leader of the party. But he was still out of step with many Tory backbenchers. They were often successful local businessmen or landowners with a power base in their community, staid, predictable and con-servative with a small 'c'. Churchill was none of these things. He also had little interest in courting his backbenchers. He still disliked many of them because of their hostility to him in the

1930s, and he was so devoted to fighting the war that he had little time to meet them and listen to their points of view. He was a devoted parliamentarian and put great time and thought into preparing his speeches, but he did this knowing that his words would be reported around the nation, often around the world.[3] He knew that the Conservative Party was the only force that could remove him but he also realised that his only real rival within the party, Anthony Eden, was devoted to him. Although they frequently argued, and Churchill admired him for this, Eden was still largely in awe of his boss.[4]

After his return from Washington, Churchill's political antennae soon picked up the discontent within the Conservative Party. Brendan Bracken reported back to him on the questions being asked about his leadership. Churchill decided to confront this head on and announced a three-day debate in the House. Not only would his policy and his decisions be openly debated but he would turn the vote at the end of the session into a vote of confidence in the coalition. This would force all Tory MPs to decide where they stood. The debate was set for later in January.

In the meantime, Churchill had other things to worry about. The situation in the Far East was worsening daily. The sinking of the two warships *Prince of Wales* and *Repulse* had led to the collapse of British naval power in the region. Sixty RAF aircraft had also been lost at the start of the war in the Far East, many having been destroyed while still on the ground. The Japanese launched an invasion of Malaya at the same time as their fliers attacked Pearl Harbor, intending to attack Britain simultaneously with their assault upon the United States.[5] Their objective was the mighty naval fortress of Singapore, the symbol of British power and prestige in the Far East, at the southern tip of the long, thin Malayan peninsula.

The island of Singapore is roughly diamond-shaped and similar in size and outline to the Isle of Wight. It was ceded in

1819 by the Sultan of Johore to Sir Stamford Raffles, who was acting on behalf of the East India Company, which at the time still governed British India. Although the island consisted of little more than mangrove swamps, Raffles appreciated Singapore's strategic importance as it had a good harbour, and was at the centre of several trade routes with India to its west and China to its east, and close to Thailand and south-east Asia. The city soon became a prosperous port and Britain's authority expanded to all of Malaya. Effectively the peninsula became a British colony. Initially valued for its tin and gold mines, the introduction of the rubber plant in the 1870s soon turned rubber into Malaya's staple export, and it was a big earner. By 1940, Malaya produced 75 per cent of the world's rubber and 66 per cent of its tin. The British colonists did not much value the local Malay workers so encouraged Indians to emigrate to Malaya, and the urban growth also attracted huge numbers of Chinese workers into the colony.

During the First World War, Japan was an ally of Britain and France so neither country needed to bother much with the defence of their Asian colonies. By the 1920s the Imperial Japanese Navy was the third largest in the post-war world. And it looked possible that in a future war, Japan might be an enemy not a friend. Admiral Jellicoe calculated that a fleet based in Singapore would provide 'the naval key to the Far East'. It could protect all of Britain's Asian and Pacific interests and the routes to Australia. But it would need to consist of eight battleships, eight battlecruisers and a full complement of supporting warships.[6] This hit the nail on the head. There was no way Britain could afford to station such a vast permanent battle fleet thousands of miles from home waters. This was the central problem of what became known as 'the Singapore strategy'. Britain would never be willing to pay for the scale of defences that were needed to protect its vast imperial interests.

In 1921 the decision was made to build a major naval base in Singapore. If there were to be no permanent naval fleet in the Far East at least provision was needed for one that could be sent there at times of tension and danger. In addition, building the base would demonstrate to Australia and New Zealand that Britain was committed to their defence. The vast cost of the project meant that almost immediately after the plans were announced, the scale of its construction was reduced by Stanley Baldwin's Conservative government. The Chancellor of this government was Winston Churchill, who argued that he 'did not believe there was the slightest chance of a war with Japan in our lifetime' and so money could be saved as the port did not need to be built on the grand scale that had been envisaged.[7]

By the mid-1930s, the Singapore strategy was challenged by a new factor. With the rise of Nazi Germany came the possibility of a war in Europe. This would always take priority when Britain came to allocate military assets as a European war might threaten the home island. Where would that leave the defence of the Far East? When Japan walked out of the League of Nations in 1933, the government committed to finishing the building of the truncated naval base in Singapore while at the same time adopting a policy of appeasement – of Hitler in Germany and of Japan in the Far East. The Singapore base was ceremoniously opened in February 1938, well before being finished, and it was hoped that its very existence would act as a deterrent to Japanese aggression. Unfortunately for Britain and her empire, it did not.

Economic developments in Malaya, particularly the development of rubber plantations as worldwide demand grew exponentially, had led to the clearing of bush and swamp and the construction of roads and railways across the peninsula. This meant that the only way to defend Singapore was to defend the whole Malayan peninsula. Thus the Singapore strategy now expanded to involve a full air and land defence of Malaya in order to protect a naval base that was in any case not fit for purpose. Muddle, confusion and compromise had replaced a clear strategy for the defence of imperial interests.[8]

Singapore society was itself torn by divisions, both racial and economic. Immensely rich white colonists who traded in rubber and tin enjoyed a pleasant life alongside wealthy Chinese businessmen and Malayan potentates. Below them were hundreds of thousands of coolies and labourers who sweated in plantations and supported the consumerist society of the elite. Downtown Singapore was brightly lit at night and supposedly sophisticated but everything was separated by racial prejudice and class divisions. And the elite were complacent, feeling the war in Europe was far removed and the Japanese threat had been exaggerated.[9]

The fall of France and the Netherlands in June 1940 greatly worsened the situation. The Japanese took over bases in French Indo-China (Vietnam, Laos and Cambodia) and the Dutch were no longer in a position to defend their own East Indies (Indonesia, Sumatra and Java). And at home, Britain faced the prospect of invasion for the first time since the Napoleonic scare of the early 1800s. The use of airfields in French Indo-China put northern Malaya and the seas around it in range of land-based bombers and torpedo bombers. The RAF calculated it needed 582 aircraft to defend the region. In the face of wartime realities this was reduced to 336 front-line aircraft in twenty-two squadrons. The army said it needed four divisions and two tank regiments. But reinforcements were simply not available as the army had lost most of its equipment in the retreat to Dunkirk and the RAF were fighting for Britain's survival in the Battle of Britain. There just were not enough assets available to reinforce the Far Eastern garrison. By the end of 1941 and the beginning of hostilities in the Far East, the RAF had just 158 aircraft in Malaya, mostly old, obsolete Brewster Buffalos and Vickers Vildebeests, air-craft that would never have been used in the defence of Britain or in combat in the Middle East. The army, moreover, had only two divisions, mostly Indian troops led by British officers.

After the sinking of the *Prince of Wales* and *Repulse* in mid-December, the navy too changed its strategy. Instead of attempting to bring a fleet to Singapore the Admiralty decided to assemble vessels in the Indian Ocean to secure essential imperial shipping routes. The army now found itself in the bizarre situation of defending airfields spread over a huge area across Malaya that were only there to protect a naval base to which there was now no intention of sending a fleet.

With the Japanese advancing rapidly down the west coast of Malaya, Churchill had told the Australian Prime Minister, John Curtin, that Malaya might well fall to the Japanese. 'I do not see how anyone could expect Malaya to be defended, once the Japanese obtained command of the sea and while we are fighting for our lives against Germany and Italy,' he told Curtin. In a remark that was, frankly, racist, he said that the Japanese had advanced so rapidly because up to that point they had faced only tiny numbers of 'white' troops, 'the rest being Indian soldiers'. In reality the Indian units had all been 'milked', that is the best officers and NCOs had been sent off to fight in the Middle East. But Churchill still expressed his confidence that Singapore could be defended and that a 'counter-stroke will be possible in the latter part of February'.[10]

Only two days after his return from Washington, General Ismay went in to see Churchill for a morning meeting and found the Prime Minister 'in a towering rage'.[11] He announced he had just received news that left him 'staggered'. Churchill had learned from Wavell that there were no permanent defensive fortifications on the landward side of the giant naval base at Singapore and that all its guns 'could only fire sea-wards'. The millions that had been invested in building up Singapore from the 1920s onwards as the centre of British imperial power in the region had been predicated on defending itself only from a seaborne attack. And now the Japanese were rapidly heading towards the city from the landward side, across jungle terrain that had previously been thought impassable. Churchill suddenly saw 'the hideous spectacle of the almost naked island and of the wearied, if not exhausted, troops retreating upon it'. He immediately dictated a note to the chiefs of staff expressing his outrage, saying that he thought it was 'incredible' that there was no defence against a land attack on 'a fortress which had been twenty years [in the] building'. He carried on, 'How is it that not one of you pointed this out to me at any time when these matters have been under discussion?'[12]

Should Churchill have known about the defences of the Singapore base? He had been involved with its construction since his tenure as Chancellor of the Exchequer fifteen years before when, wearing his Treasury hat, he had reduced expenditure on the base. Without doubt he should have been well informed about the strengths and weaknesses of the island fortress. Should the chiefs of staff have reminded the Prime Minister of the vulnerability of Singapore from the landward side, once fighting had begun in the Far East and Churchill was openly talking about the need to defend Singapore at all costs? Certainly they should have. But they believed that the need to prepare a land-based defence of the island had always been understood. However, it's impossible not to see in Churchill's fumings the anger of a politician who desperately seeks to avoid blame by pointing the finger at his advisers and accuses them of not telling him something of substantive value that he thinks they should have told him. And, as always with Churchill, by putting pen to paper he hoped to defend himself from the criticism of future historians.

Churchill demanded that the chiefs of staff immediately
draw up a plan to prepare a landward defence for Singapore.
He concluded by writing that the city of Singapore should
be turned into a citadel 'and defended to the death'. No surrender should be contemplated 'and the Commander, Staffs
and principal Officers are expected to perish at their posts'.
The chiefs considered his suggestion, prepared a defensive
plan and sent this to Wavell, but omitted the order for senior
officers to 'perish at their posts'.[13]

In an evening meeting of the Chiefs of Staff Committee on
21 January, Churchill came up with a new proposal, a political
response to the military crisis that seemed to be fast approaching. If the situation was so bad that Singapore was effectively
lost, he asked whether it should not be abandoned and the
naval fortifications demolished to prevent them from being
of use to the enemy. The troops already there and the reinforcements on their way could then be diverted to the defence
of Burma. 'If Singapore could only hold out for another three
or four weeks,' Churchill argued, 'was it not only throwing
good money after bad to send more reinforcements there;
should they not be sent to Burma?' For Britain, Burma was
vital for the defence of India. But Churchill also knew that the
Americans saw it as providing a crucial overland supply line
to the Chinese, who must continue their war with the Japanese.
If China was knocked out of the war, hundreds of thousands
more Japanese soldiers currently engaged in Manchuria
would be freed up to attack the Allies. Taking the broad view,
Churchill argued that to Britain's imperial interests Burma
'was more important than Singapore'.[14] When news of this
discussion leaked to the Australian government, Curtin was
furious. He telegraphed Churchill to say that the abandonment
of Malaya and Singapore 'would be regarded here and elsewhere as an inexcusable betrayal'.[15] It was clear that Churchill's
idea was going to be politically impossible to implement.

After that evening's meeting of the Defence Committee, Churchill had drinks with Anthony Eden, his friend Lord Beaverbrook and A. V. Alexander, First Lord of the Admiralty. In addition to his political and military woes, Churchill had picked up a cold after his flight back from the United States. Eden later wrote, 'Winston was tired and depressed, for him. His cold is heavy on him. He was inclined to be fatalistic about the House, maintained that the bulk of the Tories hated him, that he had done all he could and would be only too happy to yield to another, that Malaya, Australian Government's intransigence and "nagging" in the House was more than any man could be expected to endure.' In this depressed mood, Churchill even reminded his friends that Lloyd George was only fifty-three when he had become Prime Minister in the last war, but that he was now sixty-seven.[16]

The problems facing Churchill and his conduct of the war were not limited to the Far East. The war in North Africa had presented one of the few opportunities for Britain to take up arms against Axis ground forces after its withdrawal from northern Europe. After the evacuation from Dunkirk, believing that Britain and France were both as good as defeated, Mussolini had declared war on the two countries. On a warm summer evening on 10 June 1940 a vast crowd gathered outside the Palazzo Venezia in Rome, in front of the giant Vittorio Emanuele monument. The crowd of supporters cheered wildly when Il Duce declared from the palazzo balcony 'People of Italy, to arms!' and 'Vinceremo!' ('We will win!') The Times called it a 'supreme example of stabbing in the back' and told its readers that in his declaration of war 'Mussolini proves himself a good second [after Hitler] in the art of treachery'.[17]

But from the start it did not go well for the Italian leader's dream of turning the Mediterranean into an Italian lake. In July, his navy, the Regia Marina, the most modern component of his armed forces, suffered under the superior gunnery

of the Royal Navy at the Battle of Calabria. Malta held out
against Italian bombing and to Rome's surprise was reinforced from Britain. In September, Italian troops advanced
cautiously from their colony of Libya 60 miles into British-
occupied Egypt. There, uncertain, their commander ordered
them to halt. In the following month an invasion of Greece
turned into a catastrophe for the Italians as the Greeks resisted
fiercely. At the end of the year, General Richard O'Connor
counter-attacked the Italian forces in North Africa with
only two divisions. His offensive was a stunning success.
He advanced 500 miles along the coast through Cyrenaica
in Italian Libya. The assault smashed ten Italian divisions
and captured 125,000 prisoners along with 400 tanks and 845
guns. It was the first British military triumph of the war and at
home people cheered the cinema newsreels showing endless
lines of Italian prisoners winding off into the far distance.

But this was just the beginning of a long see-saw war
across North Africa. Hitler came to the aid of his Italian ally,
sending troops to assist in Greece and ordering the man he
described as his most daring general, Erwin Rommel, to
Libya. At first Rommel had only two divisions of troops but
they would grow into an efficient, well-armoured grouping,
the Afrika Korps or Panzerarmee Afrika. Rommel's orders
were to remain on the defence, but the desert was a long way
from Berlin and the commander soon saw an opportunity
to take the offensive, pushing British forces right back to the
Egyptian border. To add to the humiliation, General O'Connor
was himself captured with his staff. In his advance into Egypt,
Rommel had left only an enclave of Australian troops in the
Libyan port of Tobruk. Besieged, the Australians, supported
by British and Indian troops, managed to cling on, supplied by
the Royal Navy at night. In June 1941, British forces launched
another offensive, Operation Battleaxe. But Rommel was
prepared and put up stiff resistance. After a few days the

offensive was called off. Shattered, disappointed and angry at its failure, Churchill appointed a new commander in the Middle East, General Claude Auchinleck.

Four days after the collapse of Battleaxe, Hitler launched his invasion of the Soviet Union. The scale of this assault set the scene for what would remain the most intense battle front of the war. It would also put into context all the other fighting fronts. Hitler invaded the Soviet Union with 120 divisions, about three million men, along a 450-mile front from the Baltic to the Black Sea, supported by 3,350 tanks. By comparison, Rommel had at his disposal in North Africa three German and six Italian divisions. Hitler's armies advanced at speed capturing one Soviet city after another – Minsk, Smolensk, Odessa. Within a month he had taken more than 600,000 Soviet prisoners. In September his troops captured Kiev, the capital of the Ukraine region, and with it another three quarters of a million prisoners. Hitler called it 'the greatest battle in world history'. In terms of numbers he was not far wrong.

Churchill was worried that after a stunning and quick victory on the Russian front Hitler would turn his triumphant armies on Britain. He urged Auchinleck to attack in the desert but his new commander told him he would not be ready until November. In the interim, British cryptographers broke the Italian naval code that listed exactly when and from where supply convoys would sail to reinforce Rommel in North Africa. One convoy of seven ships carrying thousands of tons of supplies, including 17,000 tons of fuel and 389 vehicles, was attacked and every vessel was sunk. The Desert Air Force was reinforced with American as well as British-made aircraft until it had a strength of about 800 planes.

When he was finally ready to attack, Auchinleck launched Operation Crusader with his Eighth Army on 18 November. Within days his men had advanced 50 miles and at the end of the month relieved the siege of Tobruk. Churchill cabled

Auchinleck: 'as long as you are closely locked with the enemy, the Russians cannot complain about no second front ... the only thing that matters is to beat the life out of Rommel and Co'.[18] The Axis lost almost 40,000 men killed, wounded or taken prisoner, but the British armoured squadrons also suffered severe losses when they came up against well-entrenched anti-tank units. When their commander seemed to suffer a nervous breakdown, Auchinleck stepped in and replaced him. The Allied army made up of Britons, Australians, New Zealanders, Indians, Rhodesians, South Africans, Czechs and Poles suffered losses of nearly 18,000 men.

In December, Hitler withdrew several Luftwaffe squadrons from the Eastern Front and sent them to the Mediterranean. They rapidly brought about a shift in the fortunes of the Axis forces. More closely protected, Axis supply convoys began to get through and the island of Malta came under renewed attack. Naval losses mounted in the Mediterranean, and on 19 December Italian frogmen got into the harbour at Alexandria and laid charges on the battleships *Queen Elizabeth* and *Valiant*. Both ships were badly damaged and sank to the harbour floor. They took months to recover, a setback almost as great as the loss of the *Prince of Wales* and the *Repulse* off Malaya.[19] Reinforcements of an entire British infantry division were diverted from North Africa and sent instead to Singapore to shore up the defence of Malaya, further weakening the Desert Army. Then, on 21 January 1942, Rommel once again launched a counter-offensive and began to advance eastwards, throwing Auchinleck's forces back across Libya. Ahead of them lay Egypt, the Suez Canal and, ultimately, the oilfields of the Middle East.

It was against this background that Churchill faced the critical motion about how he had conducted the war. To open the debate he spoke for nearly two hours. He admitted to a range of disasters, blunders and misfortunes and confessed 'to feeling the weight of the war upon me even more than in the tremendous summer days of 1940. There are so many fronts which are open, so many vulnerable points to defend, so many inevitable misfortunes, so many shrill voices raised to take advantage, now that we can breathe more freely, of all the turns and twists of war.'[20] Harold Nicolson wrote in his diary, 'One can actually feel the wind of opposition dropping sentence by sentence and by the time he finishes it is clear that there is really no opposition at all – only a certain uneasiness. Winston does nothing to diminish that uneasiness. He says we shall have even worse news to face in the Far East and that the Libyan battle is going none too well. He thrusts both his hands deep into his trouser pockets and turns his tummy, now to the right, now to the left, in evident enjoyment of his mastery of the position.'[21]

A less friendly view came from Henry 'Chips' Channon: 'One's first impressions [of Churchill's speech] were entirely favourable but I soon detected an undercurrent of hostility, and of criticism, for he had mollified nobody ... why is the PM so unpopular in the House, he, a life-long House of Commons man? Perhaps his intolerance, his arrogance and his bad judgement are the reasons, and yet his many magnificent qualities are obvious to all.'[22]

The debate carried on for two more days but the steam had been taken out of the opposition. There was no alternative leader being put forward and no coherent plan for change being proposed. There were repeated criticisms of the War Cabinet and many MPs called for the appointment of a Minister of Production. Trenchant criticism came from a high-standing Tory MP, Sir John Wardlaw-Milne, of both military strategy in the Far East and industrial production at home. The question, he said, was whether Churchill was 'trying to do too much, perhaps even carrying a burden which is beyond the power of any one human being'.[23] Many in the Conservative Party wanted to avoid a vote. Even if few would vote against the Prime Minister, some might abstain, and this could be seen as a sign of weakness. Churchill was prepared to risk this and desperately wanted a vote because he knew he would win strongly and wanted the reassurance this would bring.

On 29 January, Churchill wound up the debate with a forty-minute speech. Praising the parliamentary system, he said, 'In no country in the world at the present time could a Government conducting a war be exposed to such a stress. No dictator country fighting for its life would dare allow such a discussion.' After breaking off from 'busy days and nights' to prepare for the debate he admitted that mistakes had been made in the field, referring specifically to the rout in Malaya, but he said he would stand by his commanders. He talked of the difficulty of fighting Germany, Italy and Japan at the same time, while also continuing to supply armaments by sea to the Soviet Union. But he insisted that the nation could not turn its back on any of these separate challenges. He refuted the specific charge that he had sent the *Prince of Wales* and the *Repulse* into action without appropriate air cover by saying that Admiral Phillips knew the risks he was taking by sailing north on his mission to deter the Japanese from landing in Malaya. He said it was a gamble that had it paid off could have led to the failure of the landings 'and a relief from the whole catalogue of misfortunes which have since come upon us, and have still to come'.[24]

Harold Nicolson painted a vivid picture of the scene at the conclusion of his peroration: ' "I have finished" he says, "I have done", and he makes a downward gesture with his palms open as if receiving the stigmata. He then crouches over the box and strikes it. "I offer no apologies, I offer no excuses, I make no promises. In no way have I mitigated the sense of danger and impending misfortunes that hang over us. But at the same time I avow my confidence, never stronger than at this moment, that we shall bring this conflict to an end in a manner agreeable to the interests of our country and to the future of the world."' These words were met by loud cheering in the chamber.[25]

The debate did go to a vote of confidence as Churchill wished, and when the result was announced no one was surprised. It was 464 in support of the government and only one vote against, that of James Maxton of the Independent Labour Party (a small group to the far left of the Labour Party). It would have been three against had not the other two members of the ILP been appointed tellers, meaning they could not vote. There was huge cheering within the Commons. After it had subsided, Harold Nicolson noted that Churchill and his

.... *but the melody lingers on!*

The Daily Mirror *cartoon, 30 January 1942. Churchill easily defeats the no-confidence vote in the Commons but criticism of his leadership will continue.*

wife Clemmie left the House 'arm-in-arm and beaming they push through the crowd in Central Hall'. The old man had triumphed again, although no one seriously thought that he would not. But Conservative MP Cuthbert Headlam confided in his diary, 'a few more votes of confidence such as today's, unless he can show some successes and a greater efficiency, will be the end of Winston'.[26]

As he left the Commons, Nicolson glanced at the Reuters ticker tape machine. It had been placed in the Lobby to keep members up with the latest news. It was ticking madly, spewing out a long line of tape, and Nicolson read the headlines that were coming through. The Germans had just announced they had entered Benghazi. The Japanese claimed to be only 18 miles from Singapore. It was an inauspicious end for a day of triumph.[27]

4

The Channel Dash

Even with Japanese forces closing in on Singapore and
Rommel once again outmanoeuvring the Eighth Army in
North Africa, there was yet another catastrophe to come. Once
more, British forces acted heroically but proved totally inadequate. Once more, Churchill would be blamed for the failure.

From the middle of 1940, with the whole of the north
European seaboard, from northern Norway to the Pyrenees,
under Nazi occupation, there were dozens of fjords for large
capital ships to hide in, and harbours for U-boats to be penned
ready to head out into the North Atlantic. Keeping the shipping lanes open across the Atlantic was vital for Britain: not
only to keep all the guns, tanks, armaments and military supplies crossing the ocean from the United States, and not only,
from the beginning of 1942, to maintain the vast flow of men
and materiel coming from North America to the UK, but also
to sustain the supply of foodstuffs, metals, fuel, chemicals and
other imports that were essential for Britain's very survival.
This was a struggle that Britain, as a trading nation reliant
upon imports, simply could not afford to lose.

Hitler was determined that his navy, the Kriegsmarine,
would succeed where the Imperial German Navy of the First
World War had failed, in starving Britain into surrender by

blockading the country. Looking back on the long battle for control of the Atlantic, Churchill wrote, 'The only thing that ever really frightened me during the war was the U-boat peril. I was even more anxious about this battle than I had been about the glorious air fight called the Battle of Britain.'[1] During the last six months of 1940 U-boats ranging right across the thousands of miles of Atlantic Ocean sank 400 ships, nearly 2 million tons of shipping.[2] In the early months of 1941, losses were rising even more alarmingly. In February, the command centre for the 'Western Approaches', the sea-lanes across the Atlantic that led to Britain, was moved to Liverpool and put under the command of Admiral Sir Percy Noble. Churchill spoke of the 'Battle of the Atlantic', putting it into the same league as the Battles of France and Britain, and insisted that this struggle be given the highest possible priority.

It was not only U-boats that threatened merchant convoys in the Atlantic. A series of surface raiders also sailed out into the ocean to cause havoc with Allied shipping. At the end of December 1940, the two battlecruisers *Scharnhorst* and *Gneisenau* left Kiel and headed into the Atlantic. Known as the 'ugly sisters', these two powerful ships, each with nine 11-inch guns and capable of 32 knots, could outrun most ships in the Royal Navy. They spent three months hunting merchant vessels. The *Scharnhorst* sank fourteen British ships and the *Gneisenau* eight, a total of more than 115,000 tons of shipping. In March 1941 they returned to Brest harbour to undergo repairs at the port's extensive dry dock facilities. But Brest was within range of RAF bombers which began regular raids on the docks. Photo-reconnaissance aircraft kept up a daily watch on the ships, and when the *Gneisenau* was spotted as having moved to the inner harbour another air raid was ordered. On 6 April a squadron of Beaufort fighter bombers attacked, each armed with a torpedo. The Germans had sur-rounded the *Gneisenau* with 270 anti-aircraft guns that put up a tremendous barrage of fire against the raiders. But one Beaufort from 22 Squadron, piloted by Flying Officer Kenneth Campbell, got through the hail of gunfire at low level and his torpedo scored a direct hit. The German warship was left with a 40-foot hole on one side and was out of commission for eight months. However, Campbell's attack became a suicide mission: he was shot down and all four members of the crew were lost. Campbell was awarded a posthumous VC for leading the attack.[3]

The following month another more famous naval engagement took place to prevent a surface raider from getting into the Atlantic. On 21 May, the pride of Hitler's navy, the *Bismarck*, the biggest German battleship yet built with eight 15-inch guns, was spotted by an RAF photo-reconnaissance pilot as it was about to leave a Norwegian fjord with its support vessel, the heavy cruiser *Prinz Eugen*. Under the command of Admiral Lütjens the two ships were about to head into the Atlantic to attack Allied merchant shipping. At the time there were eleven separate convoys crossing the ocean and the damage the *Bismarck* could cause was immense. The Admiralty ordered several vessels to converge on the bleak, ice-bound stretch of water between Greenland and Iceland known as the Denmark Strait where the *Bismarck* would attempt to pass into the Atlantic. Thus began one of the greatest chases in naval history.

The first round in the ensuing battle went to the *Bismarck*. HMS *Hood*, one of the navy's latest battleships, was hit by a single armour-piercing shell from the *Bismarck* which penetrated its rear ammunition store. More than 100 tons of cordite exploded and the ship was literally ripped in two. It went down in minutes and only three men from its crew of 1,400 survived. A combination of shipboard radar, sightings by Catalina flying boats and radio intercepts now brought a number of capital ships from both Scapa Flow and Gibraltar into the chase. These included two aircraft carriers, two more battleships, several heavy cruisers and many destroyers. It was a sign of both the seriousness of the threat and the overwhelming power the Royal Navy could bring to bear.

On the evening of 24 May, Fleet Air Arm Fairey Swordfish aircraft led by Lieutenant Commander Eugene Esmonde flying from HMS *Victorious* spotted the German battleship. The Swordfish was a biplane with canvas wings held together with bracing wire and known by its crews as the 'Stringbag'. Although they looked like leftovers from another era, the planes were sturdy and reliable although very slow. But out of range of the much faster and more manoeuvrable German fighters, the Swordfish was very effective. Each one carried a single torpedo. One of them hit *Bismarck* amidships. This forced Lütjens to head for Brest for repairs, about 700 miles away. A second wave of Swordfish aircraft found the German battleship and this time scored two direct hits. One of these damaged the port rudder leaving the *Bismarck* disabled and unable to do anything but sail around in a large circle. The ancient-looking Swordfish had proved its worth.

Soon after daybreak on the morning of 27 May, the battleships *King George V* and *Rodney* and the heavy cruisers *Dorsetshire* and *Norfolk* closed in for the kill. The *Bismarck*'s heavy guns were still able to fire and caused damage to the *Rodney* but the *Bismarck* was a sitting duck and a combination of shells and torpedoes ultimately did for her. Admiral Lütjens sent a final signal: 'Ship unmanoeuvrable. We shall fight to the last shell. Long live the Führer!' After several hours of being hit repeatedly, the *Bismarck* finally went down in the late morning.[4] All but 114 of its 2,200-man crew, including Admiral Lütjens, went down with it. It was a stirring victory for the Royal Navy, later commemorated in books and films.[5] But, with the loss of the *Hood*, it had been a costly one. All of this deterred Hitler from ever sending the *Tirpitz*, the other

German heavy battleship, into the Atlantic. The largest warship left in the Kriegsmarine spent most of the rest of the war
hiding in the fjords of Norway.

After spending no more than a week in the Atlantic, *Prinz
Eugen* returned to Brest with its own engine troubles. The
harbour became the object of repeated observation by photo-
reconnaissance sorties and several more raids by Bomber
Command. There were now three large warships in dock
there, the battlecruisers *Scharnhorst* and *Gneisenau*, whose
gaping hole was slowly being repaired, and the heavy cruiser
Prinz Eugen. In January 1942, Hitler decided to recall all three
vessels to home waters, fearing the Allies were about to launch
an attack upon Norway. He suggested to Admiral Raeder, the
commander-in-chief of the Kriegsmarine, that the warships
should attempt a 'surprise break through the Channel'.[6]
Raeder was not at first keen on such a proposal and favoured
a longer circuit out into the Atlantic, around the north of the
British Isles and south into the North Sea. But it was not easy
to resist Hitler when he became convinced of a plan of action
and Raeder finally agreed to the idea. Vice Admiral Ciliax,
whose flagship was the *Scharnhorst*, was instructed to prepare
a plan. Ciliax decided on a route, departing Brest in the early
evening so photo-reconnaissance aircraft would not spot his
departure for at least twelve hours, keeping close to the French
coast and avoiding most of the British-laid minefields. He
chose a date when there would be minimal moonlight so it
would be as dark as possible. During daylight hours the three
warships would be watched over by at least sixteen fighter
aircraft to defend them from any attempt by the RAF to attack.
The most dangerous moment of the mission would be passing
through the 22-mile-wide Dover Straits which according to the
timing of the plan would take place in daylight. Ciliax chose
a daylight passing of the Straits in order to be able to draw on
extra air cover at this point. The Luftwaffe could call upon up

to 280 fighters to assist in the transit of the cruisers.

In late January, Enigma intercepts picked up suggestions of the plan without any of the details on timing or route. When observation aircraft spotted minesweeping operations in the southern Channel it seemed to confirm that some sort of transit was being prepared. On 2 February, the Admiralty distributed an intelligence 'appreciation' in which the various alternative escape routes were considered. The intelligence report reckoned that the most likely route for the three vessels was right up the Channel and concluded with remarkable prescience, 'we might well find the two battle cruisers and the eight-inch cruiser with five large and five small destroyers and ... twenty fighters constantly overhead ... proceeding up the Channel'.[7]

The Admiralty intelligence assessment alerted all the relevant commands. Six destroyers armed with torpedoes were put on stand-by in the Thames estuary. Six motor torpedo boats were sent to reinforce the flotilla at Dover. The minelayers *Manxman* and *Welshman* were deployed to Plymouth and Dover respectively. There was a shortage of submarines but two old boats normally used for training were sent into the Bay of Biscay, and HMS *Sealion* was ordered to lie off the coast watching the port of Brest. The six serviceable Swordfish aircraft of 825 Fleet Air Arm Squadron were deployed to Manston in Kent, ready to attempt to intercept the enemy warships.

When Admiral Ramsay, based at Dover, considered the German action he concluded that if the Germans went ahead they would be most likely to pass through the Straits at night. He thus miscalculated one of the key moments of the German plan. No further naval assistance was available as all the cruisers and battleships at Scapa Flow were occupied in assisting a big troop convoy of twenty-six ships that was about to sail from the Clyde into the Atlantic to begin the long journey around the Cape of Good Hope towards the Middle

East. And also, there was always the possibility that the *Tirpitz* would use the distraction to head into the Atlantic to attack Allied shipping, so reserves had to be kept to counter such a possibility.

The RAF were also informed of the possibility of an attempt to get through the Channel. Bomber Command claimed priority in attacking ships at sea and it was put on alert to send aircraft to bomb the German ships during their voyage. Coastal Command only had a tiny number of Beaufort squadrons equipped with torpedoes available as most had been sent to the Mediterranean. And they were scattered across the country. One squadron was split between Thorney Island near Portsmouth and St Eval in Cornwall but it was crewed by teams who had little experience of attacking moving vessels at sea. Another squadron was based at Leuchars in Scotland to keep an eye on the *Tirpitz*. It was ordered to fly to East Anglia but because of snowy conditions in the south-east its dispatch was delayed. Hudson aircraft equipped with on-board radar that could detect a large ship at sea up to 30 miles away were ordered to begin daily patrols up and down the Channel.

Admiral Ciliax chose 7.30 p.m. on the evening of 11 February to leave Brest and begin his daring mission. In the event his departure was delayed a few hours by an air raid, but at 10.45 p.m. the three big warships and their escorts slipped out of harbour, rounded the Brittany peninsula and began to speed up the Channel at a rapid 27 knots. At dawn, just after they had passed Alderney, almost due south of the Isle of Wight, their Luftwaffe air escort appeared overhead. But from the beginning, things started to go badly wrong with the British response.

The submarine *Sealion* had been waiting off Brest harbour watching for any departing ships but, believing the plan was to pass through the Dover Straits at night, had calculated that no ship would leave after 9.30 p.m. and so had abandoned its watch mid-evening. Because of the delay caused by the air raid, it missed seeing the flotilla depart. A Coastal Command Hudson aircraft on patrol looking for any vessels sailing at night had to return to base with radar failure. No replacement was sent out and the failure to cover a part of the possible route of the German vessels was not reported to Dover. Another Hudson flew as planned further east up the Channel but it was just out of range for its radar to pick up the surface vessels. So, it was not until 10.30 a.m. on Thursday the 12th that it was noticed that the three capital ships with their support vessels had left Brest. By this point they were already off the mouth of the Somme river, twelve hours and 300 miles into their mission.[8]

Over the previous few weeks, the Germans had begun jamming the radar stations along the south coast. As this was a regular occurrence, on the morning of the 12th it did not prompt any specific alert. At RAF Fighter Command headquarters in Stanmore the radar operators looked at blank screens but made nothing of it. Like Coastal Command, who had failed to report the gap in their night-time surveillance, so Fighter Command also failed to report to Dover what was happening. Accordingly, in late morning, Admiral Ramsay decided that it was unlikely the German vessels would try to break through on this day. He stood his forces down. The destroyers based in the Thames estuary departed for an exercise in the North Sea.

A regular Spitfire patrol made a low-level sweep to check if anything was going on in the Channel. It spotted some activity near Le Touquet but it needed a second patrol to notice that there were large ships involved. The pilots maintained radio silence so this was not passed on until they had landed and were debriefed. By now it was well after 11 a.m. Admiral Ciliax could not have begun to imagine how effective his deception measures had been. At 11.20 his ships had to reduce speed to 10 knots to pass through a recently laid British minefield. It would have been an ideal opportunity to launch an attack upon the slow-moving vessels but no squadrons were in the air and the carefully planned response had not even begun.

Admiral Ramsay was at last alerted by his own radar and realised that the German ships were making their transit. Amazed, he discovered that without being told they were even en route they had reached a point almost opposite him, near Boulogne. He ordered the huge shore batteries at Dover to open fire. But by now a low mist had settled over the area and the gunners could not see the targets. Their shells fell short. Ramsay ordered his motor torpedo boats to attack the German vessels. Bravely, these small craft approached the German squadron but the heavy guns of the capital ships and the small arms of the escorting E-boats along with the defending fighter aircraft kept them from approaching close in. Several torpedoes were fired off but only at long range. No hits were recorded.

By now it was after noon. The Swordfish crews of 825 Fleet Air Arm Squadron at Manston were scrambled. The six aircraft were commanded by Lieutenant Commander Eugene Esmonde, the man who had led the attack that had disabled the *Bismarck*. Carrying a heavy torpedo, the Swordfish could fly at no more than 90 mph. Esmonde and his crews waited in their cockpits for the fighter escort they had been promised. Five squadrons were supposed to escort them. But everything was behind schedule and there was a delay in coordinating the fighter response. By now the German vessels had successfully passed through the Dover Straits, were out of the minefields and had picked up speed again. At 12.30 Esmonde decided he had to attack alone before the enemy ships passed out of range.

With just one squadron of fighters to escort his six Swordfish he set off across the Channel to a point 10 miles north-east of Calais. The Spitfire escort immediately engaged with the German fighters that included not just Messerschmitt 109s but also new and more powerful Focke-Wulf 190s that were faster than the current mark of Spitfire. A fierce dogfight ensued. The sky filled with the chaos of combat, and German fighters swarmed in to attack the Swordfish that began to line up for their attacks. As the German fighters sped in from behind, the observers and gunners, standing up in the rear of their Stringbag cockpits and facing backwards, shouted instructions for the pilots to take evasive action. The German fighters were puzzled by the slow speed of the Swordfish and constantly overshot their targets. This enabled the first wave to get close to the German vessels. Out of the smoke and mist, Esmonde correctly picked out the *Scharnhorst* and prepared to launch his torpedo through a hailstorm of fire. But by now the German fighters were attacking the Stringbags from the beam. All three Swordfish from the first wave dropped their torpedoes but within seconds were shot out of the sky. Esmonde was killed, as were three others; the remaining five men from the first wave were later rescued at sea. Having watched Esmonde and the other two aircraft being shot down, the second wave of Stringbags gallantly launched their attack but again all three were shot down. There were no survivors from this wave. Moreover, none of the torpedoes that had been launched hit their targets. The German ships sailed on.[9]

Further confusion struck the RAF attacking force. The squadron of Beauforts from Scotland had to divert from Coltishall because of snow in Norfolk. They had been due to refuel and arm up with torpedoes at Coltishall but there were no torpedoes at the airfield they were diverted to. Another group of Beauforts were dispatched from Cornwall and seven more from Thorney Island were ordered to attack once they had linked up with their fighter escorts at Manston. They reached Manston at 1.40 p.m., late for their rendezvous, so it was decided to instruct them to fly on towards the German ships and link up with the fighters there. But the Beauforts of Coastal Command were on a different radio frequency to the Spitfires of Fighter Command and did not receive the message. By the time it all got sorted out the Beauforts were too late to reach the German ships and had to return to base without having seen action.

The Germans were not having it all their own way. At about 2.30 p.m. the *Scharnhorst* struck a mine just north of the Scheldt estuary. It slowed right down but repairs began immediately. Admiral Ciliax and his staff transferred to one of the destroyer escorts. But this vessel was also damaged and so he transferred to yet another. While doing so, as confusion spread, a German Dornier bombed the vessel he was on. Ciliax then saw the *Scharnhorst*, repaired and able to carry on at 25 knots, sail right past him.

In the early afternoon, Ramsay ordered his six destroyers to break off their exercises near Harwich and attack the German vessels as soon as possible. In order to do this, the destroyers had to cross a German minefield. The senior officer, Captain Pizey on HMS *Campbell*, ordered his ships to proceed at full speed and bravely led his flotilla through the mines. This they did without incident. Shielded by the mist, soon after 3.40 p.m. the destroyers spotted the *Scharnhorst*, which had now rejoined *Gneisenau*, at about 4 miles' range. The German cruisers put up a barrage of defensive fire. HMS *Worcester* was severely damaged and set on fire but the destroyers pressed home their attack. Once more the poor weather and lack of visibility hindered their targeting. Again, torpedoes were fired but the range was too great. The Germans seemed blessed as none of these torpedoes hit home.

During the afternoon, Bomber Command ordered several squadrons of its aircraft to attack the German ships. Halifaxes, Stirlings, Manchesters and Wellingtons were all involved.

Some of the crews had only got back from raids over Germany in the early hours of the morning. They were quickly briefed and initially equipped with armour-piercing bombs but to be effective these had to be dropped from several thousand feet. The cloud cover was now down to 700 feet, so many of the aircraft were rearmed with high-explosive bombs. This caused further delays. By the time the bombers reached the Germans off the Dutch coast all was confusion. There were many German aircraft in the air, no longer just the fighters but also Dorniers, Heinkels, Junkers 87s and 88s, all there to defend the German vessels. The RAF bombers struggled to identify targets and no one had told them that the Royal Navy's destroyers were also on the scene. At least one aircraft lined up to attack a destroyer before being told to desist at the last second. At the height they needed to drop their bombs there was thick cloud and only forty of the bombers, roughly one in six, managed to identify a target and drop their load. Two hundred other crews returned to base with their bombs still on board having had no sighting whatsoever of the German ships.

By now it was dusk, and as darkness settled over the German cruisers it looked as though they had made it. But the drama of the day was not yet over. Just before 8 p.m. the *Gneisenau* struck a mine off the Dutch island of Terschelling. It was able to carry on but at a slower speed. Then at 9.30 the *Scharnhorst* struck another mine in roughly the same area. This time the big German ship was badly damaged. Both main engines stopped and her steering was put out of action. The *Gneisenau* and the *Prinz Eugen* reached the mouth of the Elbe to cross to Kiel in the Baltic in the early hours of the 13th. The *Scharnhorst*, still taking on water, limped into Wilhelmshaven a few hours later. They had made it. Hitler's daring plan had succeeded.

The ambitious German plan had been executed efficiently with a well-coordinated fighter escort. Things only went wrong for the Germans in the late afternoon, by which time the ships had passed Dover and were on the final straight. The Germans lost seventeen fighters and one escort vessel. On the British side, HMS *Worcester* returned to its base having put out the fires on board. The RAF also lost seventeen fighters but in addition fifteen bombers, three Beauforts and all six Swordfish. Esmonde, for leading his Swordfish attack against a hail of fire, was rewarded for his extreme bravery with a posthumous VC. It had all been very British, brave and courageous but ultimately futile in preventing the German cruisers from getting through.

Hitler had been right in calculating that British commanders would be slow to respond to a fast-moving and audacious mission. Remarkably, Admiralty intelligence had correctly anticipated most aspects of what became known as the Channel Dash ten days before it took place. Plans had been prepared involving the contribution of all three commands of the RAF, naval destroyers and Motor Torpedo Boats, and the shore batteries at Dover. But nothing had been properly planned out. Technical failures had not been reported. Communications had not been coordinated and were utterly abysmal. It did not help that the German ships were already twelve hours into their mission by the time anyone realised they had even left Brest. Only the attack by the desperately slow Swordfish biplanes had gone ahead as planned, albeit without full fighter escort. But despite the heroism of their attack, nothing had been achieved. It was a sorry story of blunder, inertia, failed communications and a pathetic lack of unified command.

At the time, the fact that the *Scharnhorst* and *Gneisenau* had hit mines off the Dutch coast was not known. But the rest of the miserable saga was quickly reported. Once again, military failures prompted a political crisis. There was uproar in the press. The normally loyal *Daily Mail* led the attack with a leader that was both anti-government and anti-Churchill. A comparison was made with Sir Francis Drake and the Spanish Armada in the sixteenth century. How was it that the Germans had got through when the Spaniards had not been able to 350 years before? The *Daily Mirror* again blamed Churchill in its editorial by asking: 'Is it any longer true to say that we trust the Prime Minister, though we do not trust the government?' With a clear reference to the recent parliamentary vote of confidence, it went on that if 'Mr Churchill continues to impose his will on Parliament and on strategy, his great qualities will no longer be an asset to the nation, but a peril'.[10]

The *Manchester Guardian* was more restrained but asked of the naval operation: 'Why did no British naval patrol engage with them at that time [as they passed through the Straits of Dover]?' Comparison was made between the sinking of the *Prince of Wales* and *Repulse* off Malaya by Japanese aircraft two months before, and the failure of British aircraft to inflict any hits on the three German warships. 'We have now not only seen capital ships without aircraft cover sunk,' the leader commented, 'we have seen those with that guard escape under the greatest possible air attack. Perhaps by now, those who plan our strategy understand.' It concluded: 'So great is the possible harm of the escape to us and to our Allies, so useful is it to the enemy, that the nation will expect a careful enquiry into the circumstances of the unhappy failure.'[11]

Churchill was thrown into despair by the fiasco. He ordered an immediate inquiry into the event that was to be led by Justice Singleton.[12] Sir Alexander Cadogan of the Foreign Office wrote in his diary, 'The blackest day of the war yet ... We are nothing but failure and inefficiency everywhere.'[13] Henry 'Chips' Channon woke up on the 13th to find the newspapers emblazoned with the names of the German ships. He wrote in his diary, 'Everything seems to be going against us.' Then he saw the furious attack in the *Daily Mail*. 'It is the first that has ever appeared,' he wrote. 'Everyone is in a rage against the Prime Minister. Rage; frustration. This is not the post-Dunkirk feeling, but ANGER. The country is more upset about the escape of the German battleships than over Singapore ... The capital seethes with indignation and were Londoners Latins there would be rioting. I have never known so violent an outburst.' When he got to the House of Commons he heard that there was a 'flap' on in Downing Street and that Winston, angered by the *Daily Mail* leader, was in 'a defiant, truculent mood'.[14]

Channon was right in that many people felt more upset about the Channel Dash than they did about the prospect of the fall of Singapore or the reverse of fortunes in North Africa. Such events seemed far distant. But the passing of German warships only a few miles from the White Cliffs of Dover was much closer to home, far more embarrassing. People were resigned to events on the different battle fronts but this affront seemed to endanger national security. Home Intelligence concluded in their weekly report for the Ministry of Information that people felt 'this was the most bitter failure of the whole war ... the blackest week since Dunkirk ... the desire to criticise is widespread, and although the Service Chiefs are greatly blamed, the main weight of public criticism seems to be directed against the government, and no longer excludes the Prime Minister'.[15]

When Churchill next went to the House of Commons he faced a barrage of questions. Channon again noted how each answer he gave prompted a reception that was 'increasingly hostile; never have I known the House to growl at a Prime Minister. Can he ever recover his waning prestige?'[16] 'Coming on top of the tragic news from Singapore, the bad news from Libya and Burma, and the good news from nowhere, the incredible happenings in the Strait of Dover were the straw that finally broke the public's capacity for bearing disaster,' wrote Mollie Panter-Downes, surveying reactions in London.[17]

Mass Observation recorded 'mounting public disquiet and alarm at the progress of the war practically without precedent even for this war'. Confidence in the management of the war slumped. More people began to carry their gas masks again and began to fear the prospect of an invasion of Britain, as they had eighteen months before. Criticism of the government, aired in the press, was widespread in the MO reports. 'Won't our Govt ever learn from its mistakes ... I tell you frankly, unless something is done and quickly we're going to find Hitler in Buckingham Palace,' offered up a middle-aged man. As a result of the Channel Dash and the retreat to Singapore 'there has appeared for the first time a small but significant body of strongly anti-Churchill feeling', Mass Observation concluded. Comments were recorded such as 'the sooner Churchill goes the better. Why? He's not the leader of the people, he's the leader of the Old School Tie.'[18]

In Dewsbury, West Yorkshire, a Mass Observation diarist noted down the mood of the customers in the corner shop in which she worked. 'Great indignation among customers at escape of German battleships. More comment than over Pearl Harbour and Prince of Wales. Customers voluntarily speak of it without my prompting, a sure sign they are disturbed ... Mrs B said "What have they been doing to let them ships escape? They've made fools of us, haven't they?" Old Mrs Mac: "it's been a black week and night. As if t'Japs weren't a sore point with many, that it happened under our noses." Another man: "By gosh it's time we bucked up what with one thing and another – there's only the Russians doing owt. They wouldn't have let them slip, you can bet." '[19]

In the unfolding strategy of the war, the Channel Dash had very different consequences from those seen at the time. Hitler had withdrawn three capital ships to home waters from where they could no longer get out into the Atlantic to attack

Britain's vital lines of supply from North America. Churchill was keen to point this out to Roosevelt to whom he sent a message saying, 'This will keep them out of mischief for at least six months during which both our Navies will receive important accessions of strength.'[20] As it turned out, the *Prinz Eugen* was torpedoed and put out of action ten days later by a British submarine; the *Gneisenau* was hit during a bombing raid on Kiel two weeks later and never went on active service again; and the *Scharnhorst* took eight months to repair and was finally sunk by a British naval force in December 1943. But of course none of this was known or could be expected at the time and the comments in that West Yorkshire corner shop best captured the mood of the British people in the aftermath.

The official history of the Royal Navy written in the mid-1950s concluded lamely, 'it seems undeniable that the organisation for the control of all the various sea and air forces involved did not prove adequate for the occasion.'[21] This hardly sums up the lamentable failure of command and control that the Channel Dash revealed. Not only did Britannia no longer rule the waves in the Far East, she could not even prevent the enemy from passing within a few miles of Dover. It was a national humiliation. But even worse was to come.

5

Imperial Collapse

On the morning of Friday 13 February, while Churchill was still smarting in Downing Street over the terrible headlines in the *Daily Mail* and the sense of failure and outrage generated by the three German capital ships passing through the Straits of Dover, on the other side of the world the Japanese advanced to within just 3 miles of Singapore. Japanese heavy artillery was raining shells down on the city. Three of the island's four air bases had been captured. During the course of that Friday, the commander-in-chief, Lieutenant-General Arthur Percival, called a senior officers' conference. He announced he had received orders to fight to the finish and the defence of the city must continue. His principal corps commander, Lieutenant-General Sir Lewis Heath, said his troops were exhausted, totally dispirited and there was no point in further fighting. The commander of the Australian troops defending the island, Major-General Gordon Bennett, agreed that the only option was surrender. When Percival said he had to consider his honour, Heath replied, 'You need not think about your honour. You lost that a long time ago up in the North [of Malaya].' The end of the mighty Singapore garrison appeared imminent.[1]

The personalities of the leading figures in the defence of Singapore all played a part in the events that had led up to this. In April 1941 Lieutenant-General Percival had been appointed as General Officer Commanding Malaya, in charge of the defence of the peninsula and of Singapore. Percival had enjoyed a fine career as a professional soldier. He had served bravely in the First World War and although badly wounded on the Somme had recovered and returned to the front line. After the war he served in Ireland during the Troubles of the early 1920s. He progressed gradually up the ranks during the inter-war years and served in Malaya as a senior staff officer in the late 1930s. Returning there in 1941, he was well aware of the vulnerability of the military position in the region, should the Japanese attack. Despite his competence as an administrator, he was not known for the strength of his leadership or for his ability to inspire those around him. He was a solid staff officer but not a charismatic commander of men.

In November 1941, Air Chief Marshal Sir Robert Brooke-Popham arrived to take up a new post of C-in-C Far East Command. His task was to coordinate plans for the defence of Burma, Malaya, Singapore, Borneo and Hong Kong. Brooke-Popham had retired from the air force four years before and had since been serving as Governor of Kenya where he was known as being patient and conciliatory. His principal task was explained to him before he left London: he had to do what he could with what he had. What was needed in the region was a dynamic improviser who could respond quickly to a rapidly developing situation. What was not needed was a safe pair of hands who was not fully up with latest military matters.[2]

One characteristic that most soldiers in the area possessed in abundance was their arrogance towards the Japanese. They were racially stereotyped as being puny in stature and technologically incompetent. Brooke-Popham had observed Japanese troops from a distance in Manchuria and sent a report in which he wrote, 'I had a good close-up, across the barbed wire, of various sub-human species dressed in dirty grey uniform, which

I was informed were Japanese soldiers. If they represent the average of the Japanese army ... I cannot believe they would form an intelligent fighting force.' And this arrogance went right down through the ranks. A battalion commander once proudly told Brooke-Popham when they jointly inspected his men, 'Don't you think they are worthy of some better enemy than the Japanese?'[3] This arrogant contempt for their foe would not long survive contact with the enemy.

The Japanese had landed 500 miles to the north of Singapore in Thailand and north-east Malaya. The landings in Thailand were unopposed, although at Kota Bharu the Japanese were resisted and suffered substantial casualties. But once ashore, even though their troops were relatively small in number they advanced rapidly. They were led by a ferocious, determined and quick-thinking commander, General Yamashita. The British and imperial troops that faced them were poorly equipped and had suffered from being a low priority while Britain prepared for invasion at home and a war in North Africa. Moreover, they had little or no training for jungle warfare in the mountainous north of the country. The first disaster came at Jitra in northern Malaya in the first couple of days. Totally overwhelmed by the speed and agility of the Japanese advance, two Indian brigades were forced to retreat leaving behind more than 300 trucks and armoured cars, along with food and ammunition intended to supply a division for three months. Three thousand troops were captured.[4] Penang, in the north, was bombed and thousands of civilians became casualties. British forces evacuated the area and to the amazement of the locals left them to their fate, which was years of brutal occupation by the Japanese.

Well trained but lightly equipped Japanese forces then pressed south. They were mobile, fast-moving and highly aggressive. They broke the rules of jungle warfare by using light tanks, thought to be inoperable in such conditions, to speed their advance. And the infantry often used bicycles for transport. One by one, major British static defence lines collapsed: the position along the Perak river at the end of December; defences along the Slim river in early January; the city of Kuala Lumpur in mid-January. Imperial troops, under constant air attack, were trained only to operate on the roads. They would adopt a position along a main road and prepare a defensive barrier. Japanese troops would approach, head into the jungle or mangroves and outflank the defenders who in order to avoid being cut off would be forced to retreat in disarray.[5] And this was repeated night after night. The defenders grew exhausted, lethargic, and morale hit rock bottom. The locals would look on and chant 'Orang Puteh Hari' ('The white men are running').[6] As the imperial power, Britain owed a duty of protection to its colonial citizens. Sometimes the European settlers were evacuated. The Asian populations were abandoned.[7]

Indian troops led by British officers were quickly overwhelmed by the Japanese tactics. Reinforcements arrived who had minimal training and were led by young officers who had often not mastered the language of their men, with disastrous results. As the imperial forces withdrew from one position to another, communications collapsed, telephone lines came down and radio links failed. Bridges were not blown when they should have been to hinder the enemy advance, or they were blown too soon, stranding troops and their equipment on the wrong side and leaving them with little alternative but to surrender. Supplies of petrol and huge depots of food, equipment and vehicles were abandoned. Retreating units were separated from their artillery as they leapfrogged each other in withdrawal. Entire units were wiped out, either killed, wounded or left behind to surrender. When the defenders had withdrawn to the final defensive line north of Johore, Australian troops were thrown into the action. They fared no better and could not prevent the seemingly unstoppable Japanese advance. It was a rout of disastrous proportions.

Meanwhile, reinforcements had continued to arrive in Singapore. On 13 January a convoy of British and American liners docked at the port having survived repeated air raids from Japanese bombers. It brought a brigade from the 18th British Division that had originally been sent from the UK to the Middle East but en route had been diverted to the Far East. After three months at sea the men disembarked but there was no time for acclimatisation or training and they were deployed within days. Later in the month the rest of the 18th arrived after an equally gruelling sea voyage but the ship carrying much of the division's equipment and weaponry had been sunk. On 24 January, 1,800 replacement Australian troops arrived. They had been rushed from Australia and some had only just completed their basic training. Many had never fired a rifle or seen a Bren gun. Nevertheless, they were sent in to reinforce the Australian units that had been badly mauled in the battle for Johore. Percival now had about 100,000 men to defend the small island of Singapore where, with the influx of refugees from the north, the civilian population had roughly doubled in size to about one million.

The civil administration in Singapore proved woefully inadequate to the challenge it now faced. Officials found it difficult to change their ways or improvise and there was a tendency to preserve red tape. China had been at war with Japan for ten years and many Chinese workers saw the Japanese as their natural enemies, so the Chinese population could have been mobilised to assist. But racist colonial attitudes prevailed. Chinese workers were thought to be unreliable and cowardly in times of danger. Little was done to involve them in the defence. In the city, the provision of shelters and air raid precautions was also inadequate and corpses were left to pile up on the streets after an air raid.

None of this helped civilian morale. Only a small number of women and children were evacuated. Again racial divisions prevailed. Of the 10,000 evacuated, two out of three were European, 2,300 were Indian and only 1,250 were Chinese, all from the wealthy elite. The vast majority of the population were left to their fate.[8]

The British, Indian and Australian forces withdrew from their previous defensive line around Johore and blew up the causeway that linked the island with the mainland. After eight weeks of almost continuous retreat most troops were reassured that the drawbridge was up and they could now stand and defend the castle. Reinforced and with substantial provisions, they prepared for what many imagined would be a long siege lasting several months until new forces arrived to relieve them. But officers were amazed at how little had been done to prepare defences on the island. According to one report, Percival had refused to sanction their preparation claiming 'Defences are bad for the morale of troops and civilians.'[9] Engineers were rapidly deployed and barbed wire, mines and booby traps were laid, but all in haste. In anticipation of a night crossing of the Straits of Johore, lights were brought in to illuminate possible crossing zones. The army requested that cars should be brought up so their headlights could be used but the civilian authorities refused at first to sanction the requisitioning of private vehicles. Form still had to be maintained. Seizing private cars would smack of panic. For the army, it was all too little and too late.[10]

Percival tried to reorganise his command and repeated the order that all units were to fight to the death. But at senior levels a sense of hopelessness prevailed. The Australian divisional commander, Major-General Bennett, felt he should be in command and had no confidence in his commander-in-chief. Percival decided the crucial battle must be fought to destroy the landing forces when they were most vulnerable, as they crossed the Straits. But he failed to come up with an effective plan to create a killing zone before the enemy could land. Instead, at brigade level, commanders made their own plans to withdraw to central lines if overwhelmed, but failed to coordinate them. The artillery that would need to play a crucial role in smashing the enemy before they had properly left their boats did not know what the infantry were planning. The situation was not yet one of chaos but it was certainly one of muddle, confusion and, again, a lack of communication. But the Japanese still faced a major challenge to get enough men on to the island to defeat a far larger force.

There were divisions within the Japanese command as well. General Yamashita despised the senior military commanders in Tokyo and worked himself up into a frenzy of anger. This hostility was reciprocated. At one point General Tojo, the Prime Minister, announced he would have Yamashita executed after the campaign was over. Yamashita believed his divisional commanders had disobeyed his orders during the advance through Malaya and were not up to the task. Despite their stunning successes, the strains of a rapid advance were beginning to tell on the Japanese side. Yamashita realised that his troops could not sustain a long siege.

After barely a week's pause, to gather his forces and prepare a crossing of the Straits, Yamashita launched his attack on the island at 10 p.m. on the night of 8 February. It was a dark night and the moon only came up at about 1.30 a.m. Yamashita saw crossing the Straits as no more than a river crossing, for which his forces were well trained and highly experienced. He decided to launch his principal thrust against the north-west of the island where the Australian 22nd Brigade held the line. The Japanese crossed the Straits in small canvas boats shielded by a heavy barrage from their artillery. Most boats took thirty minutes to cross the Straits and it was at this point that they were most vulnerable. But the beach lights failed.

The defenders did not open fire as they were not aware of what was happening. The artillery did not fire as the gunners could not identify targets. Phone lines were destroyed, leaving commanders in the metaphorical as well as literal dark. Three waves of Japanese infantry from two divisions, supported by engineers and mortar units, landed on the island before dawn. Some Australian defenders fought fiercely; others pulled back. The Japanese rapidly established a beachhead on the north-west of the island. The first few hours proved to be decisive.

During the following day a half-hearted counter-attack was launched. It failed. The rear lines began to fill with retreating soldiers. No one seemed to know quite what was happening at the front. A second Japanese crossing of the Straits by the Imperial Japanese Guards Division went badly wrong for them. An Australian officer set light to petrol pouring into the swamps from a supply depot. The whole area became a blazing inferno. The attack faltered. Then, mysteriously, the Australian brigade commander ordered his men to retreat, opening up the Indian troops on his flank to attack. In the confusion, the Japanese recovered and more troops flooded on to the island.[11]

Yamashita, realising the lack of coordination among his enemy, ordered his men forward at speed before tanks and support vehicles could catch up with them. When they entered Tengah airfield they were surprised to find aircraft still around the air base in good working order, and when they went into the officers' mess, fresh bread and soup were still on the dining tables. The next major objective was the one piece of high ground on the island, Bukit Timah, overlooking the city and harbour of Singapore. Yamashita anticipated a major battle for this vital piece of ground but the defending forces were so disorganised that only a single battalion of Argyll and Sutherland Highlanders found themselves between the advancing troops and their objective. They could not hold them up for long and the Japanese seized Bukit Timah and its vast supply dumps of food and ammunition with barely a fight.

On 10 February, the Supreme Commander, Wavell, paid one of his several visits to the island. It proved to be his last. He tried to rally Percival and his senior commanders. The result was another counter-attack. And another failure. The Australians did not communicate with the Indians. Units misunderstood what they had to do and found themselves in the wrong place. Percival failed to inspire enthusiasm for a joint final assault. Troops were rapidly losing confidence in their British commanders.

After Wavell returned from Singapore he received an urgent telegram from Churchill in London. The Prime Minister calculated that Percival must have 100,000 troops on the island, including 33,000 British and 17,000 Australian. They must greatly outnumber the Japanese 'and in a well-contested battle they should destroy them'. He went on: 'There must at this stage be no thought of saving the troops or sparing the population. The battle must be fought to the bitter end at all costs ... The honour of the British Empire and of the British Army is at stake. I rely on you to show no mercy to weakness in any form. With the Russians fighting as they are and the Americans so stubborn at Luzon, the whole reputation of our country and our race is involved.'[12] Wavell passed this on to Percival, adding that 'the Chinese with almost a complete lack of modern equipment have held back the Japanese for 4 and a half years. It will be disgraceful if we yield our boasted Fortress of Singapore to inferior enemy forces.'[13] Percival adapted this as his Order of the Day on 11 February, declaring, 'In some units the troops have not shown the fighting spirit which is to be expected of men of the British Empire. It will be a lasting disgrace if we are defeated by an army of clever gangsters, many times inferior in numbers to our own.'[14] Such words evoking racial pride and imperial honour could not have brought much cheer to men who everywhere saw their army disintegrating. Many officers refused to pass this order on to their men.

One by one the final outposts across the island fell to the relentless advance of the Japanese troops who captured further dumps of food, supplies and ammunition. The first of the reservoirs containing the city's water supply was seized on the 11th. By Saturday 14 February, the defenders had retreated to a small enclave around the city of Singapore. There was a major water shortage. The artillery ran out of shells, as did the anti-aircraft units, meaning that Japanese bombers could roam as they pleased. The RAF had already withdrawn most of its squadrons to Sumatra and were rarely to be seen. When the final squadron of Hurricane fighters and remaining air force personnel were evacuated, the RAF commander turned to Percival and as he said farewell commented in sombre mood, 'I suppose you and I will be held responsible for this, but God knows we did our best with what little we had been given.'[15]

The final forty-eight hours of struggle were not edifying. It is always hard to maintain discipline at the end of losing a battle. And in this case, a large multi-national imperial army that had been retreating almost continuously for more than two months knew it was trapped in the city of Singapore without escape. Many British and Indian troops blamed the Australians for failing so hopelessly to stop the Japanese landings. Some Indian units began to desert. Other stragglers from a variety of outfits left their formations and were found wandering around the city or holding out in abandoned cellars. Japanese bombs and shells continued to rain down and the many refugees packed into the city had nowhere to hide. Several reports spoke of 'pandemonium' in the city streets. A pall of thick black smoke from the burning oil dumps hung over the metropolis. Some battalions fought fiercely as the Japanese advanced into the wealthy, smart suburbs only to find that the unit on their flank had simply disappeared. The Australians retreated to their barracks and, short of ammunition, refused to fire their artillery to defend anyone but themselves.

On the other side, the Japanese troops were exhausted and now at the end of long supply lines. They had not expected the battle for the island to go on as long as it had. They were running desperately short of ammunition. Occasionally they resorted to terrible atrocities. After coming under heavy artillery fire, one unit charged into the nearby Alexandra hospital. As the staff tried to surrender about fifty of them were massacred and one patient was bayoneted on the operating table. Two hundred more were rounded up, taken away, and executed in small groups over the following day.

Yamashita knew that his army would not survive a prolonged street-by-street battle for the city. Even with the vast supply of captured goods they could not continue fighting for long. Percival feared that an angry and desperate enemy would commit the sort of appalling massacre that the Japanese had carried out in Nanking, China a few years before, raping and murdering tens of thousands of civilians while beheading soldiers who had surrendered. One of his officers urged him to admit defeat 'while Japanese soldiery could be controlled by their commander'.[16] At a commanders' meeting, Percival was warned that with the bombing and the lack of water in the city there was already some looting and the Asian population might start to riot against the British authorities. Once again, his generals unanimously advised capitulation. There seemed no alternative. Back in London, 7,000 miles away, General Sir Alan Brooke, Chief of the Imperial General Staff, wrote in his diary, 'We are paying very heavily now for failing to face the insurance premiums essential for security of an Empire! This has usually been the main cause for the loss of Empires in the past.'[17]

A series of increasingly desperate cables passed between Wavell and Percival. On the morning of 14 February, Wavell wrote, 'Where sufficiency of water exists for troops they must go on fighting.' Percival replied, 'Both petrol and food supplies are short owing to most of our dumps being outside the town area. Morale of Asiatic civil population is low under bombing and shelling from which they have no protection. Will continue to comply with your intention but feel must represent the situation as it exists today.' During the day, Churchill, who was at Chequers, rang his army chief, General Brooke. They realised that further defence was futile and might only provoke a terrible massacre. Churchill reluctantly instructed Brooke to cable Wavell: 'You are of course sole judge of the moment when no further result can be gained at Singapore and should instruct Percival accordingly.'[18] In London they had finally accepted that the game was up.

The following morning, Wavell informed Percival, 'So long as you are in [a] position to inflict losses and damage to enemy and your troops are physically capable of doing so you must fight on ... when you are finally satisfied that this is no longer possible I give you permission to cease resistance.'[19]

At 4.30 p.m. on Sunday 15 February a small delegation led by General Percival with a British colonel acting as translator walked up the Bukit Timah Road towards the Ford factory which had been taken over by the Japanese as their headquarters. As they walked up the hill carrying a Union flag and a white flag of surrender, Japanese photographers and cameramen filmed them. When they reached the factory they sat around a table and were filmed again. Yamashita knew how to stage-manage the event. He sat at one side of the table looking fierce and very much in charge; Percival sat on the other side looking gaunt and weak. After forty minutes of haggling, Yamashita lost his temper and said emphatically that if Percival did not sign the surrender there and then he would launch an assault on the city within an hour. Percival gave way. The surrender was signed. A ceasefire came into effect at 8.30 p.m.

The largest British surrender in history at Singapore, 15 February 1942.
General Percival, commander-in-chief, is on the right.

The Japanese blitzkrieg advance through Malaya had been every bit as impressive as the German advance through Belgium and France nearly two years before. But this time there was no Dunkirk, no miraculous deliverance that enabled hundreds of thousands of men to get away to fight another day. Instead, this blitzkrieg ended in a city packed with refugees under repeated aerial and artillery bombardment where all facilities were failing and the military defence had disintegrated. In the two-month campaign British and imperial forces had suffered losses of around 17,000 killed and wounded. The Japanese had lost around 9,000, with 3,000 dead. The surrender was of the largest number of British-led troops in history – British, Australian, New Zealand, Indian and Malayan, about 100,000 men. The military failure would lead to a calamity for hundreds of thousands of soldiers and civilians.

Two days after the capitulation, the victorious Japanese troops staged a victory parade in downtown Singapore. A young Chinese schoolteacher watched the ceremony. 'We felt as if that was the end of the world,' she later remembered. 'We didn't know what to do.'[20] The local population now faced years of occupation. European civilians were taken off to an internment camp to be incarcerated by the Japanese. Yamashita ordered a purge of the Chinese population to remove any pro-nationalist groups, called a *sook ching* (purification by elimination). Estimates of those executed by the Japanese military and secret police range from 25,000 up to 50,000. This was far from the 'Rape' of Nanking but was dreadful enough.

The Indian prisoners were separated from the rest. A Japanese intelligence officer addressed them and invited them to join the Indian National Army. This pro-Japanese army was led at the time by a Sikh officer named Mohan Singh. It would go on to fight against Allied forces including other Indians in Burma, later led by a more charismatic leader, the nationalist Subhas Chandra Bose. Some prisoners willingly signed up having lost faith in British rule; others were intimidated into joining the INA. Those who refused were shipped off and ended up as slave labourers in New Guinea. Again, estimates of numbers vary, but of the 45,000 Indian troops who surrendered, about 40,000 later joined the INA and fought against the British.[21]

The 55,000 British and Australian troops who went into captivity had to endure years of horrors and atrocities in Japanese prisoner-of-war and slave labour camps. Many were assigned to work on the Burma–Siam railway where conditions were appalling. Men were regularly beaten and tortured, denied medical supplies and forced to work long, gruelling days on minimal rations. It has been estimated that as many as 49,000 of those who surrendered at Singapore were killed in captivity.[22]

The scale of the defeat stunned the world. Pictures of the British delegation marching to surrender carrying the Union flag and of Percival looking puny at the negotiating table against an all-powerful Yamashita were rapidly sent around the world. This was a magnificent propaganda victory to add to the military triumph. The images summed up an impression of Japanese strength and British humiliation. In Japan, the people were astonished but delighted with the fantastic victory and the conquest of such a major British fortress and base. Emperor Hirohito sent a message congratulating his troops and announced that Singapore would henceforth be known as Shyonan, 'the radiant South'. Hirohito then sat outside the gates of the Imperial Palace in Tokyo on a white horse for an hour in the winter sunshine. Passing citizens gazed upon their divine ruler paying tribute to his victorious army. A well-known Japanese novelist expressed the view of many when he wrote, 'not a single blemish will stain our brilliant victories. It has been a useful lesson for the God-forsaken arrogance of Britain and America. There is cause for rejoicing that hope is born among our young people. Our spirit, bright, clear and calm, we bow with reverence before the spirits of our heroic dead.'[23]

Across Asia, the military defeat spelt imperial disgrace for Britain. For many Malays, Chinese and Indians there was a strong feeling that Britain had 'let us down' and left them to the mercy of a cruel and brutal Japanese occupation. But in Britain it was the sense of military failure that hurt hard and most immediately after the surrender. Events in Malaya and Singapore contrasted sharply with the situation in the Philippines. Here, Japanese troops had landed on 10 December 1941, under the command of General Homma. They advanced rapidly against only light resistance. The American air force stationed there was almost entirely wiped out while most of its aircraft were still on the ground, as the

RAF had been in Malaya. The US Navy under heavy aerial bombardment withdrew. But the American commander on the Philippines, General Douglas MacArthur, was made of sterner stuff than Percival. He ordered a withdrawal to the Bataan peninsula leaving Manila, the capital, as an open city. At Bataan the Americans had amassed fuel, ammunition and water. From here, about 80,000 American forces and Filipino troops fought a superb and spirited defence, beating off wave after wave of Japanese assaults and inflicting heavy casualties on their enemy. By the end of January, the defenders had withdrawn to a new line but dysentery and disease ravaged the armies of both sides. The Japanese lost almost as many men in attacking Bataan as they had in the whole Malayan campaign and the defenders continued to hold firm in incredibly tough circumstances throughout February and March. Many lived underground in a series of caves, devoid of sunlight and on pitiful rations. But still they fought on. On President Roosevelt's orders, MacArthur left Bataan by PT boat in March and was successfully evacuated to Darwin, Australia to take command of Allied troops in the Pacific. By early April, General Homma's heavily reinforced army finally overwhelmed the disease-ridden, starving defenders; 78,000 men went into captivity, which began with a brutal 65-mile 'Death March' to San Fernando camp. Beaten as they struggled along the route and bayoneted by the roadside if they fell, it was an appalling end to a heroic defence. The final collapse took place in May when the small US-held island of Corregidor in Manila Bay, known as 'the Gibraltar of the East', surrendered to Japanese forces.

Across Asia, the ripples of Britain's humiliating defeat at Singapore continued to spread out. In India, British prestige was forever shattered. Not only did many Indian prisoners rally to the Indian National Army to fight their old masters but, later in 1942, inspired by Gandhi, Congress launched a 'Quit India' campaign. Protests and demonstrations frequently spilled into sporadic anti-British violence and riots. After the war, London acknowledged that the British Raj was no longer sustainable and the post-war Labour government finally looked to find a way to depart peacefully and honourably from the continent Britain had dominated for two centuries. There is a direct line running from the fall of Singapore in 1942 to the partition and independence of India in 1947 and of Burma the following year.

In Australia, the loss of thousands of their troops surrendered by British commanders into a cruel captivity also left a lingering anger. Some had only disembarked their transports days before finding themselves in Japanese prisoner-of-war camps. With a strong sense of having been betrayed by London, the Canberra government felt it could no longer trust British promises of protection. In five months the Japanese thrust had overwhelmed every western outpost between India and Australia. Australian public opinion feared that the door was wide open to a Japanese invasion. Australian leaders decided in future to ally themselves with America, never putting their trust in British imperial promises again. Although its troops continued to fight bravely with Britain in the Middle East, nearer to home the Australians fought with American forces in New Guinea and the United States used Australia as a base to build up their resources in the Pacific. For decades to come, Australia would see its destiny more aligned to the US than the UK.

As a footnote to the desultory Australian campaign in Malaya and Singapore, General Gordon Bennett was one of the few senior commanders to plan his own getaway from the beleaguered city. Having ordered his troops not to attempt to escape, Bennett and a small party of officers disappeared into the night as the rest of his men were laying down their arms on the evening of 15 February. Bennett should have led his men into captivity but believed the lessons he had learned made him an ideal commander to lead further Australian forces against the Japanese. He made it back to Australia, where he was formally welcomed by the government but condemned by the army high command who thought he should have remained with his men. He did not lead troops in action again.

Instead, Bennett joined the long-running blame game about what had gone wrong by writing a book, *Why Singapore Fell*, in 1944. He blamed the British commanders for their poor leadership and their failure to mount an effective defence along with the weakness of the Indian troops. The round of accusations and recriminations went on after the war as analyses of the disaster continued for years. Churchill had promised an inquiry into the reasons for the fall of the city but it was never held. Instead, in his war memoirs he blamed the chiefs of staff for not telling him about the lack of landward defences on the island of Singapore.[24] Percival published his own defence, *The War in Malaya*, in 1949. He saw the defeat as a consequence of the superior morale of the Japanese soldier and the enemy's naval and air supremacy which left the army to fight an ordered withdrawal through Malaya, rendering it dispirited and incapable of defending Singapore.

In the immediate aftermath of the surrender, General Wavell was asked by the chiefs of staff to reflect on the lessons learned in Malaya and Singapore. He wrote a reflective and penetrating paper on 17 February, only two days after the collapse. 'The trouble goes a long way back,' he wrote, pointing to the long-term failure of the 'Singapore strategy'. He blamed 'lack of vigour in our peace-time training, the cumbrousness in our tactics and equipment, and the real difficulty of finding an answer to the very skilful and bold tactics of the Japanese in this jungle fighting'. He left his most damning condemnation for his conclusion: 'But the real trouble is that for the time being we have lost a good deal of our hardness and fighting spirit.'[25] When General Brooke read Wavell's report in London he was thrown into despair and confided in his diary, 'Cannot work out why troops are not fighting better. If the army cannot fight better than it is doing at present we shall deserve to lose our Empire.'[26]

Robert Chang, an air raid warden in Singapore before it fell, put the consequences of these failures even more plainly. Before 1942, he said, the British 'were more or less the over-lords or masters ... Common talk after the surrender was that British soldiers don't know how to fight.'[27]

How was Britain ever going to win a global war with an army that had lost its 'hardness and fighting spirit', when the chief of staff could not work out what was going wrong and observers felt it didn't know how to fight?

6

'Hard Adverse War'

The humiliating collapse in Singapore greatly added to popular criticism of the Prime Minister and his government. The press was convinced that Churchill was carrying too much responsibility as both Minister of Defence, controlling wartime military strategy, and Prime Minister, determining the political direction of affairs. Mass Observation recorded a range of comments supporting this view. 'I reckon Churchill's got too much on his hands to conduct this war properly,' said one fifty-year-old man. A younger man stated, 'Make Anthony Eden Minister of Defence and give him a free hand.' A twenty-five-year-old woman commented, 'I think Churchill's taking too much on himself.'[1]

This view spread to many people around the country. On an RAF base at Digby in Lincolnshire, a young WAAF officer detected a new take on the discussion by her colleagues of the state of the nation. As a Mass Observer she dutifully wrote down what she heard. 'Up to now,' she recorded, 'the government has been criticised often, but always with the reservation "Churchill's all right". But now Churchill is condemned with the rest.' As one WAAF said, 'A month ago, if people had been talking about Churchill like this, we'd have called them fifth columnists: but now ...' One of her friends remarked, 'It's time we had a new government – Churchill's taking too much upon himself these days.' Another was reported as saying 'He roars all right in his time, but he's outlived it.'[2]

The ceasefire in Singapore came into effect at lunchtime, British time, on Sunday 15 February.[3] That evening Churchill addressed the nation in a live BBC broadcast from Chequers. He used the speech as an opportunity to review the whole progress of the war, since he had last addressed the nation after signing the Atlantic Charter with Roosevelt, six months before. 'Taking it all in all, are our chances of survival better or are they worse than in August 1941?' he asked. 'Are we up or down?'

Initially, he concentrated on the plus points. The United States with its 'vast resources' was now in the war as an ally. The British Commonwealth and America were now 'all together … till death or victory'. Of this Churchill said, 'I cannot believe there is any other fact in the whole world which can compare with that. That is what I have dreamed of, aimed at and worked for, and now it has come to pass.' He also spoke about great Russian successes in holding Moscow and Leningrad, and in 'advancing victoriously, driving the foul invader from that native soil they have guarded so bravely and loved so well'. He concluded that these 'two tremendous fundamental facts will in the end dominate the world situation and make victory possible'.

He emphasised Britain's demanding role fighting in a world at war. 'A ceaseless stream of ships, men and materials has flowed from this country for a year and a half, in order to build up and sustain our armies in the Middle East, which guard those vast regions on either side of the Nile valley. We had to do our best to give substantial aid to Russia. We gave it [to] her in her darkest hour and we must not fail in our undertaking now.' Then on the assault from Japan, he asked, 'How could we have provided for the safety of the Far East against such an avalanche of fire and steel as has been hurled upon us by Japan?'

He did not attempt to ignore the difficulties that still lay ahead. 'You know I have never prophesied to you or promised smooth and easy things, and now all I have to offer is hard adverse war for many months ahead. I must warn you, as I warned the House of Commons before they gave me their generous vote of confidence a fortnight ago, that many misfortunes, severe torturing losses, remorseless and gnawing anxieties lie before us.' And he did not in any way downplay the disaster of the failings in the Far East. 'I speak to you all under the shadow of a heavy and far-reaching military defeat. It is a British and Imperial defeat. Singapore has fallen. All the Malay Peninsula has been overrun.'

He concluded by laying on some of the uplifting rhetoric that had inspired the nation in the summer of 1940. 'This,' he proclaimed, 'is one of those moments when the British race and nation can show their quality and their genius. This is one of those moments when it can draw from the heart of misfortune the vital impulses of victory ... Here is another occasion to show as so often in our long story that we can meet reverses with dignity and with renewed accessions of strength. We must remember that we are no longer alone. We are in the midst of great company.' He ended with a great flourish more suitable to a speech in the House of Commons than a fireside chat on the radio: 'The whole future of mankind may depend upon our action and upon our conduct. So far we have not failed. We shall not fail now. Let us move forward steadfastly together into the storm and through the storm.'[4]

Churchill's one-time private secretary, who was on a pilot training course in South Africa, was walking down a street in Pretoria when he heard 'a familiar voice coming from the wireless in a small café. It was Winston announcing the fall of Singapore.' Having been at Churchill's side throughout the finest hours of 1940, Jock Colville was well able to judge the Prime Minister's mood. He wrote, 'The nature of his words and the unaccustomed speed and emotion with which he spoke convinced me that he was sorely pressed by critics and opponents at home. All the majesty of his oratory was there, but also a new note of appeal lacking the usual confidence of support.' Colville observed that 'there was something about his voice and delivery which made me shiver'.[5]

Other critics back home were harsher in their verdicts. Oliver Harvey, a Foreign Office diplomat, wrote in his diary, 'In his usual style he painted a magnificent backcloth for the fall of Singapore – but it didn't meet the point that nobody believes the Government machine is working efficiently.' He also noted that 'He never mentioned the Channel [Dash] episode.'[6] Even a friendly figure like Harold Nicolson recorded a day later, 'I fear a slump in public opinion which will deprive Winston of his legend. His broadcast last night was not liked. The country is too nervous and irritable to be fobbed off with fine phrases. Yet what else could he have said? A weaker man would have kept away from the wireless and have allowed someone else to tell us the bad news.'[7]

The next few days saw a round of black and depressing meetings for the leaders of Britain's war effort. The Japanese launched further attacks in Burma and on the Dutch East Indies (Java and Sumatra). The decision was made not to attempt to fully defend Java but to concentrate on the defence of Burma, Ceylon (Sri Lanka) and Australia. After a Cabinet meeting on 16 February, Sir Alexander Cadogan wrote in his diary, 'PM truculent and angry – and havering . . . All news as bad as it can be.'[8] The press continued to claim that Churchill had gathered too much power in his own hands and there were even more strident calls for a separation between the posts of Minister of Defence and Prime Minister. Questions were asked of Churchill in the House as to whether he would appoint a Minister of Defence to advise on war strategy. His answer was simple and determined: 'No, sir.' He refused to countenance a diminution of his authority to control the war effort.[9] Lord Beaverbrook wrote to a friend on the matter. 'The trouble about this suggestion is that either the new Minister of Defence will disagree with the Prime Minister on strategy and get the sack, or agree with the Prime Minister, in which case his appointment will be superfluous.' Beaverbrook concluded, 'there is no sign of the agitation coming to an end'.[10]

On 17 February, two days after the surrender of Singapore, there was a short adjournment debate on the recent disasters. Churchill told the House that there would be a secret inquiry into how the German warships had been allowed to slip through the Channel. But he also revealed that the ships had been damaged during the course of their dash and would be out of action for many months. He insisted that the withdrawal of the two ships from Brest to the Baltic was 'decidedly beneficial to our war situation'. The ships could no longer come out of harbour and attack convoys in the Atlantic. The huge bombing effort against the port at Brest could now be refocused on bombing Germany. And by the time the German ships were back in action the Royal Navy would have been strengthened and the US Navy would be playing a more prominent role. He concluded with a positive spin that 'the naval position in the Atlantic, so far from being worsened, is definitely eased'.

With regard to the fall of Singapore, he announced that he would not allow a debate on the surrender so soon after the event. He could not see that it would help a very serious situation in the Far East. He could add nothing, Churchill said, to what had been reported in the press and did not want a public discussion at such a tense time 'in a mood of panic'. At this point members started yelling 'No' at the Prime Minister. Churchill carried on: 'I think that a very excited debate taking place here today, while our minds are oppressed by what has happened, may easily have the effect of causing a bad and very unfavourable reaction all over the world. That is what I say. I stick to it.'[11]

Many members of Parliament expressed their anger at the Prime Minister's approach and tone. The Labour MP Aneurin Bevan demanded a debate and said it was the 'duty' of MPs 'to express the anxieties of the country' in the House. Liberal MP Sir Percy Harris declared that 'the public outside are immensely disturbed' by the turn of events and the House should be able to debate issues like the fall of Singapore. Several MPs challenged the idea that asking questions was an act of disloyalty. Earl Winterton called for 'a Grand Inquest of the Nation on all that has gone on and is going on, for the country is profoundly concerned'. Labour MP Frederick Bellenger went even further and told the Prime Minister 'there is in the country and indeed in the House at the present moment a feeling that we have not got the right kind of persons to direct this war to a satisfactory conclusion ... we have not got the right kind of Government'. At this, the House cheered. According to *Punch* magazine, at this point the Prime Minister angrily pawed the ground with his left foot, while the Deputy Prime Minister Clement Attlee focused intently on a doodle he was drawing on a piece of paper on his lap.[12] Churchill continued to insist that 'this moment of great anxiety and distress' was not the time for a debate that would only contribute to the 'rattling process which is going on in some parts of the Press ... which tends to give a feeling of insecurity'. The sole communist MP and member for Fife, Willie Gallacher, announced, 'Among the mass of the people there is no confidence in the Government as a Government.' When Churchill got up to leave the chamber and was followed out by several government ministers, Gallacher turned the knife in the wound and became overtly abusive by declaring, 'The

Führer goes, the yes-men follow. Is it any wonder that we are losing the war; is it any wonder that the Empire is lost, when we have such types as that? They are simply crawlers.' It is not recorded how the House responded to this jibe.

The Soviet ambassador, Ivan Maisky, watched the events from the balcony of the House of Commons. He could barely believe what he saw going on below. No sort of criticism of the political leadership was of course allowed in the Soviet Union. He wrote that Churchill 'did not look well, was irritated, easily offended and obstinate. The MPs were caustic and sniffy. They gave Churchill a bad reception and a bad send-off. I've never seen anything like it.'[13]

Many of those present were worried by the petulance displayed by the Prime Minister. Harold Nicolson wrote in his diary, 'Winston made his statement this afternoon. It started all right but when people asked questions, he became irritable and rather restless. He spoke about "anger and panic" which infuriated people ... The pity of it is that he had a good case, and if only he had kept his head and produced his promises in the right order, all would have gone well. He was not at his best.'[14] The normally hostile MP Henry Channon noted in his diary that the Commons was 'restless, crowded and angry'. He wrote that the Prime Minister entered the House with a 'scowl' and that 'No cheer greeted him as he arrived.' His description of the Channel Dash, according to Channon, 'convinced nobody, and particularly his attempt to turn an inglorious defeat into a victory displeased the House'. As MPs questioned his speech, Channon wrote that they became 'increasingly hostile'. He wondered, 'Can he ever recover his waning prestige?'[15]

Churchill was seriously rattled by events. In his weekly lunch with the King, the PM told him that he was angry about his reception in Parliament and that it was like 'hunting the tiger with angry wasps about him'.[16] When General Brooke met him later that afternoon he found him 'in a dejected mood', and he told Brooke 'he was just back from dealing with a troublesome House'. Brooke then confided in his diary, 'I am afraid that he is in for a lot more trouble.'[17]

The following morning, Churchill went as he often did to the Map Room in the Number 10 Annexe (now known as the Churchill War Rooms) for the latest update from Captain Pim, his map officer. Pim found him 'very much depressed', feeling the 'irksomeness of having to put up with criticism as soon as events went badly'. Churchill implied to Pim that he was seriously thinking of handing over his responsibilities to someone else. 'But my God, sir, you cannot do that,' Pim told him assertively. This was no doubt just what Churchill wanted to hear from a loyal officer and he wondered aloud whether the 'ordinary citizen' felt the same way and would 'support him in bad days as well as fair', or whether ordinary people would agree with the criticisms in the press. Pim did all he could to reassure the Prime Minister.[18]

No government could survive the joint humiliations of the Channel Dash so near to home and the fall of Singapore on the other side of the world without impact. Churchill's government responded as many administrations do, with a reshuffle. There were two key facets to the government changes that followed. First, the disastrous collapse in Churchill's popularity. Second, the emergence of a figure whom many had come to believe could do a better job as war leader than the current Prime Minister.

Sir Stafford Cripps was known as an ascetic figure, currently riding on a wave of popular support because of his championing of the Soviet Union. The contrast with Churchill could not have been greater. Churchill was an old-school Conservative and an imperialist. He had a rounded figure that came from his love of champagne, brandy, good food and cigars. Cripps was a committed left-winger who had dallied with Marxism. He was tall and lean, a teetotaller and a vegetarian. He suffered from colitis, an inflammation of the bowel, which left him with chronic digestive problems often brought on by stress or intense work. But his persona seemed to chime with the increasingly austere climate of war. Churchill grew to respect and admire his rival if not to enjoy his company. He always had a rather saintly personality as far as Churchill was concerned, who once said of Cripps, 'There, but for the grace of God, goes God.'[19]

Stafford Cripps had been born into a family of established wealth and privilege. His father was a successful ecclesiastical lawyer and a Conservative MP who later became a Labour Party minister. His mother was the sister of Beatrice Webb, the Fabian socialist and social reformer. Cripps, the spoiled youngest of five children, grew up on a 400-acre estate at Parmoor in the Chilterns. He went to Winchester College where he was the golden boy and went on to read Chemistry at University College, London. He excelled in the subject and while in his early twenties wrote a paper for the Royal Society. In 1911 he married Isobel Swithinbank, the rich heiress of the ENO Liver Salts fortune. She would eventually come into an inheritance that was worth approximately £12 million in today's money.[20] They were devoted to each other and for forty years Isobel provided the domestic love and support that underscored Cripps's successful career.

After managing an explosives factory during the First World War, Cripps reverted to his legal work and began to rise up the ranks of the profession, soon earning huge fees as a patent lawyer. He was known for his forensic understanding of a case and his ability to out-argue opponents. He became the youngest King's Counsel in the country in 1927. With a growing family, a country estate in Gloucestershire and a successful legal career he looked every inch the typical Tory squire. But he was far from this. His deep and passionate Christian faith led him to feel that it was his duty to make the world a better place for those less fortunate than himself. In 1930 he joined the Labour Party, was elected to Parliament, and in Ramsay MacDonald's government became Solicitor General. For many years he combined an active political life with his legal career.

The 1930s proved to be Cripps's radical decade. He refused to join MacDonald's National Government which he regarded as a sell-out and concentrated on the radical left policies of the Socialist League, of which he became chairman. He called for class war against all those whom he saw as sympathetic to fascism and was opposed to appeasement but refused to support any sort of rearmament until war was inevitable. In 1939 he was expelled from the Labour Party for his extremist views.

After the outbreak of war, he spent time in India and China and visited Moscow, which at this point had allied with Berlin. When Churchill formed his coalition government in May 1940, Cripps was asked to return to Moscow as Britain's representative there, eventually becoming ambassador. He took a sympathetic line towards Soviet affairs and became an important link with Stalin after Hitler's invasion in June 1941. He argued that Britain should recognise Soviet territorial seizures since 1939 and played a significant role in winning Anglo-American support for Stalin. He repeatedly tried to return to Britain from what increasingly felt to him like political exile. But both Churchill and Attlee were happy to keep him at arm's length from Westminster politics, both seeing him as a rival. Finally, after America had entered the war, Churchill allowed him to come back to Britain in the new year.

On 23 January 1942 Cripps returned to London basking in the glory of Soviet military success which had gained the admiration of millions of Britons. The *Daily Mirror* had a picture on their front page of Cripps returning home wearing a Russian fur hat. Churchill was suspicious of his motives and when they met at Chequers soon after his return greeted him with the words, 'Well, Stafford, how have you returned? Friend or foe?' Cripps answered by saying he was 'a friendly critic or a critical friend'.[21]

Cripps and a small team of young male advisers around him ran a very modern type of campaign in the media. This group of what today would be called special advisers was known as the 'Crippery'.[22] They often succeeded in getting their boss into the newspapers and the press quickly took to him. Not surprisingly, he became a hero of the *Daily Mirror*, a paper that was read by up to one in four of the British adult population. He was presented as a modest man who had given up the possibility of earning a fortune as a barrister to help his country. He was seen as a man of faith and a reformer who wanted to help build a new and better Britain out of the sacrifice of war. More surprising was the support given him by *The Times*, the *Daily Telegraph* and the *Daily Mail*. Being closely associated with the heroic defence of their country by the Soviet military enabled Cripps to present himself in marked contrast to the dismal failures of Britain's military. He was seen as being forward-looking, progressive, clear-minded, super-efficient and non-aligned. Many began to see him as an alternative leader of Britain's failing war machine.

A broadcast he gave on 8 February on *Postscript*, a popular BBC talk programme that followed the main *Nine O'Clock News* on a Sunday evening, attracted a lot of attention and went down particularly well with Mass Observation. The organisation recorded a 93 per cent approval rating for the talk, higher than any given by Churchill or J. B. Priestley, another popular *Postscript* talker. Cripps argued that Britain was not yet fully mobilised for total war and there was a lax spirit in the country. Among the comments recorded were sentiments like 'It made me feel we weren't making half the sacrifice the Russian people are' and 'Marvellous, he told us outright that we're not doing enough.'[23] A diarist wrote,

Sir Stafford Cripps speaking at a rally. After his time in Moscow he benefited from being associated with heroic Soviet resistance rather than endless British failures.

'Thought Sir S Cripps spoke well tonight and truly. Enjoyed his speech as much as any of Winston's although he was not as "heroic" and he gave us some pretty plain speaking.'[24] Mass Observation concluded that 'he won overwhelming public approval' after his return from Russia 'largely by contrast to Churchill' who was in a 'low trough' of popularity. The organisation put him down as 'the first alternative leader-figure since the fall of Chamberlain'.[25]

Because of this newfound popularity, Churchill felt compelled to ask Cripps to join the government to help revitalise his administration, and offered him the position of Minister of Supply. It was a responsible position supervising the production of arms and munitions for all three services, but it was not a senior post and was outside the War Cabinet. Cripps turned down the offer, to Churchill's evident dismay. Still, at least it kept Cripps onside during the no-confidence debate in the Commons in late January. But it was not long before Cripps would move to the centre of affairs.

Following the disastrous week of fiasco and failure in the Channel and in Singapore, there was a considerable public demand for a reconstruction of the government. It needed 'a good spring cleaning, not just tidying up', one woman told Mass Observation.[26] The first set of changes were announced on 19 February. The War Cabinet, which had been operating with nine members, was reduced to seven. Five ministers remained: Churchill, Attlee, Eden, John Anderson (who had been Home Secretary in charge of air raid precautions and was now Lord President of the Council) and Ernest Bevin, who was playing a major role in keeping the nation mobilised for war as Minister of Labour. Attlee became Deputy Prime Minister with responsibility for representing the Dominions in the War Cabinet. Two members left: Lord Beaverbrook resigned supposedly for health reasons but in reality against the promotion of Attlee; also out was Arthur Greenwood, the deputy Labour Party leader, who had not been effective in Cabinet. Kingsley Wood, the Chancellor of the Exchequer, left the War Cabinet too but kept his post. Oliver Lyttelton was brought back from Cairo to become Minister of Production with a seat in the War Cabinet. The other critical development was that Churchill fought off all demands for him to appoint a new Minister of Defence, retaining the position alongside that of Prime Minister. But he did give up the position of Leader of the House, and it was this that he offered to Sir Stafford Cripps. Churchill wanted him to use his powers of persuasion and his support within the press to promote the government line. This time Cripps had no hesitation in accepting the offer as with it came entry to the War Cabinet as Lord Privy Seal.

In many ways it was a curious appointment. Cripps was an independent MP, still not readmitted to the Labour Party, and so without any party backing. Cripps joked to the Crippery, 'At last I have a party that cannot be split and is in total agreement.'[27] In a broadcast on the BBC World Service to India, George Orwell declared, 'The fact that such a man without any party machine backing him can be put into government in direct response to the wishes of the common people is a testimony to the strength of British democracy.'[28] He was certainly the man of the moment. One report for the Ministry of Information noted: 'Cripps – day after day the name hits the headlines in Britain's newspapers, day after day when men talk about war or politics they talk about Cripps.'[29] His plain and austere lifestyle appealed to a public now attuned to rationing and restrictions. But as Mass Observation also recorded, he was highly regarded as being 'brainy'.[30] It would now remain to be seen how he would get on with the Prime Minister and what his sudden rise would contribute to central government.

There was one final bit of business to sort out in the Pacific. Everywhere the Japanese were on the advance. If Java and Sumatra were lost, oil supplies to the whole area could be cut off. Japanese troops were advancing into Burma, the doorway to India and the country from where vital supplies were transported overland to China. The Chinese were tying up fifteen to twenty Japanese divisions and it was essential that this front was kept supplied. The Allies had lost control of the seas after the disastrous naval losses at Pearl Harbor and off Malaya. They were now down to only about 140 aircraft across this vast region, while the enemy could muster at least 900. This gave the Japanese aerial superiority which they used to cover their seemingly unstoppable ground troops wherever they went on the offensive.

President Roosevelt cabled Churchill with a supportive message reflecting on the loss of Singapore. He recommended winding up the command under General Wavell that had been established only two months earlier at the Arcadia conference in Washington. He proposed a reorganisation of the war in the Pacific. The United States would take command of the final resistance by US and Filipino troops in Bataan. And the US would take primary responsibility for the defence of Australia. Britain should concentrate on the defence of India and Burma. 'No matter how serious our setbacks have been and I do not for a moment underrate them,' he told the Prime Minister, 'we must constantly look forward to the next moves that need to be made to hit the enemy.' Churchill replied, 'I do not like these days of personal stress and I have found it difficult to keep my eye on the ball ... Democracy has to prove that it can provide a granite foundation for war against tyranny.'[31]

Wavell's strategy of defending the region until new forces could arrive had collapsed with the surrender of Singapore. Now he was to give up his command. He wrote to a friend, 'I feel I ought to have pulled it off but the dice were rather heavily loaded and the little yellow man threw them with considerable cunning. I hate making excuses. I was given a job and have fallen down on it.'[32] To Churchill he wrote humbly, 'I have failed you and the President here where a better man might perhaps have succeeded.'[33] Churchill ordered him to resume his role as commander-in-chief in India and to pursue the war against Japan from there. Two days after his command came to an end the Japanese inflicted a major defeat on the Allied navies at the Battle of the Java Sea, their navy outgunning a combined Anglo-American, Australian and Dutch fleet. Two light cruisers were sunk and more than 2,000 sailors were lost including the Dutch admiral commanding the fleet. The Japanese ships suffered only light damage and few casualties. The disastrous loss opened up the island of Java to invasion. Everywhere at sea, on land and in the air the Japanese looked invincible.

Despite these continuing troubles, Churchill had survived. He had reorganised his government and had now invited to sit at the War Cabinet table a man who seemed popular enough to challenge his leadership of the national war effort. But he had bought some time and for now it seemed as though the 'rattling' in the Commons and in the press that had so upset him would subside. The main question was where and when would the next crisis arise, and how calamitous would it be? And could Churchill survive another serious blow?

7

Shipping Perils

During 1941, the photo-interpreters at RAF Medmenham closely studied developments across occupied Europe. Specialist teams focused on different activities taking place on the ground, like developments at airfields, or construction work at war factories, learning from the photographic evidence much about what was taking place inside the German war machine. Almost every week Spitfire photo-reconnaissance pilots flew over the major German shipyards at Kiel, Hamburg and Bremen recording on their high-resolution photos the ships under construction below. David Brachi at Medmenham led the section looking at German ship building, and one of his specialisms was following the construction of U-boats. The laying of the keel was the first part of the process, which was clearly identifiable on aerial photographs, its long, narrow shape always easy to spot. Next came the building of the superstructure and, again, Brachi became skilled in following this. It took about eight months to construct a U-boat and then about three months of trials before active service. So Brachi was able to forecast U-boat launches about a year in advance.

In February 1941, Brachi counted twice the usual number of keels being laid down for new U-boats. This meant that by the beginning of 1942 the output of U-boats would have doubled. He wrote up his observations in a report that was passed up to the head of naval intelligence, Admiral John Godfrey.[1] Godfrey informed the First Sea Lord, Admiral Sir Dudley Pound, then chair of the Chiefs of Staff Committee. When Pound told the Prime Minister that U-boat production would double by 1942, Churchill became seriously worried. He formed a special War Cabinet committee to tackle the challenge of what he was now calling the Battle of the Atlantic, which he regarded as crucial for Britain's survival. 'I'm not afraid of the Air, I'm not afraid of invasion,' Churchill told the War Cabinet in March 1941, 'but I'm anxious about the Atlantic.'[2]

At the Western Approaches command centre in a bunker below Derby House in Liverpool, the movement of convoys and the sighting of U-boat packs were monitored on large wall maps. As a nation that was far from self-sufficient in basic supplies, Britain needed to import agricultural produce, fuel, metals and an array of other materials in order to survive, in addition to the vast quantities of arms, weapons, munitions and, by 1942, the hundreds of thousands of men arriving from the United States to fight the war. This battle would be fought not just in deadly exchanges on the high seas, but in purchasing offices, shipyards, docks and wharves on both sides of the Atlantic.[3]

Issues of shipping, or the lack of it, became a real crisis during the first six months of 1942. But the strains on shipping resources had become apparent early in the war. The convoy system had been introduced soon after the declaration of war, so that naval protection could be supplied to groups of ships. But this meant a convoy had to travel at the speed of its slowest ship. The consequence was that the faster ships took longer to cross the Atlantic than usual and so could make fewer crossings. An added burden was that ships that had crossed the Atlantic with cargoes intended for ports on the east of

A Wren plots shipping movements at the Western Approaches Operations
Room, Derby House, Liverpool. The Battle of the Atlantic was the
battle that had to be won to ensure Britain's survival. The lights are on
because a film simply called Western Approaches *was being shot.*

England such as London could no longer transit the Channel
so had to sail around Scotland. The London docks were then
by far the biggest port in the country with the largest number
of cranes for unloading ships. Unloading cargoes was slow
because of blackout restrictions, air raid warnings and the use
of old technologies and working practices in the docks. And
goods unloaded at ports in the west of Britain, such as Bristol,
Liverpool or Glasgow, then had to be transported by rail to
their destination, putting an immense strain on the railway
network. The stevedores and dockers who were reluctant to
change their methods became the villains of the story in the

government's eyes and new rules were introduced to speed up the unloading and distribution of goods.

In addition, Britain's traditional supply of imports from Europe had obviously been cut off after the Nazi conquests, so foodstuffs had to come from much further afield. And with the Mediterranean closed to merchant shipping, the route to the east was no longer through the Suez Canal but around the Cape, adding 10,000 miles and several weeks to the average journey. In 1940, the government had set the minimum annual quantity of imports needed at 42 million tons. In 1941 this was reduced to 31 million tons, of which 15 million should be food imports. When it looked as though even this would be impossible to achieve the meat ration was reduced to one shilling's worth of meat per person, per week. The Minister of Food, Lord Woolton, who had run the Lewis's shopping chain before the war, appealed directly to Churchill arguing that any further reduction in the ration would be bad for morale. Churchill responded as he usually did when it came to the question of food supplies by guaranteeing the level of meat imports.

The war had a dramatic effect on the patterns of global shipping but it was still the vast Atlantic Ocean bringing supplies from America that would be the focus of Britain's battle for survival. At the beginning of the war the only real weapon against the U-boat was Asdic, a system of sending sound pulses that bounced back when they hit something making a particular 'ping', a bit like an underwater radar. From the 'ping' an experienced operator could assess the distance and bearing of an underwater object.[4] But Asdic was limited in its range and could be disrupted by movements in the water from other vessels nearby. In 1941, new measures against the U-boats slowly began to appear. One of these was a radio direction finding system that picked up enciphered messages sent by U-boats as they came to the surface to send signals to their headquarters near L'Orient in France. It was impossible to decipher the messages but it was possible to locate where the signals were coming from. If two or more radio stations could pick up the signals then they could triangulate a 'fix' on the position of the U-boats. This could be done at long range and with impressive accuracy. The system, called High Frequency Direction Finding, or HF/DF, was nicknamed 'Huff Duff'.

Also in 1941 there were developments in Air-to-Surface Vessel radar (ASV) that meant patrolling aircraft could spot a U-boat when it was on the surface. All submarines until the latter part of the war had to surface not only to send signals but also to recharge their batteries and many did this at night when they would be pretty well invisible. For every twenty-four hours of operation, a U-boat needed to recharge its batteries for about four hours. New ASV operating at a wavelength of 1.5 metres meant that both at night and during bad weather, aircraft could pick up a radar signal from a U-boat on the surface. The equipment was still primitive and consisted of two sets of aerials attached to the side of an aircraft. By continuously and rapidly switching transmission from one to the other, an operator could pick up a signal from a vessel and then direct the aircraft towards the ship or submarine. It was a taxing system to operate, often for hours on end, and its range was very limited. It could identify a ship at about 30 miles but could only pick up a reflection from a U-boat conning tower at about 4 miles. Nevertheless the first U-boat 'kill' using ASV was recorded on 20 November 1941, and more followed.[5] But against the scale of losses of merchant ships it was just a tiny step in battling the U-boat menace. A truly effective ASV had to wait until centimetric radar was developed. This did not come until later in 1942.

The numbers of corvettes and destroyers escorting the Atlantic convoys increased considerably during 1941. The crews became more experienced and skilled in battling the U-boats. But still the losses in the first months of the year were appallingly high: 316,300 tons in February, rising to 387,800 tons in May; a total of 402 individual ships in the first five months of the year.[6] From April 1941, Churchill insisted that details of the losses at sea must be strictly censored so as to avoid public alarm. This gave a great opportunity for German propaganda to score over British secrecy. In that month Dr Goebbels claimed to have sunk over a million tons of British shipping, whereas the actual sum (which was bad enough) was less than half of this. One Mass Observation diarist noted sceptically, 'Listened to Lord Haw-Haw this evening, he devoted the whole time to a survey of British and American shipping losses since the war began. The figures he gave were colossal and staggering that if true we should have been out of the war long ago.'[7] Many other listeners might have been more believing. The Ministry of Information had to think hard about how to present the Battle of the Atlantic as a vital part of the war effort without revealing the full scale of the losses. Occasional stories about individual ships were reported in the British media. And many people in the towns where the seamen lived had a general sense of the seriousness of the situation. But the full scale of the U-boat threat was never fully revealed.[8]

Other developments during 1941 affecting the Battle of the Atlantic came out of another branch of the scientific war in the work carried out at Bletchley Park, the home of the neutrally named Government Code and Cypher School (in reality the national codebreaking centre). During the war and for thirty years afterwards, the work of Bletchley Park was the best-held, ultimate secret of the war. Today its day-to-day business is well known although much mythologised in novels, books, television programmes and movies.[9] The German military had developed a sophisticated encrypting system called

Enigma which involved typing messages on the keyboard of an electro-mechanical typing machine. A series of rotor blades at the back of the machine were set up to encode each letter as another letter, and the scrambled message was then sent as a radio signal in the clear. When typed through another machine with the rotors in exactly the same alignment the operator could retrieve the original message. New settings were regularly introduced which varied the alignment of the rotor blades. This could be done every week or, in more disciplined units, every twenty-four hours. As long as the person sending and the operative receiving the signal used the same settings the messages could be read as plain text. Members of the Polish intelligence studied the German Enigma system closely during the 1930s and captured an Enigma machine. In July 1939 the Poles handed over to the British Secret Intelligence Service and French intelligence all the work they had done in developing electro-mechanical codebreaking aids to decrypt Enigma. The British and French were stunned by what the Poles had achieved and in Britain this coincided with the move of the Code and Cypher School from London to Bletchley Park, a country house estate 50 miles from London. Here a remarkable group of eccentrics and geniuses were gathered to build on the work started by the Poles.[10]

The German military regularly sent detailed messages with precise reports about the strength and location of units, casualties and operational plans using this system, secure in the knowledge that it would take weeks to find the precise combination of the rotors to read a signal. By this time the information would be redundant, and even if an enemy did discover how to read a message, when the rotors were reset they would have to start all over again. Each branch of the German military used a slightly different configuration of their Enigma machines. At Bletchley Park the codebreakers concentrated first on reading messages sent by Luftwaffe stations to each other and to their headquarters. The Luftwaffe Enigma operators were somewhat sloppy in their use of their Enigma machines and sometimes used a girlfriend's name as a key setting, or began a second message with the same setting with which they had ended the first. This gave a way in for the codebreakers to start decrypting a message. In May 1940, Bletchley Park began reading Luftwaffe signals traffic. The existence of these decrypts, known as Ultra, was kept top secret and very few within even senior levels of the government or military knew of the codebreaking operation, probably no more than thirty people maximum. But every day a batch of decrypts was delivered by messenger to Churchill in a battered yellow leather briefcase for which only he had the key on his personal keyring. Even his closest aides had no idea what the yellow briefcase contained. Churchill loved reading these messages in the raw, although the reality was they needed the skills of an experienced interpreter to make sense of what they amounted to. The codename 'Boniface' was given to the decrypts so if anyone should by accident hear about them it would be assumed that they were messages from a secret agent somewhere in Europe. Churchill referred to the deciphering staff at Bletchley Park as 'the geese who laid the golden eggs and never cackled'.[11]

The Kriegsmarine used a different Enigma keying system. Operators had a book of random indicators which were themselves enciphered, a far more sophisticated system that avoided the use of repeated words or girlfriends' names. And they changed them regularly. This meant that the cryptana-lysts at Bletchley Park had no way into the naval signals traffic. For one senior figure in naval intelligence, Ian Fleming, it was clear that only by capturing the indicator lists and encipher-ing tables would it be possible to crack the code. But he could find no way of seizing the books or persuading an operator to betray the regime and hand them over. Harry Hinsley, a Cambridge history undergraduate who had given up his studies to work at Bletchley Park, did, however, come up with a suggestion. Hinsley knew that the Germans had stationed a series of converted fishing trawlers north-east of Iceland to send back meteorological data which was needed to predict weather conditions for bombing raids and shipping. They had Enigma machines on board to decode signals sent to them. He assumed that as the boats were at sea for long periods they would carry the code books for several months in advance, probably in a locked safe. Hinsley proposed that a small task force should be sent to capture the code books on these remote and unprotected vessels.

On 7 May 1941 the task force of a cruiser and four destroyers surrounded and quickly moved on to one of these trawlers, the *München*. Her crew threw the Enigma machine overboard with the current code books but Hinsley had been correct in his assumption and the boarding party captured from the ship's safe the book listing all the keys for the month of June. In the same month another destroyer captured a U-boat, U-110, and again seized the code books on board. When all this got back to Bletchley Park it was transformative. It had taken up to eleven days to be able to read even a small number of the naval signals. By using the captured books this was reduced to between four and six hours.[12] By deciphering key signals to and from the U-boats hunting together in 'wolf packs' when they transmitted information to their base, it was possible to confirm their location and their intentions; the convoys could then be routed away from the waiting menace. This reduced shipping losses dramatically, from an average of about a quarter of a million tons per month in the first six months of 1941 to roughly one quarter of that over the next few months.[13] This was a tremendous victory in the first phase of the Battle of the Atlantic.

The capture of the code books undoubtedly helped save merchant ships. For instance, convoy HX155 sailed from

Halifax, Nova Scotia in October 1941 with fifty-four ships carrying grain, sugar, tobacco, oil and aviation fuel, steel and copper and other supplies. When the Admiralty discovered from Bletchley Park that two wolf packs of U-boats were assembling along its route the convoy was re-routed to the north. Every ship got through, arriving in Liverpool two weeks after departure and bringing in the goods Britain needed. By November the rate of losses in the Atlantic was down to 91,400 tons, twenty-nine ships.[14] Additionally, at the end of the year Hitler ordered Admiral Karl Dönitz, the U-boat commander-in-chief, to redeploy some of his U-boats to the Mediterranean, reducing the danger in the Atlantic. It looked as though Britain was winning the battle. But all that was about to change.

In August 1941, the Royal Navy had captured another U-boat, U-570 on its first patrol, and towed it to a port in Iceland. All the crew were taken prisoner. Not knowing what had happened on board, Admiral Dönitz assumed the worst and believed that the code books had been seized. In fact, in this instance the crew had destroyed them before surrendering and they had not been taken. Dönitz ordered an investigation into the possibility that their codes had now been broken. An almost comic-book Prussian named Captain Stummel with a glass eye and a limp carried out the investigation. He concluded that it was impossible to break the Enigma codes. But Dönitz still decided to tighten up their process of decrypting signals. So, in January 1942, the U-boat service added another rotor blade to their Enigma machines. This increased the possible code permutations by a factor of twenty-six. Overnight, this meant that Bletchley Park could no longer read any of the naval signals. The codebreakers were plunged into darkness.[15]

The sudden blackout of all German naval signals caused an immediate crisis in the Battle of the Atlantic. To this was added an enormous opportunity for Dönitz's U-boats on the eastern seaboard of the United States. The Americans entered the war with no sense of the precautions that British shipping was accustomed to living with. There was no attempt at a blackout along the east coast. Shore lights continued to blaze. Around Miami the glow from neon lights extended 6 miles along the Florida coast. Even if the merchant ships that continuously trafficked up and down the coast were blacked out they were easy to spot at night against this brightly lit background and the US Navy did nothing to introduce a protected convoy system. The U-boat crews enjoyed some of their easiest hunting during the entire war. The captains called it 'the happy time'. They sank thirty-one American ships in January 1942, sixty-nine in February, and the numbers continued to rise. After three months the authorities ordered that coastal lights should be dimmed, known as the 'brown out'. But cries went up all the way from Atlantic City to Miami that 'the tourist season will be ruined'.[16] It took a few more months for proper precautions to be introduced and for a convoy system to be established.

While the codebreakers at Bletchley Park frantically tried to find ways to decrypt the new U-boat signals, German codebreakers succeeded in breaking Britain's naval cipher. As a consequence they could track the route and progression of convoys as they crossed the Atlantic. Losses in mid-ocean rose to frightening levels. In January total shipping losses including British, Allied and neutral ships totalled 420,000 tons. This rose to 680,000 tons in February and 830,000 tons in March. Of British vessels alone, U-boats sank 300 ships in the Atlantic in the first six months of 1942 – equivalent to more than a million tons of shipping.[17] Apart from the terrible loss of life this brought, it meant that millions of tons of supplies including basic foodstuffs, fuel, chemicals and all the materiel of war ended up at the bottom of the Atlantic.

Although the vast increase in the tonnage lost was never revealed to the British people, it had a deep impact on

Churchill. His doctor, who like the rest of the public did not know the scale of the losses, realised that the issue of shipping was a cause of serious concern. 'Wherever he goes he carries in his head the monthly figures of all sinkings, though he never talks about them,' Wilson wrote in his diary on 4 March 1942. 'One day when things at sea were at their worst, I happened to go to the Map Room. There I found the PM. He was standing with his back to me, staring at the huge chart with the little black beetles representing the German submarines. "Terrible" he muttered. I was about to retreat when he whipped round and brushed past me with his head down. I'm not sure he saw me. He knows that we may lose the war at sea in a few months and that he can do nothing about it. I wish to God I could put out the fires that seem to be consuming him.'[18]

Britain was dreadfully over-extended in 1942, finding itself fighting a world war on two fronts thousands of miles apart. Before 1939, Britain had controlled roughly 80 per cent of world shipping. But with millions of tons lost in the Battle of the Atlantic, with vessels taking weeks to go around the Cape to supply the Middle East, shipping resources became a front-line issue. And with the reduction in available shipping, the level of non-war-related imports dropped as well. The result was a tightening of belts in the spring of 1942 and an increase in the number of points needed to acquire all sorts of goods. For the first time domestic fuel rationing was discussed during 1942 and this included coal, not because it had to be imported as Britain was sitting on vast reserves, but because coal was used to generate both gas and electricity, and the output from the mines had been hit by so many skilled miners joining the military. Therefore, domestic consumption had to be reduced. A complex scheme was drawn up in which coal as well as gas and electricity would be rationed according to the number of rooms in a person's house. One Mass Observation diarist calculated for his landlady that she would only have half the coal available to her in the winter of 1942–3 compared to previous winters, which he described as 'pretty drastic'.[19] Another said he would put up with any amount of cuts in clothes coupons, writing, 'I have stopped caring whether I am well dressed or not. While the war is on there are far more important things to do and think about.' But when it came to coal he recorded a different verdict: 'I shall certainly be very miserable if it is cold and I'm not allowed a fire owing to rationing. This would certainly lower my morale more than anything else.'[20]

In June, after protests from Conservative MPs, the government was forced to abandon its plans for coal rationing but instead encouraged people to economise on their use of all fuels – keeping lids on saucepans while cooking and only filling baths with a maximum of 5 inches of hot water. A series of mild winters helped ensure that the ongoing shortage of coal did not become another national crisis.[21]

The terrible losses at sea were yet one more sign that in the first half of 1942 everything was moving backwards as far as Britain's war effort was concerned. All the failures and disappointments of the year have to be seen against the backdrop of the shipping lost during the worst stage of the Battle of the Atlantic. Although the public at large were ignorant of the massive and growing scale of the losses, everyone felt the pressure on rations and the lack of supplies from abroad. For how much longer could this go on?

8

Grave Deterioration

Churchill remained at a low ebb for several weeks, with dreadful reports of losses in the Atlantic and after the surrender of Singapore. He saw the collapse of the fortress at the heart of Britain's defence of the Far East as a terrible humiliation. In a speech at Caxton Hall to the Conservative Party Central Council in March he did not hold back. In the last twelve months, he told the party members, 'we have had an almost unbroken series of military misfortunes'. He described how Britain had been struggling for two years 'in a deadly grapple with two heavily armed opponents both of whom had been preparing for years, and bending their whole national life to the fulfilment of a gospel of war'. Then came an attack from a 'new and most formidable antagonist in the Far East'. During the previous year, British forces had been driven out of Cyrenaica, Greece, Crete and Malaya. Hong Kong had fallen and, he claimed, 'Singapore has been the scene of the greatest disaster to British arms which our history records'.[1] He couldn't make it any worse than that.

That he should be Prime Minister at such a grim moment in the country's military history truly disturbed Churchill. 'Poor old PM in a sour mood and a bad way,' Sir Alexander Cadogan noted in his diary.[2] When Churchill's daughter Mary visited

Downing Street in late February for a lunch alone with her parents she found her father in a state of depression. 'Papa is at a very low ebb,' she wrote in her diary. 'He is not too well physically and he is worn down by the continuous crushing pressure of events. He is saddened – appalled by events.'[3]

There was only one bright moment during those weeks. On the night of 27 February, British paratroopers carried out a daring raid on a German radar station on the north coast of France at Bruneval.

During raids on Germany by Bomber Command in 1941 it had become clear that the Germans had not only built a very effective radar shield to protect the Fatherland but that they were using different technologies that were more powerful and accurate than some of the British radars. The principal German radar to detect approaching aircraft was called Freya, after an ancient Nordic goddess associated with fertility. It had rotating aerials and a range of about 90 miles, and was accurate in identifying distance and bearing but poor in assessing the height of an approaching aircraft. But in late 1941 British bombers found that German night fighters were being directed against them with much greater accuracy, and losses increased alarmingly. It seemed the Germans were using an additional form of radar codenamed 'Würzburg' and that it appeared to be more accurate. Then the boffins discovered references that the pulse signals were sent and received from a paraboloid or bowl-like reflector and operated on a short wavelength of 53 centimetres.

The scientists in the Air Ministry decided that the only way to understand precisely how this new radar system worked was to capture a Würzburg and bring it in for analysis. But where would they find one, and how could it be captured? At this point the photo-interpreters at RAF Medmenham spotted a bowl radar with a 10-foot diameter on a clifftop on the north French coast east of Le Havre. It was a stunning identification of a tiny object that was less than a millimetre wide on an aerial photograph. Lord Louis Mountbatten, the ambitious, youthful head of Combined Operations, was looking for missions for the newly formed 1st Airborne Division and his team came up with a plan to drop a company of paratroopers in the surrounding hills at night with the task of moving down the valley to the coast, capturing the small radar station, dismantling the radar piece by piece, and descending the cliffs with the radar equipment where they would be taken off the beaches by landing craft of the Royal Navy. They would be away by dawn. The paras of C Company of the 2nd Battalion of the Parachute Brigade were selected for the mission, 120 men. They were known as 'Jock Company' as they consisted mostly of tough Scottish troops. The company began to train hard for the mission but on every exercise something went horribly awry; either they were dropped in the wrong place or the navy failed to turn up at the right beach to extricate them. These failures had left the officers in charge anxious about the outcome of their mission.

On the night itself, most of the paras were dropped on target but two planes dropped their men a few miles from the drop zone in the wrong valley. Nevertheless, the paras went ahead with their task, captured the radar and dismantled it. As they descended to the beaches a fire fight broke out with the German defenders. Soldiers originally from the Seaforth Highlanders screaming their old regimental war cry of 'Caber Feidh' finally overcame the German troops. The paras gathered with three prisoners including a captured radar operator and waited on the beach. But there was no sign of the landing craft that were due to take them off. Radio communications with the navy had completely failed. As German reinforcements closed in on them, the commanding officer decided there was no option but to use up their ammunition and then surrender. He later admitted to being pretty 'fed up' with the prospect of spending the rest of the war in a prison camp. At that point one of his men spotted a vessel coming in to the beach. At the absolute last possible minute the landing craft arrived. Most of the paras got away, and when their precious cargo arrived in Britain the boffins were able to study it and understand how this short-wavelength radar system worked. It was now possible to explore ways in which to jam a Würzburg in the future.[4]

The operation had been mounted with the hope that it would be a fillip to the morale of the nation. Accordingly, the newspapers and radio, desperate for some good news, were full of the story of the daring mission which, to add additional lustre, was the first successful operation by the nation's new, all-volunteer, elite airborne force. 'I'd like to see more of that sort of thing done,' wrote one Mass Observation diarist.[5] It was said that after the Bruneval Raid any man wearing the airborne wings of the paratroopers on his shoulders who walked into a pub would get drinks bought for him all evening, even if he politely pointed out that he had not been on the raid. 'Never mind, mate,' he would be told, 'you're a paratrooper and that's all that matters.'[6] At last there was a feat of arms to celebrate, albeit on a very small scale.

Bruneval had been the sort of audacious commando-style raid that Churchill loved, and the day after the men returned to their base he called the leader of the operation, Major John Frost, into Downing Street to report to him first hand about the raid. Mountbatten and Major-General Frederick 'Boy' Browning, the commander of the 1st Airborne, were also there along with the chiefs of staff and some members of the War Cabinet. It was a daunting moment for Major Frost who had been battling behind enemy lines only a few hours before. But it was Mountbatten who launched into a clear and compelling narrative of the raid and Churchill, deeply impressed, asked several questions. When he asked Frost about the quality of the intelligence they had received, the officer who had led the raid said it was excellent, so good in fact that they had even known the name of the German sergeant in charge of the radar station. After being cheered by the story of the raid, Churchill went over to a model of the site that had been brought in for the presentation. As he ran his finger over the outline of the cliffs he said slowly but clearly, 'Now about these raids, there must be more of them. Let there be no doubt about that.'[7]

But the Bruneval Raid brought only temporary relief for the Prime Minister. To some at the centre of events the government still seemed rudderless. On 2 March Eden and Cadogan met and agreed that 'for the last fortnight there has been no direction of the war. War Cabinet doesn't function – there hasn't been a meeting of the Defence Committee. There's no hand on the wheel (Probably due to the PM's health).' After a Cabinet meeting later in the day, Cadogan wrote, 'News from everywhere – except Russia – bad. There's something wrong with us, I fear.'[8]

The reshuffle that had begun in late February continued. Six Cabinet ministers and nine under-secretaries of state were replaced. David Margesson took the blame for the disasters in the Far East and was fired from his post as Secretary of War and replaced by his top civil servant, Sir James Grigg. At least Grigg would not represent a political threat to the Prime Minister in this important post. The balance of the coalition now changed from the form it had taken since May 1940. The Labour Party seemed to have a more central role; although Cripps, the key new arrival, had not yet rejoined the party he was clearly a man of the left. And with the departure of Beaverbrook, Ernest Bevin, the pre-war trade union boss, emerged in a stronger position as Minister of Labour. He would continue to play a powerful role in mobilising the workforce for war, and in promoting his policy of encouraging companies to establish Joint

Production Committees in which workers would sit alongside managers when organising production.

The final stage of Churchill's reinvigoration of his government came with changes to the Chiefs of Staff Committee. Churchill wanted Mountbatten to join the small group. He thought Mountbatten, who had so impressed him over the Bruneval Raid, would add a touch of youth and flair to the committee of the most senior military men in the country. Moreover, the general feeling was that the chair of the committee, Admiral Sir Dudley Pound, was too elderly and exhausted to any longer coordinate the group that was at the heart of the nation's war machine. So, in early March, General Sir Alan Brooke was appointed as chair of the committee. From here on, for the next three years, he and Churchill met pretty well daily. The two men would have something of a love–hate relationship for the rest of the war. Brooke found the Prime Minister insufferable at times with his interfering, bullying style and his desire to get involved in minor tactical issues. Churchill loved this sort of detail but Brooke thought it was entirely beyond what a Prime Minister should be concerned with and that it amounted to nothing less than meddling. Additionally, Brooke was pushed to the brink of exhaustion by Churchill's tendency to call meetings late at night when everyone had already worked a long day. But all this was combined with an immense respect for the PM whom he realised was an inspiration to many of those who worked for him. On his part, Churchill was frequently exasperated by this tough Ulsterman who was one of the few who would dare to answer him back. At times, aides reported hearing a shouting match taking place between the two men as they argued over a point of strategy. Brooke would come out of the room and be heard to mutter 'That man!' But then with a sigh to continue, 'But what would we do without him?'[9] One close observer of their relationship noted that unlike his

IWM

*General Sir Alan Brooke, Chief of the Imperial General Staff. He and
Churchill had a love–hate relationship for much of the war.*

predecessors, Brooke had the great gift of 'shaking himself
like a dog coming out of the water' after a bruising encounter
with the Prime Minister.[10] And Churchill respected anyone
who stood up to him, rarely bore a grudge, and when faced
with a determined, well-argued case never overruled his
Chief of the Imperial General Staff.

Not everyone was keen to see Mountbatten, a middle-
ranking naval officer, promoted to the highest echelon of the
national command structure. But Churchill insisted, saying
he wanted Mountbatten to join the chiefs of staff not to advise
purely on Combined Operations but 'to exercise influence
upon the war as a whole, upon future planning in its broadest
sense'.[11] He wanted new energy and drive in military decision-
making. To solve the problem of his relatively low seniority,
Churchill had Mountbatten promoted to acting Vice Admiral.

Mountbatten was naturally delighted to ascend to the top military table in the land and wrote to a friend proudly that he was now 'the youngest Vice Admiral since Nelson'.[12]

Meanwhile the Japanese advance into Burma continued unabated. There had been no serious planning for the defence of Burma even though the country contained the sole overland route to supply China in its long war with Japan. Moreover, control of Burma offered access to a side door into India. The Japanese had launched their invasion in mid-January and in many ways the battle for Burma mirrored that for Malaya. There were too few Allied troops, most of whom were poorly trained for jungle warfare, and they were spread over too large an area. They were overly complacent and were led by Lieutenant-General Sir Thomas Hutton, another commander who was a good staff officer but lacked charisma. The RAF had only one squadron of Brewster Buffalo aircraft in the country and they proved no match for the Japanese fighters. The Australian government refused to send a division that had been withdrawn from the Middle East fearing they would be sacrificed in Burma just as Australian troops had been in Singapore. The Japanese used the same tactics as in Malaya, outflanking well-prepared defensive positions by advancing into the jungle, surrounding them and forcing a chaotic retreat. After a disastrous defeat on the Sittang river, Hutton prepared to abandon the capital, Rangoon. Wavell this time intervened and removed Hutton, replacing him with General Harold Alexander, a far more striking, dynamic figure. But with Allied troops falling back in retreat and Burmese troops deserting in vast numbers, Alexander arrived just in time to abandon Rangoon on 7 March, narrowly escaping a humiliating capture himself. The Japanese entered the city the following day. Another imperial capital fell to the Japanese.

The Burma campaign lasted for another two months in what was called a 'fighting retreat'. Chinese troops arrived to defend their vital supply line, the Burma Road. Alexander had two able generals to assist: Joseph Stilwell, an American in command of the Chinese forces, and Sir William Slim, in command of the imperial troops. Yet again the Japanese proved resourceful, determined and ruthless in their push north. Without air cover after the RAF had withdrawn to India, the result was a foregone conclusion. Lashio, the terminus of the Burma Road, was soon captured leaving China isolated from overland supplies from the outside world. The retreating armies slowed the Japanese down as they crossed first the Irrawaddy river and then the Chindwin. Mandalay was captured on 1 May, and later that month the remains of the British, Indian and Gurkha troops withdrew across the mountains to the frontier of India. Slim described the remnants of his army as they crossed the border into India, without transports and having struggled across jungles, mountains and ravines, as being 'pitifully small' in numbers and as 'gaunt and ragged as scarecrows'.[13]

The Burma Road had been cut and Japanese troops were on the Indian border. It had been a disastrous campaign, and having covered 900 miles became known as the longest retreat in British history. But the fighting withdrawal had prevented the Japanese from getting to India before the monsoon season so, for now at least, they could proceed no further. And the battle for Burma had convinced General Slim that before taking on the Japanese again he must have both troops that were properly trained in jungle warfare and aerial superiority, which would allow him to supply his men from the air. It would be two years before he had all that he needed to take the offensive in Burma.

The navy too were reeling after the surrender of Singapore and Rangoon. They withdrew what ships they could muster into the Indian Ocean but one of the key problems was that they lacked a base. The nearest harbour where major repairs could take place was 4,000 miles away on the other side of the ocean in Durban, South Africa. Ceylon provided a military headquarters but Colombo and Trincomalee, the two ports, were too small to host large warships. A temporary, secret base was established at Adu Atoll, a ring of coral reefs surrounding a large deep-water lagoon south of the Maldives. It was given the codename 'Port T' in an attempt to hide its identity. But there was always the threat of a sudden, Pearl Harbor-style attack from Japanese aircraft carriers. The Bay of Bengal running south from Calcutta to Madras suddenly appeared very open to a Japanese naval attack. From land and sea, India looked painfully exposed and vulnerable.

The defence of India was of course a political as well as a military issue. Churchill had served in India as a young cavalry officer. He saw British rule there as the natural and just order of affairs. He had resisted throughout his career any suggestion of the break-up of the British Raj and in the mid-1930s this stance had isolated him from the rest of his own Conservative Party. But now, with the Japanese battering at the gates, Indian nationalists might take advantage of imperial weakness to attempt to overthrow British rule once and for all. Again, the need for reform in India leapt up the political agenda to avoid a collapse of the Raj. That would be an even greater imperial catastrophe than all the other military disasters added together.

Following the fiasco at Singapore, President Roosevelt made clear to Churchill his own view that India should become independent. Churchill still resisted and argued that the President did not fully understand the complexities of an India divided between a Hindu majority and a Muslim minority, and in which many princely states still guarded their precious rights. Reluctantly, he accepted Attlee's suggestion that a Cabinet committee should be set up to review the status of India. The members would include Attlee, Cripps,

Anderson, Grigg and Leo Amery, the Secretary of State for India. Churchill occasionally sat in, and after one of his visits to the committee Amery wrote in his diary that the Prime Minister was 'quite incapable of listening or taking in even the simplest point but [he] goes off at a tangent on a word and then rambles on inconsecutively ... knowing nothing of his reputation [one] would have thought him a rather amusing but quite gaga old gentleman who could not understand what people were talking about'. Amery wondered if Churchill was 'losing his grip altogether'.[14]

Most people who thought about the issue of India in the post-war world believed that Britain's colonial relationship with the subcontinent could not remain the same as before the war. As Mollie Panter-Downes put it, 'Few intelligent Britons think that postwar Asia will settle down into the cosy old pattern of Empire, with mad dogs and Englishmen in sole enjoyment of the midday sun.'[15] At the beginning of March, Cripps suggested that he travel to India to propose an agreement to the Indian Congress Party offering post-war independence as long as they agreed to support Britain's war effort. Added to this was a guarantee that any province could opt out of an independent India, meaning that the Muslims could create their own state, as was their aim, to be known as Pakistan. It would be the first time that Britain had formally offered to leave India after two centuries of presence. Sending Cripps on the mission was a gamble for both Churchill and Attlee. If he came back with a deal then he would present an even greater threat to the current leadership. But the day after Rangoon was occupied, the War Cabinet agreed to send him to India. Roosevelt sent his own emissary to assist the mission.

Cripps threw himself into a fast-paced round of meetings in New Delhi. He established himself and the Crippery in a modest bungalow just off the city centre which contrasted dramatically with the vast palace from which the Viceroy conducted his operations. The bungalow became the frantic centre of activity, its garden constantly packed with reporters and cameramen, and with a constant round of visitors as the great and the good of India turned up to argue their point of view. Cripps met with forty different Indian representatives in a matter of days. There were 350 million Indians, one fifth of the world's population at the time, and many different perspectives to grapple with. Cripps offered a very positive spin on the negotiations when he gave a press conference to a packed briefing room in which one British journalist believed he was watching the 'Awakening of India'.[16]

But the challenge of India was too great for even the smart efficiency of Sir Stafford. Gandhi insisted that the only moral position was one of non-violence. When asked if this meant not opposing the Japanese, he said that it did. Only by stepping aside could further violence be avoided, he argued. Although he was respected as a saint-like figure, not many people agreed with this position. Congress demanded immediate control of India. They would then raise a new army to fight the Japanese. The Muslim League wanted a guarantee of a Muslim state and were minded to approve the deal on offer. Those who served the British administration or, like the Sikhs and many others, fought in its army were opposed to any change in the current status quo. Then there were the politically minded Untouchables who wanted an end to the caste system, and the communists who wanted to rip up the class system. There was a small minority who supported the fascists and those who agreed to fight for the Japanese. And there were millions of peasants, hungry and poor, tied to the land whom everyone else wanted to dominate. Many in Britain and even more in America could agree that Britain had to leave India, but how and to whom was not going to be easy.

Cripps regarded Nehru, the leader of the Congress Party and another brilliant lawyer who had trained in Britain, as a good friend. They had met before and both shared many of the same characteristics and attitudes. Cripps was genuinely surprised to find that Nehru was highly suspicious of the offer and demanded immediate control of an interim wartime government by Congress. When Gandhi met Cripps, he told him that if his offer was all Britain could come up with, he might as well go home. Famously, Gandhi described the idea of a promise of future independence as 'a post-dated cheque' (to which one journalist added the phrase 'on a failing bank').[17]

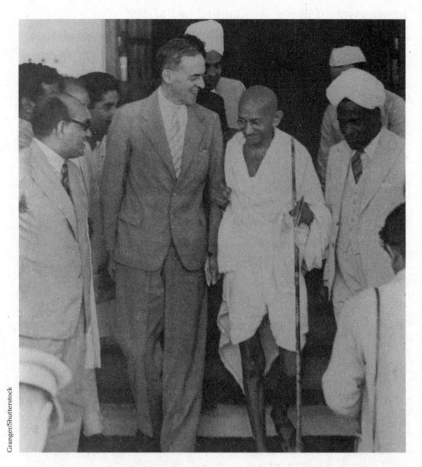

Sir Stafford Cripps on his mission to India meets Gandhi. The defence of India became a political as well as a military issue in 1942.

Only Jinnah, leader of the Muslim League, seemed supportive. Cripps's self-confident assuredness took a beating. As
the Japanese advanced relentlessly through northern Burma
towards the Indian border, hectic negotiations continued.
But Cripps could not get Nehru to agree a deal. Suspicion
of British promises was too great and the Congress Party
realised that after the failures to defend Hong Kong, Malaya,
Singapore and now Burma, the British were no longer militarily the top power. Independence now was their priority.
For Britain, winning the war first was the primary objective.

For several weeks the delegates of the different Indian fac-
tions went back and forth to Cripps's bungalow. New ideas
emerged. New compromises were sought. But Congress
insisted on its right to form a National Government straight
away. Then, in the middle of April, Cripps gave up and
announced he would return to London. At another press
conference a journalist asked, 'What happens now?' Cripps
replied, 'Nothing. The offer is simply withdrawn and I do not
think we are able to make another one. The position is just
as it was before I arrived.'[18] His frustration and exhaustion
with India were clear. Mass Observation recorded that many
people in Britain were surprised at the failure of the talks; 45
per cent of those interviewed blamed Britain for the collapse
of the talks, 30 per cent blamed the Indians and 25 per cent
blamed both sides. However, none of it reflected badly on
Cripps in a Mass Observation poll where 70 per cent still had
a favourable view of him, almost the same as before he left
for India.[19]

The Congress Party issued a statement: 'Britain must
abandon her hold in India'. The Americans were greatly
disappointed and suspected (wrongly) that Churchill had
sabotaged the mission. Churchill said he regretted Cripps's
return before the War Cabinet had been able to agree new
terms to offer. But wheels had been set in motion that would

not stop running for the next five years. The 'Quit India' campaign united nationalists but the British arrested most of the Congress and thousands of local leaders, keeping them imprisoned until 1945. And in 1943 Churchill irredeemably damaged Britain's status in India when he refused to allocate scarce shipping to relieve the appalling Bengal famine. Many nationalists blamed Britain for the dreadful suffering in Bengal and this stoked anti-imperialist views.[20] Meanwhile, the contradictions of the British Raj continued. As Congress denounced British rule, the Indian Army fighting in the Middle East and Asia still stood at over a million men and 50,000 came forward every month to volunteer.[21] Whether this would be enough to save India either from the Japanese or from internal divisions was not clear. But it was evident to the whole world that for the first time in a century and a half Britain could no longer guarantee Indian security.

There was further angst in Downing Street when General Auchinleck in North Africa announced that he would not be ready to launch an attack against Rommel's forces until July. Everywhere he turned, Churchill found himself frustrated. And from frustration came irritation, exhaustion and anger. In early March, Churchill sent Roosevelt a long and pensive telegram about the state of the war. 'When I reflect how I have longed and prayed for the entry of the United States into the war, I find it difficult to realise how gravely our British affairs have deteriorated by what has happened since December 7,' he wrote. 'We have suffered the greatest disaster in our history at Singapore, and other misfortunes will come thick and fast upon us.' Churchill regretted that the 'great power' of the US 'will only become effective gradually because of the vast distances and the shortage of ships'. The event he was most beginning to fear was that Rommel would break through in North Africa, cross the Middle East and join up with victorious German troops who would smash the Russians on the Eastern Front and head south into the Caucasus and the oilfields around the Caspian Sea. He expressed this fear to Roosevelt: 'The whole of the Levant-Caspian Front now depends entirely upon the success of the Russian Armies. The attack which the Germans will deliver upon Russia in the spring will I fear be most formidable.'[22] It was only three months since Churchill had 'slept the sleep of the saved and thankful'. But everywhere and on every front, the situation had gravely deteriorated.

The mood in Britain was thoroughly depressed. A Mass Observation diarist in a small village in Hampshire noted down some of the comments she overheard. One friend was 'in a state of great bitterness over events in the Far East and she said she thought we would be under German rule here before too long'. The diarist also noted, 'We had a chat with some friends passing by who pleaded guilty to having lost faith in Churchill and this Govt and hoped and expected a tremendous (but "typically English") upheaval in this country, culminating with Sir Stafford Cripps becoming No. 1 and a real total war effort expected from everybody, and if not why not?'[23]

In North Africa and Egypt, British forces slowly built up their strength against a skilful foe. In the Far East, Japanese troops continued to move rapidly towards the Indian border. With the failure of the Cripps mission, British rule in India was on the brink of total collapse. Wavell insisted that he could not guarantee the defence of the subcontinent without substantial reinforcements. In London, while the Prime Minister stamped and fretted, a newly reinvigorated government assessed its options. General Brooke, reviewing the situation, confided to his diary, 'I do not like the look of things.' He wrote: 'I suppose this Empire has never been in such a precarious position throughout its history ... I wish I could see more daylight as to how we are to keep going through 1942!'[24]

9

Arctic Convoys

Hitler's assault upon the Soviet Union in June 1941 had been on an epic scale. Across a gigantic front from the Baltic to the Black Sea, three massive army groups smashed through the Soviet defences in an eastern version of the blitzkrieg that had led to the collapse of France the previous year. Army Group North advanced rapidly in the direction of Leningrad (today St Petersburg). Army Group Centre occupied Belorussia (Belarus) and after capturing Minsk drove on towards Moscow. And Army Group South struck into Ukraine heading for Kiev. The ground troops were supported by hundreds of squadrons of Luftwaffe bombers and dive bombers. It was the biggest land operation in history, designed to annihilate the Red Army in huge encircling movements.

The invasion transformed the war in many ways. For Britain it meant an easing of the pressure of the Blitz that had killed thousands of civilians and left deep scars across British cities through the winter and spring of 1940–1. Now the war moved to the east and the destruction of both military targets and civilian communities was on an unprecedented scale. By mid-July, Russian losses included roughly 6,000 aircraft, 8,000 tanks and over 600,000 soldiers taken prisoner. Details picked up from intercepted German police messages, decrypted at

Bletchley Park, revealed evidence of mass killings behind the advancing front line of 'Jews', 'Jewish plunderers', 'Jewish bolshevists' and Russian prisoners in hundreds, then in thousands, then in tens of thousands.[1] This mass murder was committed by SS death squads that roamed freely behind the advancing German Army rounding up and murdering political and racial 'enemies' of the Third Reich. In a BBC radio broadcast Churchill reported that 'As [Hitler's] armies advance, whole districts are being exterminated. Scores of thousands – literally scores of thousands – of executions in cold blood are being perpetrated.' Churchill described this as a 'crime without a name'.[2]

The possibility of a German victory was a spectre hanging over the British government throughout the late summer and autumn of 1941. Sir Stafford Cripps, while Britain's ambassador in Moscow, attempted to reassure Stalin that all possible support would be given by Britain to the Soviet Union. Cripps urged Churchill to make 'a superhuman effort to help Russia'. Four hundred Hurricane fighters were offered to the Soviet Union in August, fighters that Britain desperately needed at home, in the Middle East and to meet demands from commanders for reinforcements in the Far East. But the War Cabinet knew that a German victory in the east would unleash a vast military machine against Britain. An equally unpalatable alternative was that if the Soviet Union faced a crushing defeat, then Stalin might be tempted to negotiate a unilateral peace with Nazi Germany.

On 4 September, Stalin wrote directly to Churchill urging him to open a second front in Europe by launching an invasion of occupied France or of the Balkans to remove the 'mortal menace' facing the Soviet Union by drawing away from the Eastern Front between thirty and forty German divisions. Churchill insisted that while still struggling for survival, Britain could not launch an invasion of France, nor of the Balkans. Commonwealth forces were growing in the Middle East and the RAF was regularly bombing German war factories but Britain could do no more than this for the next few months. Churchill told Cripps to explain the realities of Britain's war to the Russian leadership, adding, 'Neither sympathy nor emotions will overcome the kind of facts we have to face.'[3]

On 15 September, Stalin sent a further telegram asking for twenty-five or thirty British Army divisions to be sent urgently either to Archangel or to the Caucasus to assist the Russian defence. As this amounted to the entire home army at that point it was a crazy request reflecting the panic in Moscow. Churchill later wrote that it was 'almost incredible' that the head of the Soviet government 'could have committed himself to such absurdities. It seemed hopeless to argue with a man thinking in terms of utter unreality.'[4] Churchill was convinced that only the United States could supply the enormous scale of resources that Stalin needed. He pleaded with Roosevelt to help Russia. Realising the dreadful consequences of a Soviet defeat, the President agreed to do what he could within the legal confines of America's neutrality.

On the afternoon of 19 September, the Defence Committee met in Downing Street to discuss aid to Russia. Churchill, Eden and Beaverbrook, the politicians present, were in favour of sending the maximum amount of aid. The chiefs of staff of the army, navy and air force were opposed. One of those present noted that for the military chiefs 'Not a rowing boat, a rifle or a Tiger Moth could be spared without weakening [Britain's defences] and without grave risk.' The discussion went on for several hours with the temper of both sets of protagonists worsening. 'Churchill's shoulders became more hunched. A scowl on his brow deepened. His interjections were more frequent and more impatient. On and on we went.'[5] As afternoon became evening the meeting carried on without agreement. After an adjournment for dinner, the committee members returned to Downing Street at 10.30 p.m. Faced with threats to continue talking all night the service chiefs gave in. Britain would supply aid to the Soviet Union. But it could never be all that Stalin wanted or needed, and Churchill concluded that 'America, not ourselves, would have to be the arsenal for the Russian army'.[6]

At the end of September an Anglo-American Mission was sent to Moscow to discuss what aid could be supplied. Lord Beaverbrook represented Britain and Averell Harriman the United States. Beaverbrook took a very pro-Soviet position and as Minister of Supply before he left set up a 'Tanks for Russia Week' in which Britain's entire tank production for the week would be sent to the Soviet Union. It proved immensely popular with most workers who wanted to do what they could to help their Soviet brothers and sisters. When the negotiations began in Moscow, Stalin drove a hard bargain. And not worrying too much about the practicalities, Beaverbrook wanted to offer Stalin almost everything he wanted. A massive quantity of military supplies was eventually pledged to the Soviet Union. *Every month* these were to include 200 British Spitfires and Hurricanes, 100 American fighter planes and 100 American bombers; 1,000 tanks, 300 anti-tank guns and 2,000 armoured cars; 4,000 tons of aluminium, 13,000 tons of steel bars, and quantities of copper, lead, tin, brass and other vital metals; 20,000 tons of petroleum products; 400,000 pairs of army boots; and a vast array of medical supplies including more than a million surgical needles, surgical gloves, a range of drugs and anaesthetics and a million metres of oilcloth for covering wounds. This level of supplies was to be maintained until June 1942.[7]

The question then became, how could this staggering amount of aid be realistically sent to the Soviet Union? A joint Anglo-Soviet occupation of Persia (Iran) took place in the summer to open up a southern route for supplies and to give Britain control over the Abadan oilfields. But for aid to be sent via this route it first had to be shipped around the Cape to the port of Khorramshahr at the head of the Persian Gulf, a journey of 12,000 miles from the UK, and then sent overland by train on a 2,000-mile trip across Iran to southern Russia. An alternative was by sea around the North Cape of Norway to the Soviet ports of Murmansk and Archangel, a far shorter journey. This seemed to be the only practical solution. Initially it had been thought that the Soviets would carry the supplies in their own ships to their own ports. But it rapidly became clear that they did not have the shipping capacity to carry the vast quantities that needed to be transported. Churchill sent an 'Action This Day' message to his chiefs telling them to find a way to begin sending supplies immediately, including by 'special convoy' if necessary. On 6 October, Churchill cabled Stalin again, saying, 'We intend to run a continuous cycle of convoys, leaving every ten days.' The journey time would be seventeen days.[8] It would be a fatal promise that would later come to haunt the Prime Minister.

Britain and America had been forced to select a wild and ferocious route for these Arctic convoys that was fraught with danger from both the climate and the enemy. British ships would assemble in Loch Ewe in north-west Scotland, then sail to Iceland where they would join American vessels that had sailed from the eastern seaboard, usually under the Panamanian, Honduran or some other flag of convenience to get around the US Neutrality Act. Once the naval escorts had arrived they would set off on a journey of between 1,500 and 2,000 miles around the North Cape, across the Barents Sea to Murmansk or Archangel. The seas the convoys had to sail through, inside the Arctic Circle, were notorious for their bad and changeable weather. A seemingly unending round of gales swept the area. In winter, these took the form of snow-laden blizzards. Sea spray lashing a ship would instantly turn to ice and would sometimes build up to a coating several feet thick. This would not only mean that nothing on deck could be touched without thick gloves but the weight of the ice could also affect the stability of a vessel and threaten to capsize it. Along with the gales were frequent thick fogs, caused by the warm waters of the Gulf Stream meeting the cold polar seas. Fogs could suddenly develop and reduce visibility to a few yards. But equally quickly they could disperse and offer a few days of clear and relatively calm weather. Throughout the year the cold was a feature. In summer, with luck it might just be above freezing. In winter, it could drop to minus 40°C. The seas were so cold that anyone unlucky enough to go in would survive for only two minutes at most. The prospect of holding out for several days in an open boat having abandoned a sinking vessel was ghastly. But this was only the beginning of the mariners' problems.

Most of the merchant vessels laden with arms, tanks, petrol and metals were underpowered for the weight they were carrying and the convoys usually moved at no more than about 9 knots. If they survived the battering from the icy seas they would head for the principal northern Soviet port at Archangel. But this was ice-bound from November to May and unusable. The only alternative was Murmansk, in reality nothing more than a large fishing harbour. It had little in the way of cargo-handling facilities, no dockside cranes or heavy-lifting equipment. Most of its berths were constructed out of wood. Sometimes it took not days or weeks but months to unload a ship. Moreover, Murmansk was within short flying time from German airfields in northern Norway. And the medical facilities were extremely primitive. There was one hospital but it was desperately short of drugs, anaesthetics and basic supplies. Having faced all this, every ship then had to return, usually empty in ballast or carrying a small amount of Russian timber or ore that was needed in Britain. Running the gauntlet on the return journey, the mariners had

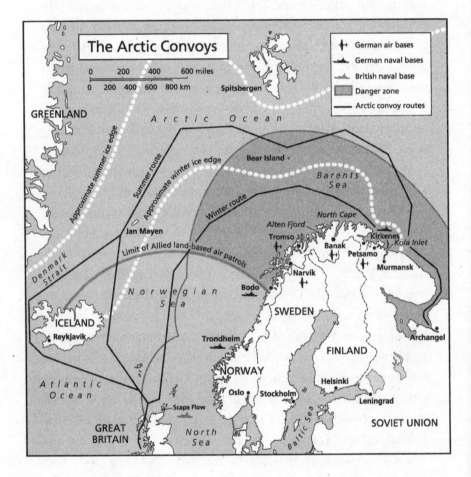

The Arctic Convoys

German air bases
German naval bases
British naval base
Danger zone
Arctic convoy routes

0   200   400   600 miles
0   200   400   600   800 km

GREENLAND

Arctic   Ocean

Spitsbergen

Approximate summer ice edge

Summer route

Approximate winter ice edge

Bear Island

Barents
Sea

Winter route

North Cape

Alten Fjord

Jan Mayen

Tromso

Kirkenes

Kola Inlet

Limit of Allied land-based air patrols

Banak

Petsamo

Murmansk

Denmark
Strait

Narvik

Norwegian
Sea

Bodo

SWEDEN

Archangel

ICELAND

Reykjavik

Trondheim

FINLAND

Atlantic
Ocean

NORWAY

Oslo

Stockholm

Helsinki

Leningrad

Scapa Flow

GREAT
BRITAIN

North
Sea

Baltic Sea

SOVIET UNION

to confront the whole process once again. For the merchant seamen on the Arctic convoys the task soon became known as the journey to hell. And then back again.[9]

The Russian convoys began in earnest in the second half of October 1941. The first few got through to the northern Soviet ports without incident, departing at roughly ten- to fifteen-day intervals. Each convoy with its naval escorts had the prefix PQ, and PQ1 to PQ5 carried their cargo in a total of thirty-eight ships. Some 750 tanks, 800 fighter aircraft, 1,400 vehicles and 100,000 tons of other military supplies were successfully transported to Soviet Russia. The return convoys had the prefix QP. And the first five all got back without loss. But in mid-November, as the German assault ground to a halt within sight of Moscow, Admiral Raeder decided that action had to be taken to prevent these supplies getting through to the Soviets. In the freezing winter waters within the Arctic Circle, the battle for the convoys now grew intense.

Since occupying Norway in April 1940, the Germans had built three airfields at the North Cape and here were based between 200 and 300 Luftwaffe aircraft including bombers, torpedo bombers, dive bombers and reconnaissance aircraft. In the winter months the polar ice came to within about 80 miles of the North Cape; in summer it receded and allowed for a slightly more northern route. But in both summer and winter the convoys were within easy flying range of these northern air bases and beyond the range of Allied aircraft to provide support. Furthermore, sheltering in the deep Norwegian fjords were a host of German warships. The most deadly of these was the battleship *Tirpitz*, the sister ship of the *Bismarck*. With its eight 15-inch and twelve 5.9-inch guns, the *Tirpitz* was sent to hide out in a fjord near Trondheim where it was ideally positioned to strike out and attack either shipping in the Atlantic or the passing Arctic convoys. Joining the *Tirpitz* in 1942 were the battlecruiser *Scharnhorst*, the pocket battleship *Lützow*, the heavy cruisers *Admiral Hipper* and *Prinz Eugen* and a flotilla of new Z-class fast destroyers based at Kirkenes, 60 miles from the Kola Inlet that led to Murmansk. Additionally, there was the Ulan Group of U-boats based at Trondheim. Initially there were three German submarines in this pack, but the number would more than double in 1942 and they would keep up a continuous patrol along the routes the convoys were likely to take.

The first loss came at the beginning of January 1942. The 5,100-ton *Waziristan* was a British ship but had picked up its cargo in New York and had sailed direct from America. A stiff gale and thick ice caused it to become separated from the other vessels in the convoy and on the morning of 2 January a U-boat spotted the *Waziristan* sailing alone. One torpedo finished off the heavily laden merchant vessel. The *Waziristan* was sent to the bottom and her entire crew of forty-seven went down with their ship.

The next few weeks were relatively quiet until PQ12 with sixteen merchant vessels was sighted by a long-range German reconnaissance aircraft. Admiral Raeder ordered the *Tirpitz* to sail from Trondheim to intercept the convoy but its movement was picked up by a watching British submarine. Alerted, the Admiralty ordered the battleship HMS *King George V* and the aircraft carrier HMS *Victorious* to pursue the German warship. When aircraft from the *Victorious* came in range they launched an attack. Although the attacking aircraft scored no hits, it was enough to send the *Tirpitz* scurrying south and out of danger. PQ12 sailed on to Murmansk, and the only loss was a Soviet merchant ship that capsized following the build-up of thick ice on her deck.

In mid-March, PQ13 departed for Murmansk. It was one of the biggest convoys so far, consisting of twenty merchant ships from Britain, America, and exiled ships from both Poland and Sweden. The escorts included destroyers, anti-submarine trawlers and the light cruiser HMS *Trinidad*. PQ13 departed from Iceland in six columns abreast, surrounded by the zig-zagging naval escorts.[10] The first few days passed peacefully enough but as spring was advancing the long dark nights that had provided some sort of cover were giving way to more hours of light. On the night of 24 March a force 9 gale blew up, straight off the polar ice. Many of the ships only had open bridges and the officers on watch had to endure hours of biting, icy winds. They were well kitted out with heavy woollen long johns, a thick jersey, a sheep-lined jerkin and on top of all that a canvas duffel coat. But the wind straight from the Arctic cut through all the layers and dulled a man's senses, slowing his reactions. The convoy sailed on, but the following day the gales grew even worse. After twenty-four hours of continuous assault from the extreme weather the ships' crews found it impossible to stay in formation. By dawn on 26 March the convoy had broken up and was scattered over hundreds of square miles of ocean, many of the ships by now hopelessly lost.

Using its radar to locate the scattered ships, *Trinidad* tried urgently to round up the convoy. But it was an impossible task. One of the small whalers had run out of petrol and had to be refuelled at sea, which took several hours. Another vessel, with the convoy commodore on board, was finally located 300 miles from where it should have been.

On the night of 27 March the gale finally blew itself out and the following morning came up fine and sunny with good visibility. This enabled the Luftwaffe to get in on the act and wave after wave of bombers attacked the dispersed ships. First came Stuka dive bombers, screeching out of the sky in almost vertical dives; then came the two-engine Junkers 88s, each carrying a single bomb; finally, there were Messerschmitt 110 fighter bombers carrying four 500lb bombs. Each merchant ship was equipped with a variety of anti-aircraft weapons including quick-firing Bofors guns, Lewis guns and light machine guns. The fire they could put up threw several of the attacking planes off course. But there were still casualties.

Several ships had met up in the clear weather and were proceeding towards their destination in small groups. One group of vessels took a route too far to the north and got stuck in the packed ice; only with the greatest of difficulty did they extract themselves and continue south towards the Soviet Union. On 29 March the weather worsened again, with mists and snow squalls reducing visibility once more. That meant an escape from air attacks, but the scattered groups of ships faced a new threat from three fast-moving Z-class destroyers that came out from their base at Kirkenes. *Trinidad* went to fend off the destroyers but its torpedo tubes had frozen up. It finally managed to fire a single torpedo but in a fluke incident the torpedo was thrown out of the sea by a freak wave and returned to hit the cruiser amidships. The *Trinidad* acquired the bizarre distinction of being the only British vessel ever to be hit by its own torpedo. Badly damaged but still seaworthy, *Trinidad* limped on and finally made it to Murmansk. The British destroyers went in pursuit of the German vessels and sank one of them. It had been an extraordinary engagement reflecting the freak conditions of the Arctic waters.[11]

On 2 April, the final surviving ships arrived at Murmansk. Five merchant ships, one in four of those that had set out, had been sunk with the loss of 101 lives. The *Trinidad* and the destroyer HMS *Eclipse* had been damaged in the battle with the German destroyers which had cost another nineteen lives. It would be months before they were seaworthy again. But this was not the end of the story. Many survivors of the ships that had been sunk had endured hours or sometimes days on the freezing sea in open lifeboats before the lucky ones had been spotted and picked up by a passing vessel. Several of the mariners were by this point suffering badly from frostbite. Twenty-two-year-old William Short, an engineer on the British merchantman the *Induna*, had bad frostbite in both legs. In the primitive hospital facilities at Murmansk he had to endure the agony of having both legs amputated, without anaesthetic. 'As soon as the knife hit me I passed out, and I was delirious for three days,' the poor man later recalled.[12]

The next chapter in the story of PQ13 was the unloading of the cargoes that had been so courageously brought to the Soviet Union. Without proper lifting facilities it was a laborious and painfully slow process. Day after day, German bombers came over and were able to sink or damage more ships, and destroy thousands of tons of cargo that was slowly being off-loaded. Only occasionally were the Russians able to put up fighters to defend the port. This went on for eight weeks until the end of May when the final cargo was unloaded. Five more ships were destroyed during the bombing raids and another eighty sailors lost their lives. In all, one half of the ships that had sailed with PQ13 were lost.

Back in the UK, Churchill faced an impossible conundrum. He was keen to demonstrate to Stalin Britain's determination to supply the Soviet Union with what it needed. But to the Admiralty, it was clear that even if the risk posed by the U-boats and the surface vessels could be contained by effective escorting, the threat from the Luftwaffe flying with total air supremacy from their Norwegian airfields was overwhelming. As the period of perpetual daylight approached through the spring, the convoy coordinator Admiral Tovey recommended that the convoys be suspended until the autumn when the longer hours of darkness returned. However, Churchill was bound by the impossible demands of the agreement made by Beaverbrook and Harriman, and President Roosevelt now put further pressure on the Prime Minister to maintain the convoys, telling him, 'any word reaching Stalin at this time that our supplies were stopping for any reason would have a most unfortunate 'effect'. Churchill cabled back that it was 'beyond our power' to keep up regular convoys and that a convoy every three weeks with up to thirty-five vessels was 'the extreme limit of what we can handle'.[13]

Meanwhile, the number of vessels waiting to sail was building up. By the end of April there were 107 ships loaded or being loaded with supplies for Russia. Churchill ordered the convoys to continue despite the immense risk. On 21 May, PQ16 set sail from Iceland with thirty-five merchant ships, and QP12 with fifteen ships left Murmansk for the return journey. The homeward convoy got through unscathed but PQ16 endured five days of furious attacks from U-boats and from more than 200 bombers. Again the naval escorts mounted a brave and determined resistance to the different forms of attack. Another cruiser, HMS *Edinburgh*, was badly damaged, this time by a U-boat, and later sank. The ship was carrying four and a half tons of gold bullion sent by the Soviet government in part payment for the supplies that had been dispatched.[14] Six merchant ships were lost en route which was considered an acceptable level. But the Admiralty feared that if the fleet of powerful surface warships joined in the fray the result would be a massacre.

That spring, several American ships arrived at Scapa Flow including the carrier USS *Wasp*, the battleship USS *Washington*, two cruisers and six destroyers. They were in part to help the Royal Navy in their defence of the Arctic convoys. The next convoy, PQ17, would be the first to sail with a combined Anglo-American escort under Admiralty command. The naval chiefs were still hesitant about the whole operation but a plan was devised by which the convoy would be ordered to scatter if the heavy German warships approached, in order to make it harder for the attacking ships to locate and destroy the merchantmen. By this extreme recourse at least it was hoped that some of the dispersed vessels would get through.

After a delay of little over a month the navy was ready to escort PQ17. Thirty-four merchant ships left Iceland on 27 June for Archangel which in mid-summer was once again ice-free and open. Their close escort consisted of six destroyers, two anti-aircraft ships, four corvettes, three minesweepers, four armed trawlers and seven submarines. Further cover about 40 miles distant was provided by four cruisers, two British and two American, under the command of Rear Admiral Hamilton. Further west still would be two battleships, *Duke of York* and *Washington*, and the carrier *Victorious*. It was a massive force ready to ensure that PQ17 could get its valuable cargo of just over 150,000 tons to the Soviet Union, which once again was fighting for its survival.

For four days PQ17 sailed in tight formation towards the North Cape. At noon on 1 July an enemy reconnaissance plane spotted the convoy which from then on remained under almost continuous observation. On 3 July, Raeder ordered the *Tirpitz* and *Hipper* to leave Trondheim and the *Lützow* and *Scheer* to leave Narvik. All four warships and their support vessels were to assemble at Alten Fjord, only a short distance from the North Cape, from where it would be easy to pounce on the convoy as it passed. Reports that the mighty German battleship had been deployed soon reached the Admiralty. In the icy sea off Norway, the convoy sailed on through largely good conditions although there were patches of thick fog. Various air attacks were made and one American ship was hit. With its engines failing, and falling behind the rest of the convoy, the crew were ordered to abandon ship and were all picked up by a rescue vessel. But the concentrated anti-aircraft fire of the merchant and naval vessels kept the bombers at a distance and hesitant about attacking. And although U-boats had now arrived to monitor the convoy from afar they were prevented from attacking by the effective patrolling of the destroyer escorts. On the evening of 3 July, the German reconnaissance aircraft spotted the four cruisers sailing to the north of the convoy. On 4 July, Raeder was told that another large Allied force had been spotted to the west, consisting of two battleships and, most alarmingly, an aircraft carrier. But then the reconnaissance aircraft lost them in the fog. Both sides had to try to calculate what the other side was about to do.

In the Admiralty in London, the news that the *Tirpitz* had been sent north created a sense of panic. The First Sea Lord, Admiral Sir Dudley Pound, took overall command of the operation. He spent the afternoon of 4 July poring over maps with senior officers trying to work out what the Kriegsmarine would do next. The battleships and the *Victorious* were by now about 350 miles to the west of the convoy. If the *Tirpitz* arrived on the scene before they could come in range, the four Allied cruisers would not stand a chance. And Pound knew that he was in command, for the first time, of American as well as British ships. While the convoy steadily steamed on its way north-east, the crews felt reassured that they had seen off the attacking aircraft with minimal loss. But in the Admiralty the tension was clearly rising.

By the evening of 4 July, Pound knew that if the *Tirpitz* chose to attack he was running out of time. So at 9.11 p.m. he sent a 'Most Immediate' order: 'Cruiser Force withdraw to the westward at high speed'. Then at 9.23 he sent another 'Immediate' order: 'Owing to the threat from surface ships, convoy is to disperse and proceed to Russian ports'. Thirteen minutes later he sent a final order clarifying this, using the previously agreed word: 'Convoy is to scatter'.[15] To Hamilton, the order seemed remarkable, but he assumed the Admiralty must have intelligence that he did not have, so imagining that the enemy's surface fleet was about to appear at any moment he turned about and, with the destroyer escorts, withdrew.

When the message to 'scatter' was passed on to the merchant vessels, their captains were even more amazed. At this point they still felt confident in the large, tightly knit convoy's ability to survive the threats from the enemy. To the alarm of the crews of the heavily laden merchantmen, they saw their powerful escorts disappear over the western horizon away from them. Nevertheless, the order to 'scatter' was carried out with precision and each vessel turned in a different direction for a prescribed period of time, before continuing in an easterly direction towards their destination. But soon the folly of the order would become apparent.

All had not been going well on the German side. The *Lützow* and three destroyers had run aground in heavy fog on islands off the Norwegian coast and were forced to return to Trondheim. On the morning of 5 July Raeder finally got Hitler's permission for the *Tirpitz* to leave Alten Fjord to attack. Hitler had been shocked by the loss of the *Bismarck* the previous year and was reluctant to risk his one remaining capital ship. He had made it clear that only he could give the order for the *Tirpitz* to sail into battle. This he now reluctantly did but insisted the sortie should only be a short one. As the German battleship finally sailed out to attack, reconnaissance aircraft reported that the convoy had mysteriously scattered. It was now easier for aircraft to attack the ships as there would be no concentrated fire from the whole convoy, and for the U-boats to attack single ships sailing without destroyer escorts. So, wanting to avoid any losses from the heavy battleship and carrier force to the west, at 9.30 p.m. on the evening of 5 July Raeder ordered the *Tirpitz* to return. It had seen no action whatsoever and its role in the story of PQ17 was over.

Now all that remained was for the Luftwaffe and the U-boats to track the scattered and virtually defenceless vessels and pick them off one by one. This they did with deadly efficiency. By dawn on 6 July, twelve ships had been located and sunk. The pursuit went on mercilessly. Five more ships went down over the following two days. A small group of surviving ships got to within 60 miles of the Russian coast when they came under relentless attack from high-level bombers during which two more ships were sunk. Urgent appeals were made for Russian fighters to come out to their aid but the calls went unanswered.

Two ships, the American merchantman *Washington* and the Dutch *Paulus Potter*, sailing close together came under attack from Junkers 88s. Both ships were hit and abandoned. Enduring terrible privations, the crews spent days at sea in lifeboats before making it to land. The *Paulus Potter* did not sink but floated, low in the water, for seven days until spotted by U-255. After coming cautiously to the surface, the captain sent his senior watch officer to board it. The boarding party found a modern-day *Mary Celeste* with everything left in place as the ship had been abandoned, even with tables laid in the officers' saloon. Then they found a steel box containing a complete set of Admiralty code books and detailed sailing instructions for PQ17. They had been loaded into a heavy box to be thrown overboard but had been forgotten in the rush to abandon ship. The books were taken aboard U-255 and proved of inestimable value to the German codebreakers.[16]

The final tally of PQ17 ships that had been sent to the bottom or abandoned was twenty-four. With these ships had been lost 430 tanks, 210 aircraft, 3,350 vehicles and nearly 100,000 tons of cargo. Only ten ships had made it to Archangel, less than a third of those that had set out.[17] The order to scatter had been nothing less than a disaster. It had been made in fear of the approach of the *Tirpitz*, but while that ship was still in Alten Fjord awaiting orders. It did not sail until the following day, and then returned within hours. Ironically, the German leadership was as fearful of risking it in battle as the Admiralty were certain of the destruction it could cause. The men of the cruiser squadron that had been told to withdraw later said that they felt 'ashamed and resentful' at having to abandon the convoy, leaving the defenceless vessels to become sitting targets.[18] The American press leapt on the story, accusing the Royal Navy of deserting the merchant seamen. The abandonment of the convoy had shaken the confidence of British and American seamen in the Royal Navy. It was a blunder of enormous proportions that led to the loss of life of hundreds of sailors, undermined the reputation of the Royal Navy and provoked a crisis in transporting war supplies to the Soviet Union. But the Admiralty kept silent about the order and the fact that it had come from the very top, from the First Sea Lord. Churchill later wrote that he did not find out about the order until after the war.[19] So, compounding the tragic blunder came a cover-up. The whole sorry saga of PQ17 was as much of a national humiliation as had been the fiasco over Singapore and the failure to prevent the Channel Dash.

After the disaster, the Admiralty recommended cancelling the Arctic convoys until the autumn when the darker days would make their transit more secure. Churchill reluctantly informed Stalin of the decision in a long message that set out in some detail the fate of PQ17. Stalin's reply on 23 July was combative and surly: 'Our naval experts consider the reasons put forward by the British naval experts to justify the cessation of convoys to the northern ports of the USSR wholly unconvincing ... I never expected that the British Government would stop dispatch of war materials to us just at the very moment when the Soviet Union, in view of the very serious situation on the Soviet-German front, requires these materials more than ever.'[20] It was a blatant put-down by a close ally whose armies were bearing the brunt of the Nazi war machine. Churchill consulted Roosevelt who recommended not riling the Soviet leader further. Churchill later wrote, 'I therefore let Stalin's bitter message pass without any specific rejoinder. After all the Russian armies were suffering fearfully and the campaign was at its crisis.'[21] The order to scatter PQ17 had not only provoked the American press against the Royal Navy but it had angered Britain's other major ally. It was extremely unusual for Churchill to be short of words. The blunder of abandoning PQ17 had reduced him to a rare silence.

Sending supplies to the Soviet Union via Arctic convoys had been one of the most challenging episodes of 1942. The ordeal for the seamen was almost beyond endurance. The losses had been dreadful. The bungling of PQ17 had been a national embarrassment. But the gratitude from the Russians had been minimal. Only the possibility of a complete Soviet collapse and the disastrous fallout this would bring could justify their continuation.

10

Bombing

On the evening of Friday 24 April 1942, sixteen-year-old Pat Child cycled back through Exeter to her home on Cowick Hill, a suburb high on a steep slope above the west of the city. Life had been looking up for Pat. Both her parents had died when she was young and she had been brought up by a strict elder brother and his wife in London. During the Blitz her school had been evacuated to Exeter and there she had eventually been settled on a family with a son but who had always wanted a daughter. For almost the first time she experienced the joys of living within a happy, loving family. Leaving school as soon as possible, she had just got a job as a receptionist and girl Friday in a photographer's shop off the high street in the centre of the city. She had only had the job a few weeks but she loved it, and with it came the sense of being an adult and earning her own way in the world. The war seemed a long way away. But that night it suddenly came a lot nearer.

At about midnight the air raid sirens in Exeter sounded. From the family shelter in the garden Pat had a grandstand view over the city centre. That night forty Dornier bombers, flying from their base in northern France, attacked the city, dropping at least sixty 250kg high-explosive bombs and 2,000 incendiaries. With the city on fire, Pat could clearly see the low-flying German bombers and later remembered even being able to see the outlines of the crews in their cockpits. During the raid seventy-three people were killed, more than fifty injured and about 600 properties were damaged. The following morning Pat cycled into the centre of the city and was amazed by the chaos she found. Fire fighters were still dousing the flames, hose pipes criss-crossed the streets, passers-by looked on stunned. When she got to the photographer's shop, there was just a pile of rubble. There would be no more work here for Pat.[1]

Exeter was not a significant military target. It was the attractive county town of Devon with a splendid cathedral, a medieval Guildhall, several Roman remains and dozens of fine houses. It was also a shopping centre and a railway junction. Its usual population of roughly 70,000 had been boosted by 1942 by the arrival of about 12,000 evacuees, some children (like Pat Child when she first arrived) and some whole families from London and the south-east who came because they thought it was a safe place to be.[2] It was listed in the famous German tourist guide Baedeker, and this was the key. The raid on Exeter was the first of a series of what would become known as 'Baedeker Raids' in the spring of 1942. There would be two more, heavier raids on Exeter, and several raids on Bath, Norwich and York over the next few weeks. In early June the last raids in the series were carried out against Canterbury. All were towns of great historic interest packed with buildings and churches that had helped to shape British history. All of them featured in Baedeker guides.

Mass Observation carried out a study on the bombing of Norwich and Bath as there were observers in both towns reporting back. In both places people were stunned to begin with. Most locals had no experience of being bombed. But as in the Blitz earlier in the war, after the first raids many people started to leave their homes in the late afternoon and 'trekked' into the surrounding countryside, either to friends or families in farms or nearby villages, or simply to sleep in the open countryside or in woods. There was some talk of panic in the towns' air raid shelters but mostly the observers reported that people were calm and resilient. There seems to have been no great sense of anger that beautiful and historic buildings had been damaged or destroyed. 'Most people said this is war and raids are to be expected,' reported one observer, who wrote that the people of Bath even felt 'pride' that they were suffering as other cities had. All of the observers recorded wild rumours about the scale of the damage caused. One was a teacher in a college in Norwich that suffered no damage at all but three days later she overheard it being said totally seriously, 'They're still digging the students out of the college.' The observers found only a few calls for revenge, one reporting that a more frequent remark was 'What good does it do? What a silly business this all is – they bomb us – we bomb them – and where does it get us?' Just like the people of London, Coventry and all the other big cities that had been bombed, so the people of these smaller cities bore the hardship well.[3]

In 1942, the bombing offensive against Germany was the only means Britain had by which it could strike at the German war machine and at the heart of the Third Reich. But the offensive did not start well. From the very first raid of the war on a land target in March 1940, against the German seaplane base at Hornum on the island of Sylt in the North Sea, the RAF discovered that they lacked the navigational aids to hit a precise target at night. Not a single bomb fell on Hornum that night and most bombs hit another island altogether, which embarrassingly was in neighbouring and neutral Denmark.[4] To start with, the RAF had the wrong type of aircraft. The Hampden was desperately slow, cruising at only 155 mph, making it vulnerable to attacking fighters; the Whitley was a little faster but prone to technical faults; the Wellington was more robust and a popular plane to fly, and would continue operational flying long after the other two had been declared obsolete. Moreover, the crews had no technology to guide them so had to rely on identifying ground locations – extraordinarily difficult over a blacked-out Europe. Only on bright moonlit nights was there much hope of spotting specific locations on the ground from the height at which they were forced to fly to avoid anti-aircraft fire. The alternative was to navigate by the stars using a sextant, which obviously only worked on clear nights. Finally, if they found their target, the bombloads they carried of about 4,000lb were puny and caused only limited damage.

Churchill was a keen enthusiast for bombing at the start. In September 1940, while the Battle of Britain raged, he wrote in a directive to ministers that 'the Bombers alone provide the means of victory. We must therefore develop the power to carry an ever-increasing volume of explosives to Germany, so as to pulverise the entire industry and scientific structure on which the war effort and economic life of the enemy depend.'[5] But for a year, the bombers failed to get through. Aerial photographs taken after raids repeatedly recorded how little damage had been caused. Bomber Command hit back, saying the photographs were on too small a scale to record the damage or that the photographic interpreters did not know what they were looking for. The reality was that after some raids, the RAF's bombs were so widely dispersed that the Germans could not only fail to work out what the target had been but sometimes which city the RAF had been aiming for.[6] The official history of the bombing offensive concluded that in the early stages of the war 'Bomber Command was incapable of inflicting anything but insignificant damage on the enemy'.[7]

In August 1941 Churchill ordered an inquiry into the effectiveness of the bombing operation. David Butt of the War Cabinet secretariat carried out a study of 650 aerial photos taken in June and July. The results were shocking. The main conclusion of Butt's report was that only about one in three bombers whose crews claimed to have successfully carried out their mission succeeded in getting their bombs within 5 *miles* of their target. On a full moon this improved to about two out of three. If this was not disappointing enough, it was found that on a night without moonlight, only about one aircraft in fifteen, or less than 7 per cent, managed to drop its bombs within 5 miles of the target.[8] This was a damning indictment of Bomber Command's effectiveness. With the losses of bomber crews so high, Churchill was deeply concerned that very little damage was being done for such hazard. He forwarded the report to the Chief of the Air Staff, Air Chief Marshal Sir Charles Portal, with a note saying, 'This is a very serious paper and seems to require your most urgent attention. I await your proposals for action.'[9]

The air marshals of course repudiated the report and challenged the accuracy of the findings by claiming the weather had been particularly bad in June and July and only a small sample of the many raids flown had been assessed. They argued that crews in the post-op debriefings continued to make clear reports of the damage they had caused. Butt recognised that his report was not definitive but insisted that with the damage assessment photos taken usually on the morning after the raid, 'A camera cannot make mistakes and cannot like a human being under conditions of extreme strain be misled by appearances.'[10] The truth was that Bomber Command could do little at this stage to improve the accuracy of its bombing until new navigational aids came in. And the crews themselves knew they were achieving little. Morale in Bomber Command slumped.

In the ensuing debate about bombing policy, the RAF decided to redirect its bombing strategy away from attempted night-time precision raids on specific factories, railway yards, airfields or naval bases and instead carry out indiscriminate raids on whole cities, which became known as 'area bombing', or more colloquially as 'carpet bombing'. German bombing of British civilians in 1940–1 had removed any moral hesitation about bombing German cities. A group of scientists led by Solly Zuckerman and J. D. Bernal were brought in to analyse the German bombing of British cities and learn lessons from the techniques used by the Luftwaffe. They concluded that a much higher use of incendiary bombs and active targeting of the working-class areas of a city were the two things most likely to have a disruptive effect on industrial output. A report stated, 'Continuous and relentless bombing of the workers and their utility services, over a period of time, will inevitably lower their morale, kill a number of them, and thus appreciably reduce their industrial output.'[11] This became the basis of a new directive for Bomber Command. In the summer of 1941, RAF policy became to kill the workers.

Portal claimed that if he were given a force of 4,000 heavy bombers he could bomb different cities every night and bring Germany to its knees in six months. This made him sound dangerously like Göring, who had claimed in the summer of 1940 that his Luftwaffe could blitz Britain into submission. Everyone knew that the bombing had not destroyed the economy and in the long run had strengthened the determination of the British people to stand up against the Nazi threat. Why would the Germans be any different? The only argument put up was that the British worker was made of sterner stuff than his German equivalent whose morale was far more likely to collapse.[12]

Bomber Command losses during the autumn of 1941 rose to alarmingly high levels. The Germans constructed a new defensive shield of coordinated anti-aircraft weapons and night fighters along the western German border called the Kammhuber Line. The aircraft were guided to the attacking bombers by the use of a new generation of radar, Würzburg. (It was the need to capture a Würzburg radar to understand how it worked that prompted the Bruneval Raid – see Chapter 8.)

In August, 525 aircraft were damaged or destroyed (including a large number in accidents as well as on active service). In the following three months a further 264 aircraft were lost on bombing missions over Europe. Each aircraft lost led to the death or capture of its crew of four or five. The lack of success in hitting targets was of course a closely guarded secret but the head of Bomber Command, Air Marshal Sir Richard Peirse, insisted on carrying on. But on the night of 14–15 October an intended incendiary attack on Nuremberg bombed a nearby town instead and only one aircraft bombed Nuremberg itself. On the night of 7–8 November three simultaneous raids over Berlin, Cologne and the Ruhr led to the particularly high loss of thirty-seven aircraft – nearly 10 per cent of the raiders. Berlin was thought to be too dangerous a target and was not bombed again until January 1943. With such great loss for so little impact, Churchill and the War Cabinet ordered Bomber Command to rest up. Peirse was dismissed from his command and sent to the Far East. For the rest of the winter there were only a few small-scale raids and, with this vote of no confidence, the whole future of the bombing offensive came under question.[13]

By early 1942, however, significant developments had begun to change the equation. The Germans had used beams to guide their aircraft in the 1940 Blitz. But it was not until 1942 that the RAF, at last, got a set of new navigational aids. The first of these was called Gee ('G' for 'Grid'). Three ground transmitters in the south of England sent pulse signals which overlapped to form a sort of lattice network across northern Europe. A bomber could pick up this network on a cathode ray tube to help navigate to its target. It was accurate up to about 2 miles, far better than anything before. It had been developed in early 1941 by British scientists at the Telecommunications Research Establishment, then in Dorset. But the RAF had delayed its introduction because of a debate about whether it should be used by just a small number of pathfinder aircraft, to guide the rest to the target, or whether it should be available in all bombers. In early 1942 Gee was finally rolled out for use by the mass of bombers.

The other significant development was the arrival of a set of heavy bombers in large enough numbers to make a real difference. Short Brothers came up with the Stirling just before the war, powered by four Bristol Hercules engines, and Handley Page produced the Halifax, powered by four Rolls-Royce Merlin engines. Both bombers had a cruising speed of about 260 mph and could carry between 13,000lb and 14,000lb of bombs over long ranges. Both models needed to resolve difficult technical problems but were ready for operational use by early 1942. Most impressive of all was the transformation of a two-engine bomber, the Manchester, designed by Roy Chadwick for Avro. This had limited performance and its Vulture engines constantly proved unreliable. When in 1941 Chadwick adapted the aircraft into a four-engine bomber powered by Merlin engines, it was renamed the Lancaster. It was able to carry bombloads of up to a massive 22,000lb at a top speed of over 280 mph. With its normal bombload of about 16,000lb it could fly well over 1,000 miles at up to 25,000 feet. The Lancaster would go on to be the mainstay of Bomber Command and a legend of British aviation.

The other important change was that a new and dynamic commander-in-chief arrived at Bomber Command. Air Marshal Arthur Harris, appointed in February 1942, was a committed and unapologetic enthusiast for bombing. He shared several characteristics with Churchill. He believed that only offensive action would win wars. He wanted to bomb German cities as powerfully and destructively as his bomber force would allow. He believed that bombing alone could win the war and make long land campaigns unnecessary. He had a no-nonsense style and regarded those who opposed his views, of whatever rank, as weaklings or at the very least as impertinent. He made many enemies, not only in the other armed forces but even within the RAF as he refused to deviate from his single-minded obsession. He regarded allocating aircraft for other missions, like long-range anti-U-boat patrols over the Atlantic or even later to bomb the Ruhr dams, as distractions from his main task. He realised that to win the war a price had to be paid and he remained resolute despite growing losses among his crews. He had no worries about the morality of area bombing. Britain was simply following what the Germans had started at Warsaw, Rotterdam, London and Coventry. 'We have got to kill a lot of Boche,' he wrote in April 1942, 'before we win this war.'[14] In a biblical quote that he made famous when it was recorded for the newsreel cameras, Harris summed up his view when he said, 'They sowed the wind and now are going to reap the whirlwind.' He would soon acquire the public nickname 'Bomber Harris'. But to his crews he was known as 'Butcher' or 'Butch'.

After his initial enthusiasm for bombing, Churchill had been disillusioned by the failures recorded in 1941 and had written to Portal, 'It is very disputable whether bombing by itself will be a decisive factor in the present war. On the contrary, all that we have learnt since the war began shows that its effects, both physical and moral, are greatly exaggerated.'[15] But he was in a dilemma as he knew that the bombing offensive was the principal way in which he could show Stalin that Britain was piling pressure on Germany, hitting at its war industries and causing fighters to be recalled from the Eastern Front. 'You need not argue the value of bombing Germany, because I have my own opinion about that, namely that it is not decisive,' he wrote to Portal and Sir Archibald Sinclair, the Secretary of State for Air, in March 1942. 'But [it is] better than doing nothing and indeed is a formidable method of injuring the enemy.'[16] There was a renewed policy debate during which Churchill's leading scientific adviser and confidant Frederick

Lindemann (later Lord Cherwell) argued that the bombing of German workers' homes could 'break the spirit of the people' while prompting a breakdown of communications, supply lines and the collapse of public services. 'Investigation seems to show that having one's house demolished is most damaging to morale,' Lindemann wrote sardonically. Using some very dodgy mathematics, he claimed that one ton of bombs dropped on a built-up area could demolish between twenty and forty houses and so turn '100–200 people out of house and home'. By scaling this up he calculated that if a force of 10,000 bombers dropped their bombs on the biggest cities in Germany every few nights then by the middle of 1943 'about one third of the German population would be made homeless'.[17] Churchill was impressed and sent the minute to the War Cabinet for discussion. The bombing offensive was on again.

By the time he was appointed head of Bomber Command the decision to pursue area bombing of the working districts of German cities had already been taken, but it was Harris who would enthusiastically implement it. And this time he had the new navigational aid and an increasing number of 'heavies' to call upon. When the bombing offensive restarted on the night of 3 March, the use of Gee helped create a striking success in the bombing of the Renault factory to the north of Paris. Here German military vehicles were built. Two hundred and thirty-five aircraft, the largest bomber force yet assembled, destroyed much of the factory. Leaflets were dropped warning the French that factories working for the German war effort would be considered as legitimate targets and workers were encouraged to strike or leave. However, nearly 400 French workers were killed in the raid, more than had been killed in any raid on Germany to this point.

The following few raids, however, were disappointing. On 8 March more than 200 bombers attacked the Krupps works at Essen but not a single bomb fell on the factory. Two nights

later another raid missed Essen altogether and bombed the surrounding countryside. A few bombs were dropped nearly 100
miles off target. A raid the following week on Cologne proved
more accurate. But the first successful attack on Germany took
place on the Baltic town of Lübeck on 28 March. The city was
one of the historic Hanseatic port towns with an old medieval
centre. The port was used to supply German forces in Russia
and there were some shipyards around the town but otherwise it did not have any military role. It was selected primarily
because the old town was largely made up of wooden-framed
buildings which it was hoped would burn well. Two hundred
and thirty bombers attacked in three waves carrying a large
proportion of incendiaries and the old town quickly went up
in flames. The fires burned for at least twelve hours. More than
300 civilians were killed, the largest number in any raid on
Germany to date. Aerial photographs after the raid revealed
that about 200 acres of the town had been destroyed and many
historic houses and churches had been razed to the ground.

Although the Blitz on Britain had been suspended the previous May before Operation Barbarossa, Hitler was infuriated
by the destruction of Lübeck. It was this raid that prompted
him personally to call for a series of retaliatory raids against
British historic towns. In his Führer Directive of 14 April he
ordered that 'Terror attacks of a retaliatory nature are to be
carried out against towns other than London.'[18] This brought
about the first raid on Exeter and then the other attacks named
by the Germans as the Baedeker Raids. German propaganda
declared, 'We shall go out to bomb every building in Britain
marked with three stars in the Guide.'[19] Of course they did
not achieve this but the raids surprised the cities which were
largely defenceless. They destroyed the Georgian Assembly
Rooms in Bath, the Guildhall in York and the sixteenth-
century Old Boar's Head in Norwich. The bombers missed
Canterbury Cathedral but destroyed its Victorian library.

Later raids in Exeter were far more destructive and devastated much of the shopping centre, damaged the cathedral and hit nine other churches. In all, over 600 tons of bombs were dropped on these British cities and 938 civilians were killed. This was severe by comparison to the negligible losses from German bombing over the previous year. But, once again, as Mass Observation had found, the terror raids did not cause a collapse in morale among Britons.

At the end of April, the RAF directed a series of four attacks at another Hanseatic port town, Rostock. This larger town did contain war factories including a U-boat yard and a Heinkel aircraft plant but once again the old city was largely made up of centuries-old wooden buildings. About 60 per cent of the centre of the city was destroyed in the raids. A state of emergency was declared and members of the Hitler Youth and the SA were sent in to help organise an evacuation. Many of those who were not evacuated fled into the surrounding countryside. A little over 200 civilians were left dead. The attacks on Lübeck and Rostock were the first raids of the war that led to heavy urban destruction and loss of life and they were of real concern to the German authorities who for the first time recorded the Rostock raid as a 'great catastrophe'.[20] The raids on the Baltic ports were well reported in Britain and overall proved popular. Vere Hodgson had lived through the London Blitz and summed up the views of many Britons when she wrote in her diary, 'We are all heartened by the terrible raids on Lübeck and Rostock. It is dreadful to be so glad – but we cannot be anything else.'[21]

Criticism of Bomber Command continued to grow, despite the publicity that the raids on Lübeck and Rostock had generated. Another review of bombing accuracy followed in May, this time by a judge, Justice Singleton. As a complete outsider he was astonished to discover the failures in the bombing campaign and took a pessimistic view about how easily they could be rectified. He doubted that over the next six months 'great results can be hoped for'.[22] Additionally, there were demands from within other branches of the services that bombers should be sent to Egypt or to India where they would be more effective. In the War Office, the Director of Military Operations was 'severely perturbed' at the resources allocated to bombing Germany. He argued that if only 10 per cent could be reallocated to air support for the army and the navy 'the war situation would be greatly improved'.[23]

Harris decided that he needed a unique event to promote the renewed offensive against Germany. Accordingly, he came up with the idea of the biggest assault of the war so far, a sensational Thousand Bomber raid against a single German city. The problem was that Bomber Command only had 450 bombers. So Harris needed to persuade Coastal Command to 'lend' him their 250 bombers; the rest would be made up by calling in training aircraft and diverting crews from their training schedule. The initial target selected was Hamburg which was, like Lübeck and Rostock, on the coast and so relatively easy to locate. However bad weather meant the target shifted to Cologne.

On the night of 30 May, 1,047 bombers set off, the majority of which were two-engine Wellingtons. Eight hundred and sixty-eight crews claimed to have bombed the target. Over 3,300 buildings were destroyed and another 9,000 damaged; 486 people were killed and 5,000 wounded. It was the most serious raid of the war to date. But two more Thousand Bomber raids, over Essen on 1–2 June and Bremen on 25–26 June, were disappointing. At Essen only eleven houses were destroyed and fifteen people killed. At Bremen, 500 houses were destroyed and eighty-five people were killed. It was clear that a large proportion of bombs were still missing their targets. Moreover, over the three raids the RAF had lost 123 bombers, that is about 700 crew members. The Thousand Bomber raids were quietly discontinued.[24] It was not until late 1944 that a thousand British bombers took part in a raid on a single city again.

AP/Shutterstock

Air Marshal 'Bomber' Harris. He was convinced that bombing enemy towns and cities could win the war.

However, Harris's raids had a great impact on public opinion. The cinema newsreels lauded the first attack on Cologne without a hint of dissent. British Movietone News allocated one half of its entire newsreel to a five-minute report. It followed each phase of the mission, from briefings, through the loading up of the aircraft with 'tons and tons of beautiful bombs', to the 'colossal force' heading off 'from aerodromes all over the country' at dusk and returning at dawn. The ability of the RAF bombers to hit back at the Germans was a constant theme. 'Maybe the Hun is less proud now of the Luftwaffe's savage attacks on Warsaw, Rotterdam, Belgrade and elsewhere,' intoned the commentator. Harris, with a sense of the need for publicity well ahead of his time, appeared in the newsreel in person, saying to camera, 'When the storm bursts over Germany, they will look back to the days of Lübeck, Rostock and Cologne as a man caught in the blasts of a hurricane will look back to the gentle zephyrs of last summer.' And the newsreel made clear that bombing was a war-winning strategy. Harris summed it up: 'A lot of people say the bombing can never win a war. Well, my answer to that is, it has never been tried yet. We shall see.'[25]

The attacks on Lübeck and Rostock, and the Thousand Bomber raids, were all in their way stunts to promote the bombing offensive. But for much of 1942 the campaign functioned on a far more mundane level. Airfields had to be rebuilt and runways lengthened to accommodate the four-engine 'heavies'. Crews had to be retrained for their new aircraft and new technologies. For these reasons up to a quarter of Bomber Command's squadrons were unavailable for active service in every month during 1942.[26] Gee was a big improvement but its range was limited. And from August the Germans found ways to jam it. So, another navigational aid, Oboe, was developed. Two radar transmitters, one in Norfolk known as 'Cat' and one in Kent known as 'Mouse', sent out pulses across Europe. A pilot flying along the Cat pulse was tracked by the Mouse radar that would send a signal to bomb when the aircraft was over its target. It was accurate down to a few hundred yards. The most sophisticated aid of all was a form of ground-mapping radar called H_2S that could be switched on in an aircraft as the bomber approached its target to provide a last-minute map of the ground below. This could work in all weathers and was not affected by cloud cover. But it required the use of a highly advanced ultra-shortwave radar using a British invention called the cavity magnetron. So worried were the scientists that if a bomber equipped with H_2S came down over enemy territory the Germans would capture and copy this huge leap forward in radar technology that the use of H_2S was delayed until 1943. And the use of the first

Pathfinder squadrons to identify targets accurately and light them up with coloured flares to enable the main squadrons to hit them was delayed for months because Harris did not want to separate out elite crews from the rest of his command to fly the target-locating aircraft.

However, although the bombing campaign was uneven during 1942 its political capital rose throughout the year. As plans for a second front in Europe were put on hold, the bombing of Germany remained the one way in which Churchill could insist to Stalin that Britain was doing its bit. He would regularly send Stalin details of raids, the tonnage of bombs dropped, along with facts and figures about homes and factories destroyed. Sometimes he even sent post-raid aerial photographs to show off the damage caused. 'We have built up a great plant here for bombing Germany,' Churchill argued to Attlee in April, 'which is the only way in our power of helping Russia.'[27]

The American bombing campaign also did not get fully under way in 1942. The Eighth Army Air Force was activated in January in Savannah, Georgia. After several months of planning and preparation, Major General Carl Spaatz, the commander, came to Britain in June but by the end of July there were only forty heavy American bombers in the UK. The Americans relied on the Boeing B-17 as the workhorse of their bombing campaign. Equipped with eleven heavy machine guns for its defence, the aircraft was soon nick-named the 'Flying Fortress'. Spaatz developed a different policy from the RAF by sending his bombers across Europe in close formation. This was better for defence against fighters and offered the opportunity to achieve greater precision. The bombers were also equipped with a new bombsight that took into account not only speed and height but other factors like windspeed and drift. American commanders insisted it greatly added to the accuracy of their bombing technique.

The Norden bombsight had been developed in the clear blue skies of the western United States and it was never as effective amid the cloudy skies of Europe. But all of these techniques encouraged the US to elect to bomb in daylight. A first small-scale raid by the Eighth against railway yards in Rouen in August seemed to confirm the accuracy of daytime bombing. But there were not enough American bombers in Britain to begin an effective campaign in the autumn and winter of 1942. It was only later in the war that the Eighth would grow into a vast force of more than 3,000 aircraft in sixty combat groups including heavy and medium bombers with fighter support groups, all known as 'the Mighty Eighth'.[28]

The bombing offensive against Germany during 1942 was still on a relatively small scale with only occasional successes. Not only did it not seriously impair the Nazi war machine, but weapons production actually increased in Germany by 60 per cent under the new Minister of Armaments and War Production, Albert Speer.[29] It was not until 1943 that the bombing truly started to hit Germany hard, when the US began regular attacks by day and the RAF by night. This was the year that saw some stunning strikes, including the famous Dam Busters raid in May and the shocking destruction of Hamburg over four nights in July. But all that lay in the future. In the meantime, the British bombing campaign in 1942 failed to solve many problems. There was no strategic plan beyond trying to destroy working-class districts in industrial towns and a vague sense that towns and cities could be wiped out by bombing. The use of technological and navigational aids was repeatedly held up because it was feared they might be of value to the enemy. In the middle of this confusion were the crews themselves. Fourteen thousand lives were lost in Bomber Command between September 1939 and September 1942. None of the promised aims of the bombing campaign had been achieved. As one former squadron commander put it when describing the attitude of the bomber crews, 'They feel they can do more than they are doing; they grope somewhat blindly in an effort to find where the failure lies.'[30]

In the broader picture of Britain's war effort in 1942, however, the bombing offensive was a limited success story. But, despite the moral controversy it posed later about the ethics of killing civilians, at the time it was a hugely popular campaign. As far as most Britons were concerned, the RAF was at least giving back to the Germans a dose of their own treatment.[31]

11

Island Fortress

By the spring of 1942 Malta had the dubious distinction of being the most bombed place on earth. Lying 50 miles from the southern tip of Sicily, it was just a few hours after Italy's declaration of war in June 1940 that the first bombing raid on the island took place. The sirens wailed their alarm at seven o'clock on the morning after Mussolini made his announcement of war. As they went about their business going to work or school, few Maltese islanders took much notice until the bombs began to fall around the Grand Harbour at Valletta with its huge fortress dating back to the Knights of St John. There were several more raids during the day, and by evening the roads from Valletta were full of locals loaded down with bundles of possessions hurriedly leaving the city to get to the safety of relatives' homes on the island. Almost one half of the entire population was on the move. It was the beginning of a long nightmare for the small island. Between then and November 1942 there were 3,215 raids on Malta and Gozo and 14,000 tons of bombs were dropped, averaging just under 100 tons per square mile, although much of the bombing was concentrated on the dockyards of Valletta and around the island's three major airfields. Nearly 1,500 Maltese civilians were killed and 24,000 properties were damaged or destroyed including a high proportion of the islanders' homes.

There are many parallels between the story of Malta and that of Singapore. Like Singapore, Malta was a small island that had come under British control in the early nineteenth century, in Malta's case during the Napoleonic wars. Like Singapore, Malta offered the Royal Navy a splendid natural harbour in a geographically central location. In its deep waters, the harbour could shelter and repair the biggest warships of the day. And from Malta the navy could attack enemy shipping across the central Mediterranean. The island also contained three airfields, and from these RAF aircraft could strike at Sicily, much of Italy and a great part of the North African theatre of war. Its strategic position, as a staging post midway between Gibraltar and Egypt, and its importance as both a Royal Navy and RAF base gave the tiny outcrop of bronze rock in the blue waters of the Mediterranean a central and heroic role in the war from 1940 to the winter of 1942.

With several warships regularly moored in its harbour, Malta, also like Singapore, had become an outpost for British servicemen to enjoy themselves as hundreds of officers and sailors in their Mediterranean whites went ashore of an evening. The main street in Valletta came alive at night with music, clubs, restaurants, bars and lots of girls. One resident described the island before the war as 'a boozer's paradise'.[1] Unlike Singapore, the vast harbour had been completed well in advance of the war. And unlike Singapore, a close association and respect had grown between the people of the island and their British protectors. Although the Maltese were deeply Catholic, the vast majority supported Britain and many worked loyally in the docks and on merchant ships. But, as with Singapore, a long-running debate had taken place in London about how best to defend the island, or even whether it could be defended if Germany or Italy decided to invade. In

July 1939, the decision was taken to reinforce the island with 112 heavy and sixty light anti-aircraft batteries and with four squadrons of fighters. But when war came other demands took priority and the ack-ack guns and the fighters never appeared. Nor did any naval reinforcements, and when Italy declared war there were only twelve British submarines in the Mediterranean (against more than a hundred Italian) and on Malta there were only three British fighters, old Gladiator biplanes that had been discovered crated up in storage. There were no pilots to fly the Gladiators so a call went out for volunteers.

For the first couple of months these Gladiator biplanes became the most lauded fighters to defend the island against the Italian Savoia-Marchetti bombers. Named *Faith, Hope* and *Charity*, the three aircraft and their pilots became popular heroes, their photos even being put up in shop windows. In the midst of the Battle of Britain that summer fighter reinforcements were difficult to find but a small number of Hurricanes were sent to the island. Together these Hurricanes and the three famous Gladiators destroyed or damaged thirty-seven Italian bombers. The propaganda concentrated on the biplanes, but it was the Hurricanes that did most of the shooting down. Some of the defenders mocked the Italian aviators and thought the 'ice-cream boys' were a bit of a joke.[2] That might have been a good way to sustain morale but it was certainly not fair. The fight was always uneven and the Italian bombers, flying at height, continued to get through to hit the docks and the RAF airfields, causing considerable damage and disruption. Malta found itself under siege.

As the fighters struggled against the massed ranks of the Regia Aeronautica, Malta additionally started to act as a base for aerial reconnaissance flights. One of the most courageous photo-reconnaissance pilots of the war, Adrian Warburton, arrived on the island in the autumn of 1940. He was an unconventional figure who grew his hair long and rarely wore his uniform correctly buttoned, but he thrived in the less formal atmosphere of the RAF in Malta. He soon embarked on an affair with a British cabaret dancer, Christina Ratcliffe. He moved out of the officers' mess and they lived together in a flat in Valletta. Warburton proved to be a brave and brilliant flier who would stop at nothing to get his aerial photographs. After one of his extremely low-level sorties over an Italian naval base, he returned to Luqa on Malta with an Italian ship's radio aerial wrapped around the rear wheel of his aircraft. His reconnaissance flights over Taranto in November 1940 brought back vital intelligence identifying the location of six Italian battleships in the harbour. Using these photographs, the Fleet Air Arm attacked the Italian naval base putting three of the battleships out of action. It was this mission and the disabling of the Italian fleet that encouraged the Japanese to plan a raid on Pearl Harbor.[3]

Warburton continued to photograph Italian naval and military bases around Naples, Brindisi, Palermo and Messina where convoys gathered to take supplies to Axis troops in North Africa. Several of these convoys were attacked after taking on board supplies. He also photographed Italian and German troops in North Africa. He was awarded a Distinguished Flying Cross (DFC), a Distinguished Service Order (DSO) and then a double bar to his DFC. He became a famous figure on the island known as 'Warby' and his exploits were, like those of the fighter pilots, great for morale. His work illustrated the strategic value of Malta, as a base from where the RAF could keep its eye on what was happening across the central Mediterranean.

As the Italian war effort began to go badly wrong, first in Greece and then in Libya, so Hitler sent ground and air forces to support his ally. In the air, the Luftwaffe came to the aid of the Regia Aeronautica. On taking up his command, Rommel had warned, 'Without Malta, the Axis will end up losing control of North Africa.'[4] So the bombing of Malta was intensified and the handful of fighter defenders regularly found themselves up against seventy or eighty Luftwaffe bombers and dive bombers led by Ju 88s and Ju 87 Stukas. Not only was dreadful damage done to the Grand Harbour but Luqa was frequently put out of action. Me 109 fighters regularly swept the island, machine-gunning anti-aircraft positions and almost anything that moved.

In May 1941, Air Vice Marshal Hugh Pughe Lloyd arrived to take command. Known universally as 'Hugh Pughe', he was a bullish figure and a popular commander among his aircrews. He soon established a reputation as a leader committed to taking offensive action whenever possible. But coming from a background in Bomber Command he lacked a knowledge of fighter tactics and had a weakness in not planning ahead for the long term. He fought the battle for Malta on a day-to-day basis. In a brief respite from the bombing, Lloyd also ordered that several pilots who had fought for months on end without a break should be replaced by new arrivals from Britain. Flight Lieutenant George Burges was one of those reluctantly ordered home. He had been a seaplane pilot and the personal assistant of the RAF commander on the island in 1940 when he had volunteered to become one of the Gladiator fighter pilots. He had flown in almost every action for a year. Two days before he was to leave he was asked to go to a popular bar in Valletta for a farewell party. When Burges arrived the bar was packed with Maltese people none of whom he knew but who wanted to thank him – another indication of the level of popular support for the courageous defenders of the island.[5]

Maintaining supplies was always a problem as nearly everything the island needed had to be brought in by sea. In the first half of 1941 the situation became serious. Food was short and increasingly severe rationing was introduced. Fuel and ammunition dropped to desperately low levels and supplies had to be carefully nursed. Manpower was always a problem too. Fourteen hundred Maltese men joined the RAF to help the groundcrews keep their aircraft operational. Hundreds of others volunteered to work in the shipyards. As bombs continued to fall on homes, offices and schools, the *Times of Malta* repeatedly kept up the propaganda battle by claiming 'we shall follow the example set by the citizens of London and Coventry', repeating the phrase 'Malta can take it'.[6]

In the summer of 1941 the situation eased as Luftwaffe squadrons were withdrawn from the Mediterranean to support Hitler's rapid advance into the Soviet Union. A few convoys managed to get through to the island bringing urgently wanted foodstuffs, medical supplies and desperately needed aviation fuel. Without this the island's defence would not have been possible. The arrival of these convoys made it look as though Malta could survive. With sufficient fuel now available, torpedo bombers flying out of the island's airfields at last were able to operate in the skies across the mid-Mediterranean and succeeded in sinking over 300,000 tons of Axis shipping.

In the second half of 1941 Malta also acted as the base for a squadron of six light cruisers and a submarine flotilla. In the autumn they also began to hit back at Axis convoys carrying supplies to North Africa. In September, HMS *Upholder*, one of the Malta-based submarines, sank two large Italian liners that had been adapted to carry troops, the *Oceania* and the *Neptunia*, both of 19,500 tons. Two months later, an Ultra decrypt identified the date and location of the sailing of a substantial Italian convoy. Churchill was concerned that by attacking the convoy the Allies might give away the fact that they had decoded the Enigma signals, so an aerial reconnaissance aircraft was sent to photograph the port where the convoy was gathering and only left when the pilot knew he had been spotted.[7] The Malta-based cruisers HMS *Penelope*, HMS *Lance* and HMS *Lively*, known as Force K, then intercepted the convoy off the toe of Italy. The cruisers sank nine of the ten ships in the convoy along with an Italian destroyer providing escort duties. During that month nearly 80 per cent of the shipping carrying supplies to the Axis armies in North Africa was sunk. Axis forces in North Africa were starved of fuel, food and ammunition. Rommel's troops were forced to retreat in renewed fighting with the Eighth Army.

Towards the end of the year, however, the situation took a major turn for the worse. Hitler ordered that Malta must be crushed. First he told Dönitz to send almost half of his U-boats from the Atlantic into the Mediterranean. The U-boat commander was furious as he felt he had the Battle of the Atlantic under control. But the presence of the increased number of U-boats had an almost immediate and dramatic consequence in the Mediterranean with the sinking of the 22,000-ton aircraft carrier HMS *Ark Royal* in mid-November by U-81. Fortunately, all but one of the ship's crew were successfully picked up by support vessels. Only a few days later, however, U-331 penetrated the screen of destroyers around HMS *Barham* and torpedoed the battleship, which capsized on its side. Men were fleeing into the water when a magazine detonated and the ship exploded with the loss of more than 800 lives.[8] At the same time, Hitler ordered the transfer of one of his most senior air commanders to take command of Axis air forces in the Mediterranean, much to the annoyance of the Italians who felt they should be in charge of the Regia Aeronautica in their own country. Their protests and anger were entirely ignored.

Field Marshal Albert Kesselring had commanded a Luftflotte (air fleet) during the Battle of Britain and the Blitz. Having pounded RAF stations, his aircraft went on to mercilessly bomb London and Coventry. In the summer of 1941

he commanded a Luftflotte during the invasion of the Soviet
Union. His fliers destroyed approximately 2,500 Soviet aircraft on the ground and in the air and provided close ground
support for the Wehrmacht as it advanced rapidly against the
Red Army. With the advent of winter and the freezing over of
the ground, the air war was suspended. Confident of victory,
Hitler ordered Kesselring to withdraw his squadrons and
transfer to the Mediterranean. With him came a Fliegerkorps
(air corps) that was sent to air bases in Sicily. Kesselring
now set about carrying out Hitler's order to crush Malta and
spoke of 'smoking out that hornet's nest'.[9] The presence of
a Luftwaffe Fliegerkorps in Sicily, with at least 200 aircraft,
transformed the situation on the island. Nineteen forty-two
would become the crisis year for Malta.

In January, severe storms and gales lashed the island but
the Luftwaffe began to appear again at the end of the month.
Fine weather returned in February and Kesselring was able
to launch his plan to subdue the island. His first objective, as
in the Battle of Britain, was to destroy the RAF and its bases.
After this, his aircraft would move on to attack the dockyards
and harbours. Finally, the plan was to destroy barracks, stores
and lines of communication on the island. Whether or not to
invade was left open; success in the bombing might make an
invasion unnecessary. In the meantime, plans were drawn up
for Italian and German paratroopers to invade the fortress
island. Just in case.

During February the Luftwaffe made daily visits over
Malta, sometimes with several air raids in a day. On the 7th
there were sixteen separate alerts in the twenty-four-hour
period. The RAF suffered a dreadful mauling. The Hurricane
fighters were no longer a match for the new mark of Me 109Fs.
They were outmanoeuvred in the air and shot up badly on the
ground. Army relief teams were sent in to do the heavy lifting
in building pens where the aircraft could shelter. Nearly 300

pens and 27 miles of dispersal runways were constructed in a three-month period. Meanwhile, the groundcrews laboured daily to fill in the craters on the runways from the last raid. There were just a few steamrollers available to flatten the surface of the runways, but then even they were destroyed in the bombing.[10] It seemed to be a hopeless struggle. The Wellington bombers that had been equipped with ASV to locate enemy convoys at sea also took a pasting. At one point in February only three fighters and one Wellington were airworthy. What was desperately needed were the latest mark of Spitfires. But none were forthcoming. From December 1941 onwards, Axis convoys had been getting through to North Africa unmolested and in late January Rommel had been well enough supplied to launch a new offensive in Libya. Once again, the Afrika Korps were advancing and the Eighth Army was in retreat. The fate of the Allied armies in North Africa increasingly seemed to be dependent upon what took place on Malta.[11]

Meanwhile, in the towns of the island conditions were becoming unbearable. The relentless bombing had reduced much of the city's homes and shops to rubble. The narrow streets were blocked by fallen masonry and collapsed walls. Air raid shelters had been dug into the sandstone rock and those who stayed in Valletta regularly spent their nights there, in rows of bunk beds. Wherever possible caves were adopted as underground shelters. But the shelters were grim. There was rarely enough fuel for lighting. They were damp, smelly, overcrowded and insanitary. Rations across the island had to be reduced further, kerosene for heating and cooking was in desperately short supply. And the mental strain of putting up with repeated raids every day, and never knowing if the next bomb was going to be the one that would get you, wore everyone to a frazzle. Yet still the people of Malta clung on, and although conditions were dire, morale never completely collapsed.

In February, a convoy laden with supplies had set off for
Malta from Alexandria but had been forced to turn back
after repeated attacks by Axis aircraft in what was becoming
known as 'Bomb Alley', the area between Crete and Libya.
In March, another convoy was assembled. Four ships again
sailed from Alexandria with their naval escort. They managed
to get through Bomb Alley but two days into the journey a
major Italian task force appeared to the north of the convoy
consisting of a battleship, the *Littorio* with nine 15-inch guns,
two heavy cruisers and ten destroyers. The naval escorts led by
Rear Admiral Vian in the light cruiser HMS *Cleopatra* turned to
confront the Italian warships while the convoy tried to escape
to the south-west under a smokescreen. The Italians were held
at bay, and after a few hours withdrew. *Cleopatra* was hit but
none of the convoy's four ships were damaged. However, as
they approached Malta the air attacks began again with a new
intensity. This time one of the convoy's vessels was sunk. Two
finally made it to the Grand Harbour, watched by the locals
thronging the ancient battlements. The fourth vessel was hit
within sight of the island and its steering gear put out of action.
Tugs eventually managed to get alongside and towed the vessel
into a harbour on the south coast. It looked as though sufficient
food, ammunition and fuel had finally made it through. But
what followed was nothing short of a catastrophe.

Arrangements had not been put in place for the rapid
unloading of the vessels. The military were not on stand-by
to help. As the Maltese dockers got to work, the Luftwaffe
pounced again. Repeated air attacks on the ships in harbour,
relatively large and easy static targets, not only slowed the
work of the stevedores but also led within seventy-two hours
to the sinking of all three vessels before a fraction of their
precious cargoes had been unloaded.[12] The organisation of
the unloading had been appalling. No plans had been made
in advance, the dockers only worked in the daytime and

there were no attempts to unload the ships at night when the raids ceased. The struggle and sacrifice in getting the ships to break the siege of the island had been in vain. In London, the chiefs of staff looked on in horror. The First Sea Lord, Admiral Pound, decided that there would be no more attempts to get a convoy through to Malta for the next couple of months. The losses were simply too high and the risks too great. The few supplies that had been unloaded at the end of March were the last that would get through to Malta for three months.

The intensity of the air raids around the island's harbours meant the Royal Navy could no longer operate effectively. Axis aircraft and fast-moving minelayers laid mines around the entrances to all the island's harbours. Force K, which had caused so much damage to the Axis supply ships in November, had already lost two of its cruisers. At the end of March, the survivors finally withdrew from Malta. The submarine flotilla also lost HMS *Upholder* and the rest of the force withdrew a few weeks later. It was simply too dangerous to stay on under the relentless bombing, and in any case there was no fuel to keep the vessels on combat duty. Malta was rapidly losing its offensive capability.

In April, the situation grew even worse. The Luftwaffe Fliegerkorps in Sicily had suffered significant losses over Malta but Kesselring was determined to smash the island and brought in massive reinforcements. There were now double the number of aircraft there had been three months before, over 300 bombers and dive bombers and more than a hundred Messerschmitt fighters. Kesselring ordered his bombers to move on from attacking the RAF airfields to destroying the docks. But many bombs fell in civilian areas and the pounding of Malta reached new heights. There were 12,000 bombing sorties over the island in the two months of March and April when more than 6,400 tons of bombs were dropped.[13] This was the period in which Malta became the most bombed place on earth. Many of the best-known sites on the island were damaged. The Royal Opera House, a beautiful, classic nineteenth-century theatre, probably the most famous building in Valletta, was entirely gutted. Several churches were hit, including the Rotunda in Mosta and St Publius in Floriana, with its two clocktowers, a landmark to the islanders. Many baroque façades in Valletta came crashing down, and the palaces of the Knights of St John were pounded into rubble. One of the big bakeries on the island was destroyed and the telephone exchange was also hit.[14] But this did not mark any easing up for the RAF bases. In one two-day period Takali airfield received more bombs than had been dropped on the whole of Coventry in November 1940. The three airfields were barely able to operate. The towns and ports were in ruins. On five days during April there was only a single airworthy fighter available; on two days there were none at all. The anti-aircraft gunners had been successful in bringing down many of the enemy's bombers but they were running out of ammunition. Meanwhile, convoys were getting through to Rommel in North Africa bringing him supplies of everything he needed – vehicles, troop reinforcements and, most importantly of all, petrol. Malta's ability to hit the Axis supply routes to North Africa, its principal strategic function, had virtually ceased.

On 17 April, in a surprise announcement, King George VI awarded the George Cross to the island, a unique honour. The George Cross, given to civilians and servicemen for acts of extreme bravery, had never been given to a community like the island of Malta before. The citation from the King stated that the award would 'bear witness to a heroism that will long be famous in history'. The *Times of Malta*, which still managed to produce its daily four pages despite the bombing of the presses, was full of pride, declaring that the 'determination and fortitude ... and courage' of the islanders would be 'an

The most bombed place on earth, Malta, spring 1942. Somehow, the statue
of Queen Victoria in the centre of Valletta survived the destruction.

inspiration to many' around the world. There was a surge of
patriotism and a boost to morale. But the bombing continued
and the rationing grew more severe. What Malta really needed
was further supplies. The governor and the military chiefs
assessed the situation and concluded that they could fight on
for about ten weeks, but then would have to capitulate as they
would have run out of food, ammunition, fuel and other means
to defend the island. The governor concluded, 'If Malta is to be
held, drastic action is needed now. It is a matter of survival.'[15]

Air Marshal Arthur Tedder, the RAF commanding officer
in the Middle East, had ordered an investigation earlier in

the year into what was needed on Malta. In addition to an improved radar system and an experienced ground controller, Malta needed the latest mark of Spitfire. Finally, the Air Ministry in London, still reeling from the loss of Singapore and disasters in the Far East, and still sending hundreds of aircraft on the Arctic convoys to the Soviet Union, decided to act. Malta would be the first overseas base from which the RAF would fly Spitfires since 1940. But it was not easy to get the aircraft to the island. There were no airfields within range for them to fly in from and they were too large to be able to take off from most British aircraft carriers. In early March the first fifteen Spitfire Vs were flown in from the deck of HMS *Eagle*, the largest carrier in the Mediterranean. On arrival they all needed to be repainted and their guns realigned, which took up valuable time. But the first day on which they flew in combat, one of the aircraft scored a kill. Still, like everything else on the island's airfields, Spitfires were shot up and bombed on the ground. Many of them were completely destroyed, others took days to repair. Some Spitfire pilots could only fly once a week or once every ten days because of the lack of spare parts. Again, the whole episode proved intensely frustrating.

On 1 April, Churchill cabled President Roosevelt to ask if the big American carrier USS *Wasp* which had assisted on the Arctic convoys could be taken into the Mediterranean. It had sufficient space on its hangar decks for the Spitfires to be assembled and flown off. By this means Churchill explained that 'a powerful Spitfire force could be flown into Malta ... [to] give us a chance of inflicting a very severe and possibly decisive check on the enemy'.[16] The President agreed, and the *Wasp* sailed to Greenock near Glasgow where it was loaded with forty-seven Spitfires. It departed the Clyde, crossed the Bay of Biscay, entered the Mediterranean through the Straits of Gibraltar, and on 20 April the aircraft took off and the pilots flew the last 600 miles to Malta.

The forty-seven aircraft landed in batches. Some of them actually flew in as air raids were taking place. They were parked up and the groundcrews gathered to prepare them. Their guns still had to be harmonised and tropical filters added to the engines. On arrival, the pilots were stunned at the carnage they saw around them. Everywhere there were potholes and craters, smashed buildings, dust and rubble. On the afternoon of their arrival another air raid was sounded and bombs fell across the fighter airfields including on the newly arrived aircraft. A few when prepared for combat managed to get airborne but most were destroyed before even getting an opportunity to fly. Within forty-eight hours only seven Spitfires were left. Yet another lifeline had been lost. Having their hopes raised only to be crushed again was soul-destroying for everyone involved. Air Vice Marshal Lloyd had to take his share of the blame for the fiasco: it had been a major blunder on the part of those managing the reception of the aircraft.

On the island the mood was glum. There was a respite in the bombing in early May. Many believed this was the calm before another storm and that this time the Germans and Italians would invade. Aerial photographs of Sicilian airfields recorded gliders being lined up. On Malta, soldiers trained to repel parachutists. In reality, the story was rather different. Kesselring spotted that Malta was at its weakest yet, and the time was right to invade and finally eliminate the problem. He met with Hitler and argued his case. Rommel, on the other hand, wanted to continue his advance through Libya and argued that the capture of Egypt would be a bigger prize. Hitler, who was cautious about airborne assaults ever since the high losses suffered by his elite paras in Crete a year before, ended up supporting his favourite general. The invasion of Malta would have to wait until later in the summer. Meanwhile, the order was given for several air groups to depart Sicily and transfer to North Africa to support Rommel's advance; others were sent back to the Eastern Front to support a new ground offensive against the Soviet Union. In London, the chiefs of staff were told of Ultra decrypts in which such orders were passed on. They informed the commanders in Malta that the bombing of the island was likely to ease up.[17] This must have been hard to believe in the mayhem of the island fortress.

During the next couple of weeks another sixty-four Spitfires were flown in from the *Wasp* and the *Eagle* in what were known as 'Club Runs' to Malta. Delighted that more Spitfires were being sent in, Churchill cabled the captain of the American carrier: 'Many thanks for your timely help. Who says a wasp couldn't sting twice?'[18] This time the RAF chiefs had learned their lesson. A new programme for the arrival of Spitfires meant groundcrews received every plane on landing and directed it to a pen where a team was waiting. Here the plane was to be rearmed and refuelled within minutes. Also, a pilot with experience of dogfights over the island was waiting to leap into the cockpit. Every aircraft had to be ready to be scrambled within thirty minutes of landing. The preparations paid off and the first aircraft down were ready before even the last batch had landed.[19] On 10 May, for the first time in months, the number of fighters sent up to defend the island exceeded the number of bombers. More than thirty German and Italian aircraft were shot down during the day. It so happened that on that same day Kesselring reported to the OKW (Oberkommando der Wehrmacht or German Armed Forces High Command) that Malta had been neutralised. 'There is nothing left to bomb,' he reported.[20] But he was wrong. In reality, a turning point had been reached.

During the next month another seventy-six fighters flew in to Malta. As the number of Luftwaffe squadrons in Sicily grew smaller, so the fighter defences of Malta grew stronger. A minelayer, HMS *Welshman*, broke the Axis naval blockade around the island and more than once brought in ammunition for the anti-aircraft guns along with fuel. During the rest of May and June, the defenders managed to restore aerial superiority over the island. Although supplies were still alarmingly low, a combination of the Axis decision to change their strategic priorities and the RAF's ability to ready their replacement fighters for immediate combat use saved the day.

The Malta story was by no means over. Food supplies dropped to disastrously low levels. Bread rationing had to be introduced for the first time. The Maltese people had to queue for all their staples – bread, pasta, tomato paste. The number of calories available each day to the population dropped to 1,690 for adult male workers and 1,500 for women and children. This was below the level the Germans allocated to the people of occupied Greece.[21] It looked as though the island fortress would be starved into surrender. In June, two convoys simultaneously headed for Malta, one from Gibraltar and the other from Alexandria. Both convoys and their escorts suffered heavy losses and the convoy from Egypt had to turn back. Six merchant ships were sunk. Only two out of seventeen got through. But the food and ammunition they brought at least meant Malta could survive for a few more weeks.

In August the most intense effort so far was made to relieve the island. Fourteen of the biggest and fastest merchant ships available sailed from Gibraltar with an escort of fifty-nine warships, including three aircraft carriers, a battleship, a dozen cruisers and scores of smaller vessels. But the operation began terribly when the carrier *Eagle* was torpedoed on the first morning and sank within minutes. The convoy then had to sail through a ferocious gauntlet of almost continuous attacks by Italian submarines, German motor torpedo boats and Luftwaffe bombers and dive bombers. Two British cruisers and a destroyer were sunk. Nine merchant ships went to the bottom. One stricken vessel spilled oil into the sea which rapidly caught fire. With flames rising dozens of feet into the air and threatening all those who had abandoned ship, the captain of a destroyer, Commander Roger Hill of HMS *Ledbury*, ordered his vessel to return and while still under attack from dive bombers rescued forty-four men from the burning sea. The destroyer had been one of the escorts on the disastrous Arctic convoy the previous month and Commander Hill later said, 'I was redeeming myself for leaving those ships in PQ17.'[22]

After days of almost continuous attacks, four vessels made it to Malta. Most famously, the American tanker the *Ohio*, carrying 11,500 tons of fuel oil, was hit several times but struggled on. She finally lost power 70 miles from Malta and began to sink. The exhausted and traumatised crew abandoned ship. But a boarding crew were sent back who secured the vessel, which was now very low in the water. The *Ledbury*, another destroyer and a minesweeper came alongside and while still under air attack managed to tow her into the Grand Harbour where cheering crowds greeted her arrival. The fuel was rapidly and efficiently unloaded from the *Ohio*'s hold.[23] Although the *Ohio* never sailed again, the life-and-death struggle to complete her journey made her story one of the most celebrated naval achievements of the war. Malta was saved. For the present at least.

On 8 May, Churchill had written to General Auchinleck, commander of forces in North Africa, instructing him to engage in battle with Rommel. Churchill wrote in this letter that the loss of Malta 'would be a disaster of first magnitude to the British Empire, and probably fatal in the long run to the defence of the Nile Valley'.[24] He knew, as did the chiefs of staff, the link between the destiny of Malta and the struggle in North Africa. He also needed no reminding that another humiliation like the fall of Singapore would be difficult to recover from politically.

12

The Desert War

The war in the desert was an unusual one. It was tiny in scale by comparison with the vast struggle taking place on the Eastern Front but both sets of armies grew in size during 1941, reflecting the fact that each side saw the conflict as vital to their interests. By the autumn of that year the Afrika Korps consisted of three divisions, two of which were panzer units, and the Italians had two corps, six divisions. The Eighth Army consisted of two corps, or four divisions, supported by three tank brigades and a full division in reserve. This was a truly imperial army made up of British, Indian, Australian, New Zealand and South African troops supported by small numbers of Poles and Free French. The Axis forces were based at Tripoli, in western Libya. The Allied army was based at the luxurious and decadent Egyptian capital Cairo, on the Nile. In roughly 1,300 miles of desert between the two were a series of coastal towns and ports that were fought over, captured, abandoned and recaptured in the see-saw war – Benghazi, Gazala, Tobruk, Bardia, Sidi Barrani, Mersa Matruh and many more that amounted to nothing much beyond a few date palm groves around a watering hole. They were small towns of white buildings, the occasional mosque, a church and a market.

Between these seaside towns was a vast quantity of desert, largely unpopulated except for wandering tribes of Bedouin or Berber. This was not the classic sand dune desert of Arabia but hundreds of miles of scrub and saltbush, yellow rock and grey earth along the coastal strip running south into swamps of moving sand for endless more miles. There was a tarmac road along the coast. There was also a railway line for 100 miles from Alexandria, and then nothing. To the south there was little more than camel tracks between distant desert oases. It was exhaustingly hot in the spring and summer with temperatures going up to above 40°C, but it could be bitterly cold at night when desert shorts needed to be complemented with extra coverings or corduroy. And in the winter it was often freezing and wet. All the time, summer and winter, the wind blew and picked up endless tiny grains of sand. The sand got into the meals eaten by every soldier, into his brew of char, into his tent, his hair and skin. Sand penetrated into engines and clogged up weapons. And when the khamsin wind blew in from the desert it picked up so much sand that it obscured everything and could reduce visibility to just a few yards. Even more irritating were the millions of flies that gathered around everything and everyone, food, drink, men and equipment. They were a larger and more aggressive variety than the flies known in Europe. Additionally, for north Europeans the desert brought a range of strange ailments. Everyone suffered from upset stomachs, the 'Pharaoh's revenge', at some point. Boils, sores, sunburn, jaundice and eye strain were all commonplace. And in the heat or the cold, with sand getting everywhere, wounds took a lot longer to heal. It was often said that the desert was neutral: both sides had to cope with it and learn to live in its harsh climate and environs.

The desert fostered an unusual sort of warfare. There was not the ferocity seen on other fronts, particularly in Russia or the Far East. There were relatively few civilians to get in the

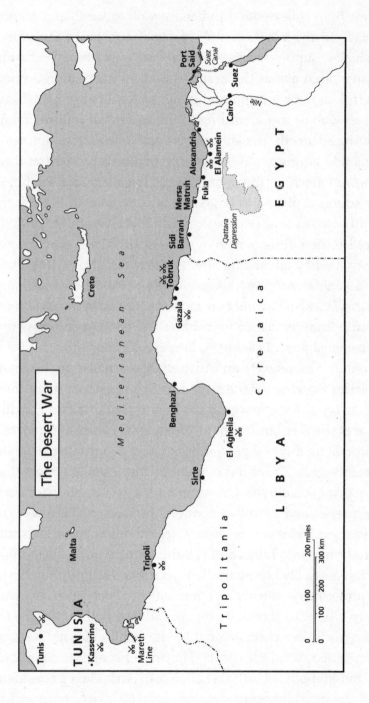

The Desert War

way. Both sides tended to behave well towards and respect their enemy. It was a war of machines, tanks, armoured vehicles, supply trucks and wagons. Everything had to be transported across the desert – food, supplies, ammunition, petrol and, most important of all, water. Engagements were often won or lost according to the success or failure of supplying advancing armoured units with adequate quantities of fuel and ammunition. If the armour was knocked out there was not much for the infantry to do but surrender. And most prisoners captured in large numbers by both sides were not wounded. In set-piece battles, casualties were high, but otherwise the killing was on a small scale. There was also the irony that by advancing after a victory an army would have to struggle with ever longer supply routes; after a defeat, a retreating army would become stronger and better integrated as it withdrew nearer to its base. The consequence was that most engagements led to no decisive conclusion.

Alan Moorehead, an Australian journalist in his early thirties working for the *Daily Express* in London, spent three years reporting the war in the desert. He described it as like war at sea: constantly moving, frequently confusing, and very difficult for any one person, a soldier or a journalist, to follow or understand. 'One did not occupy the desert any more than one occupied the sea. One simply took up a position for a day or a week and patrolled about it,' he wrote. 'There were no trenches. There was no front line. We might patrol five hundred miles into Libya and call the country ours. The Italians might as easily have patrolled as far into the Egyptian desert without being seen ... We hunted men, not land, as a warship will hunt another warship, and care nothing for the sea on which the action is fought.' The armies of both sides, he concluded, 'used the desert. They never sought to control it.'[1]

But for both sides the war in North Africa had a considerable strategic importance. Having been thrown out of northern

France in June 1940, it was the one place where Britain could confront the enemy on land after Mussolini had chosen to invade British Egypt. Much prestige as well as huge supplies of men and materiel were committed to the desert fighting. And the Suez Canal, always seen as a vital link in Britain's empire, had to be defended. This meant Egypt had to be fought for and protected. On the other side, after Hitler had committed Rommel to the war in the desert, it too became a battlefield on which German arms had to be seen to prevail. Hitler was unduly concerned, almost obsessed, with the Mediterranean and with preventing the Allies from striking against his southern flank, through Greece or Yugoslavia (today Slovenia, Croatia, Bosnia and Serbia). He saw the war in North Africa as an essential part of winning control of the Mediterranean.

During 1941 the Allies enjoyed considerable success beyond the desert war in the wider Middle East. An attempt by the Germans to take control in Iraq in order to seize that country's oilfields had been put down. Syria, controlled after the fall of France by the Vichy French and a potential route for an Axis attack upon the flank of the British forces, had been invaded. It was a short but bitter campaign that saw Free French soldiers in the Allied forces fighting Vichy French. And British soldiers resented having to spill blood to fight Frenchmen when they should be fighting Germans. But quickly Syria and Lebanon were brought into the Allied orbit. And, in a third campaign, after the Germans had attacked the Soviet Union, British and Soviet forces had jointly and rapidly occupied Persia and replaced the elderly and corrupt ruler with his son, Mohammad Reza Pahlavi, who would rule as Shah for nearly forty years. The Axis threats in the region had been defeated. The Persian Gulf was under British control. Oil supplies had been secured and refineries kept open. And in a little noted event, British and Soviet troops had linked up on the banks of the Caspian Sea in Persia. Toasts had been drunk to Stalin and to Churchill and both sides had then politely withdrawn to their agreed positions.

This left Britain ready to concentrate on the war in the desert once again. With Malta largely controlling the ebb and flow of the war in North Africa, so Rommel and his Italian allies became desperately short of fuel, equipment and supplies of all sorts in November 1941. That was the month in which Allied naval and air operations succeeded in sinking nearly 80 per cent of all shipping sent to supply the Axis forces. Rommel was still planning a limited attack to capture Tobruk which had held out under siege for eight months 70 miles behind his lines, but Auchinleck beat him to it and launched an offensive, Operation Crusader, on 18 November. It was intended to relieve Tobruk and recapture Cyrenaica, the eastern part of Libya. It was the largest British ground offensive of the war so far and was led by the newly named Eighth Army under General Alan Cunningham (the brother of the admiral who led the Mediterranean Fleet). Churchill had been pressing Auchinleck to take the offensive for some weeks to relieve the pressure on the Eastern Front where the Germans had captured most of the Ukraine and were heading towards Moscow. But Auchinleck hesitated, not wanting to risk the lives of his men, waiting until he had a clear superiority of roughly 3:1 in front-line tanks and armour over the Axis forces.[2] On the eve of battle Churchill sent a message to the troops: 'For the first time British and Empire troops will meet the Germans with an ample supply of equipment in modern weapons of all kinds.' He concluded, 'The eyes of all nations are upon you.' And he added with a suitably grand flourish, 'The Desert Army may add a page to history which will rank with Blenheim and with Waterloo.'[3]

The battle began in lashing, heavy rain. It remained a confused affair for several days. Churchill as always was desperate for news and his private secretary noted in his diary, 'PM very impatient at absence of news of its progress'.[4] The British advance was successful at first but came unstuck in the face of determined Italian resistance. The 7th Armoured Division got to within 10 miles of Tobruk but was decimated by German anti-tank guns, which were more powerful than the 2-pounder guns on the British tanks, losing 113 out of its 141 tanks. By the end of the first week of fighting the British superiority in numbers of tanks had been reversed and the Germans held the advantage of 3:1.[5] Private Crimp of the 7th Armoured wrote, 'We may have had the greater number but most of them were ... lanky, lightweight, gangling cruisers, pretty fast but mounted with feeble 2-pdr guns, no earthly good against the thicker armour and much more powerful 75-mm armament of the German panzers. How many crews have been wasted in useless tanks.'[6]

Then, displaying his characteristically aggressive instinct, Rommel took a gamble by launching a counter-attack. But the attack soon lost momentum as his panzers ran out of fuel. New Zealand troops moved towards Tobruk. The commander of the Eighth Army, General Cunningham, hesitated, unsure how to proceed. Auchinleck, as commander-in-chief, believed he did not show enough offensive spirit and intervened mid-battle to relieve him of his command. He replaced him with his chief of staff, Lieutenant-General Neil Ritchie, a staff officer who had spent most of his time behind a desk in Cairo. He had to be quickly promoted to be of sufficient rank to take command. Ritchie was very familiar with Auchinleck's battle plan and could now carry it out for him. He reorganised his forces to restart the offensive. The Desert Air Force provided close support to the ground forces and relentlessly attacked Axis positions. Then the weather turned again and the air assault had to be called off. On 4 December Rommel ordered yet another counter-attack with what remained of his two panzer

divisions and two Italian armoured divisions. But the Italians
failed to turn up. The attack never took place. On 7 December,
the New Zealanders relieved Tobruk. Two days later, Rommel
ordered an organised retreat to a defensive line at Gazala. But
XXX Corps followed in pursuit and a week later managed to
outflank the Axis troops. Rommel reported to the OKW, 'After
four weeks of uninterrupted and costly fighting, the fighting
power of the troops – despite superb individual achievements –
is showing signs of flagging, all the more so as the supply
of arms and ammunition has completely dried up.'[7] With a
dwindling supply of petrol, in order to save the Afrika Korps
he ordered another retreat and this time his troops did not stop
for about 150 miles. Allied forces reoccupied the garrisons of
Barce and Benghazi and finally came to a halt at El Agheila in
early January 1942. They were back to almost exactly the spot
they had reached after their advance against the Italians a year
before. All of Cyrenaica had been recaptured. The Axis had
suffered 38,000 casualties, the Allies around half of this. About
300 Axis and 278 British tanks had been completely destroyed.
It was without doubt an Allied victory but, as was so often the
case in the desert war, an indecisive one. The Axis forces had
not been annihilated. They survived to fight another day. And
that day would not be long in coming.

British propaganda lauded the victory, claiming that 'The
destruction of the enemy's forces in the Western Desert has
been accomplished. The German armour has been destroyed.'[8]
Such reports left the British troops in the most advanced
positions rather complacent. But it was not the case. Alan
Moorehead wrote that the public disliked intensely 'having
its hopes raised high only to be plunged into the disappointment of reality later'.[9] As Luftwaffe bombers transferred from
the Eastern Front to Sicily, so Malta came under intense pressure, and reinforcements began to get through once again to
North Africa. This had begun on 22 December 1941 with the

arrival of forty-five brand-new panzers. Throughout January the Afrika Korps received dozens more tanks, thousands of tons of ammunition, reinforcements and enough fuel to begin actions in depth again.

On 21 January Rommel launched a modest incursion, little more than a heavy reconnaissance, to assess the strength of British forces facing him. By now it was the Eighth Army that had extended supply lines, with its most advanced units some 800 miles from headquarters. And the battle-hardened troops that had fought in Crusader had been replaced with newly arrived units who proved no match for Panzerarmee Afrika. Rommel was surprised at how weak the British defences were. Within a couple of days his prodding had built up into a full offensive and the Eighth Army was forced into a hectic retreat. On 29 January, the day of the no-confidence vote in the House of Commons, Benghazi was recaptured. On 5 February, Rommel called a halt at Gazala. His army had run out of fuel and could advance no further. But his troops were only 40 miles from Tobruk. The 'Desert Fox', as Rommel had become known, had done it again. He had recaptured nearly all of Cyrenaica, had taken 1,400 prisoners and destroyed seventy-two tanks and forty field guns.[10] All hope of advancing to Tripoli and forcing the Axis out of North Africa was lost. In the month that would see further humiliations in Malaya and Singapore, Alan Moorehead reflected on the reverses in the Western Desert and decided 'there had been a straight fight and the Axis army was better than the British army'. He concluded, 'The cold fact was that somehow the British had to build a better army. And build it quickly.'[11] Meanwhile, both armies had fought themselves to a standstill. As they stared across the desert at each other at Gazala it was once again time to re-equip and build up their strength.

As we have seen, Churchill had plenty on his mind over the coming weeks: the Channel Dash, the humiliation of

surrender at Singapore, the collapse in Burma, the struggle
to supply the Soviets and growing domestic opposition at
home. The Prime Minister was also growing increasingly
worried about the situation in the Soviet Union as he expected
the Germans to launch their spring offensive on the Eastern
Front before long. There was further frustration in Downing
Street when General Auchinleck announced that he would
not be ready to launch an attack against Rommel's forces until
July. Churchill requested that Auchinleck should return to
London immediately to discuss strategy. Auchinleck replied
that the situation was too grave and he was not prepared to
leave Egypt. Churchill was furious and was overheard saying
he would fire 'the Auk', but Brooke talked him out of it.[12] On
15 March, Churchill cabled Auchinleck to express his 'deep-
est anxiety' about the delay. 'A heavy German counterstroke
upon the Russians must be expected soon,' he predicted, 'and
it would be thought intolerable that the 635,000 men ex Malta
on your ration strength should remain unengaged preparing
for another set-piece battle in July.' To Auchinleck's argument
that he needed time to build up his reserves and fully prepare
for an offensive, Churchill argued, 'there is no certainty that
the enemy cannot reinforce faster than you, so after all your
waiting you will find yourself in relatively the same or even
a worse position'.[13]

By April it had become clear to all the troops spread
across North Africa that a battle was coming. A procession
of trucks, camouflaged with desert netting, wound its way
along the coast road for 300 miles from the depots on the
Nile to the front at Gazala. The railway line that ran along
the coast was hurriedly extended towards Tobruk so that
tanks and ammunition could be hauled by train. Journalists
noted that the famous watering holes like the Turf Club and
the Sports Club on Gezira island were quiet and the streets
of Cairo had almost emptied of British soldiers. On the Axis

side, reinforcements had been steadily arriving. The three divisions of the Afrika Korps had been brought back to just about full strength. Elements of eight Italian divisions had been put under Rommel's command. Numbers of Mark III panzers with their powerful 50mm guns were assembling. And aerial reconnaissance reported that long convoys of trucks and wagons were heading towards Gazala from Tripoli and Benghazi. As the desert heat rose incessantly, an air of expectancy hung over the troops at the front.

Rommel was a brilliant strategist, a gambler, and a charismatic leader. In the desert he was able to put all his ideas of how to fight a fast, mobile war into action. He was constantly on the move around the battlefield, was supremely quick to assess a situation and when he had made a decision would act with speed. Conscious of his image, he often allowed himself to be photographed, frequently wearing a pair of goggles over his service cap, and in winter a thick leather overcoat, but always displaying his medals. He made a striking figure and was popular with his own soldiers, known as a commander who led from the front. To the Allies this all helped build a myth of invincibility around him and he became probably the best-known German general in the field. Moreover, he was surrounded by able commanders who had built up considerable experience of fighting in northern Europe, in Soviet Russia and in the desert.

On the other side, Churchill knew that to achieve the victory he longed for, to evict the Axis from North Africa and to reduce the pressure on the Soviets, his generals would have to smash the Afrika Korps and the Italians. But the British generals were not of the same calibre. Auchinleck was a fine thinker and a totally professional soldier who had served nearly all his career in the Indian Army. But he had made a poor choice as commander of Eighth Army in Lieutenant-General Ritchie. He was close to his commander-in-chief 'the Auk',

Rommel became a legend among Allied as well as Axis troops in the desert war. He led from the front, was quick to assess the situation and fast to respond.

but Ritchie was not much respected by his corps commanders Lieutenant-Generals William 'Strafer' Gott and 'Will' Norrie. Both of them had more battle experience than Ritchie and each of them thought he should have been put in command. But the Eighth Army was at least by now a formidable fighting machine. By the middle of May, the British had built up a clear superiority in armour once again. The Panzerarmee Afrika had 560 tanks, of which a third were obsolete Italian vehicles. They were up against 850 British tanks. Nearly half of these were new American Grant tanks that had arrived to support the British Valentines and Crusaders. Most of the British armour with their 2-pounder guns had been outgunned by their German rivals. But the Grants had a much more effective 75mm gun located in a sponson at the side of the tank. And the Eighth Army was also starting to make use of a new

6-pounder anti-tank gun that could fire faster and was more accurate than its predecessor. The problem was that there were only a small number available. Rommel had forty-eight of the brilliant German 88mm guns. This excellent armament could be used as an anti-aircraft weapon or, as in the desert, as an anti-tank gun. It was highly mobile and much feared by the Allied armour. The Axis had about 90,000 men in the field but the Eighth Army had 126,000, an increase of nearly 50 per cent since the beginning of the year. Only in the air did the Axis have a clear superiority with 500 aircraft available for service against 190 in the Desert Air Force.[14]

In the Libyan desert, morale among the men of the Eighth Army was good. A radio speech by the Prime Minister in early May greatly encouraged the troops. Looking back over the last two years of war, Churchill said, 'We are no longer unarmed; we are well armed. Now we are not alone; we have mighty Allies.' This went down particularly well. An Australian Army morale report concluded that 'no single event in the last six months has had such a marked influence on the morale of the men as the Prime Minister's stirring words ... the speech, full of fire and determination and ironic humour, has created a great feeling of confidence and satisfaction'.[15] Reinforced and now with morale restored, the desert soldiers felt a turning point had come and looked forward to the next stage in their war with Rommel and the Italians.

At the point where the two sides had stopped fighting in early February, at Gazala, the British did what they usually did in North Africa. They set about building a 'line' that began at the sea and extended south into the desert. Up to now both armies had used the same tactics, each trying to outflank the other, heading south into the desert and then coming up behind the waiting troops. To prevent this, Ritchie ordered that his troops should form self-sufficient groups of brigade strength and build up what were called 'boxes' made up of armour, artillery and infantry which could fight off attackers from any direction. Surrounding each box, hundreds of thousands of mines were laid. The southernmost box, nearly 40 miles from the sea, was made up of Free French troops located around an old desert fort called Bir Hacheim. These boxes were intended to hold out for some time before the massed armour of the 1st and 7th Armoured Divisions could arrive to provide support and drive back the enemy.

In late April and early May, Churchill and the chiefs of staff regularly read decrypts from Bletchley Park in which Rommel's staff were reporting the build-up of Axis forces. Churchill forwarded these to Auchinleck as 'special information'. But Auchinleck held out against pressure from London and insisted he would not be ready to attack until mid-June. This time he wanted an overall 3:2 superiority in men over Rommel before launching an offensive. On 8 May the War Cabinet received more decrypts in which Rommel's quartermaster general analysed the state of his fuel supplies and declared he had sufficient petrol for thirty-eight days of operations.[16] The War Cabinet agreed that an attack was imminent and the Eighth Army must take the offensive quickly to disrupt Rommel's plans. Churchill told Auchinleck 'to attack the enemy and fight a major battle ... the sooner the better'. He made it clear that London was 'prepared to take full responsibility' for the decision.[17] Still Auchinleck felt he did not have the strength to overwhelm the enemy. He delayed further.

Then, on the morning of 26 May, a British tank commander surveying the western horizon at dawn saw through his binoculars a column of dust rising into the sky. 'Looks like a brigade of Jerry tanks coming,' he reported over the phone to his headquarters. As he watched, the column transformed into several giant pillars of dust spreading rapidly along the horizon and rising high into the sky. He called his HQ back. 'It's more than a brigade,' he reported. 'It's the whole bloody

Afrika Korps.'[18] Once again, Rommel had got there first. The Battle of Gazala had begun.

The Axis offensive opened with an attack against the South African division in the north of the line. But this was a feint. As the South Africans held firm, the main thrust came a few hours later when, during a moonlit night, Rommel's panzers headed south in a vast sweep across the desert. They bypassed the French at Bir Hacheim and attempted to assault the Allied lines from the rear. As was usual in desert battles, the situation remained confusing and difficult to follow for some days. Several commanders on both sides were captured in their headquarters by enemy troops who suddenly appeared out of the dark or in the midst of a sandstorm. But after forty-eight hours it became clear that Rommel had miscalculated. His panzer units came across a British stronghold that their reconnaissance had not spotted. Fighting concentrated on an area that became known as the 'Cauldron'. The defenders of a box here, 150th Brigade led by Brigadier C. W. Haydon and consisting of three north-country infantry battalions, fought heroically. Running desperately low on fuel, Rommel stared into the face of defeat. But this only seemed to bring out the best in the Desert Fox.

On the night of 28 May, Rommel himself climbed into the cab of the leading truck in his supply convoy and navigated it across the desert through a sandstorm to rendezvous with his leading panzers. Refuelled and with water and rations restored, Rommel ordered a complete change of plan. Instead of heading for Tobruk his forces would take up a defensive position and bide their time until the Eighth Army attacked. Now pretty well surrounded by British troops, he waited for the British armour. But, inexplicably, Ritchie failed to order an attack. Ritchie and his corps commanders argued over what was the best action to take. When decisive leadership could have won the day, the generals argued among themselves and Ritchie did not have the temperament or the experience to impose a single will on his command. The moment passed when the leading Axis forces in North Africa could have been annihilated. The Afrika Korps instead had time to overpower the British resistance in the Cauldron in a few days of intense fighting. Stukas screamed down to dive-bomb the 150th Brigade box. The panzers moved in from all sides. Running out of ammunition and water, the survivors had no option but to destroy their weapons and surrender. Rommel arrived to pay his respects in person to his gallant opponent. But Brigadier Haydon lay among the dead of his brigade.[19]

For several days the battle seemed to be evenly balanced. The Afrika Korps continued to strengthen its position but was not strong enough to continue its advance. Isolated fighting took place but Ritchie still held off ordering a decisive counter-attack. When it finally came on 5 June it was poorly led and appallingly coordinated. The Afrika Korps' 88mm guns wrecked tank after tank in the British assault. The infantry were not fully informed of the mauling the armoured units were getting and carried on regardless. Collaboration between Allied armoured and infantry units was almost non-existent. Ritchie held back his reserves just at the point at which they could have made a real difference. By dusk that day the Eighth Army had lost 6,000 men of whom 4,000 were taken prisoner, and 150 tanks had been knocked out including many of the new American Grants.

From this point, the outcome of the battle looked increasingly certain. Rommel turned south to mop up the Free French in the desert castle at Bir Hacheim. The French withdrew and two thirds of their force managed to escape. The panzer units were now down to only 120 German and sixty Italian tanks. But their reduced numbers did not seem to diminish their ardour. Using an old tactic, they lured the British armour towards them and then laid into the British tanks with their

IWM

General Ritchie, centre with pipe, puzzles over a map with his corps commanders at Gazala, May 1942. General Norrie (left) and General Gott (right) are seen, with two staff officers on either side.

screens of anti-tank weapons. Seventy more British tanks were taken out. Ritchie rapidly came to the conclusion that the battle was lost. The only way to get his army out in one piece was to withdraw to the Egyptian border.

From London, Churchill and the chiefs of staff followed events with increasing despair. On 13 June, Churchill cabled Auchinleck: 'Retreat would be fatal. This is a business not only of armour but of will power.'[20] The soldiers of the Eighth Army were fighting with great grit and determination. Several VCs were won during the three weeks of the Gazala battle. Middle-ranking officers also performed well. A mass of experience of fighting in the desert was building up among these officers who led several local victories over German and Italian troops. But, sadly, the senior British commanders did not display the willpower that Churchill called for. They were simply not up to the task. The Eighth Army once again faced defeat in the desert. And this time its withdrawal could be fatal.

13

Global Battles

At the beginning of May, Churchill's standing was still low among many people in Britain as the run of disasters seemed never-ending. A commercial traveller who daily met a variety of people noted in his diary, 'I find from conversations, reception of newsreels etc that Churchill's power to inspire has rather slumped.'[1] The call for a second front was continuing to build momentum. Partly it was led by the Communist Party and supported by left-wing newspapers like *Tribune* and the *News Chronicle*, but it was also a policy advocated in Beaverbrook's *Daily Express*. And a broad mass of industrial workers felt great sympathy with the plight of Soviet workers and soldiers and supported the demand. A Mass Observation diarist in North Yorkshire recorded that 'Open Second Front Now' had been painted on the wall of a local hospital, noting that 'an effort has been made to rub it out which has only succeeded in making it more noticeable'.[2] On the mess wall at RAF Oakington, a bomber station near Cambridge, a graffiti artist had painted an even more forthright message: 'Russia Starves While Britain Bullshits'.[3] A rally was organised in Trafalgar Square at which 43,000 turned up to support the demand for a second front, the biggest demonstration held during the war. Much of this protest was directed against

Churchill and the War Cabinet who were thought not to be doing enough to support the Soviets. And it was around this time that Stalin, the man who had led the Terror of the 1930s and ordered the execution of tens of thousands of his citizens, was given the cheery nickname of 'Uncle Joe'.

At 9 p.m. on Sunday 10 May 1942, Churchill broadcast to the nation to mark the second anniversary of his appointment as Prime Minister. The BBC broadcast the speech not only within the UK but throughout the Commonwealth, to the United States, through its twenty-three European services and to other nations around the world.[4] Churchill wanted to look back at the last two years and to 'peer cautiously' into the future. 'As in the last war, so in this, we are moving through many reverses and defeats to complete and final victory,' he predicted. He spent much time talking about the heroism of the Soviet defence of the Russian homeland. 'They poured out their own blood on their native soil,' he told his listeners. 'They kept their faces to the foe.' And they were fighting on 'with unflinching valour'. He lauded the merchant and Royal Navy seamen who were struggling to help keep the Soviets supplied with weapons on the perilous Arctic convoys. He taunted Hitler for forgetting about the Russian winter and leaving his troops freezing as they struggled to repel Soviet counter-attacks. Hitler 'must have been very loosely educated', he mocked. 'We all heard about it at school.' He acknowledged the calls for a 'Second Front Now' and the demonstrations demanding this. 'Naturally,' he responded, 'I shall not disclose what our intentions are,' but, he asked, 'Is it not far better that demonstrations of thousands of people should gather in Trafalgar Square demanding the most vehement and audacious attacks, than there should be the weepings and wailings of peace agitations?' He talked of the growing power of the bombing offensive against the cities and war factories of the Third Reich. He told the people of Germany to go out into the fields 'and watch their home fires burning from a distance'. There they could reflect on the suffering their armies were imposing across Europe and Russia, and 'There they may remember that it is the villainous Hitlerite regime which is responsible for dragging Germany through misery and slaughter to ultimate ruin.' He praised the people of Malta for their resistance. He invoked the might of the United States, which he said was 'many times greater than the power of Japan'. He then summed up his review of progress by saying that 'tonight I give you a message of good cheer', and concluded, 'We shall drive on to the end, and do our duty, win or die.'[5]

Churchill had written a section about the criticisms levelled against his war leadership in recent months. 'Our critics are not slow to dwell upon the misfortunes and reverses which we have sustained, and I'm certainly not going to pretend that there have not been many mistakes and shortcomings.' He went on, 'I am much blamed by a group of ex-ministers for my general conduct of the war.' In this passage, while not engaging with his critics point by point, he wrote that he was a servant of the House of Commons and could at any time be dismissed by Parliament. But at the last minute he deleted this section and the overall tone of the speech was consequently more confident and upbeat.[6]

Mass Observation diarists were broadly positive in their response to the Prime Minister's broadcast. 'Made one proud to be British,' wrote a Gateshead housewife.[7] An ARP warden from Surrey wrote, 'It was a new Churchill who spoke yesterday – a Churchill as usual full of confidence, but this time he did not dwell on the troublesome and worrying times ahead for us – the latter was for the enemy.'[8] But not everyone agreed. A Hampshire housewife felt that the broadcast was full of clichés, though she recognised that she was in a minority. 'I am shocked by the number of people who asked me this morning if I hadn't heard the PM's speech, didn't I think it was good & wasn't he more hopeful this time, and so ad nauseam.'[9] A teacher wrote, 'The reference to German citizens fleeing from their cities to watch their home fires burning I thought disgusting.' A hospital worker also recorded that his boss, despite being a Czech Jewish refugee and a committed anti-Nazi, found it distasteful and denounced 'all this nonsense of hating your enemies'.[10] But Home Intelligence in its weekly report for the Ministry of Information concluded that praise for the speech was 'practically unanimous' and many people found it to be 'his best ever'. Moreover, the official morale-assessing organisation noted that the speech helped reduce demands for a second front because Churchill's words meant that many believed it was 'on the way'.[11]

Internationally, too, the speech went down well. Peter Fraser, Prime Minister of New Zealand, wrote that Churchill's words had 'struck an immediate response in every New Zealand heart'. And Lord Halifax, the ambassador in Washington, sent a message to the PM noting that 'reaction here had been splendid. This is supported by universal comment reaching me. It was exactly what was wanted.'[12] It seemed the Prime Minister had hit the right note for most of his listeners and the speech marked something of a bounce back in his popularity.

The defeat of the Wehrmacht at the gates of Moscow in December 1941 had been as important a turning point on the Eastern Front as had been the defeat of the Luftwaffe over the skies of southern Britain in the summer of 1940. It marked the failure of the first phase of Hitler's blitzkrieg campaign against the Soviet Union. The German Army had lost more than 760,000 men killed, wounded and taken prisoner on the Eastern Front. The Red Army had probably lost nearly four times that number. And about half a million square miles of Soviet territory was now under German occupation. But the Soviet Union still had vast reserves it could draw upon. About 1,300 war factories were literally packed up, freighted to the east beyond the Ural mountains and rebuilt hundreds of miles away from the front.

Trains carried millions of machine tools, thousands of tons of iron and steel, and complete production lines to the east. At a giant new factory built on the site of an old iron and steel works near the town of Nizhny Tagil in Siberia, tens of thousands of workers and engineers, men and large numbers of women, worked twelve-hour shifts to produce the great T-34 tank. With rations reduced to 400 grams of bread per day, and in winter temperatures that dropped to minus 30°C, output still rose to sixty tanks per day. The complex, which included a steel-making plant and accommodation for the workers, became known as 'Tankograd'. Month by month war production in these new factories increased as Soviet workers, despite terrible hardships, stepped up to meet the demands placed upon them. Guns, artillery, tanks and aircraft poured out in ever-increasing numbers.

Fighting during the bitter winter months was limited but both sides prepared to resume their campaigns as soon as the spring thaw would permit. By the beginning of May 1942, the Red Army consisted of five and a half million men, equipped with about 5,000 tanks and supported by roughly 2,500 combat aircraft. Facing them were 217 divisions of the German Army including Romanian, Hungarian, Italian and Slovakian forces, more than six million men, with more than 3,200 tanks and 3,400 combat aircraft. Despite these numbers, Hitler decided not to press on with his three-pronged assault along the whole length of the front as had been the strategy in 1941. Instead he wanted to concentrate on the south. He planned to launch a massive offensive into the Caucasus, smashing the region's industries, capturing key agricultural lands and seizing the Soviet Union's main oil supplies. This would take the flank of the German advance towards the mighty Volga river and the strategically important city of Stalingrad. For Hitler, capturing Stalingrad would have great ideological and propaganda value. Having won a victory along the Volga his armies would then turn north and mop up Moscow and finally Leningrad. Many of his senior commanders disagreed with this strategy. They wanted to focus on assaulting Moscow and capturing the Soviet capital. But as Supreme Commander of the Armed Forces, Hitler had his way, and on 5 April 1942 he issued a Führer Directive outlining his plans for the spring and summer southern offensive.

In the event, Stalin ordered the Red Army to launch its spring offensive before the Germans were ready to open theirs. On 12 May the Russians attacked south of Kharkov on a 120-mile front with about 640,000 men. They advanced 15 to 20 miles but the offensive soon ran out of steam. The Soviet commanders were slow to follow up their initial successes. The Germans quickly regrouped and on 17 May launched a counter-attack. Within a week they had thrown back the Red Army and captured 240,000 prisoners. It was now the turn of Hitler's armies to launch their spring offensive.

Field Marshal von Bock, who had commanded Army Group Centre in its thrust to Moscow, was put in overall command. General Friedrich Paulus led the Sixth Army as it smashed through the Red Army at Kharkov at the end of May and advanced towards the Don river basin. Further south, most of the Crimea had been occupied in 1941 but the capital city, Sebastopol, had remained in Soviet hands. Now 200,000 troops of the German Eleventh Army launched an operation to capture the city, imagining it would take about two weeks. After a five-day aerial and artillery bombardment, the assault troops went in on 7 June. They met fanatical Soviet resistance and it was only when the Seventeenth Army arrived with reinforcements that they began to make progress. Three weeks of intense street-to-street, house-to-house fighting followed. Bombing and shelling of the city was intense. Superior German firepower finally overcame the resolute Russian resistance and the last defenders were evacuated at the beginning of July. Axis troops (Germans and Romanians) had lost 36,000 men killed, wounded and missing. Soviet casualties were nearer to 118,000 but of these 95,000 had been taken prisoner.

However, forces on the Eastern Front had the same difficulties in advancing as troops in the desert. They could move rapidly forward but when they got too far from their supply depots they began to slow. Vehicles and tanks started to break down. Bringing up spare parts took time. Petrol supplies began to run low. Everything proved difficult over the distances involved, from evacuating the wounded to bringing up reinforcements. After 300 or 400 miles, the balance would shift from the aggressor to the defender. As in the desert, a few hundred miles meant little in the vastness of the steppe. German field commanders could report back that they had successfully crossed a river, but there was always another river ahead. And then another. And then yet another. The big difference in the Soviet Union, of course, was that the land was heavily populated. After every village or town had been captured, the inhabitants would be rounded up, some of their houses would be burned down in front of them, and often the men would be separated from the women and children. There would be tearful farewells as many knew they would never see their family again. Potential resistance groups or partisans would be taken away and frequently shot.[13] And behind the Wehrmacht were the execution squads, rounding up and murdering tens of thousands. This was not just a military exercise, for Hitler it was an ideological and a racial war, to destroy Bolshevism and smash the Slavic race into submission to their Aryan masters.

By summer 1942 Axis troops everywhere were on the advance. The Crimea was finally under German control. Paulus was advancing across the Don basin and his forward troops came within sight of Stalingrad in mid-August. Von Bock's army was advancing into the Caucasus and captured the oilfields in Grozny. In North Africa, Rommel was leading the Afrika Korps into Egypt. Hitler dreamed of a gigantic pincer movement whereby Rommel's forces would occupy Egypt, then move forward through Palestine, Syria and Iraq into northern Persia where they would link up with von Bock's forces advancing south through the Caucasus. Not only would huge tracts of the Soviet Union and the Middle East be under Nazi control but this new Greater Reich would have secured its fuel supplies by capturing the oilfields of Iraq and the Caucasus. But this was to remain a pipe dream. On 24 August, Stalin ordered that Stalingrad, the city that bore his name, should be defended at all costs. One of the greatest battles of the war was about to commence.

In the Far East the situation also looked extremely bleak. At the beginning of February the Japanese had threatened Australia by bombing Port Moresby in New Guinea. Then on 19 February, four days after the fall of Singapore, their aircraft bombed and strafed the port of Darwin in northern Australia. An American destroyer and five merchant ships were sunk. In a second raid, the local RAAF airfield was blitzed. Two hundred and forty people were killed and 150 injured during the raids.

Two and a half thousand miles to the north-west the situation was equally critical. As the Japanese Army threw the British out of Burma and pressed at the gates of India, their navy moved into the Bay of Bengal. Several unarmed freighters chugging up and down the eastern coast of India between Madras (Chennai) and Calcutta (Kolkata) came under attack. In three days, twenty-three merchant ships were sunk. It was the Indian version of the 'Happy Time' along the US coastline. More threateningly, a huge Japanese carrier force of five aircraft carriers supported by four battleships, three cruisers and eleven destroyers under the command of Vice Admiral Nagumo moved into the Indian Ocean. Bombing raids on the towns on the east coast of India prompted an invasion scare.

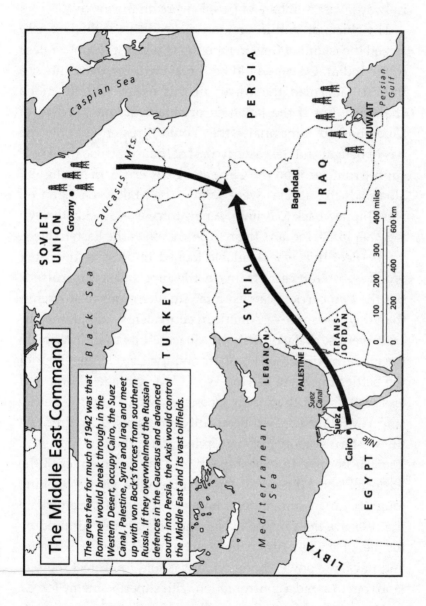

The Middle East Command

The great fear for much of 1942 was that Rommel would break through in the Western Desert, occupy Cairo, the Suez Canal, Palestine, Syria and Iraq and meet up with von Bock's forces from southern Russia. If they overwhelmed the Russian defences in the Caucasus and advanced south into Persia, the Axis would control the Middle East and its vast oilfields.

In the pandemonium, refugees flooded out of Madras and other coastal towns into the interior, filling the roads and railways. Vast numbers of people were on the move.

The chiefs of staff in London realised that if the Japanese seized the island of Ceylon then the whole British power base in the Indian Ocean would be threatened. For two centuries Britain had ruled the waves in this ocean without much challenge. But if the Japanese occupied the naval bases of Colombo and Trincomalee they could threaten not only the Bay of Bengal and the eastern coast of India, but also the whole supply route around the Cape along eastern Africa to Egypt, along which supplies were sent to the Middle East and oil was shipped back to Britain. A new force was quickly thrown together in the Indian Ocean to be known as the Eastern Fleet.

The fleet that was available looked impressive on paper with two aircraft carriers, five battleships and seven cruisers. But the two carriers carried a far smaller number of aircraft than their Japanese or American equivalents, and all the aircraft were slow Swordfish or Albacore biplanes, inferior to the modern Aichi dive bombers and the Zero fighter. Four of the battleships were of First World War vintage, slower and less well armed than their Japanese rivals. Only the battleship HMS *Warspite* had been fully modernised in a refit on the western seaboard of the United States the previous year. *Warspite* became the flagship for the new commander of the Eastern Fleet, Admiral Sir James Somerville. He was a blunt, tough-talking commander who had led part of the attack on the *Bismarck* the previous year, and was greatly admired by his men. He was a firm believer in new technology like radar and naval air power. Somerville was told to protect the sea-lanes but to avoid a confrontation with superior enemy forces.

At the end of March, Somerville received intelligence reports that the Japanese were likely to attack Ceylon on 1 April. When the Japanese fleet did not appear, he withdrew to Port T, the temporary base south of the Maldives, to refuel. In fact, the Japanese had timed their attack for 5 April, Easter Sunday, when they thought the defenders would be distracted. At dawn that morning Japanese bombers and dive bombers attacked Colombo. The RAF Hurricanes and Fulmars that took off to defend the port were overwhelmed by the Zeros that supported the bombers. Nineteen RAF fighters and six Fleet Air Arm Swordfish were shot down for the loss of seven Japanese fighters. Just after lunch that same day HMS *Dorsetshire* and *Cornwall*, two heavy cruisers, were spotted by enemy reconnaissance aircraft off the Ceylonese coast. An hour later Japanese carrier-borne dive bombers arrived and, diving out of the sun, managed to sink both ships within twenty minutes. Four hundred and twenty sailors were lost, but more than 1,100 survived to be rescued the next day after having endured twenty-four hours under a tropical sun in shark-infested waters.

Nagumo sailed north and ordered his aircraft to attack the harbour at Trincomalee. At news of the approaching raid, the light carrier HMS *Hermes* and a destroyer, HMAS *Vampire*, were ordered to put to sea. The 11,000-ton *Hermes* had no aircraft on board to defend it. On 9 April, Japanese Aichi dive bombers, known to the Allies as 'Vals', spotted the two ships and attacked. Without air escort the Vals soon scored direct hits on both ships. The *Hermes* went down first and the *Vampire* soon after with the joint loss of more than 300 sailors. It was yet another humiliation for the Royal Navy. Had the admirals learned nothing since the loss of *Repulse* and the *Prince of Wales* four months before? Warships without an effective air fighter defence were sitting ducks for the skilled Japanese naval fliers. Somerville's Eastern Fleet had been badly mauled and Britain's control over the Indian Ocean was substantially weakened. The provision of old ships without proper escort had failed utterly to deter the Japanese. Britain had overreached itself and commanders had again adopted failed tactics.

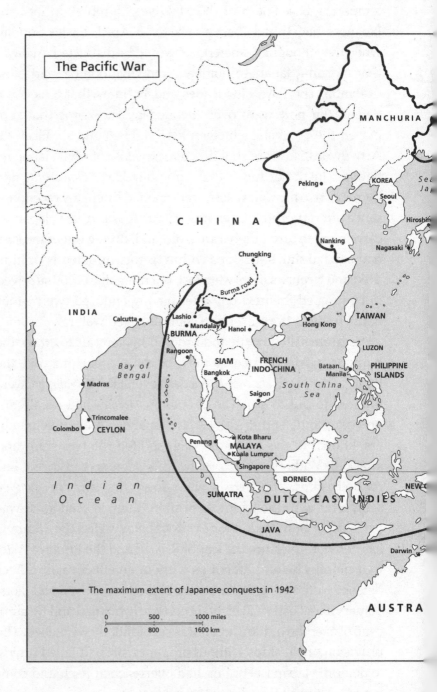

The Pacific War

MANCHURIA

CHINA

Peking •

KOREA

Seoul •

Sea
Ja

Hiroshi

Nanking •

Nagasaki

Chungking •

Burma road

INDIA

Calcutta •

Lashio •

TAIWAN

Hong Kong •

LUZON

Mandalay •

BURMA

Hanoi •

Rangoon •

SIAM

FRENCH
INDO-CHINA

Bangkok •

Bataan

Manila

PHILIPPINE
ISLANDS

Bay of
Bengal

South China
Sea

Madras •

Saigon •

Trincomalee •

Colombo • CEYLON

MALAYA

Penang •

Kota Bharu •

Kuala Lumpur •

Singapore •

BORNEO

NEW

Indian
Ocean

SUMATRA

DUTCH EAST INDIES

JAVA

Darwin •

AUSTRA

—— The maximum extent of Japanese conquests in 1942

| 0 | 500 | 1000 miles |
| 0 | 800 | 1600 km |

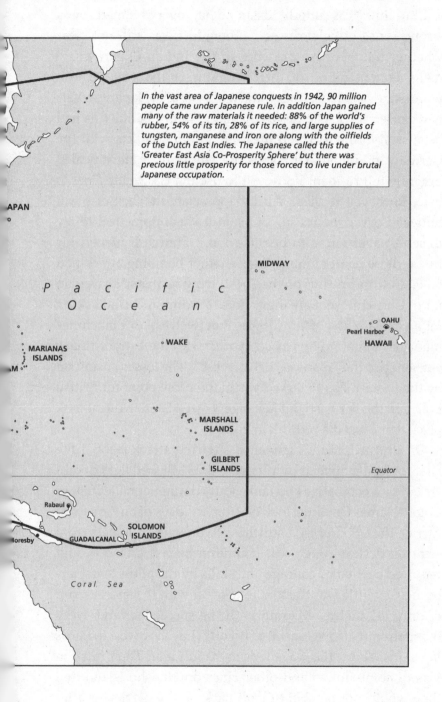

In the vast area of Japanese conquests in 1942, 90 million people came under Japanese rule. In addition Japan gained many of the raw materials it needed: 88% of the world's rubber, 54% of its tin, 28% of its rice, and large supplies of tungsten, manganese and iron ore along with the oilfields of the Dutch East Indies. The Japanese called this the 'Greater East Asia Co-Prosperity Sphere' but there was precious little prosperity for those forced to live under brutal Japanese occupation.

APAN

P a c i f i c
O c e a n

MIDWAY

○ WAKE

OAHU
Pearl Harbor
HAWAII

MARIANAS
ISLANDS

M

MARSHALL
ISLANDS

GILBERT
ISLANDS

Equator

Rabaul

SOLOMON
GUADALCANAL ISLANDS

oresby

Coral Sea

Churchill was utterly despondent, overwhelmed by a strong sense of helplessness, although it was still not clear whether the Japanese presence in the Indian Ocean was a mere demonstration of their strength or the prelude to a planned invasion of either India or Ceylon. The Japanese Vals had caused terrible losses to the navy. 'Nothing like this had been seen in the Mediterranean in all our conflicts with the German and Italian Air Forces,' he later wrote.[14] He appealed urgently to President Roosevelt to use the US Pacific Fleet to help. Roosevelt replied, 'I fully appreciate the lack of naval butter to cover the bread,' but said it was impractical to try to send naval forces to help Ceylon.[15] Churchill turned his ire on those nearer home. After another bombing attack had failed to score any hits on the *Tirpitz* lying up in its Norwegian fjord, Churchill sent an angry note to Admiral Pound asking for an explanation of 'how it was that twelve of our machines managed to get no hits as compared with the extraordinary efficiency of the Japanese [air] attacks?'[16] The losses sustained by the Eastern Fleet marked yet another low point for British policy in the Far East. But just over a week later an event took place that caused a rethink in Tokyo.

On 18 April, the US launched a daring attack right at the heart of Japan. Sixteen twin-engine B-25 Mitchell light bombers led by a combative and audacious commander, Lieutenant Colonel James Doolittle, took off from the deck of an American carrier, the USS *Hornet*. Launching two-engine bombers from a carrier deck in rough seas had never been tried before and required particular courage and skills by the pilots to get airborne. Doolittle was the first to take off with the shortest run of only 142 metres. Magnificently, he succeeded, and every other aircraft also managed to lift off. They flew west towards Japan just above the wave tops to avoid radar. Their mission was to bomb Tokyo and other cities on Honshu island, but they would not be able to land back on the carrier so after dropping their bombs they had to fly on to mainland China. There, most of the aircraft crash-landed or the crews baled out when they ran out of fuel. Eight crew members were captured by the Japanese and three were executed; sixty-nine managed to return with the help of Chinese soldiers and civilians, provoking vicious reprisals from the Japanese.

The mission was a stunning success, not because the bombers caused much in the way of destruction in Japan's capital. But the very fact that the Japanese home islands could be raided was an enormous shock and affront to the country's leaders, just as the bombing of Berlin by the RAF in August 1940 had been to Hitler, Göring and the Nazi leaders. Suddenly, the Japanese felt vulnerable and reassessed the need to protect their mainland. News of the raid was a huge morale boost to the American people. Japan was being treated to some of its own terrible medicine. The Imperial Japanese Navy withdrew from the Bay of Bengal and the Indian Ocean to concentrate on defending waters nearer home. Churchill wrote that the Japanese Navy 'vanished as suddenly as it had come'.[17]

As one threat receded, another appeared. For some time, Churchill and the War Cabinet had been worried about the island of Madagascar lying off the East African coast. As a former French colony it was now ruled by Vichy France. At its northern tip, at Diego Suarez, was a well-fortified naval harbour. If the Vichy French invited either the Germans or the Japanese to use the port it could become a base from which submarines or surface raiders could attack the supply route around the Cape to the Middle East. Combined Operations under Lord Mountbatten began to train a commando force for an amphibious landing to capture Diego Suarez. After a long sea journey from the UK this force eventually assembled with other troops that had been en route to the Middle East, at Durban. Churchill and the War Cabinet were still debating whether to go ahead with the operation when, in April, Pierre

Laval was appointed under German pressure as head of the Vichy government. As a known Nazi collaborator, it was thought he was more likely to allow the Germans or Japanese to use the island. So, on 5 May, British forces undertook their first amphibious landing of the year, not against occupied Europe as the second front movement wanted but against a remote island in the Indian Ocean.[18] The landings were a success. After forty-eight hours of fighting, the French sailors, Malagasy and Senegalese troops defending the port laid down their arms. For now only the harbour of Diego Suarez remained in British hands but over the next few months troops occupied the rest of the island. Churchill was clear, however, that Madagascar had not been captured out of any intention of territorial aggrandisement, it was purely being held 'in trust' for the French people.

Also at the beginning of May a new form of naval engagement took place in the Coral Sea, the ocean north-east of Australia. The Japanese planned to land troops on Tulagi in the Solomon Islands and Port Moresby in New Guinea so as to threaten Australia by putting its northern territories in range of land-based Japanese aircraft. Vice Admiral Shigeyoshi Inoue requested support from a carrier force to cover the landings. American codebreakers had cracked the Japanese naval code and on reading the decrypts of Inoue's request, Admiral Chester Nimitz, the new commander of US forces in the Central Pacific, decided to send a task force to intercept the Japanese carriers. The two fleets never sighted each other but their aircraft engaged and over a three-day period one Japanese light carrier, the 11,000-ton *Shoho*, was sunk and a bigger carrier, the 26,000-ton *Shokaku*, was damaged. The Americans suffered the loss of their 37,000-ton carrier USS *Lexington*, and another carrier, the USS *Yorktown*, was badly damaged. Although the American losses were greater, there was no clear winner of the Battle of the Coral Sea, the first naval battle in which no warships had engaged, only the aircraft of the two navies. However, it was the first time a major Japanese move had been stopped by the Allies and the landings on Port Moresby were postponed, never to be attempted again.

A far more conclusive naval action took place in the Pacific one month later. The Japanese naval commanders were still fretting that the main aircraft carriers of the US Navy had not been in Pearl Harbor when they had attacked the base in December. The hero of that raid, Admiral Yamamoto, argued to the Emperor's chiefs of staff that the carriers must be destroyed. The Japanese Army commanders, on the other hand, argued that capturing territory and obtaining the natural resources and raw materials Japan needed in Asia and the Pacific should take priority. The Doolittle Raid reframed this argument over strategy. It was agreed that the American carriers posed a real threat to Japanese security and Yamamoto should go ahead with his plan to lure them into a trap by drawing them out to Midway island in the mid-Pacific where he would destroy them with a far superior force. Once again, American cryptographers intercepted the naval messages about the Japanese plans which listed the complete order of battle and date for the planned attack. Admiral Nimitz had to decide if the messages were authentic or some sort of decoy to distract him from a possible attack against the US west coast. He decided they were genuine and assembled his carriers to launch their own ambush of the Japanese.

The two fleets met off Midway island, a remote and relatively insignificant atoll about 1,300 miles north-west of Hawaii. Nimitz had the USS *Hornet* and *Enterprise* and also the *Yorktown* after miraculously fast, round-the-clock repairs had been carried out to the damage inflicted in the Coral Sea. Rear Admiral Raymond Spruance was in command of the task force. Yamamoto sent four carriers under Vice Admiral

Nagumo, who had returned from the Indian Ocean, with a back-up fleet of two battleships, two heavy and one light cruisers plus supports.

The key phase of the Battle of Midway took place over only a few hours, beginning with a Japanese raid on the island at dawn on 4 June. The US carriers launched torpedo-carrying bombers, Grumman Avengers and Douglas Devastators, against the Japanese carriers at 9 a.m. They failed to score a single hit. Thirty-five of the slow-moving bombers were shot down by Zero fighters flying off the Japanese carriers. Only six returned. Then the situation suddenly reversed. Two squadrons of Dauntless dive bombers flying from the *Enterprise* and the *Yorktown* in search of the Japanese carriers were flying through heavy clouds when at 10.25 a.m. the clouds suddenly dispersed and there, quite clear in the sea below, the pilots saw two Japanese carriers. The carrier crews were in the process of refuelling and rearming aircraft on their flight decks. This was the moment of maximum vulnerability for any carrier, with aviation fuel pipes spread across the decks and ordnance piled high. The dive bombers struck the Japanese carriers with precision accuracy. Two 1,000lb bombs hit the *Akagi*. One of them penetrated below decks and within minutes the carrier had become a blazing inferno of burning fuel and exploding bombs and torpedoes. The rest of the American dive bombers attacked the *Kaga*. This time four bombs found their target, one hitting a petrol refuelling truck near the main superstructure, igniting a sheet of flame that killed everyone on the bridge. Like the *Akagi*, tremendous fires were soon ablaze below decks and the solemn ceremony began of transferring the Emperor's portrait to an attendant vessel, a ritual that preceded the abandonment of any Japanese warship. At almost exactly the same time a squadron of dive bombers from the *Yorktown* found and struck a third carrier, the *Soryu*. They attacked in three waves and without a single loss the bombers scored three hits, igniting fuel and blowing up aircraft closely packed on the flight deck. Over a period of just six minutes all three carriers received direct hits. Stunned, Nagumo had to abandon his flagship the *Akagi*. The three carriers were abandoned and later, as blazing wrecks, were scuttled.

Aircraft from the fourth carrier, *Hiryu*, pursued the Americans and discovered *Yorktown*, dived in to attack and scored three hits, creating a huge hole in the flight deck. An hour later further Japanese aircraft scored hits with two torpedoes on the *Yorktown*. Taking on water and heavily listing, the ship was abandoned but she remained afloat and the following day a salvage party returned and the carrier managed to limp on. It was hoped she could get back to Hawaii to be repaired again. Late in the afternoon, American aircraft spotted the *Hiryu*, and the Dauntless dive bombers attacked. Once again her deck was put entirely out of action and the ship was left blazing. Several hours later she sank, her captain Rear Admiral Yamaguchi choosing to go down with his ship. Spruance decided to withdraw to avoid a confrontation with the enemy battleships and, after a brief pursuit, the Japanese decided to do the same. *Yorktown* was later hit by a Japanese submarine and sank. This and a destroyer were the total US losses. But all four Japanese carriers and a heavy cruiser in their escort fleet had been sunk. In just a few minutes one half of Japan's elite fleet carrier force, the ships that had launched the attack on Pearl Harbor, that had fought at the Coral Sea and harried the Royal Navy in the Indian Ocean, had been lost and many skilled pilots killed.

It was a tremendous victory, the first major naval defeat suffered by the Japanese. It demonstrated the brilliant achievements of the US cryptographers, the superb flying skills of the American dive bomber pilots, superior tactical planning and, to a degree, the role of luck. The Battle of Midway has been called a turning point in the Pacific war and one of the truly decisive naval battles in history.[19]

Long before the news of an American victory in the Pacific had reached London, Churchill had decided it was time for another head-to-head with the President. Plans for operations later in 1942 were at a stalemate. General Marshall along with Harry Hopkins had visited London in April and powerfully argued the case for opening a second front in Europe. They had been met with implacable opposition from General Brooke and the British chiefs of staff who knew with so few American soldiers yet in Europe that British troops would have to bear the brunt of any operation and that losses would be disastrous. There were not enough landing craft to mount an operation, there was no aerial supremacy, and the troops had not trained for an amphibious landing. A major defeat of an invasion force would not help Stalin but would instead aid Hitler. Brooke argued, 'The prospects of success are small and dependent upon a mass of unknowns, while the chances of disaster are great and dependent upon a mass of well-established military facts.'[20] There was general agreement that an invasion of France should take place in 1943 after sufficient numbers of American troops had arrived in the UK. But Roosevelt's principal question remained. Where *could* they attack German forces on the land in 1942? Churchill and the War Cabinet were concerned that if they could not agree on a suitable Anglo-American offensive then the US would give up on its 'Germany first' strategy that had shaped their war effort for the last six months.

Accordingly, Roosevelt agreed to meet Churchill initially in his family home at Hyde Park overlooking the Hudson river. Then they would travel on together for meetings with their military chiefs in Washington. Churchill decided to fly again across the Atlantic. This would take twenty-four hours, not the two weeks of his last trip. He requested the same pilot of the Boeing Clipper in which he had flown back from Bermuda in January. One of his last acts before departing was to inform the King that if anything happened to him during the journey, he recommended that Anthony Eden, the Foreign Secretary, should replace him being 'in my mind the outstanding Minister in the largest political party in the House of Commons'.[21] Just before midnight on 17 June, Churchill and his small entourage, including his private secretary and his doctor along with Generals Brooke and Ismay, took off in a luxury flying boat, a commercial airliner operated by BOAC, which had taken over from Imperial Airways.[22] Brooke, who had never flown in a Clipper before, wrote in his diary, 'Huge flying boat beautifully fitted up with bunks to sleep in, dining saloon, stewards, lavatories . . . Slept very comfortably.' Churchill sat on the flight deck for a couple of hours then slept in the bridal suite. The next morning they flew over a large convoy clearly visible below them. Brooke wrote, 'PM in tremendous form and enjoying himself like a schoolboy'.[23] The giant Clipper finally landed on the Potomac river after twenty-six hours and thirty minutes in the air.

It was 18 June. The fighting in the desert had started up once more. Yet again the war was at a crucial stage as Churchill arrived for his second wartime summit with Roosevelt.

14

Disgrace

By the second week of June, Ritchie's Eighth Army was in a chaotic retreat from its once so heavily fortified position at Gazala. Huge quantities of food, petrol and ammunition that had been slowly and painstakingly brought up to the front over the last eight weeks, intended to supply the army for months, were either destroyed or simply abandoned. The coastal road heading from the Libyan border towards Alexandria and Cairo was packed with vehicles streaming east. An observer reported that 'Ambulances laden with wounded plunged through the desert and jostled for position with armoured cars and tanks, jeeps and travelling workshops.'[1] By day the vehicles kept a decent distance in case they came under attack from the air and had to quickly disperse. By night they drove without lights in the desert darkness bumper to bumper so as not to fall off the road and become separated from the stampede. An army in retreat is never a happy sight, and this was no exception.

There were still acts of bravery and heroism. The 50th (Northumberland) Division which had been situated in the centre of the Gazala line had already lost one brigade in the Cauldron and was now cut off and prevented from pulling out to the east. The remaining two brigades decided to go west instead. General Ramsden divided his division into small units of a few vehicles each and they headed off towards the enemy. The Italians were so astonished to see British troops coming towards them at this point of the battle that they broke. Enemy supply vessels were captured; petrol and rations were seized. Several Italians tried to surrender. Most were told to get lost but one group were persistent. Without resources to look after prisoners the Northumberland men confiscated their boots and left them standing in the desert, looking utterly miserable. Had this all been part of a planned strategy it could have helped to turn the battle by driving towards the Axis rear. But having smashed through the enemy lines the 50th turned south and in a vast sweep traversed the desert and joined the rest of the Eighth Army heading back towards Cairo and the Suez Canal.

By this point Rommel was jubilant. On 15 June he signalled: 'The battle has been won and the enemy is breaking up.'[2] As his exhausted troops went in pursuit of their retreating enemy there remained one final objective, Tobruk. This port town had been the focal point of three major offensives since June 1940. It was roughly midway between Benghazi and Cairo and its port facilities, modern water filtration plant and warehouses where supplies could be gathered also made it of central strategic importance. The heroic defence of Tobruk during the eight-month siege from April to December 1941 meant its story had become a legend and the 'Rats of Tobruk', as the defenders became known, mostly toughened Australian troops whose faces were darkened by the sun and who were lean and hard after months of privations under siege, stood out from the rest of the Eighth Army. To Churchill, and to Rommel, 'Fortress Tobruk' had acquired a symbolic status. For the British it was a symbol of determined and heroic defence. For Rommel, a symbol of victory over the Allied armies. Without Tobruk, he could not hope to advance on Alexandria, Cairo and Suez.

On 10 June, a week before departing for the US, Churchill had called into Downing Street Major-General John Kennedy, Director of Military Operations in the War Office, and Major-General Francis Davidson, Director of Military Intelligence. Kennedy was a staff officer to his core, efficient, clear-thinking and one who totally believed in the efficacy of planning. He was now committed to organising Britain's army operations in what was often contemptuously dismissed as 'a desk job'. When he and Davidson arrived at Downing Street they were ushered into the Cabinet Room where they found Churchill in a 'onesie' siren suit. Churchill lit a cigar and told Kennedy and Davidson that he wanted to discuss the situation in the Middle East and get the latest information on numbers taking part in the fighting. At least 25,000 men and 350 tanks had been sent to reinforce the Eighth Army since the battle had begun. Auchinleck had sent him figures from Cairo but Churchill wanted to be sure they were accurate. Both generals began to feel that the Prime Minister was losing confidence in 'the Auk'.

Churchill talked for some time about the situation in the Middle East. Like many conversations with the Prime Minister, this one soon became a monologue. Kennedy and Davidson must have wondered why they were there, if Churchill just wanted an audience. In fact, that was not the case. Churchill needed a sounding board. He didn't want yes-men to agree to his every word, he wanted feedback and arguments in response to his. But Kennedy remembered him becoming quite maudlin. 'I don't know what we can do for that Army,' he despaired. 'All our efforts to help them seem to be in vain.' New divisions had been sent out, American Grant tanks had been supplied. 'Nothing seems to help them. And I'm the one who gets his neck wrung when things go wrong.' Kennedy was quite sympathetic to the Prime Minister but was not at all sure how he could help. 'I doubt that Army's offensive spirit,' Churchill went on. It was not the fighting men but their commanders. They were too cautious, too concerned about the Germans coming in by the back door. Fear of failure was leading to caution. And indecision was resulting in failure.[3]

In the days following this meeting a series of signals passed between the Prime Minister and his commander-in-chief in Cairo. On 14 June, Churchill cabled Auchinleck: 'As long as Tobruk is held no serious enemy advance into Egypt is possible.'[4] Auchinleck replied the following day: 'I have no intention whatever of giving up Tobruk.' And he made it clear that he had passed this instruction on to Ritchie.[5] Both men recognised the strategic and symbolic value of holding the Libyan port town.

Back in the Western Desert, once again Rommel was reorganising his depleted resources. With impressive speed, on 16 June his panzers had re-formed to begin an assault upon El Adem, about 10 miles south of Tobruk. General Ritchie told his men to hold on as reinforcements were being rushed out from Cairo. An armoured brigade fought staunchly at Sidi Rezegh to the east but was given a severe mauling by the German 88mm anti-tank guns. Within twenty-four hours there were only forty-eight tanks still in fighting mode. Early on the morning of 17 June, Rommel's panzers moved through what remained of the British line. By the following day the Afrika Korps and the Italian Ariete Division had 'Fortress Tobruk' surrounded. British units continued to harass his troops but were little more than pinpricks in his side. Sergeant Albert Martin, a rifleman in the Rifle Brigade, was in one of these units. Feeling they were up against far stronger enemy troops, Martin wrote in his diary, 'Everything has been a jumble. Does anyone at the top know what they are doing?'[6]

Tobruk garrisons had plenty of experience of holding out under siege. This time there was no reason to imagine the situation would be any different. The garrison there was substantial. In terms of fighting men it contained a South African division, a tank brigade with about sixty tanks, and two additional brigades of infantry, an Indian and a Guards brigade that included the Coldstreams. In addition, there were three regiments of field and two regiments of medium artillery. This amounted to a force of about 35,000 men supported by 2,000 vehicles. They were well supplied with 1.5 million gallons of petrol, a vast quantity of ammunition including 130,000 rounds for the 25-pounder artillery guns, and at least three million ration packs. These were the supplies that had been brought up over previous months to support the big push into Cyrenaica.

However, this embarrassment of riches disguised a less than happy reality. The garrison was under the command of the South African Major-General Hendrik Klopper. He had been a brigade commander until a recent promotion and had relatively little experience of desert warfare. Forced back into Tobruk, he was amazed to discover that no comprehensive contingency plan had been made for the defence of the city. Although the centre was fairly small the defensive perimeter outside the town extended for about 30 miles of trenches, fox holes, casements, barbed wire and minefields. These had been well maintained and fiercely fought over during the long siege in 1941. But lengthy stretches of the perimeter had fallen into decline over the winter since lifting the siege. Several large gaps existed in the minefields surrounding it. But the new defenders did not have the mine charts from their predecessors to show the layout of the minefields.[7] Equally worrying was that the Desert Air Force had been forced to withdraw from all its forward air bases. Tobruk was now out of range of its fighter aircraft. Meanwhile, the centre of the city was a scene of total carnage. Most of the buildings constructed by the Italians during their period of colonisation had been destroyed in the previous rounds of fighting. Everywhere there was rubble, remains and endless dust. The harbour was full of the rusty relics of ships that had been sunk during the dozens of air raids on the city. It was not an inspiring scene and it encouraged a negative atmosphere. While all non-essential troops were being evacuated, units coming out of the retreat from Gazala were ordered into the city and allocated to defend a part of the perimeter. Confused as to what the plan was, these men did not have the steely determination of their predecessors, the 'Rats of Tobruk' who had fought to defend every inch of ground. Rumours spread rapidly. A reporter noted that the feeling among the hastily assembled defenders was that 'they had been left in the lurch, that they were being used as a rearguard in an action that was already doomed'.[8] The commander of a Royal Artillery field battery said that his men felt as though they had been caught with 'their pants down' without time to 'put their defences in[to] first class shape'.[9] Meanwhile Eighth Army headquarters, 150 miles away, issued a communiqué listing the strengths of the garrison with resources to withstand a siege of three months, concluding, 'We hope, therefore, that Tobruk should be able to hold out until operations for relief are completed.'[10]

It was, inevitably, Rommel who mounted the first assault. At dawn on Saturday 20 June, wave after wave of Stuka dive bombers attacked the south-east perimeter of the city's defences. The Luftwaffe pulled into action almost every aircraft in North Africa it could muster for this assault, with aircraft also sent from Greece and Crete. The shattering raid was an immense blow to the resolve of the defenders. In further bombing of the city centre Klopper's headquarters was hit. He had to move to an alternative location. During the transfer, radio communications between the commander and his senior officers were lost. In the south-east corner, after the bombers came the sappers, clearing a route through the minefields. Then came the panzers, followed by the infantry. The defenders lacked the heart to make a resolute stand. By mid-morning the German attackers had advanced about a mile and a half inside the perimeter line.

British tanks outside the besieged fortress came out from Sidi Rezegh to challenge the German and Italian forces. But it proved a half-hearted affair. By mid-afternoon their counter-attack had been beaten off. By early evening more and more panzers and infantry were flooding through the gap in the Tobruk perimeter. The South Africans in the south-west corner of the city had not yet fired their weapons but now found enemy troops behind them. Panzers advanced into the heart of the city and opened fire on vessels in the harbour. Two naval destroyers made a hasty exit out of what remained of the port. British demolition squads began destroying ammunition and petrol. Where it could be ignited the petrol went up, filling the air with giant black plumes of smoke; elsewhere it was just poured into the sand. Klopper struggled to keep control but it was clear that total disaster was quickly befalling the Tobruk garrison. At 8 p.m. he sent a short message. 'My HQ surrounded,' he said, ending, 'Am holding out but I do not know for how long.' Six hours later he sent another message to Ritchie that he was trying to evacuate whatever mobile troops he could but that further defence was hopeless. He signed off: 'Will resist to last man and last round.'[11]

In the early morning of 21 June Klopper changed his mind. He realised that there was only one possible outcome and that continued fighting would cause unnecessary sacrifice. He sent a final signal: 'Situation shambles. Terrible casualties would result. Am doing the worst.'[12] He ordered a white flag to be raised. Some of the South African troops in the west who had still barely even opened fire in the battle could not believe the order to surrender and refused to obey. Desultory fighting went on in the confusion for the rest of the day. Some men managed to get away. Nearly 400 Coldstream Guards made it out of the city. Two of Klopper's staff officers escaped in his car. In total about 2,000 men managed somehow to escape. But by early evening it was all over. The Cameron Highlanders and the Gurkha Rifles were the last troops to raise their hands and give themselves up. The Germans were in control. Fortress Tobruk had survived eight months of siege in 1941 but had fallen to Rommel in June 1942 in a weekend.

Moreover, the Desert Fox had captured the largest treasure trove of supplies that had ever been seized in the desert war. Despite the demolition of quantities of petrol and ammunition, enough was left to fuel the Afrika Korps advance all the way to the Suez Canal. Thousands of captured vehicles would soon have a German cross painted on them and were recruited to assist in the Axis advance. German losses had amounted to just over 3,300 men, although there had been a high proportion of officers killed or wounded. On the day following the surrender of Tobruk, a delighted Hitler promoted Rommel to the most senior rank in the German Army of Field Marshal. But Rommel took no time off to savour his victory. He issued a declaration to his men: 'Soldiers of the Panzer Army Afrika! Now for the complete destruction of the enemy. We will not rest until we have shattered the last remnants of the British Eighth Army.'[13] He left four battalions of Italians behind to handle the prisoners, corral the supplies that had been abandoned and begin the process of reopening the port. And with what was left of his Afrika Korps he headed east in hot pursuit of the rest of the Eighth Army.

On the morning of 19 June Churchill had flown up from Washington to New York State where he was met by the President. They spent two very pleasant days together admiring the Roosevelt family estate at Hyde Park and having preliminary one-to-one discussions. The President drove the Prime Minister around his majestic grounds in a limousine that had been adapted to cope with his disability. Churchill was particularly impressed by the wonderful view over the Hudson river from the bluffs of Hyde Park but anxious that

Churchill and Roosevelt at the White House, June 1942. During
their meetings Churchill received some humiliating news.

the President in his unusual vehicle should not drive too near
the edge. On the evening of 20 June they took the presidential
train to Washington and Churchill was once again put up in
the suite in the White House he had lived in at the beginning
of the year.

The following morning, Churchill accompanied by
Generals Ismay and Brooke went to join Roosevelt and Harry
Hopkins in the President's study. They had not got far into
their discussion about future strategies when a messenger
came in and handed a note on a pink piece of ticker tape paper
to the President. He read it and passed it to the Prime Minister
without comment. Churchill looked at the note, which said
'Tobruk has surrendered with twenty-five thousand men
taken prisoner'. Churchill simply could not believe what he

had read. He sent Ismay to phone London immediately to find out what was happening. Ismay came back a few minutes later with verification that news had just come in from Alexandria of the surrender. Churchill was overcome. He later wrote, 'This was one of the heaviest blows I can recall during the war. Not only were its military effects grievous, but it had affected the reputation of the British armies.' At Singapore 85,000 men had surrendered to a far smaller number of Japanese. Now a large group (the actual number was 33,000) had laid down their arms to an Axis force of perhaps half their number. Churchill recalled, 'I did not attempt to hide from the President the shock I had received. It was a bitter moment. Defeat is one thing. Disgrace is another.'[14]

There was silence for a few moments in the President's study. But when he spoke, there was no reproach or complaint from Roosevelt. He simply asked, 'What can we do to help?' Churchill, without prompting, asked for Sherman tanks, the latest model off the American production lines, to be sent to the Middle East. The President asked General Marshall to join them. Marshall explained that the first of the new Shermans had just been issued to the US 1st Armoured Division, but that they would be recalled at once and shipped to the Middle East in the fastest vessels that were available. The Americans were good to their word and 300 Shermans were soon on their way, along with a hundred self-propelled 105mm guns. Although a ship carrying some of the engines was sunk by a U-boat off Bermuda, a second ship with replacement engines was soon dispatched. Their presence would greatly help the situation in the desert war later in the year.[15] The news of the surrender could not have occurred at a more embarrassing, even humiliating, moment for the British Prime Minister and his team in Washington. But the President and his chief of staff proved both magnanimous and generous in their response. It was a tremendous display of support from the US and of unity between the two allies.

In the desert, morale was, not surprisingly, low. The news was whispered from man to man: 'Tobruk has fallen.' Men were reprimanded by their officers for predicting that Rommel would be in Cairo in a week. Everywhere there was the sense that the latest defeat had been a crushing blow.[16] The incidence of sickness and of battle fatigue (that is, psychological trauma, or what had been called 'shell shock' in the First World War) increased by just over 50 per cent in a month.[17] Morale reports within the army picked up evidence of a tendency to 'criticise the war effort and general conduct of operations'. Auchinleck reported to the War Office that one of his 'main tasks' had been 'to study the psychology of this very mixed array we call an Army', and that he had to 'spend most of my time doing this in the hope that it will not disintegrate altogether'.[18]

With the support of his senior commanders, Auchinleck made a formal request to the War Cabinet that the death penalty be reintroduced for 'desertion' or 'cowardice' on the field of battle.[19] It was not the first time a Second World War army commander had requested the reintroduction of this measure that had been used in the First World War. But the stories of those 'shot at dawn', as the well-known phrase had it, made the punishment extremely unpopular with the public, and the Labour government had abolished the use of military firing squads in 1930. When Auchinleck's request came before the War Cabinet it was quickly turned down. Churchill did not support the measure and there was zero prospect of the Labour members of the coalition government going along with it.[20] But the whole incident reveals the appalling state of morale in the Eighth Army in the spring and summer of 1942.

Ironically, the capitulation of Tobruk had another unintended consequence. Hitler decided that after Rommel's triumph there was no need to launch an invasion of Malta. The Italians, from Mussolini down, desperately wanted to invade the island and finally remove the threat to Mediterranean shipping and supply lines. But the prospect of reaching the Suez Canal was far too attractive for both the German and Italian leaders. Mussolini flew to Libya and dreamed of posing for photographers alongside the canal after its capture. At a meeting with the Italian commanders in his desert headquarters on 26 June, Rommel stated that if all went well he would be in Cairo in four days. He insisted that the Luftwaffe must be left to support his advance and not return to Sicily to renew their assault upon Malta. The Italians agreed to go along with this. So, bizarrely, the fall of Tobruk saved Malta.[21] And, certain of the defeat of the Eighth Army, Hitler lost interest in the desert war and felt he could now concentrate again on his major obsession, the war on the Eastern Front.

In Britain, the response to news of the surrender of Tobruk was one of dismay. Propaganda had built up the Libyan port town into another impregnable fortress. And the collapse in confidence was suitably great. The *Manchester Guardian* asked: 'Why were our hopes so consistently raised?' It reported that everywhere the talk was 'what had happened to its defence and defenders that it fell so easily'. The paper concluded, 'Not since the fall of Singapore has there been so much expression of public feeling as over the Tobruk disaster. The difference is that the feeling now is anger and irritation rather than dismay and depression.'[22] The *Observer* wrote, 'Britain feels shamed in the eyes of its enemies, its Allies and the neutral fringe; and not only shamed – angry and resentful ... The British people are bewildered as well as angry.'[23] A Mass Observation diarist noted, 'Faces are unanimously long about it, two people said they thought we were facing 100 years of war. One said "Do you think we can win?" '[24] In her corner shop in Yorkshire, one diarist reported a conversation in which she overheard a customer saying, ' "There's something jolly rotten somewhere. We should have put up more of a show than this. What must the

Russians think of us now? What's the good of all this blah-blah about a second front when we can't cope with what we have on our own plates now?" ... M said "Well we couldn't fight on so many fronts and help all the Empire and raid Germany and help Russia and do all successfully" ... Depressed all day and very angry ... Mr D thinks the Generals are not to blame for the Tobruk disaster, but lack of equipment ... Ma said there was not a single cheerful item in the newspaper and gloomily wondered if we were going to win the war after all.'[25]

In the desert, the next chapter of the fighting quickly began to unfold. Exhilarated by their success, Rommel and his Panzerarmee were in close pursuit of the retreating Eighth Army in what became known as the 'Gazala Gallop'. Ritchie decided not to attempt to stop him at the Egyptian border but to retreat further east to the town of Mersa Matruh, about 150 miles from Tobruk. Appreciating the significance of the surrender at Tobruk, Auchinleck offered to resign as Commander-in-Chief Middle East but this was not accepted by Brooke and the chiefs of staff. But knowing that someone had to go, Auchinleck rather reluctantly, but in retrospect very belatedly, removed Ritchie as commander of Eighth Army on 25 June. He decided to take personal control of the situation at the front. The first thing he did was to abandon the defensive line assembling at Mersa Matruh. He felt he did not have sufficient armour to hold the rapidly advancing Panzerarmee. He decided on a new plan. The forces of the Eighth Army would harass the Axis troops as they advanced while conducting what he described as a 'fluid defence'. He would pull back another 100 miles to a small railway halt at a place called El Alamein. This was only 60 miles from Alexandria. Here he would stand and fight.

El Alamein was unusual in the desert war. There was no way of outflanking a defence mounted here. To the north was the Mediterranean. Thirty-eight miles to the south of the sea was a giant natural feature, the Qattara Depression. This huge expanse was a rare feature in the desert. Much of it was below sea level and consisted of quicksands, salt marshes and sand dunes that were totally impassable. Northern stretches of it were made up of steeply rising and descending cliffs that were again impossible for armoured vehicles to cross. In theory it would have been possible to bypass it by trekking several hundred miles to the south but Rommel's forces did not have the petrol for this and would in any case have exposed themselves to merciless attacks from the air. El Alamein marked the narrowest point between the Qattara and the sea. For the first time in the desert war there really was a front where battle had to be joined. There was, literally, no way around it.

The retreat from Mersa Matruh was chaotic. The bulk of the Eighth Army reached El Alamein on 30 June. Rommel's troops arrived there the following day. The field marshal had driven his men forward with characteristic vigour. Many German soldiers complained that they had not even had time to have a swim in the Mediterranean. But morale among the British and Commonwealth forces was at rock bottom. Assessments by officers in different units reported that 'indiscreet and defeatist talk' was rife among the troops. 'This disaster goes on and on,' wrote another. 'For no good cause chaps sort of say "Where do we retreat to next?"' But Auchinleck offered new energy and determination. Most soldiers blamed Ritchie for recent army failures. Many were reported to hold the view that at the top 'someone has blundered badly'. Officers who had to censor letters home by their men reported that many wrote that Rommel was a far better general than any they had in the Eighth Army. But now men were cheered that the commander-in-chief had taken command. Auchinleck issued a message to all troops that the enemy 'thinks we are a broken army'. He concluded, 'Show him where he gets off.'[26]

It's difficult to overstate how much depended on the engagement to come. If Rommel smashed the line at El Alamein, as he had smashed every line he had come up against since January, then Alexandria and its naval base, along with Cairo and the Suez Canal with its massive supply depots, would be next. This would make the fall of Tobruk look like kids' play. Rommel could then cross the Sinai into Palestine and Syria. With Jerusalem and Damascus under his control, the Third Reich would dominate the Middle East with its vast oil reserves and in addition would control the Jewish national homeland with all the horror that would unleash. Next would come Baghdad and Iraq. If this was not bad enough, Russia's southern flank would be opened up to Axis forces. British control of the Mediterranean would be lost. And all the effort Britain had put into fighting the Axis armies would have been in vain. As one seasoned observer put it, 'It would force England back to the dark days of the Battle of Britain.'[27] On 30 June a secret American intelligence assessment predicted that the Germans would be in Cairo in a week.[28] Rommel was on the brink of one of the greatest victories of the war.

The Royal Navy left Alexandria at the end of June. Cairo was put under an evening curfew. In the blocks of offices that made up the huge Middle East GHQ and in the British Embassy on the Nile, officials began to burn papers and all secret documents that were not to fall into the enemy's hands. For a day, parts of the city were covered with burnt pieces of paper; it became known as 'Ash Wednesday'. All non-essential personnel were evacuated. Trains to Palestine were packed with people hauling all the belongings they could carry with them. Plans were being laid for a string of defensive lines right back to the canal and preparations were made for GHQ to evacuate to Gaza. There was even talk of flooding the Nile delta. A panic was spreading across the city. Only the Egyptians themselves seemed unperturbed. Although many had done well under British domination, they reckoned they would probably get along with the Germans and Italians.

The Cairo Stock Exchange slumped but did not crash. And the simple fellahin, the farmers who tilled the soil of the Nile delta and the labourers who provided all the services needed in a bustling city, seemed quite fatalistic about the departure of the British. Life for them was hard and would remain hard whoever was in charge.

But by this point the military pendulum was swinging again, as was always the case in the desert war. At El Alamein, the Eighth Army were only a few miles – about three hours' drive – from their sources of supply. The Desert Air Force was able to fly from well-equipped and established airfields. By contrast, Rommel and his Afrika Korps had been fighting continuously for six weeks. His men were utterly exhausted, shattered by the ceaseless effort and heavy fighting of the last month. Now they were hundreds of miles from their supply bases of Tripoli and Benghazi, reliant upon food, ammunition and fuel being brought up in convoys of lorries. If a tank broke down there was a long wait for spare parts. And the German and Italian drivers were not finding it easy to drive the hundreds of captured British and Commonwealth trucks. When a captured lorry developed a fault no one had the parts to fix it. The Luftwaffe that had provided immense support in the battles around Gazala and Tobruk was now unable to offer relief. The RAF once again achieved aerial superiority and attacked the Axis troops with wave after wave of bombers, all supported by fighters. Now it was the turn of the morale of Rommel's troops to drop.

Rommel was down to a tiny number of battle-worthy tanks. The Afrika Korps had about fifty-five and the Italians only about fifteen. Despite huge losses of more than a thousand tanks at Gazala, the British and Commonwealth forces had slightly more than twice the number of the Panzerarmee and more were arriving from the Canal Zone. Rommel attacked the line at El Alamein head on but this time his troops were too exhausted to make any headway. By the evening of 3 July, he had lost the first Battle of El Alamein. The Axis advance had finally been halted.

Auchinleck was eager to take advantage of his sudden superiority. During the course of July he launched four separate attacks on Axis forces. But all of them failed to dislodge the enemy. There were still several problems within the Eighth Army. The coordination between the armoured units and the infantry was abysmal. Every time there was an advance, Axis forces would counter-attack, often on the flank, isolating the infantry who would be dreadfully exposed. Losses among the infantry were severe in some units. The New Zealander troops were especially feared by the Germans for their warrior spirit. But a New Zealand brigade, fresh to the fighting, suffered particularly heavy losses on 15 July. They attacked and broke clean through the German lines but the British armour failed to turn up to support them. Instead German armour got in among them and killed or captured hundreds. One New Zealand officer displayed such gallantry before being captured that he was awarded a Bar to his VC.[29] An angry New Zealander wrote, 'the Tommy tanks were sitting about two miles back waiting orders!!! The crews out frying sausages while our lads were being torn to pieces … to see the best troops in the world slaughtered like sheep because of those Pommie bastards.'[30]

By the end of July the desert war had come to a standstill. The Axis advance had run out of steam. But the Allied attacks had failed to force them back from their advanced positions. Morale in the Eighth Army hit a new low. The numbers reporting sick or suffering from battle fatigue rose again. By mid-July more than 1,700 men were missing from their units, most of whom had deserted. In some cases officers were reporting bad cases of depression among their men and that troops were 'beginning to lose interest in the war, to some in fact the reason for the war itself has become dimmed'.[31] There was something else that was worrying the British commanders in Cairo and in London. Since Rommel had launched his offensive at Gazala in late May, the Eighth Army had lost 1,700 men killed and 6,000 wounded. But an incredible 57,000 were classed as missing, most of whom had been taken prisoner. This was far more than could be accounted for by armoured units failing to protect the infantry. It was a case of surrender on an epidemic scale. Churchill wrote, 'This extraordinary disproportion between killed and wounded on the one hand and prisoners on the other revealed that something must have happened of an unpleasant character.'[32] The Army Council put it more clearly when it concluded that 'the capitulation at Singapore, the fall of Tobruk and the large proportion of unwounded prisoners in the operations in Cyrenaica' suggested that the army was in a condition that did 'not appear to accord with its old traditions'.[33] How was the Eighth Army going to regain its fighting spirit? Was victory over a weakened and overstretched foe ever going to be possible? Or was there something fundamentally wrong with the British Army as a whole? Why was it constantly losing land battles on different fronts? Something dramatic needed to be done.

15

Censure

Following the humiliation and disgrace of the surrender of Tobruk, Churchill and his entourage spent another five days in the United States. The meetings with President Roosevelt ranged over many topics. The two leaders discussed the exchange of scientific information about the possibility of creating a bomb through nuclear fission. The United States agreed to take over the task of constructing an atomic bomb and in September 1942 launched the enormous Manhattan Project in which eventually more than 120,000 scientists spent nearly three years harnessing the power of the atom. The Americans came to regard the bomb as entirely their own creation although early work on the nature and feasibility of its construction had been carried out in the UK. This would later be the cause of a bitter dispute, but in June 1942 there was total agreement between the two leaders to push on with atomic research in the US as the Allies wanted to find the way to build an atom bomb before Hitler did.[1]

Of far more immediate impact was the discussion about how best to attack the Nazi war machine in 1942. The American position was clear: they wanted a major land and sea assault against occupied Europe, probably in the autumn. The British also said they wanted this but only if it could be certain of success. As had been made clear to General Marshall during his April visit to London, an attack by six or eight divisions on northern France in September could not succeed unless the Germans were 'utterly demoralised', perhaps by a catastrophic defeat in Russia, which was extremely unlikely. A significant landing would require an estimated 7,000 landing craft. There were only a few hundred available. The transportation of a single armoured division required forty-five troop ships plus all their escort vessels. Operation Bolero, the transport of tens of thousands of American soldiers to the UK as preparation for a cross-Channel invasion, was still in its early phase. There was simply not enough shipping, landing craft or men available yet to build up a sufficient force for a landing in occupied Europe. And none of the forces available, naval or military, had trained for an amphibious assault. 'The British Government do not favour an operation that is certain to lead to disaster,' Churchill told Roosevelt. But that raised again the question, if no major landing in France was possible in 1942, 'Ought we not to be preparing within the general structure of "Bolero" some other operation by which we may gain positions of advantage, and also directly or indirectly to take some of the weight off Russia?' This brought Churchill and his military chiefs back to the idea of an Anglo-American landing in French North-West Africa later in the year.[2]

Accompanying every summit between the President and the Prime Minister were meetings between the chiefs of staff of both nations. General Alan Brooke was present in Washington for the first time at these Combined Chiefs of Staff sessions. Both Marshall and Secretary of War Henry Stimson were still pressing for an invasion of northern France but appeared to be convinced that such an operation could not succeed during this year. 'Meeting was I think a success,' Brooke wrote in his diary.[3]

When Churchill and Roosevelt joined the conversations there was continued discussion about future strategy. The transfer of men and materiel from the US to the UK would continue under Bolero. Consideration would still be given to an operation against northern France. A British note of the meeting read: 'If a sound and sensible plan can be contrived we should not hesitate to give effect to it. If, on the other hand, detailed examination shows that, despite all efforts, success is improbable we must be ready with an alternative.' Planning would begin for an operation against French North-West Africa, and 'The possibility of operations in Norway and the Iberian peninsula in the autumn and winter of 1942 will also be carefully considered.'[4] The British appeared to be making ground against the American position.

Before the summit was complete, several other meetings took place in Washington, a city which the British found intensely hot and steamy in the mid-summer. Churchill, who had the luxury of an air-conditioned room in the White House, was introduced for the first time to Generals Dwight D. Eisenhower and Mark Clark, who would go on to lead Allied forces in the Mediterranean and in northern Europe. They both made an excellent impression on the Prime Minister. The President and the Prime Minister discussed with their naval chiefs the need for more escort vessels to try to reduce the losses in the Atlantic and the need for more effective convoying of ships in the Caribbean. There was also a meeting of the Pacific War Council in which Admiral Ernest King laid out his preferences for the war in the Far East. There were still tensions between the British and American positions and British prestige had taken such a blow with the surrender at Tobruk that it was impossible to finalise a decision about future strategy while the Prime Minister was still in the US.

After a few days in Washington, Churchill and Brooke were taken to Camp Jackson in South Carolina to see a military display mounted by two divisions who were in training before being sent to Europe. The display featured a parachute jump by a trainee battalion of paratroopers. Churchill was fascinated and saw the makings of a great army that would come to Britain's aid in future battles for Europe. Brooke was far more critical. What he saw was a military machine desperately trying to scale up at speed from a small professional peacetime army of a couple of hundred thousand to a wartime force of many millions.

'What do you think [of the display]?' Churchill asked Brooke.

'To put these troops against German troops would be murder,' replied the chief of staff.[5]

Time would tell which of them would be proved right.

But another shadow was falling across the visit to Washington. The capitulation at Tobruk had produced a wave of despair in Britain. In the House of Commons, once again questions were raised about Churchill's leadership. During a lunch with the President, a press chief arrived with a set of New York newspapers to show the Prime Minister. From them screamed a range of headlines: 'Anger in England', 'Tobruk Fall May Bring Change of Government', and 'Churchill to be Censured'. It was suggested that the Prime Minister should return home immediately. Later that night Churchill telephoned Anthony Eden to enquire about the situation in Westminster. It was 5 a.m. in London when the call was put through. Eden assured the Prime Minister that although there was much grief he had not heard a single word of serious censure. 'No doubt there [will] be blame for the Government but so far nothing [has] happened to shake us,' Eden told Churchill.[6]

On 25 June, the day that Ritchie was sacked as commander of the Eighth Army, Churchill sent a personal message to Auchinleck. 'I hope the crisis will lead to all uniformed personnel in the Delta and all available loyal manpower being raised to the highest fighting condition,' he told him. 'Every fit male should be made to fight and die for victory.'

He concluded by making it clear how important the Prime Minister believed the struggle taking place in North Africa was: 'You are in the same kind of situation as we should be if England were invaded, and the same intense drastic spirit should reign.'[7]

That evening, Churchill said goodbye to Roosevelt at the White House and with Brooke, Ismay and his entourage drove to Baltimore where the BOAC Boeing Clipper awaited them. Harry Hopkins went with Churchill to see him off. As he left to board the luxury flying boat he turned to Hopkins and remarked, 'Now for England, home, and – a beautiful row.'[8]

Despite Eden's reassurances, the House of Commons had indeed erupted over the failure at Tobruk. 'Chips' Channon noted in his diary that he found 'an atmosphere of disappointment, bewildered rage and uneasiness' in the House when news of the surrender came through. He thought the news might 'endanger or even bring down the spineless Government'. Then there was talk of a Vote of Censure against the government, and the lobbies 'hummed'. Channon wrote, 'everyone I saw was suddenly as excited as an aged virgin being led to her seducer's bed'. One MP told him, 'When your doctor is killing you, the first thing to do is to get rid of him.'[9] On 25 June a motion was put down, 'That this House, while paying tribute to the heroism and endurance of the Armed Forces of the Crown in circumstances of exceptional difficulty, has no confidence in the central direction of the war.' Forty-eight hours later, on the day Churchill landed back in Britain, news came in of a humiliating defeat in a by-election at Maldon in Essex, caused by the death of the sitting Conservative member. The government candidate received only half the number of votes of Tom Driberg, the Independent Labour candidate.[10] It is not unusual for governments to lose by-elections mid-term, but if this was an indication of the loss of support for the government in the country at large while facing a critical moment in a world war, it was severely worrying.

At a time when Rommel looked as though he would sweep into Cairo and there would be yet another catastrophic capitulation, even the suggestion that the House had lost confidence in Churchill's leadership for the second time in six months made the Prime Minister want to bring the censure issue to a vote. He was confident of winning the vote, as he had been in January, and felt that a clear victory in Parliament was the best way to reassure the world that he was very much in charge. Also, he knew that the Cabinet would give him complete support. This was vital in that he led a national coalition, so all major parties would be committed to him. The defeat of a censure motion was the best way to display that he *did* have the confidence of the House.

The Vote of Censure debate began on 1 July, the day Rommel's forces arrived at El Alamein in pursuit of the retreating Eighth Army. The vote was proposed by Sir John Wardlaw-Milne, a senior member of the Conservative Party and chair of an influential House committee. 'It is surely clear to any civilian that the series of disasters of the past few months, and indeed of the past two years, is due to fundamental defects in the central administration of the war,' said Wardlaw-Milne, pointing the finger clearly at Churchill.[11] He went through the sorry saga of one defeat following another, of stories of the constant under-provision of resources for the armed forces, of poor strategic decision-making and of the recent run of disasters in Libya. Wardlaw-Milne stressed in his opening speech that he wanted the position of Prime Minister to be separated from that of Minister of Defence. 'I want a strong and independent man appointing his generals and his admirals and so on,' he argued, repeating what many members felt. The principal difficulty facing any opposition movement was who to propose as a replacement for Churchill.

All was going well until Wardlaw-Milne nominated His Royal Highness the Duke of Gloucester. Many MPs burst into laughter at such a preposterous suggestion as putting a royal non entity in charge of the nation's military effort. Chips Channon saw Churchill's face light up as the case against him looked suddenly absurd. 'He knew now that he was saved, and poor Wardlaw-Milne never quite regained the hearing of the House,' Channon wrote.[12]

The motion was seconded by Admiral Sir Roger Keyes, who had worked closely with Churchill in the First World War and knew how he operated. He argued that instead of Churchill having his power taken away from him, he should have greater authority to override his chiefs of staff. One MP aired the general sense of puzzlement by interrupting Keyes with the comment, 'I am rather confused at the course the Debate is taking. I understood ... that a Vote of Censure [has been moved] on the ground that the Prime Minister had interfered unduly in the direction of the war. The Seconder seems to be seconding because the Prime Minister has not sufficiently interfered in the direction of the war.' Keyes responded, 'It would be a deplorable disaster if the Prime Minister had to go.' Clearly the opposition had no unified case against the Prime Minister.

Several members spoke out during the debate on the poor quality of British equipment. The 2-pounder anti-tank gun came in for much criticism. Comparison was made with the far superior German 88mm weapon. There was also criticism of the weak armour of many of the tanks with which the army went to war, the Matildas, Crusaders and Valentines. There were questions as to why the RAF lacked a dive bomber to compare with those used so effectively by the Germans and the Japanese. Other MPs criticised the generals who led the army who were too slow to adapt and improve their thinking. The most remarkable contribution to the debate came from a serving officer, Major Stephen Furness, the member for Sunderland, who had rarely spoken in the House because he had been away on active duty. Speaking in uniform, he criticised the 'appalling military record of the British Army ... [that] has never won a single campaign against the German Army'. He, too, criticised some of the weapons with which men were being asked to fight, such as 'tanks with turrets which men cannot get into' and guns which take so long to develop that the Germans have outclassed them by the time they arrive. But he was also critical of the military leadership and the fact that 'we seem to shut our men up in places like Singapore and Tobruk, and then the general hauls down his flag. It is causing enormous harm in the Army, and it also has a psychological effect.' Such words were a stinging rebuke coming from a middle-ranking officer with direct experience of fighting the war.

The most considered attack came from Aneurin Bevan, the left-wing Labour MP, who opened the second day of the censure debate. To accusations that such a vote would undermine the morale of troops at the front, Bevan responded, 'It would be a serious thing if the soldiers in the field could not hear any voices raised on their behalf in the House of Commons,' and that it was the duty of MPs to ensure that they were given 'the right weapons with which to fight'.[13] Claiming that Churchill was a wily politician but a poor war leader, Bevan came up with his best lines: 'The Prime Minister wins debate after debate and loses battle after battle. The country is beginning to say that he fights debates like a war and the war like a debate.' Bevan argued that the strategy of running the war was wrong and this was the Prime Minister's fault. He had been in office for two years and there had been nothing but failure after failure. And he too argued that the weapons the troops were being asked to fight with were wrong and that was generally the fault of the entire government. He was especially critical of senior figures in the army, which he claimed was 'class ridden'. He taunted the army that able men were held back by less able commanders. He joked that if Rommel was in the British Army he would not have progressed to a higher rank than sergeant. It was a cogent attack upon Churchill and his government, an oratorical crescendo that reached a peak when he declared of the people of Britain, 'This is a proud and brave race, and it is feeling humiliated. It cannot stand the holding out of Sebastopol for months and the collapse of Tobruk in 26 hours. It cannot stand the comparison between these lost battles, not lost by lack of courage, but by lack of vision at the top. It cannot stand this; it is a proud and valiant country, and it wants leadership. It is getting words, not leadership.'

Another cogent attack was made by Leslie Hore-Belisha who spoke with the authority of having been Secretary of War in the late 1930s. He asked how could the country place reliance on 'judgements that have so repeatedly turned out to be misguided?' He argued that 'If situations and prospects are constantly misjudged, neither the tactics nor the equipment can ever suffice to meet them. If you persist in under-estimating your enemy and over-estimating yourself, you are courting disaster.' By quoting Churchill's positive and encouraging statements over the last two years and contrasting them with the 'catastrophic' outcome of events, Hore-Belisha produced a rounded critique of the Prime Minister for persistently over-promising and underperforming.

Churchill himself wound up the debate on the second day with a ninety-minute speech. He pointed out the damage that such a debate would do to Britain's friends around the world and how much encouragement it would give to the nation's enemies. But he insisted, 'I am in favour of this freedom, which no other country would use, or dare to use, in times of mortal peril such as those through which we are passing. But the story must not end there, and I make now my appeal to the House of Commons to make sure that it does not end there.' He criticised the press for stirring things up and causing more damage internationally, especially when he had been in Washington. He said the American leaders were not perturbed by such reports because 'our American friends are not fair-weather friends. They never expected that this war would be short or easy, or that its course would not be chequered by lamentable misfortunes.' He praised the heroic people of Malta, defended the actions of his generals in Libya and spoke of 'the terrible hazards and unforeseeable accidents of battle'. He talked of the struggle to fight in the Far East, to defend India, to battle in North Africa and to send supplies to Russia at the same time, while simultaneously suffering losses at sea.

Harold Nicolson heard Churchill speaking and wrote in his diary, 'He makes a long statement which really amounts to the fact that we had more men and more tanks and more guns than Rommel, and that he cannot understand why we were badly beaten.'[14] Chips Channon was more hostile: 'His magic had no magic for me. We might as well have had Macaulay or even Caruso as Prime Minister. He skated around dangerous corners, and by clever evasion managed to ignore the question as to whether he had ordered Tobruk to be held. Nevertheless he had his usual effect of intoxicating his listeners.'[15]

The defeat of the motion was certain, and the moment did not require his finest oratory. Churchill summed up, 'After all, we are still fighting for our lives, and for causes dearer than life itself. We have no right to assume that victory is certain; it will be certain only if we do not fail in our duty . . . the duty of the House of Commons is to sustain the Government or to change the Government. If it cannot change it, it should sustain it. There is no working middle course in war-time.' When the House divided, 25 voted for the motion of censure and 475 supported the government. There were cheers in the House.

Once again Churchill had survived, even though the number who were prepared to stand up and be counted against him had risen from January.

The following morning Churchill received a short message from President Roosevelt that read: 'Good for you.' And he received a longer message from Harry Hopkins: 'Those who run for cover at every reverse, the timid and faint of heart, will have no part in winning the war. Your strength, tenacity and everlasting courage will see Britain through.' 'Thank you so much, my friend,' Churchill replied. 'I hope one day I shall have something more solid to report.'[16]

There was nothing 'more solid' to report yet. It was on the evening of 4 July that Admiral Pound gave the fateful order for convoy PQ17 to scatter. When only ten merchant ships out of thirty-four made it through to Archangel, the War Cabinet decided that there could be no further convoys to the Soviet Union in the summer months. It was another reason for Britain to hold its head in shame.

Around the country people were despondent. 'Civilians have had to listen to the monotonous falling of British arms and strongholds abroad while being harassed at home by rising prices, dwindling business, increasing curtailment of liberty and comfort, and anxiety about their menfolk overseas,' wrote Mollie Panter-Downes in London. 'From what is being said on every bus and train and on every street corner ... it is obvious that millions who a short time back wouldn't have dreamed of criticizing Mr Churchill are now openly criticizing him.'[17] In their monthly review of morale, Mass Observation reported that July was 'a month of discontent and disappointment'. In addition to worries about the war in North Africa, there was concern about a Soviet collapse on the Eastern Front and rumours that big shipping losses were going to bring in new rationing restrictions. A sixty-year-old man reported that there had been a lot of defeatist talk at the beginning of the month during the censure debate. And a fifty-five-year-old man said, 'we've made a balls of it everywhere and can't understand people not taking it more seriously'. Most of those interviewed, however, were pleased that Churchill had won his vote of support in Parliament.[18]

Churchill's leadership was secure, but the business of wartime strategy for the rest of 1942 still had to be resolved. Despite the British hope that the Americans were signed up to a major landing in North West Africa later that year, General Marshall was reluctant to give up on his hope of some kind of assault upon occupied France. There was a lingering feeling among the US chiefs of staff that they were being manipulated by the Brits whose obsession with the Mediterranean was largely down to an outdated imperial concern to protect the Suez Canal and the route to India. The arguments went on among the American chiefs for some time after the summit meetings in Washington. Admiral King, still wanting priority for the Pacific War, argued that if there could be no invasion of Europe in 1942, then maybe the US should avoid Europe altogether for a year and concentrate on the war against Japan.

Marshall was pushing for a limited incursion into northern France, an attack in September on a port like Cherbourg, which troops would occupy for a period of time, sufficient to make the Germans withdraw forces from the Eastern Front. This was referred to as Operation Sledgehammer. Churchill wrote assertively in a note to the chiefs of staff on 5 July, 'No responsible British General, Admiral or Air Marshal is prepared to recommend "Sledgehammer" as a desirable or even a practical operation in 1942. No confirmation of the hopes of additional landing craft from the United States have been obtained. The three American divisions will not be here in time to be trained for the special amphibious work required.' He was further concerned that all Britain's slender resources would be concentrated on defending a bridgehead in France to the detriment of all other actions and that such a diversion would limit the build-up of a major cross-Channel landing in 1943.[19] The chiefs of staff unanimously endorsed the PM's position.

There were still tensions between politicians and the chiefs as the situation in Egypt looked so uncertain. At a Cabinet meeting on 8 July Churchill attacked Auchinleck for a lack of offensive spirit. Brooke wrote in his diary, 'PM in one of his unpleasant moods going back on old ground and asking where the 750,000 men in the M[iddle] E[ast] were, what they were doing and why they were not fighting.' The Prime Minister demanded to know why Auchinleck could only draw on 100,000 fighting men at El Alamein. Brooke tried to explain that the men Auchinleck had were spread across Somalia, Abyssinia, Palestine, Lebanon, Syria, Iraq and Persia and were not all available in the Western Desert. But Churchill did not want to fall out with his chief of staff. Brooke wrote, 'After being thoroughly unpleasant during the Cabinet meeting, with that astounding charm of his he came up to me afterwards and said "I am sorry Brookie if I had to be unpleasant about Auchinleck and the Middle East." '[20] Brooke felt reassured that he still had the support of the PM. The Churchill charm had worked again. However, the Prime Minister was further frustrated when the chiefs of staff opposed his idea of an invasion of northern Norway to seize the airfields from which the Luftwaffe were bombing the Arctic convoys. This was dismissed as being completely unpractical. There was a sense among the politicians that the military were opposed to any new ideas. Sir Alexander Cadogan wrote in his diary, 'Chiefs of Staff have no ideas and oppose everything.' In despair, Churchill had apparently joked, 'We'd better put an advertisement in the papers, asking for ideas!'[21]

The debate about strategy continued at the highest level.

Marshall's patience had been exhausted by the on–off status of the second front planning. After tense exchanges in the White House on 15 July the President sent a delegation of three men, General Marshall, Admiral King and Harry Hopkins, to London with instructions that they must reach an agreement with the British. It did not help that each of the three men wanted something slightly different. Hopkins was broadly sympathetic to Churchill's wish for an invasion of North-West Africa; Marshall wanted the incursion into France, Operation Sledgehammer; and King preferred to concentrate on the Pacific. The President's instructions to his delegation were clear. They were to explore every aspect of Operation Sledgehammer. Then, 'If Sledgehammer is finally and definitely out of the picture, I want you to consider the world situation ... and determine upon another place for US Troops to fight in 1942 ... US ground forces must be put into position to fight German ground forces somewhere in 1942.'[22]

The Downing Street meetings with the Americans began on Monday 20 July 1942. For two days the arguments went back and forth. The British chiefs said a landing at Cherbourg was impossible to sustain and would distract RAF bombers from their offensive against the German war machine. Marshall argued that if the Russians were defeated in 1942 then the Germans would reinforce the north French coast and a landing might be impossible if postponed to 1943. King argued that the limited shipping available ought to be used against the Japanese in the south-west Pacific. Churchill continued to present the case that the true second front in 1942 should be in North-West Africa, that only here could an effective and fruitful attack be delivered in the autumn. On the evening of 22 July the American delegation reported back to the White House that they had been unable to reach a unanimous decision.

It was time for the President to resolve the dispute. The following day Roosevelt sent a message to London that he had made a decision. An attack on France would not take place in 1942. Planning should proceed for a landing in North-West Africa, to be named Operation Torch, before the end of October. As commander-in-chief his word was final. Marshall and King accepted the President's decision with magnanimity. They would follow Roosevelt's ruling without hesitation. Brooke wrote in his diary, 'A very trying week, but it is satisfactory to think that we have got just what we wanted out of the USA Chiefs.'[23] Churchill later wrote that Roosevelt's decision 'was a great joy to me, especially as it came in what seemed to be the darkest hour'.[24]

It was a significant moment. The President had agreed to side with Churchill and the British and not with his own chiefs. America would now be committed to a theatre of war, the Mediterranean, that would eventually draw in about a million men and millions of tons of supplies. Churchill's strategy of encircling the Germans rather than the American option of striking at the enemy head on had won the day.[25] In hindsight, it has to have been the right decision. An invasion of northern France at this point of the war would have been a disaster. Only the Mediterranean, where resources had already been gathered, offered even the slightest opportunity to defeat Axis forces.

After the three-man delegation had returned to Washington, Roosevelt sent Churchill a friendly message. 'The Three Musketeers arrived safely this afternoon,' he began. 'I am of course very happy in the result, and especially in the successful meeting of minds. I cannot help feeling that the past week represented a turning point in the whole war and that now we are on our way shoulder to shoulder.'[26] The President was correct. It was a turning point, and the consequences of the decision made in late July 1942 would affect the shape and the course of the war not only for the rest of that year but for 1943 as well. The Mediterranean, first North Africa, then Sicily and afterwards Italy, would become the second front until the Allies finally had sufficient forces to invade northern France, in June 1944. Out of the 'darkest hour' had come light.

16

'Have You Not Got a Single General Who Can Win Battles?'

As Commander-in-Chief Middle East, General Claude Auchinleck had a vast area for which he was responsible ranging from the Persian Gulf to East Africa. Although in retrospect attention on the conflict in the Middle East has focused on the desert war, at the time there were many other issues to concern the C-in-C. There were constant fears that German paratroopers would land in Palestine, or attempt to seize the Suez Canal, or capture the Persian oilfields. Although Syria had been occupied there was always the possibility of German landings there or in Cyprus, launched from occupied Greece. The C-in-C Middle East had always to fight the desert war while looking over his shoulder. Auchinleck had taken over command of the Eighth Army after the debacle of Tobruk. He had succeeded in holding Rommel at the new line in the desert at El Alamein but had not been able to push him back. From early July he started to cable his boss at the War Office in London, General Sir Alan Brooke, with suggestions for who should replace him as Eighth Army commander so he could once again concentrate on the bigger Middle Eastern picture. Brooke thought the Auk was a fine general but was not convinced of his ability to appoint the right commanders and so decided he must go out to Cairo to supervise the transition to a new general who, with the extra resources and reinforcements arriving in the area, would be charged with finally evicting Rommel's depleted Afrika Korps from Egypt.

Later on the day Churchill survived the Vote of Censure, he and Brooke met a young officer in Downing Street who had asked to see the Prime Minister. He was Captain Julian Amery, the son of Leo Amery, the Secretary of State for India. Young Amery had just returned from Cairo where he reported there was very low morale among the troops, especially in the armoured units who had 'lost confidence in the Command'. Amery said that the Auk was doing all he could to save the situation but there would be a huge boost to morale if Churchill went to Egypt himself to visit the fighting front. Churchill asked what good he could do. 'Your presence among the troops in the battle zone would be enough. It would have an electric effect,' Amery replied.

'You mean, just go around and talk to them?' asked Churchill.

'Yes, to the officers and to the men,' Amery responded.[1]

To Brooke, who was of course acutely aware of military hierarchy, this 'young pup' showed immense impudence addressing the Prime Minister in this informal way. He wrote in his diary, 'The cheek of the young brute was almost more than I could bear.'[2] For Churchill, who was not in any way upset by the direct nature of the report from the young officer, a seed had been planted. He immediately took to the idea of visiting the front in Egypt. As the arguments in favour of a trip grew in his mind, everyone tried to dissuade him. Anthony Eden argued that he would be in the way at a crucial moment in the war and the army in the Middle East did not want to have to bother about the security of the Prime Minister as well as everything else. Brendan Bracken, whose advice Churchill usually listened to, tried to put him off by pointing out the risks involved. The last thing that Brooke, who was planning his own visit, wanted was to have the PM in tow, and he pointed out that there would be no luxury flying boat available to fly him there. The journey would be both uncomfortable and dangerous. But the appeal of the idea of visiting the battle zone in person continued to grow in Churchill's mind. Partly out of vanity, no doubt. But partly because he had a profound concern about the Eighth Army which had been equipped with the best that was available but seemed to be constantly losing battles to the Desert Fox.

The evening after Amery had made his suggestion, Churchill dined with Eden. He was in a maudlin mood despite winning the Vote of Censure overwhelmingly. They discussed the problems of the army and what they saw as a trade union rather than a military outlook within its ranks whereby men wanted to argue things out rather than strictly obey orders. Churchill was disheartened by the criticisms he had heard in the Commons, many of which he knew to be true. He repeatedly said the army had not done as well as it should. 'I am ashamed,' he admitted to Eden.[3] Despite his outward public confidence and aggressive spirit, he was frequently thrown into despair at the lack of success of the armed forces. What particularly upset him was that he felt the old British tradition of heroic resistance against greater odds, of Rorke's Drift, the defence of Mafeking or the Battle of Mons, of drawing glory even out of defeat, was entirely missing in the army of 1942 which threw in the towel so pathetically even against smaller forces at Singapore and Tobruk. Brooke said that on more than one occasion he embarrassed him in Cabinet by demanding openly in front of all the other members, 'Have you not got a single general in that army who can win battles? Have none of them any ideas? Must we constantly lose battles in this way?'[4]

Indeed, it was an entirely justified question to ask about

the British Army in 1942. What *was* wrong with it? Were there institutional failings in its structure? Or were British soldiers not as courageous as they had been in previous generations? Or was it the case that they were badly led? Or just poorly equipped? How low had morale dropped during the series of defeats in 1941 and 1942? It was impossible to see how Britain could hold its head up post-war, even if it survived the war thanks to American support, if every battle its army fought ended in defeat, humiliation and shame.

Churchill himself had an ambivalent relationship with the army. He had trained as a soldier at Sandhurst in the 1890s, had served in several regiments as a young man including the elite 4th Hussars cavalry in India. He had come under fire while battling 'rebels' in the Swat valley in Malakand (recently a Taliban stronghold in north-west Pakistan) and had taken part in one of the last ever cavalry charges at full gallop in close order at the Battle of Omdurman. In the Boer War he had been taken prisoner and had made a spectacular escape. In the First World War, for five months he led a battalion of the Royal Scots Fusiliers in the trenches near Ploegsteert in Belgium. He was shelled repeatedly and at one point had just left a dugout when a shell landed, killing everyone left there. His praise for the heroism of the ordinary soldier was immense. Of the First World War soldiers who had fallen on the Somme in 1916 he had written, 'No attack however forlorn, however fatal, found them without ardour. No slaughter however desolating prevented them from returning to the charge ... they fulfilled the high purpose of duty with which they were imbued.'[5] But he had always been less than impressed with senior commanders. He thought in the Boer War they were unimaginative and lacked a sufficiently aggressive spirit. He never forgot the fact that in 1915 the War Office initially turned down his idea of building 'landships' to cross no-man's land as an attempt to break the stalemate of the Western Front, an idea that later led to the development of the tank. He thought the army lived in a closed world and its leaders did not sufficiently engage with new ideas and new technologies.[6]

In the First World War the army had grown into a massive fighting force of six million men made up of volunteers and, from 1916 on, conscripts. During the 1920s and 1930s it had returned to a small, regular force of just over 200,000 volunteers. Most of its tasks involved policing Britain's vast empire. It was not until late 1938 that serious attention was paid to scaling up the army and preparing for another European land war.

In the inter-war years, the common soldier, known as one of the Other Ranks, usually came from the industrial slums of the nation. He often joined up as a route out of poverty and hunger rather than from patriotic ardour. He was usually poorly educated and many could not read or write. He was offered poor rates of pay (the British soldier of the 1930s was in real terms less well off than his predecessor in Wellington's army well over a century earlier), given meagre prospects of promotion and by living for many years away from home, often abroad, found it difficult to marry and lead a normal family life.[7] The soldier had a poor reputation for being rough, tough and uncouth, a drunken, clod-hopping lout who was not fit for polite civilian company.[8]

Army life for these ordinary soldiers consisted of endless amounts of drill, square bashing for hours on end, and a full-time devotion to polishing buttons, boots and anything else that could be made to shine. Such obsession became an end in itself and anyone joining up had to submit to hours of being bawled out for not forming fours in perfect style or for not having a razor-sharp crease in his khaki trousers. Outside specialist units like the Tank Corps and the Royal Artillery, there was relatively little training in the mechanics of combat or the use of military vehicles. The thinking was that such devotion to spit-and-polish detail was good for discipline and encouraged obedience on the field of battle. The pre-war squaddie was not expected to think or display any creativity. His task was to keep his head down and do as he was told.

Many officers in the pre-war army still came from the younger sons of the gentry but this was no longer exclusively the case. Frequently they joined from the upper middle classes as well. And a few came from more impoverished backgrounds. Auchinleck was the son of a widowed mother who had struggled as a single parent to bring up four children.[9] When Bernard Montgomery went to Sandhurst he was too poor even to buy his own wristwatch. Some officers were bright, intellectually hungry, totally professional and committed. Wavell, for instance, had a fine intellect, authored histories and biographies, spoke seven languages, one of which was Russian, and wrote poetry. Many officers, however, enjoyed a pretty easy and genteel life, especially those who spent years abroad in India, Asia or the Middle East.

There was little emphasis in officer training on the science of warfare. In the First World War the British Army had been at the forefront of the application of science, from the development of sound ranging to locate the enemy's artillery to the study of aeronautical research to gain advantage in the new arm of air warfare. Britain's reputation as a leading scientific nation should have continued within the army post-war but everything went into reverse. The Royal Military College at Sandhurst developed yet another spit-and-polish obsession and was more keen to produce dull but obedient and upright officers who accepted everything without question than to turn out independent-thinking, well-rounded leaders. The Academy at Woolwich, where engineers and artillerymen trained, was a little more scientific than Sandhurst, but neither institution compared to West Point in the United States where cadets received almost a university level of education and military training.[10]

The core unit in the British Army was the regiment, which

usually had a regional or county background. Most officers and soldiers remained within their regiment for their entire period of service. It was the entity to which they owed their loyalty. The regimental colours and portraits from previous wars adorned their messes and shaped their rituals. When John Masters, later a novelist, was seconded to the Duke of Cornwall's Light Infantry in 1934, the battered relics from fighting in the American War of Independence and the Battle of Waterloo and from the defence of Lucknow during the Indian Mutiny stared down at him from the mess wall where he dined with fellow officers every night with an echo like 'silver trumpets of the past'. In them, Masters saw all 'the glory' and the 'mud of forgotten fields' and felt 'lapped in the warm continuity of tradition'.[11] Even on leaving the army, a man still 'belonged' to his regiment. It was a fraternity with its own rites and customs that looked after a man from passing out to passing on. Many men saw themselves as a member of their regimental family first and a soldier of the British Army second.

Most armies included regiments but they were usually administrative units rather than closed-minded centres of loyalty. By comparison, in the German and American armies the core unit was the division, a far larger, composite fighting unit. In the British peacetime army most regiments had two battalions, one based at home and one serving abroad. A six-year posting to India, for instance, was common. Regimental life with its cap badges, relics and proud rituals helped to keep the British Army a closed and inward-looking society, often more concerned to preserve its traditions than to embrace change or accept new technologies. Talking shop in the officers' mess was strictly frowned on. Discussing sport, military bands or regimental rivalries was permitted. Debating how to improve the efficiency of a field howitzer was emphatically not. Any young officer who demonstrated an interest in studying or writing up any aspect of military practice would have been regarded by his seniors at best as showing 'extremely bad form' and at worst as being a dangerous subversive.[12] Professional soldiering was simply not regarded as a quality worth pursuing. A leading historian has recently spoken of British officers 'lacking skill, energy and imagination' and performing their duties 'in a cloud of cultural complacency'.[13] Officers might find themselves in unusual and exotic locations but would rarely mix outside their regiment and certainly not with locals who were seen as alien and untrustworthy. Harold Macmillan was deeply unimpressed with those pre-war men who had become senior staff officers by the middle of the war. He classed them as 'wooden', 'stupid' and 'a curiously narrow-minded lot' who 'seem to go all over the world without observing anything in it – except their fellow officers and their wives'. He decided that the insular world which they inhabited equipped them at the end of their careers as fit for nothing other than, in his damning phrase, to be 'secretaries of golf clubs'.[14]

Evelyn Waugh satirised the power of the regiment in his novel *Men at Arms* (1952) when his central character Guy Crouchback takes a commission in a less than distinguished regiment, the Halberdiers. When he joins he looks around him at the small band of newcomers who he learns have been chosen from more than 2,000 applicants. 'He wondered, sometimes, what system of selection had produced so nondescript a squad,' wrote Waugh. But Crouchback soon realises that 'The discipline of the square, the traditions of the mess, would work their magic and the *esprit de corps* would fall like blessed unction from above.'[15]

In April 1939 a huge expansion of the army began when conscription was reintroduced, for the first time in British peacetime history. By 1942, 2.9 million men and 138,000 women had joined the armed services.[16] On being conscripted, a person was offered a notional choice of which service they wished to serve in. Three out of four conscripts asked to join the Royal Navy or the RAF. The navy had centuries of victories to call upon and had the appeal of being the senior service. The RAF was the newest and most glamorous service. It had cultivated an image of being modern, go-ahead and technically oriented. Many young men saw the air force as representative of what they wanted Britain to become, whereas the army seemed to represent what it had once been.[17] This in itself was an indictment of the pre-war image of the British Army.

Despite their first choices, many conscripts found themselves assigned to the army where the spit-and-polish culture still ruled the day with its mindless repetition of simple tasks and its obsession with smart, tidy battle dress and bright brass buttons. This might have suited a small regular army of poorly educated volunteers but certainly was not appropriate for an army of well-educated citizen soldiers training to fight a global war. Many of the men who flooded into the army in 1939, 1940 and 1941 were horrified at the petty rules they came across, at the barrack-room discipline they had to learn, at the hours of square bashing that faced them. The transition from civilian to soldier was completely bewildering for many recruits. They were desperately bored, and the bulk of the army, those not fighting in the desert or the Far East, was kept at home drilling continually for several years. While they spent hours cleaning their uniforms, the progress of the war went from bad to worse. Soldiers were said to complain that 'while Russia bleeds' the British Army 'polishes its boots'.[18]

On the other hand, many regular officers began to question whether these new recruits had the qualities needed to become soldiers and officers. They asked if they were too soft to serve in a well-disciplined military hierarchy. Perhaps years of going to the cinema and visiting dance halls, of reading novels and newspapers, and living in an open, democratic society had softened them so much that they no longer had the fibre of their fathers who had gone to war in 1914. Did they really have what was needed to form a disciplined military force that could be sent thousands of miles away to fight and die for king and empire? They were seen in marked contrast to the German lads who had grown up in the Hitler Jugend to be tough, outdoors-oriented, obedient but comradely, and utterly determined to fight for Hitler and the Reich. The Wehrmacht had defeated the British Army in pretty much every engagement since April 1940, but it was the superiority of German arms and armour that most depressed British commentators.

The argument about the poor quality of British weapons and armour had been raging since the summer of 1940. There were many sides to the debate. For instance, even before the war it was known that the 2-pounder anti-tank gun was not able to penetrate the thicker armour on many of the German Army's newest marks of panzer like the III and IV. Plans to upgrade to a 6-pounder weapon had been made in 1938. But this involved a major retooling in the limited number of factories where anti-tank guns were produced, which would take time and require investment. After the army got back from Dunkirk having abandoned most of its hardware in France, including 850 anti-tank guns, there was a need to re-equip as quickly as possible with the threat of a German invasion looming. It was far easier to rebuild the army with the technology available than to slowly reconstruct the production lines to produce a new generation of weaponry. It was a simple case of quantity over quality. The 2-pounder remained in production long after its sell-by date had passed. By comparison, the German 88mm weapon could be used as both an anti-aircraft and an anti-tank gun. It had better sights, was easily manoeuvrable and had a far higher muzzle velocity than its British equivalents. It was, simply, a far superior weapon.[19] Forty per cent of all tank losses in the desert war were as a consequence of direct hits from the 88mm.[20]

Likewise with the tank: the government had cut back British Army funding so much in the inter-war years that research and development in tank design had suffered. While the German Army, re-equipping in the late 1930s, developed fast-moving, well-armoured vehicles, the British Army continued to use highly mobile but lightly armoured infantry support tanks, known as I-Tanks. Again, with 700 tanks being abandoned in the retreat to Dunkirk, the need to re-equip quickly was paramount. More I-Tanks continued to be produced, firing the old 2-pounder gun. In further contrast, the German panzers had a gun capable of firing both high-explosive and armour-piercing shells and also capped shells which the British called 'arrowheads'. But many of the guns on the British tanks were limited to firing high-explosives only. They were intended to support the infantry but were not of much use in tank-versus-tank combat. A replacement tank was designed for the Middle East called the Crusader. But this proved to be mechanically unreliable and its armour could easily be penetrated. Confidence in the Crusader quickly plummeted among tank crews. So strong was the outcry that the Deputy Prime Minister, Clement Attlee, led a special inquiry into the weakness of the Crusader in the spring of 1942. It was revealed that it had been developed too quickly and had gone into production before having been adequately tested – essentially, the product of haste. Many improvements did follow including the superior Matilda tank (only the 88mm gun could penetrate its armour), and there was also the Valentine with less strong armour but with the advantage of greater speed. When the American tanks started to appear, like the Stuart and the Grant, both of which had a better gun than their British predecessors, the confidence of the tank crews in their vehicles improved.[21] Developments in design, armour and firepower all began to transform the situation in the second half of the war. But in the crucial first nine months of 1942, the British Army was still largely fighting with weapons that had been designed before the war or in the very early stages of it.

The superior German Army equipment was not limited to weapons and armour. The Germans had an efficient system of workshops for repairing damaged tanks and getting them back on to the battlefield. They only had a few models and had standardised parts so they needed fewer spares and could distribute them quickly. The British Army used several different models of tank, each one requiring different spare parts, all of which had to be transported in North Africa over hundreds of miles of desert. And every soldier seemed to know that even the German fuel containers were better than their Allied equivalents. The German can was rectangular, solidly built from pressed steel, and contained 20 litres. It was easy to fill and to empty, and could be used over and over again. The British version was a more flimsy 4-gallon container that required the use of a funnel for emptying. It would frequently spring a leak and was rarely used more than once. The German container was so efficient that it was nicknamed the 'Jerrycan', and by the second half of the war its design had become ubiquitous.

Then there was the question of battlefield tactics. In the British Army the liaison between armoured and infantry units was notoriously poor. Partly this was down to the cavalry ethic that still prevailed in some armoured units, decades after the last cavalry charge had taken place. Some cavalry regiments, like the Royal Scots Dragoon Guards, were so reluctant to give up their horses in the late 1930s that officers lobbied MPs to reverse the decision.[22] The use of horses emphasised their sense of independence and superiority within the British military machine. Partly it was also because there were few joint all-arms exercises on a scale large enough for armoured and infantry units to be able to practise collaboration. But it was also down to the make-up of armoured units in the army. An armoured division or brigade consisted primarily of armoured vehicles with support units. The infantry, whether motorised or on foot, were either part of a support group or were in separate units altogether. In the German Army, where detailed studies on the use of armour had been undertaken during the 1930s, each panzer division included an infantry regiment of at least two battalions of motorised troops. The fact that the infantry and the panzers were under the same command brought a greater level of collaboration between the two. When a British armoured unit wanted infantry support the commander had to search out the local infantry commander who was often of the same rank and hammer out a way in which they could work together. Sometimes this succeeded. Other times, with conflicting priorities, it did not. Australian and New Zealand infantry officers in the desert repeatedly grew to despair at the lack of support from British armoured brigades. One New Zealand brigadier described the relationship between armour and infantry in the Eighth Army as 'a most intense distrust, almost hatred. It was always the case,' he claimed, 'that the tanks would not be where they were wanted in time.'[23] In a clash at El Alamein in mid-July 1942, Captain Charles Upham of the New Zealand infantry, who had just won a second Victoria Cross (one of only three men ever to do so), was captured by a panzer unit while waiting for the British armour to appear. As a result, this brave and distinguished soldier spent the rest of the war in captivity.[24]

Auchinleck recognised some of these problems and in early 1942 started the process of reforming the Eighth Army so that his armoured divisions were more like panzer divisions, consisting of one armoured brigade and one motorised infantry brigade. But these reforms were slow to be implemented and the process of change had only just begun when the withdrawal set in following defeat at the Battle of Gazala.[25]

Many blamed the generals for the repeated failures of arms, just as they had come to be blamed for the sacrifices of the Great War. The figure of Colonel 'Blimp' had originated in the cartoons of David Low in the *Evening Standard*. By the late 1930s Blimp had come to epitomise the angry, oafish military commander with a bald head and a walrus-style moustache who was hopelessly out of touch with the modern world. Low, a New Zealander, wanted his Blimp to reflect all that he felt was pompous, reactionary and jingoistic about the British Establishment. When in 1942 the film makers Michael Powell and Emeric Pressburger proposed making a film entitled *The Life and Death of Colonel Blimp*, the War Office and the Ministry of Information united in their opposition to the project. Even Churchill tried to ban production of the film, thinking it would be deeply critical of army commanders, and suggested that emergency powers should be brought in to suppress it. But the film was made and it proved a great box office hit.[26] A left-leaning and widely read newspaper like the *Daily Mirror* repeatedly pointed to what it saw as a failure of leadership in the army. One leader proclaimed that the army was being led by 'brass-buttoned boneheads, socially prejudiced, arrogant and fussy' with knowledge not even of the previous war but of 'the last war but two'. 'Weed Them Out' it demanded.[27] The quality of the officer class trained up before the war concerned not only the readers of the tabloid *Mirror*. Even General Brooke, the man who led the British Army in 1942, lamented privately in his diary, 'how poor we are as regards Army and Corps commanders. We ought to remove several, but heaven knows where we shall find anything very much better.'[28] The inward-looking, technophobic, complacent culture of the officer class in the 1930s had not delivered the sort of generals who could win battles against a determined, ruthless foe.

The press regularly offered many reasons to explain Britain's military failures. In the main this open media debate

was tolerated but there were times when it was thought to
have gone too far. After a particularly critical report in the
mass-selling *Picture Post* in December 1941 entitled 'What
has Happened in Libya?', the magazine was banned from
distribution in the Middle East in case it further undermined
morale. But *Picture Post* was not banned in Britain where it
continued to ask whether 'our commanders and our holders
of high office [should be] above criticism's reach?'[29] In Britain,
many journalists picked up, as did the MPs in the censure
debate, on the poor quality of army equipment. 'The Germans
still have the better all-purpose gun; the better tank; the
better plane,' wrote Alan Moorehead in the *Daily Express*. 'The
Germans always mass their fire-power ... they have more
training than we have.'[30] The left-wing weekly *Tribune* blamed
a combination of factors for Britain's humiliation at Singapore.
'The training prescribed for the British Army has been, and
continues to be utterly inadequate for the tasks it has to face,'
its military correspondent wrote in March 1942. 'We have not
only prepared weapons for the wrong war, we have not only
developed a strategy for the wrong war, but we have also
prepared our soldiers for a war that has not happened.'[31] The
chorus of complaints and diagnoses of the problem continued
almost daily. The Axis armies, it was said, were schooled in
the offensive spirit. The *Manchester Guardian* spoke of 'a painful weakness still existing in the system which should unite
the men who design, the men who choose, and the men who
produce our weapons of war'. The newspaper's critique was
wide-ranging. It picked out the failure of equipment like the
2-pounder 'whose weaknesses had been proved in the last
desert encounter; we had not been supplied with anything
like sufficient numbers of the new six-pounder'. Army training came in for its share of blame; it compared 'unfavourably
with that given [to] the German novices'. In addition, the
generals were too slow to respond to developments on the

battlefield: 'Was this point not made during the Battle of France two years ago?' While commanders were blamed for their 'inability to act with the same dash as the Germans' it was admitted that 'it would demand a general of remarkable capacity to outdo Rommel'.[32]

In the summer of 1942, an opinion poll agency circulated a questionnaire to hundreds of houses in order to assess public attitudes towards the army. One of the questions asked was who the householders fancied as the most outstanding general. Of course they meant which British general, so the agency was astonished when a large proportion of those who answered wrote 'Rommel'.[33]

To sum up, the army that was fighting in 1942, in the jungles of the Far East and the desert of North Africa, was the product of the 1930s. Although it had expanded dramatically in numbers during the first two years of war, the weapons it fought with, the generals who led it, the middle-ranking officers who ran it and the culture that prevailed had come out of an era of cutbacks, complacency and conservatism. And beyond that, Britain was proud of the fact that, unlike Germany and Japan, it did not have a tradition of militarism. And in the inter-war years the predominant view had been 'never again'. Never again would so many lives be lost in futile head-on attacks against enemy lines. Never again would generals living in chateaux in the rear echelon be impervious to the mass sacrifice of the ordinary soldier. The sad consequence of this peace-loving sentiment was an army that was not properly equipped, properly trained or properly led to fight a resolute and skilled foe when war came again. General Henry Pownall, who had been chief of staff of the British Expeditionary Force in France in 1940 and to General Wavell in the Far East in 1942, later wrote that Britain needed 'a tougher Army, based on a tougher nation, an Army which is regarded by the people as an honourable profession to which only the best can gain admission ... One whose traditions are not based on purely regimental history but on the history of the whole British Army; where the competition is in efficiency, not in games or pipe blowing and band concerts.'[34]

The British Army closely reflected the society from which it came. In the early war years it was, as one serving subaltern, Richard Hoggart, wrote, 'a microcosm of British society in both its decencies and its gross imperfections'.[35] It's difficult to conclude anything other than it was not fit for the purpose of fighting the German or the Japanese armies, both of which had steeled their soldiers into imaginative, skilled fighters devoted to their Führer or Emperor. It's easy to sympathise with the verdict of Sir Alexander Cadogan, who wrote, 'Our soldiers are the most pathetic amateurs, pitted against professionals.' And later: 'The Germans are magnificent fighters and their Staff are veritable Masters of Warfare.' He added that by 1942 'Our army was the mockery of the world.'[36]

Lessons were being learned, and change was coming. Under General Ronald Adam, the new Adjutant General, an entirely new citizens' army was being developed that would be conscious of why it was being asked to fight and in which a form of military meritocracy ruled so that those showing the best ability would be promoted. But the problem faced by Churchill and the government in 1942 was that the institution that had been created did not look as if it was up to the task of winning the war. In the summer, this concern focused on the North African desert and even more precisely upon the Eighth Army defending the line at El Alamein. Who commanded it during its next battle mattered very much. Another defeat would have cataclysmic consequences, not only for the war in the Middle East but for Britain's standing as a fighting nation.

With this in mind, Churchill prepared to accompany Brooke to Egypt. It was not going to be an easy journey, nor one without risks. In the War Cabinet on 30 July, Eden raised questions about the risk to the Prime Minister's health but Churchill replied that it was his duty to go and he felt 'confident of his fitness to undertake the journey'.[37] The following day Churchill went to RAF Farnborough where he had to take a test to establish if he was fit enough to be able to breathe through an oxygen supply when flying at altitude. He entered what was called the 'Chamber', was fitted with an oxygen mask and 'taken up' to the equivalent of 15,000 feet. For fifteen minutes he had to remain there while Clemmie looked on anxiously through a porthole. After the test was over his blood pressure was taken and Churchill was pronounced fit to fly. Before leaving he tracked down the officer in charge and asked him to adapt the mask so he could smoke a cigar while wearing it.[38]

On the night of Saturday 1 August, Churchill and his doctor boarded an unheated, unpressurised four-engine long-distance B-24 Liberator at RAF Lyneham. It had been specially adapted with its bomb-bay removed and two shelves substituted to lie out on. That was all there was, along with a supply of blankets, far removed from the luxury cabins and silver service of the BOAC flying boats. Clemmie waved Churchill off as the heavy bomber taxied away, its engines roaring as it lumbered down the runway into the darkness. Churchill managed to rest with the help of a sleeping pill despite complaining of the 'razor-edged draughts' in the aircraft's fuselage. At dawn the plane touched down safely at Gibraltar. Brooke had already flown out and they spent a day at the fortress before flying on overnight to Egypt on a long, roundabout route to avoid the desert war combat zone.

Churchill loved to take the co-pilot seat and he later described his joy as they approached Egypt at sunrise and saw 'the endless winding silver ribbon of the Nile stretched joyously before us'. He knew the river well. 'In war and peace I had traversed by land or water almost its whole length.' The plane landed smoothly within sight of the pyramids outside Cairo. Churchill wrote, 'Now for a short spell I became "the man on the spot". Instead of sitting at home waiting for the news from the front I could send it myself. This was exhilarating.'[39] The next two weeks would help to determine whether Britain would play a significant part in winning the war.

17

From the Pyramids
to the Ogre's Den

On arriving in Cairo, Churchill quickly appraised himself of the situation in the Eighth Army. He was astonished at the appalling level of morale he discovered in the Desert Army. He wrote, 'This splendid army, about double as strong as the enemy, is baffled and bewildered by its defeats ... a kind of apathy and exhaustion of the mind rather than the body has stolen over our troops which only new, strong hands and above all the gleam of victory can dispel.'[1]

The conference that Churchill convened during his eight days in Egypt reflected the importance of the decisions to be taken. The Chief of the Imperial General Staff, 'Brookie', the Adjutant General of the British Army Sir Ronald Adam and the Military Assistant to the War Cabinet Colonel Sir Ian Jacob had come out from London along with Sir Alexander Cadogan representing the Foreign Office. The Resident Minister of State for the Middle East Richard Casey was there; Averell Harriman arrived after a few days as the senior US representative; General de Gaulle represented the Free French. The army commanders, including Auchinleck and Generals Corbett, Morshead, Ramsden and Gott, were consulted along with Admiral Harwood and Air Marshals Tedder and Coningham. General Wavell flew in from India, and the South African Prime Minister Field Marshal Jan Smuts arrived from Pretoria. Churchill wanted Smuts in Cairo as an old friend whose advice he valued. And he knew that Smuts had a ruthless streak when it came to appointing commanders. It was clear to Churchill that something had gone seriously wrong with the Eighth Army and only change at the top could reverse the downward trend. Auchinleck would have to go, but Churchill later told a friend, 'It was a terrible thing to have to do ... It is difficult to remove a bad General at the height of a campaign: it is atrocious to remove a good General.'[2]

The key question was who to put in charge of the Eighth Army. Both Churchill and Brooke disliked Auchinleck's nominee, his chief of staff Lieutenant-General Thomas Corbett, but they could not agree between themselves on an alternative. Churchill favoured Lieutenant-General 'Strafer' Gott. He had been in the desert since the beginning of the war and had been in command of XIII Corps at the Battle of Gazala. But Brooke was convinced he was exhausted by two uninterrupted years of war in the desert and needed a break. Churchill and Brooke flew out to El Alamein on 5 August to review the front-line troops. Here Churchill met Gott and convinced himself that he was fit, lively and perfectly capable of taking command. 'He impressed me at once with a feeling of confidence,' Churchill wrote.[3] It was the job Gott had wanted for some time, having resented the promotion of Ritchie above him. Brooke had the highest respect for the general but when he met him, Gott presented a different picture and said, 'I think what is required out here is some new blood. I have tried most of my ideas on the Boche.'[4]

Churchill decided to split the big Middle East Command and surprised Brooke by offering him the job of commander-in-chief of a newly reconfigured command. Brooke was sorely tempted to take on such a high-profile role but decided that he had now learned how to work with Churchill as CIGS and that it was better for the national war effort not to disrupt the process of decision-making at the highest level. He later wrote, 'rightly or wrongly I felt I could exercise some control over him ... I had discovered the perils of his impetuous nature. I was now familiar with his method of suddenly arriving at some decision as it were by intuition without any kind of logical examination of the problem.' Brooke felt it would take a successor at least six months to learn how to work with the Prime Minister and 'During those six months anything might happen.'[5] Somewhat reluctantly, Brooke turned down the offer. It was finally agreed to create a new Near East Command which would include Egypt, Palestine and Syria and to offer this to General Sir Harold Alexander, who had been in the Far East. He was an aristocrat, an ex-Guardsman, always immaculately dressed and with film-star good looks. Auchinleck was to be offered a new command of Persia and Iraq and the vital role of protecting the region's oilfields, at that point threatened by the German advance into the Caucasus. Brooke gave way to the PM over the command of the Eighth Army and this was offered to Gott. Several other senior army figures were sent home.

It was an intense few days of reorganising the Middle East command structure and reshuffling its leadership in what became known as the 'Cairo purge'. Back in London, the Foreign Office diplomat Oliver Harvey wrote that it was indeed 'a massacre of generals, though not of innocents'.[6] After the decisions had been reached, Churchill spent 7 August inspecting troops. He returned to the British Embassy in Cairo for dinner and was going upstairs to his room when Colonel Jacob passed him.

'This is bad about Gott,' he said.

'Why, what has happened?' asked Churchill.

Then he received the terrible news that Gott's aircraft had been shot down while flying the short distance from

Topfoto 0238108

Churchill at the Cairo 'purge', August 1942. Back row left to right:
Tedder, Brooke, Cunningham, Sir Alexander Cadogan.
Front row left to right: Smuts, Churchill, Auchinleck, Wavell.
So many generals there's hardly enough room on the bench!

Burg al-Arab airfield near El Alamein back to Cairo. He had
boarded a Bombay transport aircraft which had just taken
off when two low-flying Messerschmitts passed the airfield
and opened fire on the slow-moving aircraft, sending it to the
ground in flames. When they pulled Gott from the burning
wreck he was already dead. There were only three survivors
out of eighteen. As if to highlight the danger, this had been the
very route that Churchill had flown only two days before, also
without fighter protection. Their plans were now shattered. As
Churchill wrote, 'What was to happen now?'[7]

Churchill, Brooke and Smuts gathered immediately at the

embassy. Brooke had argued all along that General Bernard Montgomery should be given command of the Eighth Army. Churchill favoured General Maitland Wilson. But Smuts also supported Montgomery's appointment, and this time it was Churchill who gave way. An immediate cable was sent to the War Cabinet in London which was in session at 11.15 p.m. discussing the various changes when a white-faced private secretary entered the meeting room with the words 'I fear that this is bad news'. He told them of Gott's death. A short while later another cable arrived informing them of the decision to appoint Montgomery in Gott's place.[8]

Montgomery had just returned from inspecting troop manoeuvres in Scotland. A Liberator was put at his disposal to fly him urgently to Cairo. He had no time to pack anything but a few essentials and say farewell to his son at his school. Although only the second choice, it proved to be an inspired appointment. Montgomery had the energy, charisma and the tactical ideas to bring the much-needed 'new blood' to the Eighth Army. With the death of the most senior British general killed by enemy action in the war came the beginning of what would become the 'Monty' legend.

Churchill has been criticised for blaming the Auk for the failures of the Eighth Army. The fact was that the PM's confidence in his general had been wavering for some time and he not unreasonably put the collapse of morale in the Middle East down to a failure of leadership. He still respected him and wanted to retain his experience, but when Auchinleck was offered the command of the oilfields in Persia and Iraq he turned it down, partly out of a sense of pique, partly because he did not agree that Persia and Iraq should be separated from the rest of the Middle East. By rejecting this he offended Brooke considerably, who wrote, 'It would have been a more "soldierly" act to accept what he was offered in war, instead of behaving like an offended film star.'[9]

General Alexander arrived to take up his new command in Cairo. Churchill gave him his orders handwritten on embassy notepaper which were blissfully simple: 'Your prime and main duty will be to take or destroy at the earliest opportunity the German-Italian army commanded by Field-Marshal Rommel with all its supplies & establishments in Egypt & Libya.'[10] Then, his business completed, soon after midnight on 10 August Churchill departed from Cairo. This time the PM's entourage filled three large aircraft. But they did not head west back towards home, instead flying further east, on to the next assignment.

Before Churchill left London, Roosevelt had told him about his worry that plans for the rest of 1942 had not been clearly explained to Stalin. He was unlikely to see the postponement of a second front in Europe and the decision to invade North-West Africa instead in the same positive way that the western Allies saw it. At that moment a telegram arrived from the British ambassador in Moscow suggesting a meeting with Stalin. Cadogan at the Foreign Office wrote, 'I should attach enormous importance to a Stalin-Churchill meeting.' He warned that the moment may come 'when the Russians are no longer attracted by "jam tomorrow". We may have to put our cards on the table.'[11]

Churchill leapt at the idea and proposed to Stalin a meeting, after his visit to Cairo, in Astrakhan on the Caspian Sea in order to 'survey the war together hand-in-hand' and to 'tell you the plans we have made with President Roosevelt for offensive action in 1942'.[12] As a sweetener he added that they hoped to run another Arctic convoy to Murmansk in September. Stalin replied that he could not possibly leave Moscow 'at the moment of such an intense struggle against the Germans' but that Churchill would be welcome to visit him at the Kremlin after completing his business in Cairo. 'You may be sure beforehand that any date will suit me,'[13] he added, making the exchange of telegrams sound more like friends setting up a dinner date. Churchill now had to add several hundred miles to his journey around another war zone but willingly agreed to meet in the Soviet capital.

So Churchill, with a team that included Brooke, Tedder, Cadogan and Jacob, Harriman to represent President Roosevelt, his personal doctor and several others including Wavell, who spoke fluent Russian, embarked on a new journey once again in the desperately uncomfortable Liberator bombers. Back in London there was concern at the risks the PM was taking. 'I expect he'll get killed in a crash,' wrote Oliver Harvey, thinking of the shooting down of Gott only days before.[14] The first phase of the journey was through the night across the Middle East and over the mountains of Kurdistan for 1,300 miles to Tehran. There they paused for a day and Churchill took the opportunity to have lunch with the Shah, newly installed by the British on the Peacock Throne. On the morning of 12 August, he took the second leg of his long journey north-west across Persia, north up the Caspian Sea within sight of the oilfields of Baku, across the Soviet border and then north-west to Moscow, a flight of more than 1,500 miles. This involved crossing the mouth of the Volga, where a little more than 200 miles upriver German Army scouts were approaching the city of Stalingrad.

There's no doubt that even a man of Churchill's strident confidence was daunted by the prospect of meeting the great Soviet leader. Clemmie had likened it to visiting 'the Ogre in his Den'.[15] After the First World War, Churchill had called for the new Soviet state to be strangled at birth. He had regarded the Soviet Union for most of his life as 'the mortal foe of civilised freedom'. Now he had to explain to its supremely powerful chief that there would be no second front in Europe in 1942. 'It was like carrying a large lump of ice to the North Pole,' he later wrote.[16] But he wanted to explain

Anglo-American strategy and sell to Stalin the planned landings in North-West Africa while also emphasising the huge
effort Britain was putting into the bombing offensive. Like
many leading statesmen he was a great believer in his own
powers of persuasion and he was convinced that talking to
the Soviet leader in person would make it easier for Stalin to
accept what clearly for him was going to be bad news.

On landing in Moscow, Churchill was escorted to State
Villa Number 7, a grand building that Stalin sometimes used
just outside the city in the midst of a thick pine-tree wood of
about 20 acres. It was surrounded by a high wall guarded by
policemen and soldiers. Inside a host of white-jacketed servants with beaming smiles awaited his every request. A buffet
laden with delicacies was laid out for him to feast on including
caviar and smoked meats along with vodka and fine European
wines. The luxury was extraordinary bearing in mind the
German Army was only about 60 miles away. The aircraft
carrying Brooke, Wavell and Cadogan had turned back with
a technical fault on leaving Tehran. It would not catch up with
them until the next day. But Churchill wanted to get on with
his Moscow mission and a few hours after touching down he
was escorted to the Kremlin. Soon after 7 p.m. he was ushered
in to meet the Soviet war leader and dictator, Marshal Stalin.[17]

Their first meeting lasted for nearly four hours. It was
an intimate gathering. Churchill was accompanied only by
the British ambassador, Sir Archibald Clark Kerr, Averell
Harriman and an interpreter; Stalin had with him his Foreign
Minister Vyacheslav Molotov, Marshal Klimenti Voroshilov
from the State Defence Committee and his interpreter. Stalin
began with a depressing outline of the grave situation on the
Eastern Front. He said that enemy troops were advancing on
Stalingrad and Baku. He explained it would be possible for
the Germans to dispatch twenty divisions from their advance
at any point to strike further north. Stalin wanted his ally to

know how desperate the situation was and to understand the scale of the struggle the Red Army was engaged in.

After an hour or so, Churchill responded, insisting that he would be frank in outlining to Stalin the situation of the western Allies. He got right down to it and explained that it would not be possible to open a second front in Europe in 1942. He said plans were being made for a full invasion in 1943 with twenty-seven American divisions supported by twenty-one British, but at present there were only two US divisions in the UK and not enough landing craft. Anything beyond a small-scale incursion on the north French coast would probably end in disaster and fail to divert German forces from the east. The British report of the meeting noted that as the Prime Minister proceeded, Stalin looked glummer and 'glummer still'. The Soviet leader asked many questions. Why could the Channel Islands not be recaptured? Why could a landing not be made at somewhere like Cherbourg? If landing craft were not available why could troops not be parachuted in from the air? Churchill had answers to all his questions but Stalin did not accept the arguments. 'The British should not be so afraid of the Germans,' he said. All troops needed to be blooded in battle and the British did not appear to want this. The meeting reached a low point.

After what seemed like a long silence, Churchill moved on to talk about the growing strength of the bombing offensive against Germany. He gave the Soviet leader a mass of data, building up the recent raids. Stalin cheered up considerably at this and told the Prime Minister that 'this bombing was of tremendous importance' and that 'It was not only German industry that should be bombed but the population too. This was the only way of breaking German morale.' Churchill went on to reveal details about Operation Torch in October. He argued that a second front need not be in northern France but an invasion of North-West Africa would force Hitler to bring back more German troops to support Italy, and success here would also help to clear the Mediterranean. Churchill explained that the Allies could threaten what he called 'the soft belly' of Hitler's Europe before striking in northern France. Stalin responded by saying, 'May God prosper this undertaking.'

The meeting broke up amicably a little before 11 p.m. They agreed to reconvene the following evening. Churchill and Harriman were elated at how well Stalin had taken the bad news. The PM returned to his villa, and although it was late and it had been a long and arduous day his adrenalin was still pumping and he dictated a joint telegram to the War Cabinet and to Roosevelt. 'I expect I shall establish a solid and sincere relationship with this man,' he wrote.[18] Then, as he later remembered, 'with the feeling that at least the ice was broken and human contact established, I slept soundly and long'.[19]

The meeting the next evening began at 11 p.m. and did not go well. The rest of the British delegation had arrived and Brooke, Wavell, Jacob, Tedder and Cadogan were also present in the Kremlin. It began with Stalin handing Churchill a note in which he utterly rejected the arguments put forward during the previous meeting for not being able to open a second front. Stalin claimed that the British had broken their promises to the Soviet Union not only over the second front but also by failing to send supplies that had been guaranteed in the Arctic convoys; all the Soviets were getting were 'leftovers' not needed in the west. He also claimed that the British and Americans did not recognise the importance of the fighting on the Eastern Front where they were up against 280 German divisions and the Red Army was losing 10,000 men every day.[20] Stalin simply did not accept that the British and Americans were unable to land six or eight divisions on the French coast. Both Churchill and Harriman insisted they were doing all they could to support the Soviets.

Stalin then launched into nothing less than a tirade against

Britain's armed forces. The story of abandoning convoy PQ17 prompted him to state, 'This is the first time in history the British Navy has ever turned tail and fled from the battle.' Then he turned to the dismal performance of the British Army and told Churchill, 'You British are afraid of fighting. You should not think the Germans are supermen. You will have to fight sooner or later. You cannot win a war without fighting.' In his recollection of the meeting, Harriman said that 'Stalin was really insulting'.[21] Colonel Jacob, who had been asked to minute the meeting, wrote that Stalin was not shouting or angry but berated Churchill in 'a low, gentle voice, with an occasional gesture of the right hand, and never looked the Prime Minister in the face'.[22]

It was one thing for Churchill to have himself expressed shame about Britain's military performance, to have talked of defeat, disaster and disgrace. But it was quite another for Britain's war leader to be harangued by the head of another nation who was supposed to be an ally. Churchill responded squarely to the accusations and Harriman was deeply impressed by what he called 'the most brilliant of his war-time utterances'. He said at one point 'I pardon that remark [dismissing the British Army] only on account of the bravery of the Russian troops.' He avoided the temptation of accusing the Soviets of having provided no support for Britain when it had stood alone in 1940. Although he did not outwardly lose his temper, Churchill's inner anger was rising. In his long response to Stalin, he forgot to pause every few seconds to allow the interpreter, a British officer translating from English to Russian, to keep up; then he grew angry with the interpreter who was failing to make all the points he wanted. Churchill said he had come a long way to establish good working relations with Stalin but that there was 'no ring of comradeship in his attitude'. 'Now that the three great nations were allied,' Churchill claimed, 'victory was certain provided we did not fall out.' By this point the PM was becoming more animated and crashed his fist on the table. Even before his words had been translated Stalin stood up, sucked on his pipe and interrupted to say, 'I do not understand what you are saying but by God, I like your sentiment.'[23]

After only a few more minutes Stalin quite abruptly halted the debate and said they 'could carry the argument no further'. He would accept the Anglo-American decision not to launch a second front but assured Churchill that Russia would fight on whatever Britain and America did. And he invited the Prime Minister to a state dinner the following evening. The discussion carried on a while longer but finally, at about 1.45 a.m., the meeting ended. As he left, Stalin held out his hand. Churchill took it and departed.

It had been a harrowing experience for all those present on the British side. Stalin had been blunt, aggressive, even insulting, and had avoided normal diplomatic niceties. He had, in essence, accused the Royal Navy and the British Army of cowardice. Churchill was annoyed and offended by these comments and had responded robustly. But maybe it had all been a game for Stalin, who simply wanted to find out what sort of a man Churchill was. He certainly seemed to be impressed by the PM's outburst. And from this point on the tension eased. Brooke, who observed the whole slanging match, wrote that the two men 'are poles apart as human beings and I cannot see a friendship between them such as exists between Roosevelt and Winston'.[24] Churchill drew a different conclusion, telling the War Cabinet the following morning that Stalin was maybe putting himself on the record for the future and was letting off steam while under immense military pressure on the Eastern Front. He concluded, 'It is my considered opinion that in his heart so far as he has one, Stalin knows that we are right.' The Prime Minister said he would attend the banquet not out of friendship but 'in the public interest'.[25]

The dinner on the evening of 14 August was a grand affair in one of the Kremlin's state rooms with about a hundred leading Soviet military figures present. The tables were laden with a variety of hors d'oeuvres and fish; then came several meat courses including suckling pig in white sauce. The banquet had barely begun when Molotov leapt to his feet and proposed a toast to Churchill. Churchill responded by proposing a toast to Stalin. Molotov then proposed several more toasts, to Harriman, to President Roosevelt and to each member of the British delegation, one by one. Everyone toasted then had to propose a toast to someone else. To break this seemingly endless round, Cadogan proposed 'death and damnation to the Nazis'.[26] General Wavell made a short speech in Russian about the courage of the Red Army which went down very well. Stalin got to his feet and walked around the room proposing toasts to nearly all the Red Army generals and commissars who were present. The official Soviet account of the dinner lists more than thirty toasts, each one preceded by a short speech.[27] Marshal Voroshilov, who had been drinking yellow vodka all evening, was so intoxicated by the time Stalin got to him that he was perspiring effusively and could barely stand. The British and Americans present managed to drink water along with the vodka during the toasts and no one disgraced themselves. Churchill sat on Stalin's right but there was little opportunity for serious conversation. At one point Stalin brought up Churchill's earlier hostility to the Soviet state. The PM admitted the fact and asked, 'Have you forgiven me?' Stalin smiled and replied enigmatically, 'All that is in the past. It is not for me to forgive. It is for God to forgive.'[28]

After nineteen separate courses had been served and all the toasting was done, Stalin invited Churchill into an adjoining room for coffee and liqueurs. At this, Churchill perked up a bit. Photos were taken of the two leaders sitting on a small sofa. After a long discussion about military intelligence, Stalin suggested they might like to see a film. But at this point Churchill decided he was tired and had had enough. It was 1.30 a.m. The two men shook hands cordially and Stalin escorted Churchill down long Kremlin corridors and staircases to the door where his limousine was waiting. The British ambassador noted that he had never known Stalin display such a courtesy to any other visitor. He obviously wanted Churchill to think that any bad feelings were behind them.

Churchill and Stalin pose after the Kremlin banquet, friends again after a stormy meeting the day before.

The following day, Churchill had time in his sumptuous villa to reflect. He thought that maybe he had been unfair to Stalin during their stormy exchange of two nights before. Clearly the Soviets were under great military pressure. Leningrad had been under siege for a year. The Germans were advancing rapidly towards Stalingrad. Perhaps Stalin had 'not meant to be as insulting as he had first thought'.[29] When it was explained to him that his villa was probably bugged and that the Soviets were listening in as he dictated messages to London and to Washington, Churchill doubted that they would stoop to this. But that did not stop him from speaking out loud some insults to the Soviet Union, including describing Russians as more like orang-utans than human beings, joking that these comments might be passed on to Stalin as a few home truths.[30]

During that afternoon Brooke, Wavell, Tedder, Jacob and the other British military officials in Moscow met with their Soviet counterparts. But they quickly discovered that there would be no free and easy exchange of information and ideas as they enjoyed with the American chiefs of staff. Brooke went through all the military reasons why it was impossible to open a second front in Europe in 1942, disclosing details about the state of the British Army and US forces in Britain. The Soviet generals looked passive and asked several questions. But when Brooke asked for information about the Soviet defence of the Caucasus, the Russians replied that they had no authority to discuss this. Trying to develop any form of cooperation between the Anglo-American and Soviet systems was going to be heavy work. Brooke wrote in his diary, 'There is no doubt that they are anxious to get all they can out of us, but at the same time have no intention of giving us the smallest help of any kind. They are an astonishingly suspicious type of people.'[31] When the Soviet generals reverted once again to claiming that opening a second front in Europe was the only way to improve the situation for the Soviet Union, Brooke was rather blunt and brought the military conference to an abrupt end.

Churchill planned to depart from Moscow at dawn the following morning but his visit to Moscow had one last round to play out. At 7 p.m. the Prime Minister went for a final time to the Kremlin to say a short farewell to Stalin. This time Churchill had a new interpreter, Major Birse, who had grown up in St Petersburg. He was bilingual in Russian and gave Churchill far more confidence in speaking with the Soviet leader. They talked about the war. Churchill said he had known the news about the second front would be painful to Stalin but that he wanted to convey the situation in person. Stalin replied by saying, 'Obviously there are differences between us, but differences are in the nature of things.' Churchill told him they were planning a small raid on the French coast the following month, what he called a 'reconnaissance in force'. The troops would only remain ashore for twenty-four hours and then withdraw. Stalin was pleased to hear this. The discussion then turned to the Eastern Front. Stalin said he was confident his forces could hold out in the Caucasus and he sounded encouraging about the prospects for victory on the Volga. After an hour Churchill stood up to leave, saying that the two leaders 'must work night and day for victory'.[32] To his surprise, Stalin responded by inviting him to his home for some drinks. Keen to depart on a high note, Churchill replied that he was always in favour of such a policy.

Stalin led Churchill and the two interpreters through several Kremlin passageways until they came to his small four-room personal apartment. An aged housekeeper appeared with some snacks. Stalin started to uncork some bottles. Then his red-haired daughter Svetlana arrived, gave her father a kiss and joined the housekeeper in preparing some food. Molotov soon joined them, and with the two interpreters the tiny group began a convivial few hours of chatting and drinking. They talked further about the war and about new supplies for the Soviet Union. They discussed Operation Torch, and Stalin wished the invasion forces well. They talked again about the significance of the bombing offensive against Germany which Stalin said was of great importance. But as the evening continued they also covered many other subjects. They discussed the formation of the Soviet collective farms which Stalin said had been a great struggle. They were also able to joke about matters like Russia being a 'land animal' while the British were 'sea animals'. Churchill spoke about his ancestor the Duke of Marlborough helping to rid Europe of the tyranny of Louis XIV. Stalin said that Napoleon had been a greater threat and quipped with a mischievous look that Wellington's invasion of Spain had been like opening a second front. At about 1 a.m. a suckling pig was brought to the table and Stalin tucked in. And the conversation flowed for another hour and more.

At 2.30 a.m. Churchill said he had to go and finally returned to his villa after more than seven hours of one-on-one talks. There was no time to sleep so he dictated some messages and headed for the airport. A bleary-eyed Molotov arrived to bid them a formal farewell and the Anglo-American delegation lined up by the runway. In pouring rain a Russian Army band played 'The Internationale', 'God Save the King' and 'The Star Spangled Banner'. Complaining of a rare headache – almost certainly a euphemism for a hangover – Churchill boarded his draughty and uncomfortable Liberator aircraft. At 5.30 in the morning the four aircraft took off and headed south. Churchill slept all the way to Tehran, where the delegation paused for an overnight stop, and then continued back to Cairo.

Churchill was delighted overall with his mission. He felt he had built up a genuine rapport with the Soviet leader. He cabled the War Cabinet: 'I am definitely encouraged by my visit to Moscow. I am sure that the disappointing news I brought could not have been imparted except by me personally.'[33] The intense few days of meetings in Moscow had left Churchill feeling he knew and understood the Soviet leader. Cadogan and Eden argued that Stalin had been playing him, turning from insults to invites: Certainly Stalin was a manipulator, but also very clear-sighted in his own interests and it's unlikely that any western leader could ever have real sway over him. But Churchill left the Soviet capital with a misguided conviction that he could personally deal with Stalin. This remained with him for the rest of the war.

There was another significant consequence of the Moscow conference. Churchill continued to feel that the western Allies must push their war machines to the maximum to put pressure on Hitler in order to help Stalin. The course of the war in the Mediterranean was now set and American supplies were starting regularly to cross the Atlantic. The only other thing Britain could do would be to increase the bombing of Germany. The offensive now ceased to be a purely military campaign and took on a political role as well. Soon after Churchill returned to London he increased Bomber Command strength from thirty-two to fifty operational squadrons. All hesitation and debate about the campaign was over. The bombing of German factories and homes was to continue with as much intensity as could be mustered.

18

'Extreme Tension'

Lieutenant-General Bernard Montgomery arrived in Cairo to take up his position as commander of the Eighth Army after his speedy departure from Britain on 12 August 1942. The day after his arrival he travelled out to El Alamein to survey the situation and was astonished at the appalling level of morale among the troops. He later wrote that 'the situation here when I arrived was really unbelievable, I would never have thought it could have been so bad'. His troops 'had their tails right down and there was no confidence in the higher command'.[1] After a day spent touring the front he asked his most senior officers to gather around him that evening. About fifty to sixty officers assembled. Monty asked them to sit down on the sand and gave a short speech. It must have been a remarkable scene. Monty was short and slim and at this point very white. He had only been in Egypt for twenty-four hours. He did not yet have 'sand in his shoes'. The last combat he had taken part in was as a divisional commander two years before in the retreat to Dunkirk. On the other hand, his officers were tanned, battle-hardened, and many of them had been fighting in the desert for two years. But Monty never lacked self-confidence and in his clipped but assertive style, speaking in short, sometimes terse sentences, he introduced himself and told them that he did not like the 'atmosphere' in the army he was about to lead. 'It is an atmosphere of doubt, of looking back to select the next place to which to withdraw.' He then stated clearly, 'The defence of Egypt lies here at Alamein … Here we will stand and fight; there will be no further withdrawal; I have ordered that all plans and instructions dealing with further withdrawal are to be burnt, and at once. We will stand and fight *here*. If we can't stay here alive then let us stay here dead.' He talked about the reinforcements that were being sent out and the new Sherman tanks and materiel that were arriving in the desert. He ended his short speech by declaring, 'The great point to remember is that we are going to finish with this chap Rommel once and for all. It will be quite easy. There is no doubt about it.'[2] The understatement appealed to his audience. Over the next few days the senior figures present passed on

Everett/Shutterstock

Montgomery poses on a Grant wearing a Tank Regiment beret. Not the typical image of a British general, but all part of the growing legend.

these words to their subordinates; they passed them on to regimental commanders, and they to battalion commanders. And so the message went down the system to the fighting men.

The effect of Montgomery's message was electric. It was backed up by a strenuous round of visits and inspections by the new commander. Initially wearing an Australian slouch hat, later replaced by a simple black beret of the Tank Regiment, he looked totally unlike the usual tall and stiff figure of a British general in a peaked cap. Monty wanted to see and be seen and heard by his men. He wanted to impress his personality on the whole army. He moved his headquarters from Cairo to a modest caravan that was both office and bedroom and could be driven around and parked up near to the action. Whenever a press cameraman appeared, he was happy to pose for a photograph. Those who monitored the censorship of letters home noted a change in tone 'almost overnight'. They reported that 'a breath of fresh, invigorating air has swept through British Troops in Egypt ... Renewed optimism and confidence were everywhere apparent.' General Hugh Mainwaring, Auchinleck's former chief of staff, later wrote that it was 'the turning point of the war'.[3] Monty had raised the spirits of his men, said what they all wanted to hear and made it clear that a new type of leader was in command.

As Monty had said, huge quantities of supplies were arriving in the Middle East from the UK. In August alone more than 72,000 tons of ammunition and stores arrived after the long journey around the Cape; 446 guns and 254 tanks were sent out from Britain and another 132 tanks arrived from the US.[4] The Eighth Army now consisted of 135,000 men against Rommel's 84,000 German and 44,000 Italian soldiers. It was not a sufficient superiority for Montgomery yet, but everyone was aware of the forward movement of vehicles and armour filling the roads heading out into the desert.

When Churchill returned to Cairo after his visit to Stalin,

he and his team quickly picked up on the change in mood among the Eighth Army. After a few days touring front-line units he sent a message to the War Cabinet reporting that 'a complete change of atmosphere has taken place'. He had observed on his earlier visit that men were so obsessed with the likelihood of a further withdrawal to the Nile delta that 'Many were looking over their shoulders to make sure of their seat in the lorry.' Whereas now Monty had issued 'an invigorating directive to his commanders' and 'The highest alacrity and activity prevails.' He concluded, 'I am satisfied that we have lively, confident, resolute men in command, working together as an admirable team.'⁵ Churchill was delighted with the improvement and a sort of boyish good humour returned. After a long day with Montgomery touring troops just behind the front line the PM went for a swim in the Med, fell over in the water under the force of a wave, and lying on his back stuck his legs in the air in the shape of V for Victory. The assembled top brass were highly amused. Back in Cairo he savoured the balmy summer evenings and stayed up late talking with his entourage in the embassy gardens until the early hours. At a press conference in Cairo, Churchill announced that we would fight for Egypt and the Nile 'as if it were the soil of England itself'. When a journalist asked about the second front, the PM quipped, 'I thought you were the second front.'⁶

However, top-secret Ultra decrypts were being forwarded to Churchill and Brooke in Cairo telling them that Rommel was preparing to restart his offensive some time after 25 August. After an enjoyable week in Egypt, Churchill was finally persuaded that it was time to return to London. Wanting him out of the way before Rommel attacked, Brooke wrote in his diary, 'I feel it is a great triumph having got him to start from Egypt. He had every intention of wriggling out of it if he could!'⁷ After a brief stopover in Gibraltar the PM was back in London on the evening of 24 August.

While he had been in Egypt the raid Churchill told Stalin about had taken place. The location was Dieppe, a heavily fortified port on the French Channel coast. It was another sorry affair that brought no credit to Allied forces. After the tiny but scientifically significant raid at Bruneval at the end of February (see Chapter 8), Combined Operations under Lord Mountbatten had organised another and much bigger raid at St Nazaire at the end of March. The objective was to put the dry dock there out of action, meaning that the largest German warships could no longer be repaired in the west of France. The Royal Navy sailed the obsolete destroyer HMS *Campbeltown* across the Channel and it was rammed into the lock gates. Royal Marine Commandos landed during the raid and destroyed other heavy machinery around the docks. The losses were high: only 228 out of the 612 who took part in the raid returned to Britain. But the Germans also suffered high casualties including dozens who died when the delayed-action explosives blew up the *Campbeltown*. The dock was put out of action for the rest of the war and was not fully repaired until 1948. So, despite the high loss rate the raid was regarded as a great success.

Churchill had already expressed his support for these assaults on the French coast to keep German forces on their toes. The momentum for Combined Operations to carry out another raid coincided with the desire of the Canadians to take on a fighting role during 1942. Canadian troops had been gathering in Britain for two years but had so far not been assigned to any combat. Mountbatten resolved to plan a new and bigger raid, this time against Dieppe. The principal purpose would be to capture the town for twenty-four hours, engage with enemy troops, draw out the Luftwaffe for the RAF to destroy, and learn lessons about mounting major amphibious operations across the Channel. A plan was designed for Canadian troops to land on the beaches on both sides of the town but instead it was decided a frontal attack on the port would be more successful. But the RAF said they could not guarantee the bombing of the town in advance of the landings and the navy said it was too risky to bring major warships in close to the shore batteries. So, in July the operation was called off. However, Mountbatten continued to press for Combined Operations to run another op, and the plan was on again. The confused on–off nature of the planning did not help the outcome.

The area where the landing was to take place was defended by six large batteries of German artillery some of which had not been spotted by Allied intelligence. Indeed, intelligence failures dogged the whole operation. On 18 August an assault force of just over 6,000 men, mostly Canadian but including some Royal Marine Commandos and a few US Rangers, embarked to cross the Channel supported by 252 ships. At 3 a.m. the following morning the assault troops began to transfer to their landing craft. Half an hour later, in a stroke of terrible luck, one landing group ran into a collection of armed trawlers and firing began. Another group of landing craft formed up behind the wrong gunboat and time was lost sorting out the confusion. The early assault troops had hoped to rely on speed, surprise and darkness to get ashore. But by the time the landing craft hit the beaches the defenders had been alerted, dawn had broken, and the men struggled ashore under a hail of well-placed machine-gun fire. Hundreds were cut down in the first few minutes. Others tried to get off the beach and over the sea-wall but this was much higher than they had been told and was lined with thick barbed wire. Before long the officers commanding almost every company had been killed or wounded. Radios constantly failed and communication between those on the beaches and the commanders off shore pretty well collapsed. When the tank landing craft arrived twenty-eight new Churchills were put ashore but they had been told to expect sandy beaches and found instead large pebbles that hampered progress. All of the tanks were lost in the fighting that followed. At 8 a.m. the reserves were ordered in but they too were soon pinned down. A few men managed to advance into the Casino and the Promenade that had made Dieppe a popular resort before the war but even these structures were well defended with weapons that again had not been spotted during the planning.

Meanwhile the RAF had tried to lure the Luftwaffe into a fight over the town. Here things again did not go to plan, and the Focke-Wulf 190s were able to outperform the Spitfire VBs whose pilots discovered they were not the fastest aircraft in the sky. One hundred and six aircraft were lost including forty-four Spitfires for the loss of forty-eight German aircraft.

The plan had been to stay in Dieppe all day but soon after 9 a.m. the decision was taken to withdraw. The destroyers escorted the rescue craft into the shore. But getting men off the beaches proved as difficult as getting them on. Countless acts of courage and bravery helped some men to evacuate but by early afternoon the raid was over. Dozens of burning tanks and vehicles had to be abandoned. Nothing more could be done to rescue those who had got into the town and one by one they all surrendered. At 5.40 p.m. the local German commander reported to C-in-C West, 'No armed Englishman remains on the continent.'[8] It took six days to calculate the full scale of the losses, which amounted to 4,384 officers and men out of the 6,000. At least 2,000 of these were prisoners, many of whom were wounded. German losses were less than 600. The raid had been a fiasco.

The results of the debacle at Dieppe were unexpected. Combined Operations learned a few lessons about how *not* to organise amphibious operations and the importance of obtaining full and detailed intelligence of the defences. It was the landings in North Africa and then in Sicily from which the

Ullstein bild Dtl./Getty Images

*Another action; another surrender. Canadians with
their hands high at Dieppe, 19 August 1942.*

big lessons were learned – knowledge applied when planning
the invasion of France in June 1944. Moreover, on the Home
Front, many people in Britain did not believe this was simply
another raid and assumed that it was an attempt to open
a second front. All the publicity at first sang the praises of
the operation using slogans like 'The Canadians fight as the
Russians fight' and 'The Navy and RAF make it an all-English
Channel'. When the terrible losses became apparent, support
for the second front dwindled. Many questioned whether now
was the right time.[9] Brooke was overheard saying, 'It's a lesson
to the people who are clamouring for the invasion of France.'[10]
This was a way of saying 'I told you so' to the Americans and
the Russians. The principal lesson from Dieppe was to show
how badly a landing in France could go wrong.

On the other hand, the situation in Malta improved considerably during the summer. Air Vice Marshal Keith Park

arrived in mid-July to replace Hugh Pughe Lloyd. Not only was Park a fighter commander unlike Lloyd (a bomber man), but he was one of the most distinguished Fighter Command officers in the RAF having led 11 Group in the south of England during the Battle of Britain. He immediately set about reforming the way the fighter defenders of Malta operated. Instead of gathering in a big wing of several squadrons away from the island and attacking the bombers as they dispersed on leaving Malta, having dropped their bombs, he now had enough Spitfires to send them in a forward interception plan to hit the bombers as they approached the island, heavily laden with bombs and still in tight formation. The change in tactics had an almost immediate effect. The tonnage of bombs dropped weekly on Malta fell by more than 50 per cent during July. As the Luftwaffe bomber loss rate increased, the number of bombing sorties against Malta also dropped, by more than half from July to August and by another half in September. And the number of strikes against enemy supply ships by torpedo bombers and submarines increased the total Axis shipping losses to 52,000 tons in August and a further 34,000 tons in September.[11] Once more, bombers and submarines operating out of Malta proved their worth. The failure of the Axis powers to knock out Malta again demonstrated the central role the island played in the control of shipping in the Mediterranean.

Meanwhile, in the desert war, on the early morning of 30 August Rommel relaunched his offensive in what became known as the Battle of Alam Halfa, named after a small, strongly fortified ridge that ran behind the southern sector of the El Alamein defensive line. That there was any assault at all was little short of a miracle. By the end of August every large Italian merchant ship had been sunk. Men and supplies had to be airlifted in from Crete. The supplies reaching the Panzerarmee Afrika had dwindled to a few thousand tons every month. The main port the Axis were using when they did get supplies by sea was Tobruk, and this was bombed almost nightly by Wellingtons. Beaufighters attacked vehicles moving along the long desert road on which everything had to be transported to the front. The Axis were rapidly running out of trucks to bring up essential supplies. Rommel himself was ill with a stomach disorder with the side effect that he was suffering from low blood pressure and dizzy spells. He had asked to be replaced but no one suitable was available so he remained in post. He still hoped to be the commander who would capture the Suez Canal.

His tactics were almost a repeat of those he had employed at Gazala. After a feint in the north he planned to attack in the south in a large circuit, driving his panzers into the heart of the Allied position hoping to cause chaos and disruption and to encircle the troops in the north. It was after this sweeping force had penetrated the line at Gazala that the British generals had dithered, giving Rommel the opportunity for victory. But there were several elements that made this new battle different from the last.

First, the ground troops were equipped with far more 6-pounder anti-tank guns than before and from the Alam Halfa ridge they fired directly into the advancing panzers as they tried to navigate through the minefields. Second, the air force was far more closely coordinated than previously. Wellington night bombers hit the advancing armour on the first night. Light bombers struck them during the following day. And the Wellingtons returned on the second night. The destruction they caused was heavy. Three German generals were killed or wounded during the first twenty-four hours including, symbolically, the commander of the 21st Panzer Division, General Bismarck. Rommel himself was lucky to escape an attack on his staff car.

Although new to desert warfare, Montgomery read the

situation well and moved his defensive line so it was always ready to repel another Axis assault. After only three days, desperately short of fuel, in a landscape dotted with burning tanks and supply vehicles, Rommel called off his offensive. Blaming the shortage of petrol and the constant harassment from air attacks, he ordered a withdrawal. Montgomery realised that, as the official history recorded it, Rommel had 'shot his bolt' and he had the opportunity to turn his defence into an offensive action, but decided against it. He felt the Eighth Army was not yet ready and more work needed to be done before he could inflict the decisive blow he was already planning.[12]

With the collapse of this attack and with the balance of forces and supplies now weighing heavily on the Allied side, Rommel's threat to capture Cairo and the Suez Canal effectively came to an end. German morale was still good, but that of the Italians was rapidly falling through the floor. In the Allied forces the successful defence of Alam Halfa provided a further boost to already rising morale. Monty had fulfilled his promise that he would win the next battle.

To Montgomery, however, it was clear that there was still much to do. His troops needed better training in order to fight the decisive battle to come. First, Monty reorganised his high command, bringing in his own hand-picked candidates, sometimes replacing Eighth Army veterans. Second, he wanted to create a better armoured unit that included both tanks and motorised infantry, on the model of the Panzerarmee. Third, as a stickler for physical fitness he introduced a regime of daily PT training for all officers and men. This met with considerable resistance from battle-hardened warriors who felt they were being treated like raw recruits. But Monty insisted this applied to men of all ranks and all experience. Across the desert soldiers were seen going on early-morning runs and practising their squats and press-ups. Finally, he organised both small-scale training in firearms and mortar use and large-scale military exercises which he tried to make as realistic as possible. This was just as he had done during the Phoney War with the division he commanded in France. It was one reason why the division got away at Dunkirk almost intact. Montgomery persuaded General Alexander that he would need several weeks for the Eighth Army to prepare. Initially they looked at early to mid-October to commence battle. But the engineers would need a full moon to clear the huge minefields ahead of them. The full moon was on 23 October.

After his return from Cairo and Moscow, Churchill became absorbed with planning for the landings in North-West Africa, Operation Torch. It was a complex amphibious operation that involved coordinating the arrival of men, vehicles and the vast quantities of supplies needed. Part was to be shipped direct from the United States, and part from the UK. There was also considerable uncertainty about how the Vichy forces in the French colonies would respond to the landing of American troops. General Eisenhower, who was based in London, was put in charge of the whole operation. At one point the chiefs of staff in Washington proposed a dramatic reduction in the scale of Torch by ruling out Algiers and instead landing troops only on the Atlantic coast to the west of Gibraltar. But after protests it was resolved to carry on as originally conceived. A date was finally settled for early November when the loading and transportation of men and supplies could be brought together.

Churchill soon began to fret about delays with Montgomery's offensive in the desert. On 8 September, Brooke wrote in his diary, 'My next trouble will now be to stop Winston from fussing Alex and Monty and egging them on to attack before they are ready. It is a regular disease that he suffers from, this frightful impatience to get an attack launched!'[13] But although he did try to egg them on, his last few days in Cairo had been so encouraging that he did not press Alexander in the way he had pushed Auchinleck. And Alexander was good at keeping Monty protected from the PM's pressure. Ultra decrypts continued to make it clear how severe were the shortages of fuel and ammunition for Rommel's forces. And Bletchley Park also read the Italian naval messages, which regularly conveyed detailed information about the sailing of convoys to North Africa. One after another these convoys were attacked causing further trouble for Rommel and his Panzerarmee. On one day he had been promised 2,400 tons of fuel but received only 100 tons. The supplies available limited him to only six days of fighting.[14]

Another Arctic convoy, PQ18, sailed with supplies for the Soviet Union in mid-September – forty merchant ships, escorted by seventy-seven naval vessels including the escort carrier HMS *Avenger*. Once again running the convoy put great pressure on the navy at the point at which shipping was being assembled for Torch. And once again the convoy came under heavy attack from both aircraft and submarines in the area where aerial protection was impossible. This time thirteen merchant ships were sunk but the escorts fought back fiercely, shooting down forty-four Luftwaffe aircraft and sinking three U-boats. After the disaster of PQ17 in July and the postponement of future convoys, PQ18 succeeded in getting two thirds of its cargo through to Archangel. This was a victory of sorts.

Roosevelt addressed the American nation on Labor Day, 7 September, in a radio speech in which he appealed to the working people of America when he said, 'Battles are not won by soldiers or sailors who think first of their own personal safety. And wars are not won by people who are concerned primarily with their own comfort, their own convenience, their own pocketbooks ... All of us here at home are being tested – for our fortitude, for our selfless devotion to our

country and our cause.' After his speech Roosevelt went on
a tour of the nation's major war factories which took up most
of September. He visited the Chrysler plant in Detroit (which
had been turned over to making tanks), the Ford factory at
Willow Run (B-24 Liberators), the Kaiser shipyards in Portland
(Liberty ships), the Higgins yards in New Orleans (landing
craft), the Boeing plant in Seattle (B-17 Flying Fortresses) and
several army training camps, airfields and naval stations. It
enabled him to catch up on the progress in war production,
which was impressive but slower than hoped. But it was
Congressional election year so it also provided an opportunity
for a nationwide canvassing tour.[15] However, the elections
on 3 November did not go well for the Democrats as rum-
blings about the nation's war policy were widespread. The
Republicans gained 47 votes in the House and 10 seats in the
Senate. The Democrats held on to their majorities but only
just. Nineteen forty-two was not a year for the leaders of the
democracies to wallow in their popularity.

There was another internal political threat in Westminster
in September when Sir Stafford Cripps, who as Lord Privy
Seal had been patiently defending the government for some
months, offered up another challenge. Cripps had become
convinced that national morale had seriously declined
over recent months and there was a widespread mood of
frustration and discontent. He said factory workers were
demoralised when they heard that the weapons they had
worked long hours to produce had been found inadequate in
battle. Businessmen were exasperated by official delays and
indecision. Servicemen were disturbed by evidence of poor
military leadership. Cripps wanted to infuse a new spirit of
vigour and enthusiasm into the nation's war effort and came
up with an idea for a new and independent War Planning
Directorate to control the national war effort. It was just the
sort of scheme that appealed to his clear and methodical brain.

Churchill, of course, not only perceived it as a direct threat to his leadership but also saw in it the impossibility of winning the war by simply implementing a planner's dream. A meeting between Churchill and Cripps turned into a blazing row, and when the PM made it clear he would not accept his proposal, Cripps threatened to resign. This would have been terribly damaging for the Prime Minister at such a critical moment, and in reality represented more of a serious political threat than the motions of no confidence and censure earlier in the year. It would be disastrous for the war effort if Cripps went just before the new Allied offensives. Churchill was convinced it was all part of a Machiavellian plot to undermine his leadership.[16]

Members of the War Cabinet, including Eden and Attlee, pleaded with Cripps not to resign. He realised that if the offensives planned in North Africa failed, then Churchill would be unlikely to survive. If they succeeded, his leadership would be secure and any threat from Cripps would be diminished. But he agreed to withdraw his resignation. The moment of crisis passed and Churchill survived yet another challenge. Later in the year, however, Cripps decided to leave the War Cabinet and Churchill made him Minister of Aircraft Production, an appointment which he pursued with vigour as it enabled him to deploy his skills as a war planner to maximum effect.

Churchill was not known for his patience. And the autumn of 1942 required a lot of waiting for events to unfold, with the key battle at Alamein and the Torch landings still ahead. The period of waiting was to him 'one of suppressed but extreme tension'. 'I myself find waiting more trying than action,' he wrote.[17] Churchill felt confident about the newly structured Eighth Army but could never be certain about the outcome of battle. 'After the unpleasant surprises of the last two years it was difficult to banish anxiety,' he later wrote. 'Another reverse would not only be disastrous in itself, but would damage British prestige and influence in the discussions we were having with our American Allies.'[18] At the end of September depressing news came through from the Russian front that German forces were threatening to smash the last line of Soviet defences at Stalingrad. The situation had reached its most critical stage. Stalin responded with further requests for 800 fighter aircraft per month to help sustain the front. At the same time Churchill also heard disappointing news from Wavell that he would be unable to start a campaign to recapture Burma that winter. The monsoon had been severe and malaria was rife among his troops. On the evening of 1 October, Churchill told Eden that if Torch failed 'then I'm done for and must go and hand over to one of you'.[19] A few days later Beaverbrook told Eden that Churchill was 'bowed' and 'not the man he was'.[20] Churchill later said that for him, September and October 1942 were the two 'most anxious months of the war'.[21]

Desperately short of fuel, and with supply lines stretching hundreds of miles back to the ports where everything it needed came ashore, the Panzerarmee dug in its tanks and laid about half a million mines along vast swathes of the front, some anti-tank, some anti-personnel, and in places a mixture of both. The British called this the 'Devil's Garden'. Rommel was getting more frantic in his calls for more men, supplies and ammunition, but mostly fuel. His requests prompted promises but they were not met as the German war machine was concentrated on supplying the Eastern Front. The desert war had become a sideshow in the eyes of the OKW in Berlin. At Bletchley Park, the codebreakers continued to read the messages that went back and forth and could clearly see Rommel's growing despair. In the desert, a new team of cipher officers had started to listen in to signals traffic within the Panzerarmee itself. And in an act of deception, it was made to look as though vast reserves were being assembled in the south of the front. A dummy pipeline and fake supply depots were laid out and German reconnaissance aircraft were allowed to photograph them. Montgomery wanted it to look as though he would launch his offensive in the south in the hope of breaking through the flank of the Axis line, as had been the case in so many desert battles. But that was not what he intended. As the waiting continued, Rommel left Egypt and paid a whistle-stop propaganda visit to Berlin during which he was filmed by newsreel cameras being presented with his field marshal's baton by Hitler. He was stunned by the absurd optimism and lack of reality he encountered among the military high command. Then he disappeared to Austria for a quiet few weeks to try to restore his health. General Georg Stumme was left in charge of the Afrika Korps.

By the latter part of October, the Eighth Army had a majority of roughly 2:1 over the Panzerarmee Afrika. There were just over 200,000 Allied soldiers against 104,000 Axis; over 1,000 Allied tanks against 489 Axis; 2,300 artillery pieces against 1,200. The Allied tank units included 252 of the new American Shermans and there were 849 of the powerful 6-pounder anti-tank guns. Only in the air were the two sides more evenly matched, with 530 serviceable RAF aircraft against 350 Luftwaffe.[22] Monty wanted every man to know of the battle plan and to understand his role in it. He visited as many troops as possible and instructed officers to explain the details of the mission to each man in terms he could understand. 'We're going to hit the enemy for six out of Africa' became the common catchphrase.[23] As a consequence, morale in the Eighth Army shot up to an all-time high. A report on the mood of British troops said that 'the offensive spirit' was 'dominant' among soldiers at all levels. One soldier wrote in a letter home, 'We've got the stuff and a general who knows how to use it.'[24]

Finally, Monty felt the Eighth Army was in a position to attack. 'When I assumed command of the Eighth Army,' he announced, 'I said that the mandate was to destroy Rommel and his army, and that it would be done as soon as we were ready. We are ready NOW.'[25] At 9.40 p.m. on Friday 23 October, battle commenced with an immense artillery barrage along the El Alamein front. Almost 750 guns opened fire on a bright moonlit night. That evening, in London, Churchill messaged Roosevelt to tell him that at last the offensive had started. He informed the President that 'The whole force of the army will be engaged.'[26] Brendan Bracken told Churchill's doctor, 'If we are beaten in this battle, it's the end of Winston.'[27]

19

'The End of the Beginning'

The artillery barrage that began the Second Battle of El Alamein was of First World War intensity. 'It was incredible. It was like a huge earthquake,' remembered Sam Bradshaw in one of the tank brigades waiting to go forward after the infantry on the night of Friday 23 October 1942.[1] 'The desert seemed to be shaking all over. It was the first time I ever felt sorry for the Germans,' recalled George Greenfield of the Buffs as he waited to advance. 'It was a shattering, fantastic sound, drowning the subdued whispering of boots in the sand and the occasional clink of a rifle or bayonet as the infantry moved up.'[2]

At 10 p.m. the barrage ceased and in the north the infantry of XXX Corps, consisting of the 9th Australian and the 51st Highland Divisions, moved forward, the latter behind the sound of the bagpipes. To the south of them the 2nd New Zealand and the 1st South African Divisions advanced against Italian forces. And to keep the Axis guessing, the 4th Indian Division, further south still, carried out a series of raids along their section of the front. Behind them the British tanks of X Corps, 1st and 10th Armoured Divisions, were to break through the gaps created by the infantry and dig in for an anticipated counter-attack. It was a truly Commonwealth army that launched the Alamein offensive. What followed mirrored the story of many desert battles. It soon became utterly confusing, with troops lost in the expanse of desert failing to achieve their objectives and commanders unclear as to which units were where as the swirling sand added to the fog of war, while the Germans responded quickly to an ever-changing battlefield. By the first morning, several key sites had been taken by the infantry but the Highlanders had suffered heavy casualties and none of the tank units had been able to move forward to capture their objectives. Monty's plan did not seem to be working.

When he received reports of the attack, Rommel, in Austria trying to restore his health, prepared to fly back to Egypt. He arrived on the evening of Sunday the 25th, to find that General Stumme, in command in his absence, was missing. Trying to find out what was happening in the chaos of the battle, Stumme's car had blundered into the advancing Australians and he had suffered a heart attack and died. Intense fighting was concentrating around a small incline in the otherwise featureless plain known as Kidney Ridge. This inconsequential spur became the epicentre of this phase of the battle. Tank losses on both sides were heavy. On the Axis side, the 15th Panzer Division was down to only twenty-three tanks and the Italian Littorio Division was down to forty-four out of 116. In X Corps, 213 tanks were hit.

In his assessment of the battle, Rommel realised that his men had been deceived into anticipating an attack in the south when the real battle was taking place in the north. Knowing that he only had enough fuel to move his panzers across the battlefield once, on the afternoon of Tuesday the 27th he ordered the 21st Panzer and the Italian Ariete Divisions from the southern sector to join in the battle in the north. On hearing that two more tankers bringing supplies had been sunk outside Tobruk, Rommel sent off more frantic demands for fuel. He put on record where he felt the blame for defeat would lie: 'I have to point out that the Army has drawn attention again and again to the need for adequate supplies of fuel and ammunition. It is therefore those who are responsible for supply who are uniquely to blame for the current grave crisis.'[3]

Meanwhile, Montgomery was having his own problems. He felt that not all of his commanders were showing sufficient resolve, especially Lieutenant-General Herbert Lumsden of X Corps who he said was 'excitable, highly strung and easily depressed'.[4] He withdrew the New Zealanders and 7th Armoured Division to form a new reserve and instead of battling on with his original strategy decided to start planning out a new one to keep up pressure in the north. When Churchill heard that Monty was withdrawing troops he panicked and prepared a hostile telegram accusing him of fighting only a 'half-hearted' battle and that the offensive was 'petering out'. Brooke stepped in to prevent him sending the message and told Churchill that he was wrong. At a stormy chiefs of staff meeting on Thursday the 29th, Churchill confronted Brooke over what he called '*his* Monty' (whenever he was critical of the general he implied he was Brooke's appointment, whenever he was praising him it was 'my Monty'). Brooke explained that Monty had been standing firm against several counter-attacks and was now preparing a reserve with which he was going to launch a new assault. Churchill was finally persuaded and agreed not to send his hostile message but to be more conciliatory. Brooke wrote in his diary, 'He is the most difficult man I have ever served with, but thank God for having given me the opportunity of trying to serve such a man in a crisis such as the one this country is going through at present.'[5] The tensions reveal Churchill's stress and frustration that the battle had lasted nearly a week and the outcome was still uncertain.

During Friday 30 October, Montgomery rewrote his battle plan and called the next phase Operation Supercharge. The

Australians launched a renewed assault in the north that evening, supported by well-coordinated attacks by the RAF on Axis positions. Then on the night of Sunday 1 November, the New Zealanders launched a new assault further south on the flank of Kidney Ridge. This attack was preceded by seven hours of bombing from the air and another heavy artillery barrage. During the night the Afrika Korps communication centre was knocked out, and when dawn came up Rommel found it impossible to assess what was going on. The New Zealanders fought brilliantly and captured their objectives near a spot called Tel el Aqqaqir. The tanks of 9th Armoured Brigade had this time kept up with the New Zealanders and had not let them down, but at a terrible cost: seventy-five out of ninety-four tanks had been knocked out. When Rommel finally understood what was happening he ordered his panzers to attack at Tel el Aqqaqir. The 1st Armoured Division arrived to support the Allied effort and from 11 a.m. on Monday the 2nd the fiercest tank engagement of the battle took place. Rommel assembled all his 88mm guns to fire on the British tanks. But with the German and Italian armour so short of petrol, and with the growing weight of armour on the Allied side, the fight lasted only a few hours. By dusk, the Germans were left with only thirty-five tanks. The Italian tank units had been completely wiped out. It was the turning point in the battle.

That evening, Rommel ordered his men to begin to withdraw and sent a message to the OKW saying that despite heroic resistance his troops were exhausted and would be unable to face a renewal of the Allied assault. He explained that he had only limited fuel to manage a withdrawal and that constant air attacks along the only road westwards would bring further destruction. He wanted the OKW to know the worst and concluded that 'the gradual annihilation of the army must be faced'.[6] The message was decoded at Bletchley

Park and was read in London at about the same time as it was read in Berlin.[7]

Hitler responded by telling Rommel that reinforcements were on their way and that the enemy would now be at their last breath. He must not yield an inch. 'You can show no path other than victory or death.'[8] Rommel hesitated, but on the night of Tuesday the 3rd the New Zealanders finally smashed the Axis line and British tanks broke out into open country. Rommel decided to ignore Hitler and gave the order to retreat. But this proved difficult to carry out. The only troops who managed to get away were those with their own transport. The infantry, who had no access to trucks, were left behind. This included nearly all the Italian troops along the entire battle front. Montgomery wanted to pursue those who were fleeing but massive congestion of British armour and artillery around Tel el Aqqaqir took some time to clear. Instead, the Allied forces started to round up those who had been left behind. Within days a total of 8,000 Germans and 22,000 Italians, including six generals, had been taken prisoner.

By Wednesday 4 November, the battle was over. Alexander sent a message to Churchill that morning: 'After twelve days of heavy and violent fighting, Eighth Army has inflicted a severe defeat on the enemy's German and Italian forces under Rommel's command. The enemy's front has broken.'[9] A delighted and much relieved Churchill forwarded the message to Roosevelt, Stalin and all the Commonwealth prime ministers. The message was read out on the BBC that night. In his caravan that evening Monty met with General von Thoma, previously commander of the Afrika Korps, who had been captured. They spoke together intently for a couple of hours and discussed desert warfare. Monty thought his German rival was 'a very nice chap'.[10]

The Eighth Army headed off in pursuit of the remains of the Panzerarmee as it retreated westwards along the desert

Print Collector/Getty Images

The turning point at El Alamein. This time the Germans are surrendering.

road. The initial congestion had given the Axis a good start; then, after just a few days, heavy winter rains lashed down around the desert highway making pursuit by armoured vehicles trying to outflank the retreating forces impossible. The Desert Fox once again managed to get away with the remnants of his force. He planned to form a new line at Fuka, 60 miles to the west.

Rommel left behind around 7,000 dead and wounded in addition to the 30,000 prisoners. Eighth Army casualties were high at 13,500 dead and wounded. Some of the front-line infantry units had suffered casualty rates of nearly 50 per cent during the thirteen days of continuous battle. But morale remained high.[11] In the scale of Second World War battles, and especially by comparison with those on the Eastern Front, the Second Battle of El Alamein was a relatively small affair. But it was a battle of immense importance. Not only did it save Egypt and the Suez Canal and prevent any possibility of a German breakthrough in the Middle East, it signified the turn of the tide as far as British fortunes were concerned. It at last provided evidence that with the right weapons and equipment, and with good leadership, the British Army could defeat the German Army. The Italian elite units at Alamein had also fought well and did not deserve to be abandoned by the Germans in the aftermath. Alamein was significant also in that it was the first and the last time an exclusively British and Commonwealth army would enjoy a victory over the Germans. All future battles would be combined operations with the United States.

Finally, after a string of dreadful defeats and military humiliations, Alamein was at last the victory Britons had been longing for and Churchill needed. It was a genuine turning point, and it saved the reputation of the Prime Minister. There was nothing like victory to lift the spirits, from the forward desert dugout to the corridors of Downing Street and the factories of Britain. 'It's been exhilarating to live through the last ten days in England,' wrote Mollie Panter-Downes. 'On the morning when British families switched on their radios and heard the news that the Nazi forces were in full retreat, London was a city of smiling people.' She recounted that girls behind their shop counters, taxi drivers, everyone she met had a smile, including the bus conductor 'who tinkled his bell and shouted "Next stop, Benghazi!"' [12]

Mass Observation reported an almost instant change of mood on the Home Front. There was a renewed interest in war news, increased optimism, a drop in war-weariness and a surge in production in the war factories. A diarist in Hampshire wrote that the view in her village was that everyone 'hoped we weren't blowing the trumpet too soon' and that people were saying 'Let's hope he [Rommel] doesn't turn the tables on us in a few days.' Others were asking, 'Do you think we shall need a Second Front now?' [13]

Four days after victory had been announced at Alamein, in the early hours of the morning of 8 November, American troops began their landings in North-West Africa – Operation Torch. It was a complex military operation that involved the sailing of three large task forces bringing men and materiel from two continents to coordinate landings on the beaches of a third. The Western Task Force had set sail from ports along the eastern seaboard of the United States in early October. Thirty-six supply and troop ships were escorted across the North Atlantic by nearly seventy warships including three battleships, a fleet carrier, four escort carriers and forty-five cruisers and destroyers. Later in October, two task forces left Britain, one from the Clyde and the second from Milford Haven, consisting of eighty-six supply ships and more than a hundred escorts including four carriers. The Western Task Force landed American troops on the beaches north and south of Casablanca in Morocco. The Central and Eastern Task Forces assembled at Gibraltar before entering the Mediterranean to land Americans at Oran and British and American soldiers in Algiers. In total around 125,000 men splashed ashore that morning in the first truly Anglo-American combined operation of the war. The Royal Navy provided most of the escort shipping in the Mediterranean. The United States provided most of the invasion troops.

That the landings took place at all was remarkable. First, there had been pressure from Stalin for a second front in Europe, not the Mediterranean. Second, there had been disagreements between the Americans and the British over the advisability of the entire operation. These had only been resolved in July when President Roosevelt overruled his own chiefs of staff and insisted on going ahead as the only means by which American troops could engage with German and Italian ground forces in 1942 (see Chapter 15). Third, there had been uncertainty about how the 105,000 Vichy French troops in Morocco and Algiers (most of whom were African) would respond. Would they oppose the landings with force or welcome the invaders? The Americans believed their troops would receive a better welcome than British forces as there was residual hostility to Britain after Churchill's order to destroy the French fleet in North Africa in July 1940. So everywhere it was American troops that led the landings.

This made the political planning for Torch as complicated as the military logistics. After defeat in 1940, the French military had divided between those who supported de Gaulle in exile in London and those who remained loyal to the Vichy regime of Marshal Pétain. The North African colonies were run by men loyal to Vichy. The Americans wanted to find a French general loyal to the Allies but with sufficient authority in North Africa to ensure there would be no military opposition to the invasion. They picked General Henri Giraud, a First World War hero who had gone on to lead the Seventh Army in France in May 1940. He was captured during the Battle of France but escaped in April 1942 and managed to travel back to the 'Free Zone' of southern France not occupied by Germany. There he was approached by an American envoy sent by Roosevelt to persuade him to take command in North Africa. At the same time, in late October, US General Mark Clark was secretly landed on the Algerian coast from a British submarine to establish an agreement with the French resistance in the region to ensure their support. It was all very cloak and dagger and no one really knew if any of the plotting would pay off.

The commander put in charge of Operation Torch by Roosevelt and Churchill was the relatively unknown General Dwight Eisenhower. Many experienced commanders such as Brooke looked down on Eisenhower, a staff officer with no experience of a field command. Brooke regarded him as a 'political' general. But he was exactly the right man to be in command of such a complex operation. Although it was a combined Anglo-American operation, once the parameters had been set, Churchill was quite willing to let the Americans run the show. He wrote submissively to Roosevelt in September, 'In the whole of "Torch", military and political, I consider myself your lieutenant ... This is an American enterprise in which we are your helpmeets.'[14]

The three sets of landings by and large passed off without disaster. The troops landed everywhere displaying large Stars and Stripes, hoping they would be seen as liberators rather than invaders. Confusion, muddle and lack of experience in amphibious landings were more of a problem than enemy resistance. In Casablanca things did not go so smoothly and it took a couple of days to occupy the city. There was some resistance at Oran but little in Algiers except for attacks on two British destroyers that tried to land US infantry in the port. On 9 November, with Giraud still waiting in Gibraltar, Admiral François Darlan, a leading French figure in Pétain's Vichy government who happened to be in Algiers visiting his son at the time of the landings, stepped forward and took command. Darlan was widely detested as commander-in-chief of Vichy forces and a figure who represented collaboration with the Nazis. Under American pressure, Darlan issued orders that French troops and sailors should cease all resistance. Pétain told him to rescind the order, and in an almost farcical episode he agreed to do so but then did not make his decision public. And then Darlan handed himself over to the Americans as a captive. At least Pétain could tell the Germans that no order had come from his government to support the Allied landings. Darlan was soon freed and Eisenhower decided he was the man needed by the Allies to give support to the invasion. Within a few days, all three ports were in US hands and most of the major airfields around each city had been occupied.

The Yanks have arrived. American soldiers after landing at Casablanca,
November 1942. It was hoped that brandishing the Stars and
Stripes would encourage Vichy French forces not to resist.

On 13 November there was more good news when the
Eighth Army re-entered Tobruk – another symbolic marker
of victory. Churchill ordered that the church bells should be
rung once again on Sunday 15 November. Two years before
this had been a signal of invasion, now it was a herald of
victory. Mass Observation noted that 'this was appreciated
by a large number of people because "It was nice to hear the
Church Bells again" and not because people felt it suited the
war situation'. But once again Mass Observation reported
another big boost in morale. Whereas many people had been
hesitant about celebrating too soon after the first news of
Alamein, it now seemed that victory was certain, and after
news of the American landings 'cheerfulness changed to an
optimism which was often exaggerated. There was talk of
the end of the war being in sight, and even more moderate
people came to say that it should be over in a year.' Among

the comments recorded were a newspaper seller who said there had been 'more of a rush on papers than at any time since King Edward's abdication'. A twenty-five-year-old male commented, 'if we are successful in Egypt it will take at least a year off the war'. Many highly critical comments about Darlan were recorded. A young male said he couldn't see how he could be trusted, and several people called him a 'rat'. But the news was obviously good for the Prime Minister, and a fifty-year-old woman was heard to say that 'Churchill was a wonderful man and all that, but not much of a one for hurrying'. It was generally felt that this victory was 'the real thing and the demands for a second front almost vanished'.[15]

Hitler's reaction to the landings in French North-West Africa was swift. The Free Zone of France in the south was occupied by German mechanised forces on 11 November, the twenty-fourth anniversary of the Armistice. It effectively meant the end of the Vichy regime and the whole of France would remain under Nazi occupation until liberated by the Allies two years later. And Hitler ordered an airlift to begin to transport German troops and equipment into Tunis. The French authorities there, another Vichy-controlled colonial outpost, were ordered to permit an Axis build-up in the area. By the end of the month 15,000 troops and a hundred tanks had been flown in. They were joined by 9,000 Italians. The beginnings of a large new Axis army were being formed in Tunisia that would add another dimension to the situation in North Africa.

Meanwhile, on hearing of the landings in North-West Africa, 700 miles west of Libya, Rommel abandoned his plans to stand firm at Fuka. He ordered his forces to pull further back as speedily as possible, eventually to link up with the new army being formed in Tunis. Having retaken Tobruk almost without a fight, advanced troops of the Eighth Army a week later recaptured Benghazi. Old battlefields were crossed at speed. After attempting a stand at El Agheila, Rommel's troops were once again forced to retreat. In mid-December, what remained of the Panzerarmee Afrika left Cyrenaica heading west. It was the end of two years of fighting back and forth across the Western Desert. But it was far from the end of the battle for North Africa.

Once the Anglo-American landing forces had established themselves in Morocco and Algeria they turned east. The hope was that they would occupy Tunis by the end of the year and then could strike a new blow in 1943 in Sicily, Sardinia, Italy or even southern France. A new British grouping, First Army, was created in Algiers under Lieutenant-General Sir Kenneth Anderson. It set out to clear the Tunisian coastline, advance 560 miles to Tunis and join up with the Eighth Army advancing west from Libya towards Tripoli. The initial advances were spectacular but as German forces in Tunisia quickly built up they were able to slow the British down. A series of paratroop drops to seize key airfields were impossible to follow up and isolated groups of paras had to fight their way backwards to British lines. Meanwhile, the bulk of American forces in Casablanca and Oran were too far west and they would not fully enter the fighting until January 1943. By early December 1942, the Allied forces had been halted in the mountains of western Tunisia with Axis troops well dug in to protect Bizerta, Tunis and Oudna, each of which had major airfields from where the Luftwaffe was operating.

The political ramifications of Torch continued to reverberate across the Mediterranean. With all of France under Nazi occupation, the Allies feared that the Germans would seize what was left of the French naval fleet at Toulon harbour and so requested that it be handed over to them. As the Germans closed in and surrounded the harbour the French sailors scuttled their vessels. A quarter of a million tons of naval shipping sank to the bottom of the sea. The Allies were disappointed not to gain the French fleet but relieved that the Germans had not been able to get hold of it. But the Germans did seize over 640,000 tons of French merchant shipping which went some way to making up for the dramatic losses of Italian vessels during the year.[16]

Admiral Darlan proved an unpopular choice as the Americans' principal military commander in North Africa. He was seen as pro-Nazi, and de Gaulle, the Free French leader in exile in London, was furious at his appointment. In December, Darlan was assassinated in his office by a young pro-de Gaulle Frenchman who was receiving training from the Special Operations Executive. It was suspected that Darlan had been targeted by the British secret service. Although there is no evidence to make a direct link it certainly suited British interests to have such a detested figure out of the way.[17] The assassin thought he would become a hero but instead he was caught, quickly tried by court martial and executed. Giraud, who had been the Allies' first choice, was appointed in Darlan's place and the murky politics of France under occupation became a little clearer.

One of the reasons for Torch had been to relieve pressure on the Eastern Front. It was not the same as a major landing in northern Europe, as Churchill, Roosevelt and the chiefs of staff knew. However, the effect was significant and it came at a crucial moment. Five hundred German aircraft were transferred to the new Tunisian front, including 400 from the Eastern Front. Among these were several transport aircraft transferred from Stalingrad where they were supplying the German Sixth Army.[18] In addition, several squadrons of torpedo bombers were sent south from northern Norway to do battle in North Africa. The consequence of this was that no future Arctic convoy to supply the Soviets ever came under the sort of intense assault that had been experienced in 1942. The occupation of all of France and the build-up of a new army in Tunisia led to a further withdrawal of limited numbers of ground troops from the east. But it was the removal of many of the transports supplying the Germans at Stalingrad that had the biggest immediate impact.

Not just one but two military victories had helped to rescue the Prime Minister. His reputation and standing began to bounce back after a torrid year that had seriously threatened Churchill's future in Downing Street. General Kennedy in the War Office was deeply critical of the extent to which Churchill meddled in military affairs he should have left to his chiefs of staff. Of the turning of the tide in November 1942 he wrote, 'Prime Ministers need luck as well as Generals; Prime Ministers who usurp the role of Commanders-in-Chief need a double dose of it.'[19] It was clear that at last Churchill had got his double dose.

The first two weeks of November 1942 proved to be a decisive fortnight. There was victory at El Alamein, the successful landings in North-West Africa, and the Red Army assembled a completely new army under General Zhukov outside Stalingrad that went on to the offensive mid-month. And between 12 and 15 November a set of furious sea battles took place off Guadalcanal which brought an end to Japanese attempts to evict US forces from the Solomon Islands. In a speech on 17 November, President Roosevelt declared, 'During the past two weeks we have had a great deal of good news and it would seem that the turning point in this war has at last been reached.' Newspaper headlines across the United States screamed out 'Turning Point of War Reached Says FDR'.[20]

Churchill was more cautious in a speech at the Mansion House in London, broadcast on the BBC. He said, 'I have never promised anything but blood, tears, toil and sweat. Now, however, we have a new experience. We have victory, a remarkable and definite victory. The bright gleam has caught the helmets of our soldiers, and warmed and cheered all our hearts.' He summed up the situation with his famous words, 'Now, this is not the end. It is not even the beginning of the end. But it is, perhaps, the end of the beginning.'[21]

Epilogue

A reinvigorated Churchill spent Christmas 1942 at Chequers with his family around him: Clemmie, his three daughters, his brother John, his daughter-in-law Pamela and his grandson Winston; Randolph was away in North-West Africa. It must have been a happy Christmas for the Prime Minister as that month satisfaction with his leadership had shot up from the dreadfully low levels earlier in the year to an extraordinary 93 per cent in Gallup's poll.[1] The arrival of messages from the war front did not cease for the festivities. On Christmas Eve a signal from General Alexander told him that if the enemy made a stand in southern Tunisia there could be no attack 'before the end of January'.[2] Monty would need time to reorganise the Eighth Army for a new assault and to prepare his supply lines. It must have sounded like the record from Cairo had got stuck in the groove. Yet again Churchill would be waiting for his generals. On Christmas Day he heard the news of the assassination of Admiral Darlan and was mightily relieved. He later wrote, 'Darlan's murder, however criminal, relieved the Allies of the embarrassment of working with him.' Now it was possible, he wrote, for the French forces in North and North-West Africa 'to unite with the Free French movement round de Gaulle'.[3]

Christmas 1942 was the fourth Christmas Britons had been

at war. The first had lulled the nation into complacency with the inaction of the Phoney War. The second had seen Britons scurrying to the air raid shelters as the Blitz approached its peak. Despite shortages, the third had brought the relief of seeing both the Soviet Union and the United States as allies. But nothing could have prepared the nation for the run of calamities that marked the first six months of 1942. Everywhere the British Army fought it seemed to fail. In North Africa morale plummeted as men fought bravely and well, and then to their astonishment were ordered to retreat for hundreds of miles. The succession of disasters undermined public confidence in Churchill's leadership and prompted many usually loyal individuals and newspapers to challenge his judgement and his strategic vision. Churchill later described the long run of catastrophes in 1942 as 'galling links in a chain of misfortune and frustration to which no parallel could be found in our history'. He reflected on the series of failures, 'Was it strange that the whole character and system of the war direction, for which I was responsible, should have been brought into question and challenge? It is indeed remarkable that I was not in this bleak lull dismissed from power, or confronted with demands for changes in my methods, which it was known I should never accept. I should then have vanished from the scene with a load of calamity on my shoulders.'[4]

For some, belief in victory never totally collapsed. In the darkest moment in the early part of 1942, Mollie Panter-Downes wrote, 'About the outcome of the war there are no doubts; about the immediate present, there are unfortunately many.'[5] Many Mass Observation diarists, however, did overhear serious doubts about the war's outcome. One diarist reported in February, 'My landlady said tonight "I wonder if we shall win this war. Sometimes I feel doubtful."'[6] In April, the diarist in Hampshire recorded that her friend had announced that 'she thought we would be under German rule before long'.[7]

In the Far East before 1941, Japanese forces had been vastly underrated and dismissed with much racist slur about the yellow races. Then, following Pearl Harbor, the astonishing speed of Japanese advances meant the pins on walls in map rooms in London and Washington were out of date as soon as they had been stuck up. In a matter of a few months Japanese conquests spread eastwards into the mid-Pacific, southwards towards the coast of Australia and westwards to the gates of India. Japanese troops occupied Siam, Malaya, Singapore, the Philippines and Burma. They landed on Borneo, New Guinea, New Britain and the Solomon Islands. Japanese aircraft sank six battleships and three aircraft carriers. The Japanese Navy sailed freely around the Bay of Bengal, threatened Ceylon, and came to the waters of northern Australia. It was probably the fastest spread of conquest in world history. Only with the Battle of Midway in June was the tide of conquest halted. But it was not until August that the advance of their armies was turned by the first ground offensive against them with the landing of US Marines on Guadalcanal.

Strategists in London and Washington had contemplated the possibility of a Japanese advance westwards through India linking up with a German breakthrough towards the east, driving out of the Caucasus and advancing from Suez, capturing the oilfields of the Middle East. The Axis powers would then have been able to meet and pool their strength, controlling a vast quantity of global natural resources. We now know, of course, that this did not happen, but the simple fact that it was realistically contemplated was a sign of how bad the situation had become. In reviewing the options in the War Office, Major-General Sir John Kennedy, the Director of Military Operations, wrote, 'Would the Russians stand up to the German attacks? ... Or would they collapse?' If they could not hold the Germans, he asked, 'Could we then defend the oilfields in the Persian Gulf without which our fleet could not operate in Eastern Waters? Could we prevent a junction of the Germans and the Japanese on the shores of the Indian Ocean? ... And would we have to face [if the Russians collapsed] once more the possibility of a German attempt to invade the British Isles?' In the summer of 1942 Kennedy and his planners repeatedly asked themselves the question, if we can only send reinforcements to either India or the Middle East, which one should we choose? In other words, could Britain more easily afford the loss of India or the Middle East?[8] He recognised that 'it became more and more difficult for Churchill to maintain his position as Prime Minister. Criticism was widespread and bitter.'[9] On the other side of the pond, when Averell Harriman returned to Washington after accompanying Churchill to his meetings with Stalin in Moscow, the US War Department presented him with an intelligence summary that predicted Stalingrad would fall any day and the German drive to the south would soon be able to speed up.[10] The possibility of a cataclysmic collapse was never far away during 1942.

On the other hand, Britain was lucky that Hitler was so obsessed with the gigantic struggle on the Eastern Front. Rommel's Panzerarmee Afrika varied in size over the months he fought the desert war, but he never had more than ten divisions under his command. If he had had double that, if the Nazi war machine could have spared another ten divisions out of the 200-plus fighting in Soviet Russia, and fully resourced this army, then the outcome would almost certainly have been very different. But Britain had pulled through, Alamein had been a defining victory. The Americans had landed in North-West Africa. The church bells had been rung. People could smile again and faith in the leader many had doubted in the spring and summer had been restored.

For the mood in Britain to swing after such a run of failures there had to be success. And it had to be a British-led success. Montgomery delivered this.

Churchill might have been riding on the crest of a wave by the end of 1942 in terms of the opinion polls, but in one respect he had completely failed to understand the mood of the people. Whether in the forces, the war factories, or at home struggling to keep a family fed, Britons were starting to ask what society was going to be like when the war was over. What was all the destruction and suffering *for*? Churchill's earlier speeches about the 'broad sunlit uplands' were fine in their way, but what about housing, employment, education and pensions? For Churchill, victory meant one thing only – military victory over the nation's enemies in Europe and the Far East. But for growing numbers of people 'victory' was about more than this; it was about building a better society, about justifying all the losses incurred in years of war. The Labour Party was openly discussing a better future for Britain, by which of course they meant a socialist future. And at the grass-roots level educational associations, workers' groups and even the Women's Institute were meeting to talk about the future. Wartime planning and the huge expansion in the role of the state had convinced many who would never have regarded themselves as socialists that they needed to see the future in very different terms from the past. A sort of austere collectivist spirit was blowing across the nation. Only one person seemed not to feel it, the Prime Minister himself, who argued that there was no time for such fanciful planning while the war still had to be won. In addition, he was very aware of the debt the country was building up and the problems that would have to be faced post-war. He believed the British people 'are liable to get very angry if they feel they have been guiled or cheated' by promises that could not be fulfilled. He did not want to deceive people with 'false hopes and airy visions of Utopia and Eldorado' and by offering 'a cloud of pledges and promises' which were 'not brought into relation with the hard facts of life'.[11]

However, others *were* spending a lot of time thinking and planning for Eldorado British-style. In December 1942, after months of preparation and weeks of what today would be called 'leaks', William Beveridge published his famous *Report into Social Insurance and Allied Services*. Beveridge wanted to remove the five evils that had plagued pre-war society: Want, Disease, Ignorance, Squalor and Idleness. The report called for a welfare system that would help usher in a new, fairer society and would eradicate poverty. But Beveridge went further than this, calling for the creation of a National Health Service that would be free to all, for the introduction of children's allowances and for the state to do all it could to ensure full employment and banish unemployment. For a 300-page government White Paper the report had a remarkable and instant impact, although the leaks to the press and the newsreels had prepared the public for its message. It proved sensationally popular, and within a month 100,000 copies had been sold with popular and shorter versions becoming even bigger sellers. The timing was fortunate for Beveridge following the turning of the tide at Alamein and a sense that now was the moment to enjoy the luxury of thinking about the future.

Home Intelligence reported that 'The Beveridge Report is everywhere said to have been the main subject of conversation and "the war news has tended to take a back seat".'[12] The response to it was said to be extremely positive. Mass Observation reported that 'General opinions about the report were very favourable' and that people did not pick out one aspect of what Beveridge had said but judged it 'almost invariably as a whole'. 'Well it all seems important,' said one woman. 'I really couldn't say what is the best thing.' A man told an interviewer, 'I have read it and think it champion and [it] will take a load off the mind of many people.'[13]

Notwithstanding the positive buzz around the report, Mass Observation also picked up a residual cynicism among some. Many remembered the broken promises to build 'Homes Fit for Heroes' after the First World War. In Yorkshire, a middle-aged woman wrote, 'Seems quite sound but don't suppose it will come to anything in the long run. It won't be allowed to work.'[14] Another woman told an interviewer, 'Well it's only a report after all ... I think it's just a carrot to hold before the donkey. They'll find some excuse for sliding out of it after the war.'[15]

Politicians were less than fulsome in their support for the report. Many Conservatives were terrified of the increased powers given to the state and by the huge costs of a welfare scheme. Even Labour leaders were half-hearted in their enthusiasm. Attlee did not want to break up the coalition government by insisting the report had to be implemented. Only Herbert Morrison, a leading Labour politician but not a member of the War Cabinet, spoke out in complete support. When asked 'Can we afford to do this?' Morrison replied, 'Can we afford not to do it?'[16] But while politicians sat on the fence, for many people the new year of 1943 brought a genuine hope that the post-war world, when it came, would be brighter and fairer and would benefit from the shared experiences of wartime.

Events that had started to unfold towards the end of 1942 quickly worked their way through into the early months of the following year. Critical here was the immense battle for Stalingrad. Having encircled the German Sixth Army in late November, leaving German forces cut off and trapped, the Soviets tightened the noose through the mid-winter months. Göring said he would supply the army by air but that required 500 tons every day and the Luftwaffe was only able to fly in a few tons daily. The withdrawal of transport aircraft to help supply a new army in Tunisia made the task even more unattainable. The German troops faced starvation, disease, frostbite and defeat. Hitler refused to allow them to break out, insisting they must stay put on the Volga, telling them help was on its way. He made the commander-in-chief, General Friedrich von Paulus, a Field Marshal knowing that no German Field Marshal in history had ever surrendered. But the honour did not prevent the inevitable, and on 31 January von Paulus finally capitulated. Perhaps learning from the Japanese at Singapore, the Soviets filmed the miserable, haggard-looking Paulus coming in to sign the surrender and footage was taken of his thoroughly wretched soldiers, without winter uniforms and with some wrapped in blankets or rags, as they shambled into a frozen captivity. Some 130,000 men became prisoners.[17] Not only was it a military turning point on the Eastern Front but film of the troops surrendering provided a stunning propaganda triumph for the Soviets. The myth of German invincibility was utterly crushed in the frozen wastes along the Volga.

Also in January, Churchill and Roosevelt met for their third wartime summit, this time in a complex of heavily guarded hotels and villas on the beach outside Casablanca, recently occupied by American troops. They had asked Stalin to join them but with the Battle of Stalingrad at a critical phase he said he could not leave Moscow. Once again there was division between the British and American chiefs of staff. Once again the Americans wanted to plan for an invasion of northern Europe and there was pressure to divert resources to the Pacific. The British still wanted to concentrate on the Mediterranean and postpone an invasion until the Battle of the Atlantic had been won. After one member of the British delegation assessed the difference in the ideas of the two sides, he concluded that all we had to do 'was to convince the Americans that ours were right and theirs were wrong'.[18] Brooke described the meetings as 'very heated' and 'making no headway'. On the fifth day he wrote, 'A desperate day! We are further from reaching agreement than we ever were.'[19] Meanwhile, Churchill and Roosevelt were getting on famously in the winter sunshine in their seaside villas surrounded by palm trees and bougainvillea. Churchill was in his element with his military chiefs around him, talking with the President regularly and knowing that once again he had full support from Britons at home. Harold Macmillan arrived in Casablanca a few days after the conference had started and wrote, 'I have never seen him in better form. He ate and drank enormously all the time, settled huge problems, played bagatelle and bezique by the hour, and generally enjoyed himself.'[20]

Allied war leaders Roosevelt and Churchill with their combined chiefs of staff at the Casablanca Conference, January 1943. Back row left to right, General Arnold, Admiral King, General Marshall, Admiral Pound, General Brooke, Air Chief Marshal Portal. All smiles now, but there had been bitter arguments about the strategy for winning the war.

After a week of intense negotiations the British and American chiefs, not wanting to go to the PM and the President with unsolved problems, finally reached agreement. Defeat of Germany remained the first priority. It was agreed to continue the war in the Mediterranean. After the capture of Tunisia there would be an invasion of Sicily followed by an advance into the Italian peninsula, hoping to knock Italy out of the war. The build-up of American troops in Britain would continue and a new plan for the bombing of Germany was endorsed. Bomber Command and the US Eighth Army Air Force would carry out a combined offensive to destroy the German 'military, industrial and economic system' and undermine German civilian morale to the point at which it would be 'fatally weakened'.[21] The military agreements were rapidly approved by Churchill and Roosevelt. It was the high-water mark of British influence over the planning of the war. From this point onwards the vast scale of the US war pro-gramme would overtake Britain. But it was fitting that after the conference was over Churchill insisted that Roosevelt join him on a visit to a favourite pre-war spot of his, Marrakesh. Here the two war leaders watched the sun go down and sang songs together.[22] It is revealing that after the President left, Churchill was relaxed enough to paint a superb view of the Marrakesh skyline with the Atlas mountains behind. It was the only painting he produced during the war.[23]

However, in North Africa the Anglo-American First Army advancing eastwards into Tunisia made only slow progress. US troops met their baptism of fire in a battle around the town of Medjez and were forced to withdraw. The newly formed German Fifth Panzer Army in Tunis soon became a formidable fighting force boasting the latest piece of German kit, the massive 55-ton Tiger tank with armour so thick it was impenetrable to Allied weapons. Rommel took command, determined to hold the Eighth Army advancing from the east at the Mareth Line, and the green US troops in the west at the Kasserine Pass. The Americans discovered what the Brits had already learned so painfully, that Rommel deployed his powerful tanks and artillery with skill, imagination and cunning. In the parlance of the day, the US troops got a 'bloody nose' at Kasserine. Meanwhile, the Eighth Army advanced to Tripoli, the capital of Mussolini's one-time Mediterranean empire. The city was occupied on 23 January 1943.

After Casablanca, Churchill had gone on another long set of journeys around the Mediterranean and he reached Tripoli in early February, soon after its capture. He made a short speech to a rapidly assembled group of Eighth Army officers and men. He said that their advance from Alamein to Tripoli, a distance of 1,400 miles, was the same as that from London to Moscow. He told them, 'You have altered the face of the war in a most remarkable way.' He concluded, in Shakespearean terms, 'After the war when a man is asked what he did it will be quite sufficient for him to say "I marched and fought with the Desert Army" ... when history is written ... your feats will gleam and glow.'[24] The following day, as the sun shone down from a cloudless sky, he inspected the victory parade of the 51st Highland Division from a quickly built dais, alongside Alexander and Montgomery. Tears of relief and victory ran down Churchill's cheeks as the pipers marched proudly past. Ian Jacob observed that 'all the anxiety, the disappointments, the hardships and the setbacks of the Middle East campaign seemed to be robbed of their sting'.[25] This was what victory felt like.

The final chapter of the war in North Africa was no less dramatic. In March, after a week of heavy fighting, Monty's men were able to break through the Mareth Line and headed north towards Tunis. Rommel, once again ill, was evacuated and General Hans von Arnim was left in command. Again, the Axis forces lost the battle of supply. Without food, fuel and ammunition, and trapped in a small enclave outside Tunis, von Arnim could no longer follow Hitler's instruction to stand and fight. He had no fuel left for his vehicles or shells for his guns. On 12 May, the remainder of the Axis forces surrendered. In all, nearly 250,000 men went into captivity along with 1,000 guns and 250 tanks. It was a larger haul even than at Stalingrad. General Alexander was able to report back to Churchill on the handwritten orders he had been given in Cairo eight months before with the message, 'Sir: It is my duty to report that the Tunisian campaign is over. All enemy resistance has ceased. We are masters of the North African shores.'[26] Churchill was again in Washington for a summit. To receive this news while with Roosevelt must have been a pleasant reversal of the 'disgrace' of the news from Tobruk eleven months earlier. Nearly three years of desert fighting was over. British and American forces had successfully fought together to bring about a victory. The next stop would be Sicily, and then the European mainland.

Another aspect of the war had gone up a gear in 1942 to reach its terrible apogee in the years following. In January 1942 at a short meeting at Wannsee, a suburb of Berlin, fifteen Nazi officials and leaders of the SS had laid down a plan for the rounding up of Jews across occupied Europe and their deportation to Poland, where they would be murdered in a set of extermination camps. They called it the Final Solution to the Jewish Question. Reports of mass murders in the east soon began to leak out and were featured in the British and American press. By the autumn of 1942 the names of three of the extermination camps were known in the west – Chelmno, Belzec and Treblinka. The name and precise location of the most notorious camp of all, Auschwitz, was unknown until 1944. On 29 October 1942 a public meeting was held at the Royal Albert Hall to protest at the murders. It was called not by Jewish leaders in Britain but by the Archbishop of

Canterbury. Churchill wrote to the Archbishop to express his 'warm sympathy' for the objectives of the meeting. 'The systematic cruelties to which the Jewish people – men, women and children – have been exposed under the Nazi regime are amongst the most terrible events of history,' he wrote. He finished his message by asserting 'when this struggle ends with the enthronement of human rights, racial persecution will be ended'.[27] In recent years, the Holocaust has come to be seen as one of the central elements of the Second World War. But this was certainly not yet the case in 1942. Mass Observation diarists rarely at this stage mention the persecution of the Jews of Europe.

Churchill had clung on throughout 1942. Many on both sides of the Atlantic had admired his grit and determination. Marshall spoke about witnessing his 'courage and resolution on the day of the fall of Tobruk'.[28] He had easily survived two votes against his leadership in the House of Commons but the political threat posed by Sir Stafford Cripps was far more serious and came closer to ousting him. But even here, at the end of the year, when Cripps left the War Cabinet to take up his new post as Minister of Aircraft Production, he departed praising Churchill. 'However much we may differ in outlook on certain matters,' he wrote to Churchill on his sixty-eighth birthday, 'it has been a great joy to me to witness your tireless work for victory ... you must be vastly and rightly stimulated by the result of all your hard and incessant work through the dark days of defeat and disappointment'.[29]

Nineteen forty-two had been Churchill's most difficult time, his darkest hour. The victories at the end of the year and the conference planning at the beginning of 1943 brought relief and a revival of his fortunes. But in reality his stock would never be as high again. As American industrial and military power grew and the Red Army pounded the Wehrmacht in the land battles on the Eastern Front,

Churchill would be marginalised, much to his distress. He would remain a formidable personality in what he still called the 'Grand Alliance' but no longer the man who shaped the course of world events.

The war, as everyone knows, dragged on for another two and a half years. By 1945, the Soviet Union had lost one third of its wealth, with 32,000 factories in ruin, 1,700 townships destroyed, 70,000 villages and hamlets burned to the ground and about 27 million of its people dead. But it had the largest army the world had ever known and the moral authority of having borne the brunt of defeating the Nazis. The Red Army finally fought their way to and captured Berlin and many countries of eastern Europe fell under Russian control as pro-Soviet communist regimes were forced on them. The United States, on the other hand, had an economy that had more than doubled in size during the war and emerged as by far the biggest industrial nation in the world, ready to expand into markets on every continent. Its armies rapidly demobilised and soldiers withdrew from much of Europe and Asia, although they remained in Germany and Japan. But America had the atom bomb.[30] The United States was the great winner of the Second World War and by 1945 a superpower that could not turn its back on the world again.

What had been at stake in Britain in 1942 was the nation's ability to fully participate in the victory and thereby stand equal among the victors. Further military defeats would have reduced the country's political ability to be part of the decision-making about the future of the post-war world. Even if final victory was certain – and, as we have seen, for many this was not the case in 1942 – it would have been a victory brought by the military successes of the Americans and the Soviets. Shame and embarrassment would have relegated Britain from a front-rank victor to a second-rate supporter of its allies with little moral stature. But military victory changed all this. As Churchill wrote, 'Before Alamein we never had a victory. After Alamein we never had a defeat.'[31]

Although by 1945 the country was bankrupt and its cities were devastated, its economy was still fundamentally strong and could recover. And Britons could enjoy a powerful and long-standing confidence in themselves as having been there at the start of the war, having stood alone, in Europe at least, for a year, and having survived defeats and privations along the long road to victory. But Churchill failed entirely to address what the future should look like and how the country could be a better place after the war. He was totally out of alignment with so many Britons when it came to empire and the future of India, as well as social reform and reconstruction. His total conviction that winning the war was all that mattered did ultimately lead to victory. But it meant that the British people did not trust him to run the peace. In the summer of 1945 he was voted out of Downing Street in a Labour landslide.

In 1942, the great strengths of Churchill were his ability to hang on because he was confident that final victory was certain, and to keep the Anglo-American alliance concentrated on the Mediterranean rather than commit the folly of what would without doubt have been a catastrophic attempt to invade France. But he was a flawed leader. He did not manage people well, especially those he relied on the most. He did not always pick his best lieutenants. The man who did more than anyone to save him politically, General Montgomery, was not his first choice; he had selected another who by the accident of fate was killed. But although he stared into the abyss of defeat, he had the determination to keep fighting. The demoralised British people nearly lost confidence in him and the country's ability to fight on. But he survived, and Britain could hold its head high.

Acknowledgements

This book was largely written during the Covid pandemic in 2020 and 2021. The national lockdowns had several effects on the process as most archives were closed. I relied heavily upon printed material, especially the outstanding *Churchill Documents* published to accompany the official biography of Winston Churchill written by Martin Gilbert. This vast series began life in 1972 known as Companion volumes with original documents, letters and papers both official and unofficial written by or relating to Winston Churchill. Initially published by Heinemann, in 2008 the huge undertaking was taken over by the Hillsdale College Press, at Hillsdale, Michigan. Three volumes were most relevant to this study, Volume 16 *The Ever Widening War, 1941*; Volume 17 *Testing Times, 1942* and Volume 18 *One Continent Redeemed, January–August 1943*. These are vast and masterly works running to some 1,600 pages each. Martin Gilbert was the editor of Volumes 16 and 17 (published in 2011 and 2014, respectively) but he was suffering from a worsening heart problem as he compiled them. He had started work on Volume 18 but died before it was completed; his former research assistant, Larry P. Arnn, took over as editor of this volume, which was published in 2015. Arnn has completed the project, and the last volume, covering Churchill's second premiership and the years up to his death, was published in

2019. Anyone writing now about Churchill's extraordinary life, which acts like a backbone to British political history for the first half of the twentieth century, owes a great debt to this gigantic publishing venture that runs to over 30,000 pages or nearly ten million words. The volumes provide a marvellous insight into the thinking of Churchill on a day-to-day, almost an hour-by-hour, basis.

The large number of political diaries that I refer to in *1942* are those published over the last sixty years. I was lucky that throughout the various lockdowns, the London Library kept going and although closed to visitors did a magnificent job of posting out books to members. I'm very grateful to the London Library for its sterling service over the last two years.

However, even when archives were closed, they were still accessible. The National Archives (at Kew) has digitised a vast amount of Cabinet papers from this period that are available to download. As the building itself was closed to those who would normally visit to carry out their research, the institution waived the normal (modest) fee for downloading material. The Imperial War Museum has only digitised parts of its huge collection, but records from its Sound Archive have been accessible online throughout lockdown.

My principal source for this book, however, has been the superb and dazzling Mass Observation Archive. This rich treasure trove of material provides a unique insight into the thinking of British men and women during the war years, recorded and written down in a variety of different ways. I describe the foundation and working methods of Mass Observation in Chapter 2. The University of Sussex has run the archive for many decades now. I'm immensely grateful that much of its wartime material – ranging from thousands of pages of handwritten diaries to the dozens of typewritten File Reports on so many aspects relating to the morale of the British people and of popular attitudes to a huge variety of wartime subjects – has been digitised. My particular thanks go to Jessica Scantlebury, the Mass Observation Archivist, for giving me access to much of this material during lockdown. I could not have written this book without that help. The quotes from Mass Observation are reproduced with permission of Curtis Brown Group Ltd, London, on behalf of the Trustees of the Mass Observation Archive © The Trustees of the Mass Observation Archive.

At Little, Brown I'm lucky to be working with the same efficient and friendly team from my last book. Richard Beswick's enthusiasm for the project helped to get it started, and he has overseen it throughout. Nithya Rae has done a great and supportive job as editor. And my thanks go to Daniel Balado for excellent work as copyeditor, to John Gilkes for the maps and to Linda Silverman for tracking down so many fine images.

As always, my final thanks go to Anne, who has lived *1942* with me day-by-day throughout 2020 and 2021!

Taylor Downing
September 2021

Bibliography

Collections of Documents

Addison, Paul and Jeremy Crang, *Listening to Britain: Home Intelligence Reports on Britain's Finest Hour – May to September 1940*. London: Vintage, 2011.

Cannadine, David (ed.), *Winston Churchill: Blood, Toil, Tears and Sweat – The Great Speeches*. London: Penguin, 1990.

Davison, Peter, *The Complete Works of George Orwell Vol. 13: All Propaganda is Lies 1941–42*. London: Secker & Warburg, 1998.

Gilbert, Martin (ed.), *The Churchill Documents, Vol. 16, The Ever-Widening War, 1941*. Hillsdale, Michigan: Hillsdale College Press, 2011.

——*The Churchill Documents, Vol. 17, Testing Times, 1942*. Hillsdale, Michigan: Hillsdale College Press, 2014.

Gilbert, Martin and Larry P. Arnn (eds), *The Churchill Documents, Vol. 18, One Continent Redeemed, January– August 1943*. Hillsdale, Michigan: Hillsdale College Press, 2015.

Kimball, Warren F., *Churchill & Roosevelt: The Complete Correspondence*, 3 vols. Princeton: Princeton University Press, 1984.

Liddell Hart, Basil (ed.), *The Rommel Papers*. London: Collins, 1953.

Official Histories and Reports

Only the volumes relevant to the events of this book are listed.

Beveridge, Lord William, *Report on Social Insurance and Allied Services* [*The Beveridge Report*]. London: HMSO, 1942.

Briggs, Asa, *The History of Broadcasting in the United Kingdom, Vol. III: The War of Words.* Oxford: Oxford University Press, 1995.

Central Statistical Office (CSO), *Fighting with Figures: A Statistical Digest of the Second World War.* London: HMSO, 1995.

Harrison, Gordon A., *United States Army in World War II. The European Theater of Operations: Cross-Channel Attack.* Washington DC: Office of the Chief of Military History, 1951.

Hinsley, F. H., *British Intelligence in the Second World War: Its Influence on Strategy and Operations, Vol. 2.* London: HMSO, 1981.

——*British Intelligence in the Second World War.* London: HMSO, 1993 [single abridged volume].

Ministry of Information (MoI) and Air Ministry, *The Air Battle of Malta: The Official Account of the RAF in Malta, June 1940 to November 1942.* London: HMSO, 1944.

Playfair, Major-General I. S. O., *The Mediterranean and Middle East Vol. III: British Fortunes reach their Lowest Ebb, Sept 1941 to Sept 1942.* London: HMSO, 1960.

Richards, Denis, *Royal Air Force 1939–45, Vol. I The Fight at Odds.* London: HMSO, 1953.

Roskill, Captain S. W., *The War at Sea 1939–1945, Vol. II The Period of Balance.* London: HMSO, 1956.

Titmuss, Richard, *History of the Second World War: Problems of Social Policy.* London: HMSO, 1950.

Webster, Sir Charles and Noble Frankland, *The Strategic Air Offensive Against Germany 1939–1945*, 4 vols. London: HMSO, 1961.

Primary Accounts, Diaries and Memoirs

Alanbrooke, Field Marshal Lord, *War Diaries 1939–1945* (eds Alex Danchev and Daniel Todman). London: Weidenfeld & Nicolson, 2001.

Amery, Julian, *Approach March: A Venture in Autobiography*. London: Hutchinson, 1973.

Amery, Leo, *The Leo Amery Diaries Vol. 2 1929–1945: The Empire at Bay* (eds John Barnes and David Nicholson). London: Hutchinson, 1988.

Bennett, Lieutenant-General Gordon, *Why Singapore Fell*. Sydney: Angus & Robertson, 1944.

Beveridge, Lord William, *Full Employment in a Free Society*. London: George Allen & Unwin, 1944.

Bryant, Arthur, *The Turn of the Tide 1939–1943: A Study based on the Diaries and Autobiographical Notes of Field Marshal the Viscount Alanbrooke*. London: Collins, 1957.

Cadogan, Sir Alexander, *The Diaries of Sir Alexander Cadogan 1938–1945* (ed. David Dilks). London: Cassell, 1971.

Channon, Henry, *Chips: The Diaries of Sir Henry Channon* (ed. Robert Rhodes James). London: Weidenfeld & Nicolson, 1967.

Churchill, Winston, *The World Crisis 1911–1918*, 5 vols. London: Thornton Butterworth 1923–31.

——*The Second World War*, 6 vols. London: Cassell, 1948–54 (*Vol. II: Their Finest Hour*, 1949; *Vol. III: The Grand Alliance*, 1950; and *Vol. IV: The Hinge of Fate*, 1951).

Duff Cooper, Alfred, *Old Men Forget*. London: Rupert Hart-Davis, 1957.

Eden, Sir Anthony (The Rt Hon. the Earl of Avon), *The Eden Memoirs: The Reckoning*. London: Cassell, 1965.

Frost, Major-General John, *A Drop Too Many*. London: Cassell, 1980; republished Barnsley: Pen & Sword, 1994.

Harriman, Averell and Elie Abel, *Special Envoy to Churchill and Stalin 1941–1946*. New York: Random House, 1975.

Harvey, Oliver, *The War Diaries of Oliver Harvey* (ed. John Harvey). London: Collins, 1978.

Headlam, Cuthbert, *Parliament and Politics in the Age of Churchill and Attlee: The Headlam Diaries 1935–1951* (ed. Stuart Ball). Cambridge: Cambridge University Press, 1999.

Hey, Kathleen, *The View from the Corner Shop: The Diary of a Yorkshire Shop Assistant in Wartime* (eds Patricia and Robert Malcolmson). London: Simon and Schuster, 2016.

Hill, Roger, *Destroyer Captain: Memoirs of the War at Sea 1942–1945*. London: William Kimber, 1975.

Hodgson, Vere, *Few Eggs and No Oranges: A Diary showing how Unimportant People in London and Birmingham lived through the War Years 1940–1945*. London: Dobson, 1976.

Hoggart, Richard, *A Sort of Clowning: Life and Times Vol. 2 1940–1959*. Oxford: Oxford University Press, 1991.

Hopkinson, Tom (ed.), *Picture Post 1938–50*. London: Penguin Books, 1970.

Ismay, Hastings, *The Memoirs of General the Lord Ismay*. London: Heinemann, 1960.

Jones, R. V., *Most Secret War*. London: Hamish Hamilton, 1978; republished London: Penguin Books, 2009.

Kennedy, Major-General Sir John, *The Business of War*. London: Hutchinson, 1957.

Kesselring, Field Marshal Albert, *The Memoirs of Field Marshal Kesselring*. London: William Kimber, 1953.

Kippenberger, Major-General Sir Howard, *Infantry Brigadier*. Oxford: Oxford University Press, 1949.

Macmillan, Harold, *War Diaries: Politics and War in the Mediterranean, January 1943–May 1945*. London: Macmillan, 1984.

Madge, Charles and Tom Harrison, *Britain by Mass Observation*. London: Penguin, 1939.

Maisky, Ivan, *The Maisky Diaries: Red Ambassador to the Court of St James's, 1932–43* (ed. Gabriel Gorodetsky, translated by Tatiana Sorokina and Oliver Ready). New Haven: Yale University Press, 2015.

Mass Observation, *War Begins at Home* (eds Charles Madge and Tom Harrison). London: Chatto & Windus, 1940.

Masters, John, *Bugles and a Tiger: My Life in the Gurkhas*. London: Michael Joseph, 1956; republished London: Weidenfeld & Nicolson, 2002.

Moorehead, Alan, *The Desert War: The Classic Trilogy on the North African Campaign 1940–43*. London: Aurum Press, 2017. [Originally published in 1944 in three volumes: *Mediterranean Front*, *A Year of Battle* and *The End in Africa*.]

Moran, Lord (Sir Charles Wilson), *Winston Churchill: The*

Struggle for Survival, 1940–1965. London: Constable, 1966; republished as *Churchill at War 1940–45.* London: Robinson, 2002.

Normanbrook, Lord and John Wheeler-Bennett, *Action This Day: Working with Churchill.* London: Macmillan, 1968.

Panter-Downes, Mollie, *London War Notes 1939–1945.* London: Longman, 1972.

Percival, Arthur, *The War in Malaya.* London: Eyre & Spottiswoode, 1949.

Pownall, Sir Henry, *Chief of Staff: The Diaries of Lieutenant-General Sir Henry Pownall Vol. 2 1940–1944.* London: Leo Cooper, 1974.

Rowe, A. P., *One Story of Radar.* Cambridge: Cambridge University Press, 1948.

Sherwood, Robert E., *Roosevelt and Hopkins: An Intimate History.* New York: Harper & Row, 1950.

Slim, Field Marshal Sir William, *Defeat into Victory.* London: Cassell, 1956; republished London: Pan Books, 2009.

Speer, Albert, *Inside the Third Reich: Memoirs by Albert Speer* (translated by Richard and Clara Winston). London: Weidenfeld & Nicolson, 1970.

Thomson, Rear Admiral George, *Blue Pencil Admiral: The Inside Story of Press Censorship.* London: Sampson, Law, Marston & Co, 1947.

Secondary Sources

Addison, Paul, *The Road to 1945: British Politics and the Second World War.* London: Quartet, 1977.

Aldgate, Anthony and Jeffrey Richards, *Britain Can Take It: British Cinema in the Second World War.* London: I. B. Tauris, 2007.

Allen, Louis, *Singapore 1941–42.* London: Frank Cass, 1993.

Allport, Alan, *Browned Off and Bloody-Minded: The British Soldier Goes to War 1939–1945.* New Haven & London: Yale University Press, 2015.

Atkinson, Rick, *An Army at Dawn: The War in North Africa 1942–1943.* London: Little, Brown, 2003.

Best, Geoffrey, *Churchill and War*. London: Hambledon, 2005.

Blake, Robert and William Louis (eds), *Churchill*. Oxford: Oxford University Press, 1993.

Boyd, Andrew, *The Royal Navy in Eastern Waters: Linchpin of Victory 1935–1942*. Barnsley: Seaforth, 2017.

Bungay, Stephen, *Alamein*. London: Aurum Press, 2002.

Calder, Angus, *The People's War: Britain 1939–1945*. London: Jonathan Cape, 1969.

Carver, Field Marshal Lord Michael, *The Seven Ages of the British Army*. London: Weidenfeld & Nicolson, 1984.

Chapman, James, *The British at War: Cinema, State and Propaganda, 1939–1945*. London: I. B. Tauris, 1998.

Clarke, Peter, *The Cripps Version: The Life of Sir Stafford Cripps*. London: Allen Lane, 2002.

Connell, John, *Auchinleck: A Biography of Field-Marshal Sir Claude Auchinleck*. London: Cassell, 1959.

Downing, Taylor, *Churchill's War Lab: Code-breakers, Boffins and Innovators: The Mavericks Churchill Led to Victory*. London: Little, Brown, 2010.

——*Spies in the Sky: The Secret Battle for Aerial Intelligence During World War Two*. London: Little, Brown, 2012.

——*Night Raid: The True Story of the First Victorious British Para Raid of World War Two*. London: Little, Brown, 2013.

——*Secret Warriors: Key Scientists, Code-breakers and Propagandists of the Great War*. London: Little, Brown, 2014.

——*Breakdown: The Crisis of Shell Shock on the Somme, 1916*. London: Little, Brown, 2016.

Edwards, Bernard, *The Road to Russia: Arctic Convoys 1942*. Barnsley: Pen & Sword Maritime, 2015.

Farmelo, Graham, *Churchill's Bomb: A Hidden History of Science, War and Politics*. London: Faber & Faber, 2013.

Farrell, Brian D., *The Defence and Fall of Singapore 1940–1942*. Stroud: Tempus, 2005.

Fennell, Jonathan, *Combat and Morale in the North African Campaign: The Eighth Army and the Path to El Alamein*. Cambridge: Cambridge University Press, 2011.

——*Fighting the People's War: The British and Commonwealth*

Armies and the Second World War. Cambridge: Cambridge University Press, 2019.

Folly, Martin, Geoffrey Roberts and Oleg Rzheshevsky, *Churchill and Stalin: Comrades-in-Arms During the Second World War.* Barnsley: Pen & Sword, 2019.

Fort, Adrian, *Archibald Wavell: The Life and Times of an Imperial Servant.* London: Jonathan Cape, 2009.

Freeman, Roger, *The Mighty Eighth: A History of the Units, Men and Machines of the US 8th Air Force.* London: Arms and Armour, 1986.

Gardiner, Juliet, *Wartime Britain 1939–1945.* London: Headline, 2004.

Gilbert, Martin, *Finest Hour: Winston Churchill 1939–1941* [vol. VI of the Official Biography of Churchill]. London: Heinemann, 1983.

——*Road to Victory: Winston Churchill 1941–1945* [vol. VII of the Official Biography of Churchill]. London: Heinemann, 1986.

Gore, Jan, *The Terror Raids of 1942: The Baedeker Blitz.* Barnsley: Pen & Sword, 2020.

Hamilton, Nigel, *Monty: The Making of a General, 1887–1942.* London: Hamish Hamilton, 1981.

Harrison, Tom, *Living Through the Blitz.* London: Collins, 1976.

Hastings, Max, *Bomber Command.* London: Michael Joseph, 1979; republished London: Pan Books, 1981.

——*Finest Years: Churchill as Warlord 1940–1945.* London: Harper Press, 2009.

Hennessy, Peter, *Never Again: Britain 1945–1951.* London: Jonathan Cape, 1992.

Holland, James, *Fortress Malta: Island Under Siege 1940–1943.* London: Orion, 2003.

——*Together We Stand: North Africa 1942–1943: Turning the Tide in the West.* London: HarperCollins, 2005.

——*The War in the West, Vol. 2: The Allies Fight Back 1941–1943.* London: Bantam Press, 2017.

Holmes, Richard, *The World at War: The Landmark Oral History.* London: Ebury, 2007.

Isaacs, Jeremy and Taylor Downing, *Cold War: For Forty-Five*

Years the World Held Its Breath. London: Bantam, 1998;
republished London: Abacus, 2008.

Kahn, David, *Seizing the Enigma: The Race to Break the German
U-boat Codes 1939–1943*. London: Souvenir Press, 1992.

——*The Code Breakers: The Story of Secret Writing*. New York:
Scribner, 1996.

Keegan, John (ed.), *Churchill's Generals*. London: Weidenfeld &
Nicolson, 1991; republished London: Abacus, 1999.

Khan, Yasmin, *The Raj at War: A People's History of India's
Second World War*. London: The Bodley Head, 2015.

Kimball, Warren F., *Forged in War: Roosevelt, Churchill and the
Second World War*. New York: William Morrow & Co, 1997.

Lewin, Ronald, *Ultra Goes to War: The Secret Story*. London:
Hutchinson, 1978.

Liddell Hart, Sir Basil and Barrie Pitt (eds), *The History of the
Second World War* [eight volumes]. London: Purnell, 1966.

MacKay, Robert, *Half the Battle: Civilian Morale in Britain during
the Second World War*. Manchester: Manchester University
Press, 2002.

McLaine, Ian, *Ministry of Morale: Home Front Morale and the
Ministry of Information in World War Two*. London: George
Allen & Unwin, 1979.

Meacham, Jon, *Franklin and Winston: An Intimate Portrait of an
Epic Friendship*. New York: Random House, 2003.

Minns, Raynes, *Bombers and Mash: The Domestic Front 1939–
45*. London: Virago Press, 1980.

Overy, Richard, *The Bombing War: Europe 1939–1945*. London:
Allen Lane, 2013.

Phillips, Adrian, *Fighting Churchill, Appeasing Hitler*. London:
Biteback, 2019.

Ponting, Clive, *1940: Myth and Reality*. London: Hamish
Hamilton, 1990.

Reynolds, David, *In Command of History: Churchill Fighting and
Writing the Second World War*. London: Allen Lane, 2004.

Roberts, Andrew, *The Holy Fox: The Life of Lord Halifax*.
London: Head of Zeus, 2014.

Roodhouse, Mark, *Black Market Britain 1939–1955*. Oxford:
Oxford University Press, 2013.

Stafford, David, *Churchill and Secret Service*. London: John Murray, 1997.

Sutton, Richard, *Motor Mania: Stories from a Motoring Century*. London: Collins & Brown, 1996.

Taylor, A. J. P., *English History 1914–1945*. Oxford: Oxford University Press, 1965.

Todman, Daniel, *Britain's War: Into Battle 1937–1941*. London: Allen Lane, 2016.

—— *Britain's War: A New World 1942–1947*. London: Allen Lane, 2020.

Tooze, Adam, *The Wages of Destruction: The Making and Breaking of the Nazi Economy*. London: Allen Lane, 2006.

Toye, Richard, *The Roar of the Lion: The Untold Story of Churchill's Wartime Speeches*. Oxford: Oxford University Press, 2013.

Waugh, Evelyn, *Men at Arms*. London: Chapman & Hall, 1952 and Penguin Books, 1964.

Wheeler-Bennett, John W., *King George VI: His Life and Reign*. London: Macmillan, 1958.

Wilson, Thomas, *Churchill and the Prof.* London: Cassell, 1995.

Woodman, Richard, *Malta Convoys 1940–1943*. London: John Murray, 2000.

Ziegler, Philip, *Mountbatten: The Official Biography*. London: Collins, 1985.

—— *London at War 1939–1945*. London: Sinclair-Stevenson, 1995.

Notes

Prologue

1. Mass Observation Archive: Diarist 5433, 26 July 1942.
2. Mass Observation, *War Begins at Home*, pp.338–42.
3. Mark Roodhouse, *Black Market Britain*, pp.77–112.
4. Juliet Gardiner, *Wartime Britain*, p.61.
5. Mass Observation, *War Begins at Home*, pp.187, 198–202 & 221.
6. Gardiner, *Wartime Britain*, p.55.
7. R. V. Jones, *Most Secret War*, pp.92–105.
8. Asa Briggs, *The War of Words*, p.141. The numbers of listeners went up and down during the war years according to the urgency of the news.
9. Raynes Minns, *Bombers and Mash*, p.149.
10. A. J. P. Taylor, *English History 1914–1945*, p.459.
11. John Keegan (ed.), *Churchill's Generals*, p.27.
12. Halifax's diary is quoted in Andrew Roberts, *The Holy Fox*, and in Robert Blake's 'How Churchill became Prime Minister' in Robert Blake and William Louis (eds), *Churchill*.
13. Martin Gilbert, *Finest Hour: Winston Churchill 1939–1941*, p.305.
14. The King's diary is quoted in John Wheeler-Bennett, *King George VI: His Life and Reign*, p.444.
15. Winston Churchill, *The Second World War, Vol. I: The Gathering Storm*, p.527.
16. This view is expressed very clearly by Lord Normanbrook, a senior civil servant in 1940 who became Deputy Secretary of the War Cabinet two years later, in *Action This Day*; see, for instance, pp.11ff.
17. Sir John Kennedy, *The Business of War*, p.173.
18. Ibid., p.229.
19. The best collection of his wartime speeches is to be found in *Winston Churchill: Blood, Toil, Tears and Sweat – The Great Speeches* (ed. David Cannadine), and for an analysis of each major wartime speech see Richard Toye, *The Roar of the Lion*.

20. Quoted in Cannadine (ed.), *Winston Churchill*, p.xxxix.
21. David Reynolds's '1940: The Worst and Finest Hour' in Blake and Louis (eds), *Churchill*, p.254.
22. Most clearly in Richard Titmuss, *Problems of Social Policy*, published in 1950.
23. Taylor, *English History*, pp.503–4.
24. First in this new school of thought was Angus Calder, *The People's War*, in 1969, then came Tom Harrison, *Living Through the Blitz*, in 1976, and this trend came to its fullest expression in Clive Ponting, *1940: Myth and Reality*, in 1990.
25. Examples of this middling interpretation would be Peter Hennessy, *Never Again: Britain 1945–1951*, in 1992; Philip Ziegler, *London at War*, in 1995; Gardiner, *Wartime Britain*, in 2004; and a new take on Churchill's speeches in Toye, *The Roar of the Lion*, in 2013.
26. A notable exception here is Daniel Todman whose vast but very readable two-volume history *Britain's War* does give proper attention to the domestic crisis of 1942.
27. In June 2020, at the peak of the 'Black Lives Matter' public campaign, Churchill's statue in Westminster Square was defaced and the word 'racist' was spray-painted on it. On the other hand, in 2002 in a BBC television series Churchill was voted by the public as the Greatest Briton, easily defeating his nearest rivals Isambard Kingdom Brunel, Diana Princess of Wales, Charles Darwin and William Shakespeare.
28. Mollie Panter-Downes, *London War Notes*, 5 July 1942, p.235.

1 'The Sleep of the Saved'

1. For the rituals of Churchill's day and the importance of dinner see Taylor Downing, *Churchill's War Lab*, pp.95–7.
2. Eyewitness interview with Colonel Manteuffel in Thames Television's *The World at War*, episode 5 'Barbarossa' (producer Jeremy Isaacs, director Peter Batty); see also Richard Holmes, *The World at War*, p.191.
3. Averell Harriman and Elie Abel, *Special Envoy to Churchill and Stalin*, p.111.
4. Churchill, *The Second World War, Vol. III: The Grand Alliance*, pp.537–8 and Harriman and Abel, *Special Envoy to Churchill and Stalin*, p.112.
5. Churchill, *The Second World War, Vol. III: The Grand Alliance*, p.540 and David Reynolds, *In Command of History*, p.264.
6. Premier Papers 3/458/5: Churchill to Roosevelt, 10 December 1941, in Martin Gilbert (ed.), *The Churchill Documents, Vol. 16, The Ever-Widening War*, pp.1595–6.
7. Churchill, *The Second World War, Vol. III: The Grand Alliance*, p.551.
8. Churchill Papers 20/46: Churchill to Roosevelt, 12 December 1941, in Gilbert (ed.), *The Churchill Documents, Vol. 16*, pp.1612 and Warren Kimball, *Forged in War*, p.125.
9. Churchill Papers 20/50: Churchill to Ismay for Chiefs of Staff

Committee, 15 December 1941, in Gilbert (ed.), *The Churchill Documents, Vol. 16*, p.1,630.

10. Harriman and Abel, *Special Envoy to Churchill and Stalin*, p.117 and Martin Gilbert, *Road to Victory: Winston Churchill 1941–1945*, pp.24–5.

11. Since the creation of the Irish Free State in the early 1920s and its refusal to become a member of the Commonwealth, Churchill had always feared that it would provide a back door through which an enemy could invade Britain. He hoped that having the first American troops billeted in Northern Ireland would deter both the Dublin government and Germany from using the island of Ireland as a route to attack Britain.

12. Adrian Fort, *Archibald Wavell*, pp.259–61.

13. Churchill Papers 20/88: Churchill to Attlee, 4 January 1942, in Gilbert (ed.), *The Churchill Documents, Vol. 17, Testing Times*, p.30 and Robert E. Sherwood, *Roosevelt and Hopkins: An Intimate History*, p.474.

14. Churchill, *The Second World War, Vol. III: The Grand Alliance*, p.594.

15. Sherwood, *Roosevelt and Hopkins*, p.442.

16. Ibid., p.442. There are many versions of this splendid story which is not repeated in Churchill's memoir history of the war. David Reynolds speculates this was because Churchill thought it lacked dignity (see Reynolds, *In Command of History*, p.271).

17. Churchill Papers 20/88: Churchill to Attlee, 3 January 1942, in Gilbert (ed.), *The Churchill Documents, Vol. 17*, p.14.

18. For a good analysis of the differences in character and outlook between Churchill and Roosevelt, see Max Hastings, *Finest Years: Churchill as Warlord 1940–1945*, pp.229–33.

19. Wheeler-Bennett, *King George VI*, p.535.

20. Cannadine (ed.), *Winston Churchill*, pp.226–33.

21. *Washington Post*, 27 December 1941, quoted in Jon Meacham, *Franklin and Winston*, p.154.

22. Gilbert, *Road to Victory*, p.30.

23. Lord Moran, *Churchill at War 1940–45*, p.17 and Gilbert, *Road to Victory*, p.31.

2 Happy New Year, 1942

1. Taylor, *English History*, p.502. For a slightly different view of these figures into early 1942 see Todman, *Britain's War: A New World*, p.13.

2. Mass Observation Archive: File Report (FR) 1030 *Christmas and New Year's Eve 1941*, January 1942, quotes from pp.33, 26, 37 & 6.

3. Mass Observation Archive: FR 1030 *Christmas and New Year's Eve 1941*, January 1942, pp.53–8.

4. Minns, *Bombers and Mash*, p.92.

5. Mass Observation Archive: FR 1224 *Housewives' Feelings About Food*, February 1942, pp.1–4.

6. The survey had been carried out by Sir John Boyd Orr in 1938 who noted that unemployment, poverty, ignorance, overcrowding

and inadequate health care all contributed to poor nutrition. See Gardiner, *Wartime Britain*, p.174.

7.   Richard Sutton, *Motor Mania*, pp.120–7.

8.   For a discussion on the control of information during the First World War in the newspapers and the new medium of film, see Taylor Downing, *Secret Warriors: Key Scientists, Code-breakers and Propagandists of the Great War*, pp.269–314; the Kitchener quote is on p.271.

9.   Films from the fighting front also proved immensely popular. *The Battle of the Somme*, made during the first month of that epic battle in 1916, was probably the most successful propaganda film ever made. Crowds flocked to see it wherever it was shown. Approximately a million viewers saw it in the first week after its release while the battle still raged in France. Within a year it had been seen by an estimated 20 million Britons (out of a population of 43 million). Its impact was enormous. People wrote about it in their diaries, wrote letters to the papers about it and were convinced they had witnessed the reality of trench warfare. A series of further *Battle* films also proved popular. There is a considerable library of work about the *Battle of the Somme* film, how it was shot, the use of fakes, and the impact it had on audiences, all summarised in Downing, *Secret Warriors*, pp.301–10.

10. See ibid., pp.304ff.

11. Ian McLaine, *Ministry of Morale*, pp.12–33.

12. Ibid., p.27.

13. Mass Observation, *War Begins at Home*, pp.75–111.

14. Ibid., pp.80–98.

15. Ibid., p.416.

16. *The Times*, 6 January 1940.

17. Adrian Phillips, *Fighting Churchill, Appeasing Hitler*, pp.107–11.

18. Alfred Duff Cooper, *Old Men Forget*, p.285.

19. Rear Admiral George Thomson, *Blue Pencil Admiral: The Inside Story of Press Censorship*, p.3.

20. McLaine, *Ministry of Morale*, p. 40. McLaine also points out that many of the failings blamed on the MoI were in fact caused by the service ministries, the Admiralty, War Office and Air Ministry wanting to control or deny the outflow of information, and so were not strictly the MoI's fault.

21. See the BBC Written Archives, Centre, Caversham.

22. For instance, the films entitled *Oatmeal Porridge* (1939) and *Tea Making Tips* (1941).

23. James Chapman, *The British at War*, pp.24–6. In the late 1960s Kenneth Clark became famous to a new generation as the presenter of the major BBC television series *Civilisation*.

24. Many of these films are available on the British Film Institute (BFI) DVD/BluRay *Ration Books and Rabbit Pies*, a compilation of twenty-nine short films from the Home Front including an illustrated

booklet with essays and film notes.

25. See the figures from the UK Cinema Association: https://www.cinemauk.org.uk/the-industry/facts-and-figures/uk-cinema-admissions-and-box-office/annual-admissions/
26. These Crown Film Unit films are available on the BFI compilation sets *Land of Promise* and *The Humphrey Jennings Collection*.
27. *The Oxford Dictionary of National Biography: Mary Adams* by Sally Adams. Mary Adams returned to BBC Television after the war where she led a distinguished career as a producer, but her most creditable achievement was probably the recruitment of a young zoology graduate to the BBC to make wildlife films. His name was David Attenborough.
28. National Archives: INF/1/290 'The Work of the Home Intelligence Division 1939–45'; see also Paul Addison and Jeremy Crang, *Listening to Britain*, pp.xi–xviii.
29. Charles Madge and Tom Harrison, *Britain by Mass Observation*, p.9.
30. This was the principal thrust of the special by Mass Observation *War Begins at Home*, published in 1940.
31. Briggs, *The War of Words*, pp.86–7.
32. Paul Addison, *The Road to 1945*, p.121.
33. Richard Broad and Suzie Fleming (eds), *Nella Last's War*, 27 April 1941, p.135.
34. Robert MacKay, *Half the Battle: Civilian Morale in Britain during the Second World War*, pp.2–3.
35. Titmuss, *Problems of Social Policy*, p.328.
36. Central Statistical Office (CSO), *Fighting with Figures*, pp.38–9 & 47.
37. Ibid., pp.233–9.

3 Confidence

1. Henry Channon, *Chips: The Diaries of Sir Henry Channon*, p.316.
2. Ten million Britons voted to support international disarmament in the so-called Peace Ballot of June 1935; see Taylor, *English History*, p.379.
3. Most of Churchill's major speeches were made in the House of Commons and were reported widely in the press. Only a few of them were later recorded and broadcast by BBC radio, seven in 1940. Some of them not heard at the time other than by those present in the Commons have become familiar to us today because Churchill re-recorded many of his speeches for release by Decca Records on a series of LP vinyl discs in 1949. See Downing, *Churchill's War Lab*, pp.117 & 363.
4. In the foreword to his memoirs dealing with the war years, *The Reckoning*, Eden said that working 'constantly and around the clock' with Churchill meant that he grew to 'love' him. See also Todman, *Britain's War: A New World*, pp.51–3.
5. Japanese naval commanders escorting the landing force intended

to launch the invasion a few hours after the attack on Pearl Harbor, not wanting to give away the total surprise of the attack upon the American fleet. In fact they thought they had been spotted by Allied aircraft, and the invasion of Thailand and Malaya was launched a few minutes before the attack at Pearl Harbor, thus bringing about the first engagements of the war in the Far East.

6. Brian Farrell, *The Defence and Fall of Singapore*, p.15.
7. Ibid., p.20.
8. Ibid., pp.51–5.
9. A picture of this elite society is vividly painted in J. G. Farrell's novel *The Singapore Grip* (1978), dramatised in a BBC television series in 2020.
10. Churchill Papers 20/88: Churchill to Curtin, 13 January 1942, in Gilbert (ed.), *The Churchill Documents, Vol. 17*, p.69. The sentence contrasting the performance of 'white' and 'Indian' troops was omitted when Churchill reproduced parts of this document in his war memoirs.
11. Hastings Ismay, *The Memoirs of General the Lord Ismay*, p.246.
12. Churchill Papers 20/67: Churchill to Ismay for Chiefs of Staff Committee, 19 January 1942, in Gilbert (ed.), *The Churchill Documents, Vol. 17*, pp.106–8; Churchill, *The Second World War, Vol. IV: The Hinge of Fate*, pp.43–5; and Gilbert, *Road to Victory*, pp.46–7.
13. Gilbert, *Road to Victory*, p.47.
14. Churchill Papers 20/67: Churchill to Ismay for Chiefs of Staff Committee, 21 January 1942, in Gilbert (ed.), *The Churchill Documents, Vol. 17*, p.125.
15. Gilbert, *Road to Victory*, pp.49–50.
16. Anthony Eden, *The Eden Memoirs: The Reckoning*, p.318.
17. *The Times*, 11 June 1940.
18. Churchill Papers 20/46: Churchill to Auchinleck, 4 December 1941, in Gilbert (ed.), *The Churchill Documents, Vol. 16*, p.1,558.
19. Todman, *Britain's War: A New World*, pp.89–90.
20. For the online Hansard record of the debate on 27 January 1942 see: https://hansard.parliament.uk/Commons/1942-01-27/debates/7871880f-e9ff-46ff-9096-ed079dd7f68a/CommonsChamber
21. Nigel Nicolson (ed.), *Harold Nicolson Diaries 1907–1964*, 27 January 1942, p.287.
22. Channon, *Chips: The Diaries*, pp.318–19.
23. https://hansard.parliament.uk/commons/1942-01-28/debates/b729eac8-7b54-4797-a8e8-9d56ef76cdea/MotionOfConfidenceInHisMajestySGovernment
24. https://hansard.parliament.uk/Commons/1942-01-29/debates/8f12746-995b-408c-8e6e-4e5d93592df9/MotionOfConfidenceInisMajestySGovernment; and Cannadine (ed.), *Winston Churchill*, pp.235–45.
25. Nicolson (ed.), *Harold Nicolson Diaries*, 29 January 1942, pp.287–8.
26. Cuthbert Headlam, *Parliament and Politics in the Age of Churchill and Attlee: The Headlam Diaries*, 29 January 1942, p.291.
27. Nicolson (ed.), *Harold Nicolson Diaries*, 29 January 1942, p.288.

4 The Channel Dash

1. Churchill, *The Second World War, Vol. II: Their Finest Hour*, p.529.
2. CSO, *Fighting with Figures*, p.190.
3. See Taylor Downing, *Spies in the Sky*, pp.131–58 for the work of the photo-reconnaissance pilots, and Denis Richards, *Royal Air Force 1939–45, Vol. 1*, p.225 for the story of the raid.
4. When the wreck of the *Bismarck* was discovered in June 1989 by a team led by Robert Ballard it was possible to assess the damage to the ship: it appears that although there was evidence of hits by many shells and extensive damage to the stern of the ship, much of the heavy steel plating of the hull below the waterline was intact. This suggests that the ship might have been scuttled, as some of the survivors had claimed at the time.
5. In 1959, C. S. Forester published a novel, *Last Nine Days of the Bismarck*. This was adapted for the film *Sink the Bismarck!* (1960), one of the classic British war movies of the time. It was produced by John Brabourne, the son-in-law of Earl Mountbatten, who was then Chief of the Defence Staff, and he ensured the Admiralty gave full cooperation to the film makers. It was directed by Lewis Gilbert and starred Kenneth More, Dana Wynter and Karel Stepanek. See Taylor Downing, 'War on Film: *Sink the Bismarck!*', in *Military History Monthly* 74, November 2016.
6. Capt. S. W. Roskill, *The War at Sea 1939–1945, Vol. II*, p.150.
7. Ibid., p.151.
8. Ralph Barker, 'Operation Cerebus: The Channel Dash', in Basil Liddell Hart and Barrie Pitt (eds), *History of the Second World War, Vol. 3*, pp.913–15.
9. Ibid., pp.915–17.
10. *Daily Mirror*, 14 February 1942, p.3.
11. *Manchester Guardian*, 14 February 1942, p.6.
12. Its condemnatory findings were finally made public in 1946.
13. Alexander Cadogan, *The Diaries of Sir Alexander Cadogan*, p.433.
14. Channon, *Chips: The Diaries*, p.321.
15. National Archives: INF1/292, HIWR 72, 18 February 1942, pp.1–2; quoted in Todman, *Britain's War: A New World*, p.115.
16. Channon, *Chips: The Diaries*, p.322.
17. Panter-Downes, *London War Notes*, p.206.
18. Mass Observation Archive: FR 1111 *Opinion on the Cabinet Changes*, February 1942; quotes are from pp.1, 4, 5 & 6/7.
19. Mass Observation Archive: Diarist 5331, 14 February 1942. This diary has been published: Kathleen Hey, *The View from the Corner Shop* (eds Patricia and Robert Malcolmson).
20. Churchill Papers 20/70: Churchill to Roosevelt, 16 February 1942, in Gilbert (ed.), *The Churchill Documents, Vol. 17*, p.264.
21. Roskill, *The War at Sea, Vol. II*, p.160.

5 Imperial Collapse

1.   The account of this conference comes from Percival's Papers
     in the Imperial War Museum, quoted in Louis Allen, *Singapore
     1941–42*, p.176.
2.   Farrell, *The Defence and Fall of Singapore*, p.70.
3.   Allen, *Singapore*, pp.53–4.
4.   Ibid., p.127.
5.   Farrell, *The Defence and Fall of Singapore*, pp.139–205 passim.
6.   Fort, *Archibald Wavell*, p.265.
7.   Allen, *Singapore*, pp.121–35.
8.   Todman, *Britain's War: A New World*, pp.99–100.
9.   Allen, *Singapore*, p.168. This quote was apparently from a
     conversation between Percival and his senior officers but other
     accounts of the same meeting do not include this phrase and it is
     possible that it was invented later to discredit Percival.
10. Farrell, *The Defence and Fall of Singapore*, pp.328–35.
11. The officer who disobeyed orders by telling his troops to retreat
     was Brigadier Maxwell – see Farrell, *The Defence and Fall of
     Singapore*, pp.346–9.
12. Churchill Papers 20/70: Churchill to Wavell, 10 February 1942, in
     Gilbert (ed.), *The Churchill Documents, Vol. 17*, p.236.
13. Fort, *Archibald Wavell*, pp.275–6.
14. Farrell, *The Defence and Fall of Singapore*, p.356.
15. Ibid., p.368. The RAF commander, Air Vice Marshal Conway
     Pulford, did not survive the evacuation. The small vessel he was on
     was hit and forced to run aground on a tiny island near Sumatra
     where he died of exhaustion and malaria.
16. Ibid., p.375.
17. Field Marshal Lord Alanbrooke, *War Diaries 1939–1945*, p.229.
18. Ibid., and several telegrams in Gilbert (ed.), *The Churchill Documents,
     Vol. 17*, pp.249–50.
19. Churchill Papers 20/70: Wavell to Percival, 15 February 1942, in
     Gilbert (ed.), *The Churchill Documents, Vol. 17*, pp.250–1.
20. The schoolteacher's name was Elizabeth Choy and she was
     interviewed for the National Archive of Singapore oral history
     programme. The interview is available as part of the Imperial War
     Museum Sound Records, ref: IWM 20385.
21. Todman, *Britain's War: A New World*, p.104.
22. Gilbert (ed.), *The Churchill Documents, Vol. 17*, p.251.
23. Allen, *Singapore*, pp.14–15. The novelist was Shiga Naoya.
24. Churchill, *The Second World War, Vol. IV: The Hinge of Fate*, pp.42–9.
25. Farrell, *The Defence and Fall of Singapore*, p.396.
26. Alanbrooke, *War Diaries*, p.231.
27. From Lee Giok Boi, *The Syonan Years: Singapore under Japanese Rule
     1942–45*, quoted in Todman, *Britain's War: A New World*, p.105.

6 'Hard Adverse War'

1. Mass Observation Archive: FR 1244 *Minister of Defence*, March 1942, pp.1–2.
2. Mass Observation Archive: FR 1091 *WAAF Morale*, February 1942, pp.1–2.
3. The ceasefire in Singapore came into effect at 8.30 p.m. local time which was 12.30 p.m. London time.
4. BBC Written Archives: Churchill broadcast, 15 February 1942, in Gilbert (ed.), *The Churchill Documents, Vol 17*, pp.251–7.
5. Sir John Colville Papers: diary for 15 February 1942, in Gilbert (ed.), *The Churchill Documents, Vol. 17*, pp.258–9.
6. Oliver Harvey, *The War Diaries of Oliver Harvey*, p.95 and Gilbert (ed.), *The Churchill Documents, Vol. 17*, p.258.
7. Nicolson (ed.), *Harold Nicolson Diaries*, p.289.
8. Cadogan, *The Diaries*, p.434.
9. The question was asked by Richard Stokes MP on 17 February.
10. Lord Beaverbrook Papers: Beaverbrook private letter to Sir Samuel Hoare, 17 February 1942, in Gilbert (ed.), *The Churchill Documents, Vol. 17*, p.267.
11. All the parliamentary quotes are from Hansard online: https://api.parliament.uk/historic-hansard/commons/1942/feb/17/fall-of-singapore
12. *Punch*, 25 February 1942, p.158.
13. Ivan Maisky, *The Maisky Diaries*, p.411.
14. Nicolson (ed.), *Harold Nicolson Diaries*, p.212.
15. Channon, *Chips: The Diaries*, p.322.
16. Wheeler-Bennett, *King George VI*, p.537.
17. Alanbrooke, *War Diaries*, p.230.
18. Sir Richard Pim Papers: 18 February 1942, in Gilbert (ed.), *The Churchill Documents, Vol. 17*, p.280.
19. Peter Clarke, *The Cripps Version*, p.xiv.
20. Ibid., p.19. The fortune was passed on to Isobel through a complex series of interlocking trust funds, partly directly from her grandfather, the founder of the family fortune, and partly via her father who died in 1928 and her mother who died in 1942.
21. Ibid., p.259.
22. Ibid., p.248.
23. Mass Observation Archive: FR 1111 *Opinion on Cabinet Changes*, February 1942, p.10.
24. Mass Observation Archive: Diarist 5331, 8 February 1942.
25. Mass Observation Archive: FR 1362 *Who Likes and Who Dislikes Sir Stafford Cripps*, July 1942, p.4.
26. Mass Observation Archive: FR 1111 *Opinion on Cabinet Changes*, February 1942, p.12.
27. Clarke, *The Cripps Version*, p.269.
28. BBC Empire Service: weekly broadcast to India, 'Newsletter', 21

February 1942, in Davison (ed.), *The Complete Works of George Orwell, Vol. 13: All Propaganda is Lies*, p.187. Although Orwell broadcast almost weekly to India on a variety of news and culture-related topics, he later lamented 'the utter futility of what we are doing' and the fact that outside the various BBC European services, 'hardly anyone is listening' (see ibid., pp.366–7).

29. Clarke, *The Cripps Version*, p.271.
30. Mass Observation Archive: FR 1118, article by Tom Harrison, 'Trusting the Brains', in *New Statesman*, February 1942.
31. Churchill Papers 20/70: Roosevelt to Churchill, 19 February 1942 and Churchill to Roosevelt, 20 February 1942, in Gilbert (ed.), *The Churchill Documents, Vol. 17*, pp.285–7.
32. Fort, *Archibald Wavell*, p.280.
33. Churchill, *The Second World War, Vol. IV: The Hinge of Fate*, p.127.

7 Shipping Perils

1. Downing, *Spies in the Sky*, pp.113–15.
2. Gilbert (ed.), *The Churchill Documents, Vol. 16*, p.370.
3. Todman, *Britain's War: Into Battle*, pp.461ff.
4. There is a powerful scene in the movie *The Cruel Sea* (dir. Charles Frend, 1953) in which the Asdic operator on board the fictional HMS *Compass Rose* tracks what is believed to be a U-boat close by as seamen in the water, survivors of the latest sinking, call for help. As the pings reach a dramatic crescendo, Captain Ericson (Jack Hawkins) has to decide whether to depth-charge the U-boat, which would kill all the survivors struggling in the sea. See Downing, 'War on Film: *The Cruel Sea*', in *Military History Monthly* 39, December 2013.
5. A. P. Rowe, *One Story of Radar*, pp.101–2.
6. CSO, *Fighting with Figures*, p.190.
7. Mass Observation Archive: Diarist 5004, 4 April 1942.
8. Anthony Aldgate and Jeffrey Richards, *Britain Can Take It*, p.246. The MoI eventually persuaded the Admiralty to allow the making of a major film about the Battle of the Atlantic but it took several years for the film to be written, approved and then made as it turned out to be a nightmare to shoot in Technicolor on the rough waters of the Irish Sea. The film when finally premiered in December 1944 was called *Western Approaches* (written and directed by Pat Jackson) and is one of the great documentary-features of the war. Brendan Bracken, the Minister of Information, told the producer it was 'the best film he has ever seen' (Aldgate and Richards, *Britain Can Take It*, p.268). See also Downing, 'War on Film: *Western Approaches*', in *Military History Matters* 121, April–May 2021.
9. At the time of writing (2021), Amazon UK lists 656 books related to Bletchley Park. The Robert Harris novel *Enigma* (1995) did a lot to bring the story of the codebreaking station to public attention and was turned into the thriller movie *Enigma* (dir. Michael Apted, 2001,

starring Dougray Scott and Kate Winslet). *The Imitation Game* is another popular movie about Alan Turing and Bletchley Park (dir. Morten Tyldum, 2014, starring Benedict Cumberbatch and Keira Knightley).

10. David Kahn, *Seizing the Enigma*, pp.68ff.
11. Ronald Lewin, *Ultra Goes to War*, p.64 and Gilbert, *Finest Hour*, pp.609–13.
12. David Kahn, *The Code Breakers*, pp.975–7.
13. From 387,800 tons lost in May to 95,500 tons lost in July 1941 (CSO, *Fighting with Figures*, p.190).
14. CSO, *Fighting with Figures*, p.190.
15. Kahn, *Seizing the Enigma*, pp.195–213.
16. Sherwood, *Roosevelt and Hopkins*, p.498.
17. CSO, *Fighting with Figures*, p.190.
18. Lord Moran, *Churchill at War*, p.38.
19. Mass Observation Archive: Diarist 5205, 21 August 1942.
20. Mass Observation Archive: Diarist 5004, 17 March 1942.
21. Todman, *Britain's War: A New World*, pp.189–93.

8 Grave Deterioration

1. Churchill Papers CHAR9/157: Churchill speech, Caxton Hall, 26 March 1942, in Gilbert (ed.), *The Churchill Documents, Vol. 17*, pp.444–5.
2. Cadogan, *The Diaries*, p.440.
3. Lady Soames Papers: 27 February 1942, in Gilbert (ed.), *The Churchill Documents, Vol. 17*, p.321.
4. See Taylor Downing, *Night Raid*, pp.222–88.
5. Mass Observation Archive: Diarist 5433, 1 March 1942.
6. Downing, *Night Raid*, pp.309–10.
7. John Frost, *A Drop Too Many*, pp.56–8.
8. Cadogan, *The Diaries*, p.438.
9. Keegan (ed.), *Churchill's Generals*, p.90.
10. Kennedy, *The Business of War*, p.208.
11. Gilbert, *Road to Victory*, pp.71–2.
12. Philip Ziegler, *Mountbatten*, p.170.
13. William Slim, *Defeat into Victory*, pp.109–10.
14. Leo Amery, *The Leo Amery Diaries Vol. 2*, 26 February 1942, p.779.
15. Panter-Downes, *London War Notes*, p.211.
16. The journalist was Alan Moorehead in the *Daily Express*, 30 March 1942.
17. Clarke, *The Cripps Version*, p.305.
18. Alan Moorehead, *The Desert War*, pp.312–13.
19. Mass Observation Archive: FR 1362 *Who Likes and Dislikes Sir Stafford Cripps*, July 1942, p.5.
20. Yasmin Khan, *The Raj at War*, pp.215–16.
21. Todman, *Britain's War: A New World*, pp.511–12 and Churchill, *The Second World War, Vol. IV: The Hinge of Fate*, p.182.

22. Churchill Papers 20/71: Churchill to Roosevelt, 5 March 1942, in Gilbert (ed.), *The Churchill Documents, Vol. 17*, p.348.
23. Mass Observation Archive: Diarist 5433, 11 April 1942.
24. Alanbrooke, *War Diaries*, 7 April 1942, p.245.

9 Arctic Convoys

1. F. H. Hinsley, *British Intelligence in the Second World War: Its Influence on Strategy and Operations*, Vol. 2, p.671.
2. Churchill Papers 9/152: BBC broadcast 24 August 1941, in Gilbert (ed.), *The Churchill Documents, Vol. 16*, pp.1,101–2.
3. Premier Papers 3/401/1: Churchill to Cripps, 5 September 1941, in Gilbert (ed.), *The Churchill Documents, Vol. 16*, p.1,172.
4. Churchill, *The Second World War, Vol. III: The Grand Alliance*, p.411.
5. The observer was Harold Balfour, Under-Secretary of State for Air, written in an article for *The Times*, 28 September 1965; see Gilbert (ed.), *The Churchill Documents, Vol. 16*, p.1,237.
6. Cabinet Papers 120/36: Minutes of War Cabinet, Defence Committee, 19 September 1941, in Gilbert (ed.), *The Churchill Documents, Vol. 16*, p.1,236.
7. Gilbert, *Finest Hour*, pp.1,207–11.
8. Churchill Papers 20/43: Churchill to Stalin, 6 October 1941, in Gilbert (ed.), *The Churchill Documents, Vol. 16*, pp.1,308–9.
9. Bernard Edwards, *The Road to Russia: Arctic Convoys 1942*, pp.1–14.
10. Ibid., pp.18–38.
11. Ibid., pp.39–53.
12. Ibid., p.62.
13. Churchill Papers 20/74: Roosevelt to Churchill, 27 April 1942, and Churchill Papers 20/88: Churchill to Roosevelt, 2 May 1942, in Gilbert (ed.), *The Churchill Documents, Vol. 17*, pp.596–7 & 616–17.
14. After a series of salvage operations in the 1980s most of the gold bullion was recovered by British divers from the wreck of HMS *Edinburgh* which lay on the seabed at a depth of 800 feet (245 metres). In 2020 money, the value of the bullion was about £70 million.
15. Vice Admiral B. B. Schofield, 'Ten Got Through', in Liddell Hart and Pitt (eds), *History of the Second World War, Vol. 3*, p.999.
16. Edwards, *The Road to Russia*, pp.140–9.
17. Schofield, 'Ten Got Through', in Liddell Hart and Pitt (eds), *History of the Second World War, Vol. 3*, pp.996–1,001.
18. Edwards, *The Road to Russia*, p.122.
19. Churchill, *The Second World War, Vol. IV: The Hinge of Fate*, p.236.
20. Churchill Papers 65/31: Stalin to Churchill, 23 July 1942, in Gilbert (ed.), *The Churchill Documents, Vol. 17*, p.985.
21. Churchill, *The Second World War, Vol. IV: The Hinge of Fate*, p. 243.

10 Bombing

1. Family stories from Pat Downing (née Child), the author's mother. She soon got another job and stayed in Exeter for the rest of the war. The city later became one of the centres for US troops preparing to launch the D-Day invasion and as a glamorous eighteen-year-old, Pat had at least two jeeps and a landing craft named after her! She had received many proposals of marriage before she met my father Peter Downing, an RAF officer, at a dance at the Rougemont Hotel, Exeter in April 1945. He had just returned from two and a half years in the Middle East. They married a few weeks later.
2. Jan Gore, *The Terror Raids of 1942*, pp.46–51.
3. Mass Observation Archive: FR 1285 *Two Baedeker Raids*, May 1942, pp.3–3b; quotes are from pp.6, 7 & 9.
4. Max Hastings, *Bomber Command*, pp.94–7.
5. Churchill, *The Second World War, Vol. II: Their Finest Hour*, pp.405–6.
6. Downing, *Spies in the Sky*, pp.174–9.
7. Charles Webster and Noble Frankland, *The Strategic Air Offensive Against Germany, Vol. 1*, p.125.
8. Ibid., pp.178–9; the full Butt Report appears as Appendix 13 in Webster and Frankland, *The Strategic Air Offensive Against Germany, Vol. 4*, pp.205–13.
9. Churchill to Portal, 3 September 1941, in Churchill, *The Second World War, Vol. IV: The Hinge of Fate*, p.250.
10. Webster and Frankland, *The Strategic Air Offensive Against Germany, Vol. 1*, p.179.
11. Richard Overy, *The Bombing War: Europe 1939–1945*, p.257.
12. Ibid., pp.262–5.
13. Ibid., pp.269–79.
14. Harris Papers quoted in ibid., p.287.
15. Webster and Frankland, *The Strategic Air Offensive Against Germany, Vol. 1*, p.182.
16. Churchill Papers 20/67: Churchill to Sinclair and Portal, 13 March 1942, in Gilbert (ed.), *The Churchill Documents, Vol. 17*, p.387.
17. Thomas Wilson, *Churchill and the Prof*, p.74, includes Lindemann's Minute in full.
18. Gore, *The Terror Raids of 1942*, p.9.
19. Gardiner, *Wartime Britain*, p.613.
20. Overy, *The Bombing War*, pp.289–90 & 428.
21. Vere Hodgson, *Few Eggs and No Oranges*, pp.229–30.
22. The Singleton Report appears in Webster and Frankland, *The Strategic Air Offensive Against Germany, Vol. 4*, pp.231–8.
23. Kennedy, *The Business of War*, p.238.
24. Overy, *The Bombing War*, pp.292–3.
25. British Movietone News is available via the Associated Press on YouTube: https://www.youtube.com/c/britishmovietone. For this newsreel see: https://www.youtube.com/watch?v=bLnZ-iFWlbs

26. Todman, *Britain's War: A New World*, p.167.
27. Churchill Papers 20/67: Churchill to Attlee, 16 April 1942, in Gilbert (ed.), *The Churchill Documents, Vol. 17*, p.541.
28. Roger Freeman, *The Mighty Eighth*, pp.4–8.
29. Albert Speer, *Inside the Third Reich*, p. 210. See also Adam Tooze, *The Wages of Destruction*, p.554 and Overy, *The Bombing War*, p.299.
30. Overy, *The Bombing War*, p.301.
31. For an analysis of the ethical arguments over the bombing of civilians see Overy, *The Bombing War*, pp.628–33. The arguments about the morality of the bombing offensive are summarised in Downing, *Churchill's War Lab*, pp.269–73.

11 Island Fortress

1. Christina Ratcliffe in a March 1958 article in the *Daily Star*, quoted in James Holland, *Fortress Malta*, p.26.
2. Charles MacLean, 'George Cross Island', in Liddell Hart and Pitt (eds), *History of the Second World War, Vol. 3*, p.1,010.
3. Downing, *Spies in the Sky*, pp.159–73.
4. Capt. Donald Macintyre, 'The Malta Convoys', in Liddell Hart and Pitt (eds), *History of the Second World War, Vol. 3*, p.1,008. Rommel thought it was a mistake to have invaded Crete in May 1941 and instead Malta should have been invaded; see Basil Liddell Hart (ed.), *The Rommel Papers*, p.120.
5. Holland, *Fortress Malta*, p.167.
6. Ministry of Information (MoI) and Air Ministry, *The Air Battle of Malta*, p.24.
7. Gilbert, *Finest Hour*, p.1,242.
8. The massive explosion and sinking of HMS *Barham* was filmed by a newsreel cameraman on board HMS *Valiant*. It is one of the most spectacular but deadly naval losses ever captured on film.
9. Albert Kesselring, *The Memoirs of Field Marshal Kesselring*, p.105.
10. MoI, *The Air Battle of Malta*, p.46.
11. Holland, *Fortress Malta*, pp.211–23.
12. Richard Woodman, *Malta Convoys 1940–1943*, pp.293–314.
13. Overy, *The Bombing War*, p.504.
14. MoI, *The Air Battle of Malta*, pp.54–7.
15. Holland, *Fortress Malta*, pp.279–80.
16. Churchill, *The Second World War, Vol. IV: The Hinge of Fate*, pp.268–9.
17. Hinsley, *British Intelligence in the Second World War*, pp.203–4.
18. Churchill Papers 20/75: Churchill to captain and crew of USS *Wasp*, 10 May 1942, in Gilbert (ed.), *The Churchill Documents, Vol. 17*, p.652.
19. The film *Malta Story* (dir. Brian Desmond Hurst, 1953) accurately reconstructs this process. Featuring footage actually shot on Malta during the war, the film also captures the scale of destruction on the island. Alec Guinness plays a photo-reconnaissance pilot, Flt Lt Peter Ross, very loosely based on Adrian Warburton, who falls in love with

a local girl, Maria, played by Muriel Pavlow. Jack Hawkins plays the part of the RAF commander, Air Vice Marshal Frank, based on Hugh Pughe Lloyd. Although the Maltese characters are played by British actors the film powerfully conveys the struggle of Malta to survive in the spring and summer of 1942; see Downing, 'War on Film: *Malta Story*' in *Military History Matters* 120, February 2021.

20. Holland, *Fortress Malta*, p.311.
21. Major-General I. Playfair, *The Mediterranean and Middle East Vol. III*, p.325 and David Woodward, 'Malta', in Liddell Hart and Pitt (eds), *History of the Second World War, Vol. 3*, p.1,260.
22. Roger Hill, *Destroyer Captain*, quoted in Woodman, *Malta Convoys*, pp.435–7.
23. Woodman, *Malta Convoys*, pp.447–54.
24. Churchill Papers 20/75: Churchill to Auchinleck, 8 May 1942, in Gilbert (ed.), *The Churchill Documents, Vol. 17*, p.645.

12 The Desert War

1. Moorehead, *The Desert War*, p.9.
2. Jonathan Fennell, *Fighting the People's War*, pp.150–3.
3. Prime Minister's Personal Telegram T.815, 15 November 1941, quoted in part in Gilbert, *Finest Hour*, p.1,239.
4. John Martin Papers quoted in Gilbert, *Finest Hour*, p.1,239.
5. Playfair, *The Mediterranean and Middle East Vol. III*, p.52.
6. IWM 96/50/1 Crimp quoted in Fennell, *Fighting the People's War*, p.155.
7. Liddell Hart (ed.), *The Rommel Papers*, p.174.
8. Alfred Gause, 'Rommel Strikes Back', in Liddell Hart and Pitt (eds), *History of the Second World War, Vol. 2*, p.864.
9. Moorehead, *The Desert War*, p.249.
10. Playfair, *The Mediterranean and Middle East Vol. III*, pp.152–3.
11. Moorehead, *The Desert War*, p.268.
12. Lord Moran, *Churchill at War*, p.54 and Alanbrooke, *War Diaries*, pp.239–41.
13. Churchill Papers 20/71: Churchill to Auchinleck, 15 March 1942, in Gilbert (ed.), *The Churchill Documents, Vol. 17*, pp.393–4.
14. Playfair, *The Mediterranean and Middle East Vol. III*, pp.217–21.
15. Australian War Memorial Middle East Morale Reports, May 1942, in Fennell, *Fighting the People's War*, p.163.
16. Hinsley, *British Intelligence in the Second World War*, Vol. 2, pp.361–2.
17. Churchill Papers 20/75: Churchill to Auchinleck, 8 May 1942, in Gilbert (ed.), *The Churchill Documents, Vol. 17*, p.645.
18. Moorehead, *The Desert War*, p.342.
19. David Chandler, 'The Fight at Gazala', in Liddell Hart and Pitt (eds), *History of the Second World War, Vol. 3*, p.1,026.
20. Churchill Papers 20/76: Churchill to Auchinleck, 13 June 1942, in Gilbert (ed.), *The Churchill Documents, Vol. 17*, p.785.

13 Global Battles

1. Mass Observation Archive: Diarist 5150, 3 May 1942.
2. Mass Observation Archive: Diarist 5256, 2 September 1942.
3. Todman, *Britain's War: A New World*, p.195.
4. Briggs, *The War of Words*, p.440.
5. BBC Written Archives: Churchill broadcast, 10 May 1942, in Gilbert (ed.), *The Churchill Documents, Vol. 17*, pp.653–61.
6. Gilbert, *Road to Victory*, p.107.
7. Mass Observation Archive: Diarist 5296, 11 May 1942.
8. Mass Observation Archive: Diarist 5004, 11 May 1942.
9. Mass Observation Archive: Diarist 5433, 10 May 1942.
10. Mass Observation Archive: Diarist 5205, 12 May 1942.
11. National Archives: INF I/292, Home Intelligence Division Weekly Report No. 85, 20 May 1942, in Toye, *The Roar of the Lion*, pp.139–41.
12. Churchill Papers 20/75: Fraser to Churchill and Halifax to Churchill, 11 May 1942, in Gilbert (ed.), *The Churchill Documents, Vol. 17*, pp.661–2.
13. Unique footage shot by a German cameraman recording the process of rounding up and separating men from women and children by the Wehrmacht after a village had been captured is featured in episode 26 ('Remember') of the Thames Television series *The World at War* (producer and director Jeremy Isaacs, 1974). It is heart-breaking to watch as tearful farewells are said by men and women who suspect that they will never see each other again. The footage is allowed to run at length. It must have been a scene repeated hundreds of times by German troops as they advanced through Russia.
14. Churchill, *The Second World War, Vol. IV: The Hinge of Fate*, p.160.
15. Ibid., p.163.
16. Churchill Papers 20/67: Churchill to Pound, 13 March 1942, in Gilbert (ed.), *The Churchill Documents, Vol. 17*, p.385.
17. Churchill, *The Second World War, Vol. IV: The Hinge of Fate*, p.164.
18. Todman, *Britain's War: A New World*, p.179.
19. Donald Macintyre, 'Battle of Midway', in Liddell Hart and Pitt (eds), *History of the Second World War, Vol. 3*, p.981.
20. Alanbrooke, *War Diaries*, p.250.
21. Royal Archives: Churchill to King George VI, 16 June 1942, in Gilbert (ed.), *The Churchill Documents, Vol. 17*, p.797.
22. Imperial Airways was founded in 1924 to transport mail, government officials, military figures and wealthy businessmen around the empire. By the early 1930s it had flights to the Middle East and South Africa and finally connected to India and Australia in 1935. Flying boats were used because there were relatively few large airfields around the world but everywhere there was water to land on, rivers, lakes, lagoons and the sea. Imperial Airways became a symbol for luxury as it needed to compete with the first-class

service on the ocean liners of the day, although it reduced long-haul travel from weeks to days. Imperial flew both Short Empire flying boats and Boeing 314 Clippers which were then the 'jumbos' of the skies. In April 1940 Imperial Airways' assets, including its aircraft, staff and routes, were transferred to the new state airline, the British Overseas Airways Corporation (BOAC).

23. Alanbrooke, *War Diaries*, p.266.

14 Disgrace

1. Moorehead, *The Desert War*, p.366.
2. Liddell Hart (ed.), *The Rommel Papers*, p.224.
3. Kennedy, *The Business of War*, pp.239–41.
4. Churchill Papers 20/76: Churchill to Auchinleck, 14 June 1942, in Gilbert (ed.), *The Churchill Documents, Vol. 17*, p.789.
5. Churchill, *The Second World War, Vol. IV: The Hinge of Fate*, p.331.
6. Albert Martin Diary, 19 June 1942, in James Holland, *The War in the West*, p.239.
7. Playfair, *The Mediterranean and Middle East Vol. III*, pp.260–3.
8. Moorehead, *The Desert War*, p.373.
9. Fennell, *Fighting the People's War*, p.174.
10. David Chandler, 'The Fight at Gazala', in Liddell Hart and Pitt (eds), *History of the Second World War, Vol. 3*, p.1,029.
11. Playfair, *The Mediterranean and Middle East Vol. III*, pp.266–72.
12. Ibid., p.273.
13. Liddell Hart (ed.), *The Rommel Papers*, p.232.
14. Churchill, *The Second World War, Vol. IV: The Hinge of Fate*, pp.343–4.
15. Ibid., p.344 and Ismay, *Memoirs*, p.255.
16. James Holland, *Together We Stand*, pp.164–5.
17. Fennell, *Fighting the People's War*, pp.173–5.
18. Letter Auchinleck to James Grigg, 2 March 1942, in John Connell, *Auchinleck*, p.460.
19. Fennell, *Fighting the People's War*, pp.160–2.
20. In the First World War, 343 serving soldiers had been shot for desertion, cowardice in the face of the enemy and a few other charges. The suspicion was widely held among the public that many of these men were suffering from some sort of shell shock or mental breakdown and that medical treatment rather than military punishment would have been more appropriate. During the 1920s there was a public inquiry and various parliamentary investigations into the subject, most of which tended to exonerate the army. But the injustice of military executions became a cause célèbre with several Labour MPs and the policy was finally abolished in 1930, although the official army line was that the abolition would undermine discipline. The records of the trials which led to the First World War executions were not made public until the 1990s but when released revealed quite clearly that many of those executed had been in

a poor mental state and were suffering from trauma. See Taylor Downing, *Breakdown*, pp.234–56.

21. Playfair, *The Mediterranean and Middle East Vol. III*, p.278.
22. *Manchester Guardian*, 23 June 1942.
23. *Observer*, 28 June 1942.
24. Mass Observation Archive: Diarist 5433, 23 June 1942.
25. Mass Observation Archive: Diarist 5331, 21–24 June 1942.
26. Fennell, *Fighting the People's War*, pp.177–9.
27. Moorehead, *The Desert War*, p.381.
28. Sherwood, *Roosevelt and Hopkins*, p.595.
29. Playfair, *The Mediterranean and Middle East Vol. III*, pp.349–51.
30. Fennell, *Fighting the People's War*, p.183.
31. Ibid., pp.184–5.
32. Churchill, *The Second World War, Vol. IV: The Hinge of Fate*, p.327.
33. National Archives: WO 32/15773: Army Council, 31 July 1942, in Fennell, *Fighting the People's War*, p.186.

15 Censure

1. Graham Farmelo, *Churchill's Bomb*, p.209. Farmelo makes the point that although Churchill later relied upon the agreement reached at this meeting as evidence of joint cooperation on the building of the atom bomb, it had been more of a friendly discussion without advisers present and nothing had been written down as a formal record of the discussion.
2. Franklin Roosevelt Papers: Churchill to Roosevelt, 20 June 1942, in Gilbert (ed.), *The Churchill Documents, Vol. 17*, pp.811–12.
3. Alanbrooke, *War Diaries*, p.267.
4. Churchill, *The Second World War, Vol. IV: The Hinge of Fate*, pp.344–5.
5. Ibid., p.347.
6. Eden, *Memoirs*, pp.331–2.
7. Churchill Papers 20/77: Churchill to Auchinleck, Personal, 25 June 1942, in Gilbert (ed.), *The Churchill Documents, Vol. 17*, p.826.
8. Ismay, *Memoirs*, p.257.
9. Channon, *Chips: The Diaries*, pp.332–3.
10. The official Conservative candidate, R. J. Hunt, received 6,226 votes; Tom Driberg, the Independent Labour candidate, received 12,219 votes.
11. All parliamentary quotations for this day are from Hansard online: https://hansard.parliament.uk/Commons/1942-07-01/debates/9aed4861-e175-4a60-a243-90fd3528ede1/CentralDirectionOfTheWar
12. Channon, *Chips: The Diaries*, p.334.
13. All parliamentary quotations for this day are from Hansard online: https://hansard.parliament.uk/Commons/1942-07-02/debates/64dacb26-408e-4010-aae7-dc5b54c7da0f/CentralDirectionOfTheWar
14. Nicolson (ed.), *Harold Nicolson Diaries*, 2 July 1942, p.295.
15. Channon, *Chips: The Diaries*, p.334.

16. Churchill, *The Second World War, Vol. IV: The Hinge of Fate*, p.366.
17. Panter-Downes, *London War Notes*, pp.234–5 & 205.
18. Mass Observation Archive: FR 1131 *Morale in July 1942*, August 1942, pp.1–4 and 'Feelings' p.2.
19. Churchill Papers 20/67: Churchill to Ismay for Chiefs of Staff Committee, 5 July 1942, in Gilbert (ed.), *The Churchill Documents, Vol. 17*, pp.922–3.
20. Alanbrooke, *War Diaries*, 8 July 1942, p.278.
21. Cadogan, *The Diaries*, 8 July 1942, p.461.
22. Sherwood, *Roosevelt and Hopkins*, pp.604–5.
23. Alanbrooke, *War Diaries*, 24 July 1942, p.285.
24. Churchill, *The Second World War, Vol. IV: The Hinge of Fate*, p.404.
25. Rick Atkinson, *An Army at Dawn*, pp.16–17.
26. Churchill Papers 20/78: Roosevelt to Churchill, 28 July 1942, in Gilbert (ed.), *The Churchill Documents, Vol. 17*, p.1,008.

16 'Have You Not Got a Single General Who Can Win Battles?'

1. Julian Amery, *Approach March*, pp.308–9.
2. Alanbrooke, *War Diaries*, 3 July 1942, pp.276–7.
3. Eden, *Memoirs*, p.332.
4. Alanbrooke, *War Diaries*, post-war commentary, p.226.
5. Winston Churchill, *The World Crisis (Vol. III, 1916–1918, Part 1)*, pp.195–6.
6. Downing, *Churchill's War Lab*, pp.1–51.
7. Michael Carver, *The Seven Ages of the British Army*, p.201. A private soldier in the 1930s was paid two shillings per day – less in real terms than the one shilling per day paid in 1800. Of course, he also received free rent and accommodation.
8. Alan Allport, *Browned Off and Bloody-Minded*, pp.18–20.
9. Connell, *Auchinleck*, p.7.
10. Allport, *Browned Off and Bloody-Minded*, pp.34–5.
11. John Masters, *Bugles and a Tiger*, pp.26–7.
12. Holland, *Together We Stand*, pp.28–9.
13. Hastings, *Finest Years*, p.260.
14. Harold Macmillan, *War Diaries*, pp.313 & 347.
15. Evelyn Waugh, *Men at Arms*, p.44.
16. CSO, *Fighting with Figures*, p.41.
17. Allport, *Browned Off and Bloody-Minded*, pp.69–70.
18. Ibid., p.95.
19. Playfair, *The Mediterranean and Middle East Vol. III*, pp.26–8 & 214.
20. As against 38 per cent of losses from hits by enemy tanks.
21. Playfair, *The Mediterranean and Middle East Vol. III*, pp.434–44.
22. Holland, *Together We Stand*, p.30.
23. Major-General Sir Howard Kippenberger, *Infantry Brigadier*, p.180.
24. Stephen Bungay, *Alamein*, p.101.
25. Fennell, *Fighting the People's War*, pp.164–5.

26. Brendan Bracken, the Minister of Information, suggested that banning production of the film would be to adopt the techniques of Joseph Goebbels so he argued that it should go ahead. The film (written, produced and directed by Powell and Pressburger, and starring Roger Livesey, Anton Walbrook and Deborah Kerr) was made and released in 1943 with Livesey giving a performance of dignity and compassion as Major-General Clive Wynne-Candy, the Blimp figure, who simply believes in traditional values of fair play. He is more of an innocent in a brutal modern world than the reactionary David Low stereotype. The film was the third biggest box office hit of 1943, after *Casablanca* and *In Which We Serve*. See Downing, 'War on Film: *The Life and Death of Colonel Blimp*', in *Military History Monthly* 66, March 2016.
27. *Daily Mirror*, 6 March 1942.
28. Alanbrooke, *War Diaries*, p.188.
29. *Picture Post*, 31 January 1942, reproduced in Tom Hopkinson (ed.), *Picture Post 1938–50*, pp.114–15.
30. *Daily Express*, 23 June 1942.
31. *Tribune*, 20 March 1942.
32. *Manchester Guardian*, 24 June 1942.
33. Panter-Downes, *London War Notes*, p.236.
34. Sir Henry Pownall, *Chief of Staff*, p.98.
35. Richard Hoggart, *A Sort of Clowning Vol. 2*, p.5.
36. Cadogan, *The Diaries*, pp.374, 389 & 433.
37. War Cabinet Papers 65/27: 30 July 1942, in Gilbert (ed.), *The Churchill Documents, Vol. 17*, p.785.
38. Gilbert, *Road to Victory*, p.158.
39. Churchill, *The Second World War, Vol. IV: The Hinge of Fate*, p.412.

17 From the Pyramids to the Ogre's Den

1. Letter Winston to Clementine Churchill, 9 August 1942, in Gilbert, *Road to Victory*, p.167.
2. Nicolson (ed.), *Harold Nicolson Diaries*, 6 November 1942, p.302.
3. Churchill Papers 20/54: Churchill to Pamela Gott, 29 August 1942, in Gilbert (ed.), *The Churchill Documents, Vol. 17*, p.1,131.
4. Alanbrooke, *War Diaries*, insert into 5 August 1942, p.292.
5. Ibid., insert into 6 August 1942, p.294.
6. Harvey, *The War Diaries*, p.147.
7. Churchill, *The Second World War, Vol. IV: The Hinge of Fate*, p.418.
8. Eden, *Memoirs*, p.339.
9. Alanbrooke, *War Diaries*, insert into 8 August 1942, p.296.
10. Playfair, *The Mediterranean and Middle East Vol. III*, p.369.
11. Gilbert, *Road to Victory*, p.156.
12. Churchill Papers 20/88: Churchill to Stalin, 30 July 1942, in Gilbert (ed.), *The Churchill Documents, Vol. 17*, p.1,019.
13. Churchill Papers 20/78: Stalin to Churchill, 31 July 1942, in Gilbert (ed.), *The Churchill Documents, Vol. 17*, p.1,021.

14. Harvey, *The War Diaries*, pp.148–9.
15. Baroness Churchill Papers: Clementine letter to Winston, 4 August 1942, in Gilbert (ed.), *The Churchill Documents, Vol. 17*, p.1,035.
16. Churchill, *The Second World War, Vol. IV: The Hinge of Fate*, p.428.
17. There are several records of the series of meetings between Churchill and Stalin from 12 to 15 August 1942. The official British record is at the National Archives: CAB 127/33. The British ambassador in Moscow also made his own record – see National Archives: FO 800/300. A translation of the Soviet record has been published in Martin Folly, Geoffrey Roberts and Oleg Rzheshevsky, *Churchill and Stalin*, pp.129–49. In addition, Churchill sent daily reports to the War Cabinet and to Roosevelt – see Gilbert (ed.), *The Churchill Documents, Vol. 17*, pp.1,059–87. Churchill also wrote up his own colourful account of the talks in *The Second World War, Vol. IV: The Hinge of Fate*, pp.425–51. Brooke wrote his account in Alanbrooke, *War Diaries*, pp.297–308 and Cadogan his in Cadogan, *The Diaries*, pp.469–74. Harriman's record is in Harriman and Abel, *Special Envoy to Churchill and Stalin*, pp.151–64. Although there are minor differences in the accounts they all confirm the fundamental course of the four days of meetings.
18. Churchill Papers 20/88: Churchill to Roosevelt, Meeting with Stalin on 12 August 1942, in Gilbert (ed.), *The Churchill Documents, Vol. 17*, p.1,066.
19. Churchill, *The Second World War, Vol. IV: The Hinge of Fate*, p.435.
20. This point about the incredible number the Soviets were losing every day only appears in the Soviet record (see Folly, Roberts and Rzheshevsky, *Churchill and Stalin*, pp.141–2) and in Harriman's account (see Harriman and Abel, *Special Envoy to Churchill and Stalin*, p.156).
21. Harriman interview with Martin Gilbert in July 1973, in Gilbert (ed.), *The Churchill Documents, Vol. 17*, p.1,063.
22. Gilbert, *Road to Victory*, p.186.
23. Arthur Bryant, *The Turn of the Tide*, pp.460–1 and Cadogan, *The Diaries*, p.471.
24. Alanbrooke, *War Diaries*, pp.299–300.
25. Churchill Papers 20/79: Churchill to War Cabinet, 14 August 1942, in Gilbert (ed.), *The Churchill Documents, Vol. 17*, p.1,077.
26. Cadogan, *The Diaries*, p.472.
27. Folly, Roberts and Rzheshevsky, *Churchill and Stalin*, pp.144–5.
28. Harriman and Abel, *Special Envoy to Churchill and Stalin*, p.161. For slightly different wording see Churchill, *The Second World War, Vol. IV: The Hinge of Fate*, p.443. Having been a seminarian in the Russian Orthodox Church before the Revolution, Stalin regularly invoked God in his conversation which struck many as odd for a communist leader.
29. Jacob Papers quoted in Gilbert, *Road to Victory*, p.193.
30. Cadogan, *The Diaries*, p.471. It is not known if the villa was bugged

but it is extremely likely that it was. Brooke was also warned that his accommodation was possibly bugged but found it hard to believe.

31. Alanbrooke, *War Diaries*, 15 August 1942, pp.303–5.
32. Notes by Major Birse on the meeting, in Gilbert, *Road to Victory*, pp.195–9.
33. Churchill Papers 20/87: Churchill to the War Cabinet, 16 August, in Gilbert (ed.), *The Churchill Documents, Vol. 17*, p.1,088.

18 'Extreme Tension'

1.   IWM Montgomery Papers, in Fennell, *Fighting the People's War*, pp.268–9.
2.   The speech was written down in shorthand by an officer of the 4th Indian Division and is in the National Archives: CAB 106/703. It is reproduced in full in Nigel Hamilton, *Monty: The Making of a General*, pp.622–5.
3.   Fennell, *Fighting the People's War*, p.270.
4.   Playfair, *The Mediterranean and Middle East Vol. III*, p.371.
5.   Churchill Papers 20/87: Churchill to War Cabinet, 21 August 1942, in Gilbert (ed.), *The Churchill Documents, Vol. 17*, pp.1,102–3.
6.   Gilbert, *Road to Victory*, pp.216–17.
7.   Alanbrooke, *War Diaries*, 24 August 1942, p.313.
8.   H. Fairlie Wood, 'The Canadians at Dieppe', in Liddell Hart and Pitt (eds), *History of the Second World War, Vol. 3*, p.1,104.
9.   Todman, *Britain's War*, p.227.
10. Lord Moran, *Churchill at War*, p.79.
11. Playfair, *The Mediterranean and Middle East Vol. III*, pp.315 & 326–7.
12. Ibid., p.388.
13. Alanbrooke, *War Diaries*, 8 September 1942, p.319.
14. Hinsley, *British Intelligence in the Second World War*, Vol. 2, pp.419–21.
15. Sherwood, *Roosevelt and Hopkins*, pp.632–3.
16. Eden, *Memoirs*, p.342.
17. Churchill, *The Second World War, Vol. IV: The Hinge of Fate*, pp.493 & 501.
18. Ibid., p.489.
19. Harvey, *The War Diaries*, 2 October 1942, pp.165–6.
20. Eden, *Memoirs*, p.344.
21. Lord Moran, *Churchill at War*, p.85.
22. Sir Francis de Guingand, 'Alamein – The Tide Turns', in Liddell Hart and Pitt (eds), *History of the Second World War, Vol. 3*, p.1,162.
23. George Greenfield, 'The Fighting at Alamein', in ibid., p.1,169.
24. Fennell, *Fighting the People's War*, pp.310–11.
25. Bungay, *Alamein*, p.159.
26. Churchill Papers 20/81: Churchill to Roosevelt, 23 October 1942, in Gilbert (ed.), *The Churchill Documents, Vol. 17*, p.1,300.
27. Lord Moran, *Churchill at War*, p.91.

19 'The End of the Beginning'

1. Sam Bradshaw in *The Lost Evidence: El Alamein* produced by Flashback Television, 2006 (producer Taylor Downing, director Steve Baker).
2. George Greenfield, 'The Fighting at Alamein', in Liddell Hart and Pitt (eds), *History of the Second World War, Vol. 3,* p.1,172.
3. IWM Rommel Papers quoted in Bungay, *Alamein,* p.177 and Liddell Hart (ed.), *The Rommel Papers,* p.308.
4. Bungay, *Alamein,* p.182.
5. Alanbrooke, *War Diaries,* 29 October 1942, p.335.
6. Liddell Hart (ed.), *The Rommel Papers,* p.319.
7. Hinsley, *British Intelligence in the Second World War,* Vol. 2, p.448.
8. Liddell Hart (ed.), *The Rommel Papers,* p.321.
9. Alexander to Prime Minister, 4 November 1942, in Churchill, *The Second World War, Vol. IV: The Hinge of Fate,* p.537.
10. Hamilton, *Monty: The Making of a General,* p.846.
11. Fennell, *Fighting the People's War,* p.309.
12. Panter-Downes, *London War Notes,* pp.248–9.
13. Mass Observation Archive: FR 1522 *Morale in November 1942,* p.1 and Diarist 5433, 5 November 1942.
14. Churchill Papers 20/80: Churchill to Roosevelt, 15 September 1942, in Gilbert (ed.), *The Churchill Documents, Vol. 17,* p.1,202.
15. Mass Observation Archive: FR 1522 *Morale in November 1942;* quotes are from pp.1, 3, 5 & 12.
16. Todman, *Britain's War: A New World,* p.293.
17. David Stafford, *Churchill and Secret Service,* pp.290–4.
18. Gordon A. Harrison, *United States Army in World War II,* p.143.
19. Kennedy, *The Business of War,* p.239.
20. Sherwood, *Roosevelt and Hopkins,* p.656.
21. BBC Written Archives: Speech, 10 November 1942, in Gilbert (ed.), *The Churchill Documents, Vol. 17,* pp.1,375–6.

Epilogue

1. MacKay, *Half the Battle,* p.95.
2. Gilbert, *Road to Victory,* p.283.
3. Churchill, *The Second World War, Vol. IV: The Hinge of Fate,* p.578.
4. Ibid., p.494.
5. Panter-Downes, *London War Notes,* p.197.
6. Mass Observation Archive: Diarist 5205, 13 February 1942.
7. Mass Observation Archive: Diarist 5433, 11 April 1942.
8. Kennedy, *The Business of War,* pp.208–27.
9. Ibid., pp.194–5.
10. Sherwood, *Roosevelt and Hopkins,* p.627 and Harriman and Abel, *Special Envoy to Churchill and Stalin,* p.168.

11. Churchill Papers 23/11: Churchill to War Cabinet, Paper No. 18, 12 January 1943, in Martin Gilbert and Larry P. Arnn (eds), *The Churchill Documents, Vol. 18, One Continent Redeemed*, pp.96–7.

12. National Archives: INF 1/292, Home Intelligence Report, 10 December 1942, in Todman, *Britain's War: A New World*, p.303.

13. Mass Observation Archive: FR 1538 *First Reactions to the Beveridge Report*, December 1942, pp.1–3.

14. Mass Observation Archive: Diarist 5445, 1 December 1942.

15. Mass Observation Archive: FR 1538 *First Reactions to the Beveridge Report*, December 1942, p.3.

16. Gardiner, *Wartime Britain*, p.584.

17. Of these only 6,000 survived to return to Germany, mostly not until the 1950s.

18. Kennedy, *The Business of War*, p.277.

19. Alanbrooke, *War Diaries*, p.361.

20. Macmillan, *War Diaries*, p.9.

21. Overy, *The Bombing War*, pp.303–7.

22. Lord Moran, *Churchill at War*, pp.99–100.

23. In March 2021 the painting was sold by Angelina Jolie for £8.3 million, making it the most expensive painting by Churchill to date.

24. Churchill speech: Tripoli, 3 February 1943, in Gilbert and Arnn (eds), *The Churchill Documents, Vol. 18*, pp.328–9.

25. General Sir Ian Jacob Papers: 4 February 1943, in ibid., p.334.

26. Churchill Papers 20/11: General Alexander to Churchill, Most Immediate, 13 May 1943, in ibid., p.1,285.

27. Churchill Papers 20/54: Churchill to Most Rev. William Temple, 29 October 1942, in Gilbert (ed.), *The Churchill Documents, Vol. 17*, p.1,326.

28. Churchill Papers 20/82: Marshall to Churchill, 7 November 1942, in ibid., p.1,370.

29. Churchill Papers 20/56: Cripps to Churchill, 29 November 1942, in ibid., p.1,460.

30. Jeremy Isaacs and Taylor Downing, *Cold War*, pp.25–7.

31. Churchill, *The Second World War, Vol. IV: The Hinge of Fate*, p.541.

Index

Page numbers in *italic* refer to maps and images

Abadan oilfields 159
Abdication Crisis 12, 58
Adam, General Sir Ronald 300, 303
Adams, Mary 51, 54
Admiral Hipper (German cruiser) 163, 169
Admiral Scheer (German cruiser) 169
Adu Atoll 149
Afrika Korps 68, 201, 236, 285
    Battle of Gazala 225–8, 296, 304, 330
    fighting strength 69, 211, 221, 323, 337, 358
    First Battle of El Alamein 262–3, 265, 273, 280, 284, 296
    retreat 218, 342–4, 351
    Second Battle of El Alamein 17, 322, 338, 339–45, 369
    supply problems 199, 216, 329–30, 333, 336, 341, 365–6
    surrender 366
    and Tobruk 68, 69–70, 216–18, 253–7, 330, 351
    Tunisian campaign 350, 351, 352, 353, 355, 364–6
    war materiel 219, 222
Aichi bomber 238, 239
air raid precaution (ARP) wardens 5
air raid warnings 46
Air-to-Surface Vessel radar (ASV) 131
Akagi (Japanese carrier) 246, 247
Albacore torpedo bomber 238
Alexander, A.V. 67
Alexander, General Harold 147, 148, 305, 308, 332, 333, 343, 355, 365, 366

Alexandria 70, 263, 264
Algeria 346, 347, 348, 351
allotments 4
Alten Fjord 169, 171, 172
Amery, Captain Julian 285
Amery, Leo 8, 150, 285
Anderson, John 123, 150
Anderson, Lieutenant-General Sir Kenneth 351
anti-aircraft weapons 76–7, 165, 180–1, 223
anti-imperialism 154
anti-tank guns 223, 274, 293, 294, 330, 337
appeasement 9, 12, 59, 62
'Arcadia' *see* Washington conference
Archangel 161, 169, 172, 278, 333
Arctic convoys 159–74, 230, 278, 308, 312, 333, 352
    attacks on 164, 165, 166, 167, 168, 169, 171–2, 280
    losses 164, 166, 167, 168, 171, 172, 333
    routes 160, *162*
    weather conditions 160–1
Ark Royal, HMS 199
Army Film and Photographic Unit 49
Arnim, General Hans von 365, 366
Arnold, General *363*
ASDIC sonar 130
Asia-Pacific war
    Allied Supreme Command 29–30
    Battle of the Coral Sea 244–5
    Battle of the Java Sea 125
    Battle of Midway 245–8, 357

Borneo 26, 93
Burma 66, 89, 93, 108, 114, 124, 125,
    147–8, 153, 236, 336
Guadalcanal 353, 357
Hong Kong 26, 93, 140
Japanese campaign 20, 24, 26, 56,
    57, 63, 64, 65, 74, 92–110, 112–13,
    114, 124, 125, 147–8, 153, 155,
    236–7, 238–45, 238–48, 353, 357
Malaya 60, 61, 62–4, 66, 93, 94, 95,
    140
map 240–1
New Guinea 105, 108, 236, 244
Pacific War Council 270
Philippines 106–7, 125
Singapore see Singapore
Solomon Islands 244, 253
threat to Australia 62, 125, 236, 244
Asquith, Herbert 58
Astrakhan 308
Atlantic Charter 24, 112
atomic bomb 268, 368
Attlee, Clement 12, 31, 116, 120, 123,
    149, 190, 294, 335, 361
Auchinleck, General Claude 25,
    69–70, 154, 210, 216, 217, 220,
    221–2, 224, 227, 252, 253, 260, 262,
    263, 265–6, 271, 280, 284–5, 289,
    296, 303, 304, 305, 306, 307
Auschwitz 366
Australia 62, 66, 108–9, 125, 244
    Japanese bombing of 236
Australian troops
    defence of Singapore 96, 98, 99, 100,
        101–2, 104, 105, 108
    Malay campaign 95–6
    North African campaign 68, 211,
        223, 251, 296, 339, 342
Avenger, HMS 333
Avenger bomber 246
Avro 182

B-17 bomber (Flying Fortress) 190, 334
B-25 Mitchell bomber 242
Baedeker Raids 176–7, 185–6
Baghdad 264
Baldwin, Stanley 4, 58, 62
Ball, Sir Joseph 49
Barce 218
Bardia 211
Barham, HMS 199
Bataan peninsula 107, 125
Bath 176, 177, 185
Battersea Power Station 48

Battle of Alam Halfa 329–31
Battle of the Atlantic 32, 55, 75–9,
    127–39, 140
    convoy system 75, 76, 77, 115, 128–9,
        131–2, 136, 137, 209
    U-boat attacks 32, 75, 76, 127–39
    see also Channel Dash
'Battle of the Beams' 6
Battle of Britain 15, 17, 32, 63, 178, 199,
    329
Battle of Calabria 68
Battle of the Coral Sea 244–5
battle fatigue 260, 266
Battle of Gazala 225–8, 296, 304, 330
Battle of the Java Sea 125
Battle of Midway 245–8, 357
Battle of Mons 286
Battle of Omdurman 287
Bay of Bengal 149, 236, 238
BBC 7, 46, 48, 51, 230
    censorship 48
    Forces Programme 7
    Home Service 7
    and maintenance of public morale
        54
    Nine O'Clock News 7, 21, 121
    Postscript 121
    World Service 124
Beaufighter 330
Beaufort torpedo bomber 76–7, 81, 84,
    85, 87
Beaverbrook, Lord 25, 30, 44, 67, 115,
    123, 158, 159, 167, 336
    Minister of Supply 25
Beddington, Jack 49
Belgium, German occupation of 10, 15
Bellenger, Frederick 116
Belzec 366
Bengal famine 154
Benghazi 74, 211, 218, 219, 265, 350
Bennett, Major-General Gordon 92,
    97, 108–9
Berlin
    bombing of 181, 243
    Soviet capture of 368
Bernal, J.D. 180
Bevan, Aneurin 116, 275–6
Beveridge, William 18, 360
Beveridge Report 360–1
Bevin, Ernest 123, 144
Bir Hacheim 224, 225, 226
Birmingham 38
Birse, Major 318
Bismarck, General 330

Bismarck (German battleship) 77–8, 171, 238
Bizerta 351
black market 4, 16, 42
blackout 3, 4–5, 6
  incidental harms of 5, 42
Blair, Tony 31
Bletchley Park 132, 133–5, 136, 137, 156–7, 224, 333, 336, 343
'Blimp', Colonel 297
Blitz 6, 17, 38, 156, 175–6, 180, 183, 199, 356
  'Blitz spirit' 17
  fatalities 54
  structural damage 54–5
BOAC (British Overseas Airways Corporation) 249, 272
Bock, Field Marshal von 234, 235
Boer War 287
Bolton 52
Bomb Alley 202
bombing campaigns 175–92
  against Germany 177–85, 186–9, 190–1, 230–1, 311, 320
  aircrew losses 187, 191
  American 190–1, 242–3
  anti-aircraft defences 180–1
  area bombing 179–80, 182, 183–5
  Baedeker Raids 176–7, 185–6
  Blitz 6, 17, 38, 54–5, 156, 175–6, 180, 183, 199, 356
  bombing accuracy 178–9, 186–7, 187, 190
  Dam Busters raid 191
  daytime bombing 191
  Doolittle raid 242–3
  effects on civilian morale 180, 183–4, 186
  effects on industrial output 180, 184, 191
  incendiary bombs 180, 181, 185
  Malta, bombing of 68, 193–4, 195, 196–7, 200–1, 202, 203–4, 203–5, 205, 207, 208, 329
  moral issues 183, 192
  navigational aids 180–1, 184, 189–90
  night-time precision raids 178–9
  pathfinders 190
  Thousand Bomber Raids 187, 189
Boothby, Bob 9
Bore War *see* Phoney War
Borneo 26, 93
Bose, Subhas Chandra 105
Brachi, David 127–8

Bracken, Brendan 47, 49–50, 60, 285, 338
Bradshaw, Sam 339
Bremen 127, 187
Brest 76–7, 78, 79, 81, 115
Brindisi 196
Bristol 55, 129
British Army 12, 288–300
  armoured divisions/brigades 296
  Army Film and Photographic Unit 49
  battlefield tactics 295–6
  British Expeditionary Force 299
  Burma 147
  cavalry ethic 295
  conscription 291–2
  Dunkirk 63, 67, 293, 294, 321, 332
  expansion of 291–3, 299
  failures of leadership 297–9
  fighting strength 288
  infantry 296
  insularity and complacency 290–1, 297, 299
  Malaya 93, 94, 95
  officers 289–91, 297
  overseas postings 290
  peacetime 290, 299
  pre-war image 288–91, 292
  public attitudes towards 299
  quality of weapons and armour 293–5
  regimental life 289–90, 291
  Royal Artillery 288
  Singapore 92–106
  spit-and-polish culture 288, 289, 292
  squaddies 288, 292
  Tank Corps 288
  training 288, 289, 298
  Western Desert campaign (Desert War) *see* Eighth Army
British Movietone News 188
Brooke, General Sir Alan 102, 103, 110, 117–18, 145–6, *146*, 155, 220, 248, 249, 258, 262, 269, 271, 272, 280, 282, 284–6, 297, 301, 303, 304–5, 306–7, *306*, 309, 310, 312, 314, 317, 324, 328, 332, 341, 347, 363, *363*
  Chief of the Imperial General Staff 26, 145, 146, 305
  relationship with Churchill 145–6, 305, 341
Brooke-Popham, Air Chief Marshal Sir Robert 93–4

Browning, Major-General Frederick 'Boy' 143
Bruneval Raid 141–4, 145, 325
Buchan, John 44
Buffalo fighter 64, 147
bureaucracy, wartime 2–3
Burges, Flight Lieutenant George 197
Burma 66, 89, 93, 108, 114, 124, 125, 147–8, 236, 336
  Japanese advance on 114, 124, 147–8, 153
Burma Road 148
Burma–Siam railway 105
Butt, David 178, 179

Cadogan, Sir Alexander 88, 114, 140, 144, 280, 300, 303, *306*, 308, 309, 310, 312, 315, 320
Cairo 211, 220–1, 253, 261, 263, 264–5, 303–4, 323–4
'Cairo purge' 305, *306*
Cambodia 63
Campbell, Flying Officer Kenneth 77
Campbell, HMS 85
Campbeltown, HMS 325
Canada 36
Canadian troops 325–6, 328
Canterbury 176, 185
Casablanca 346, 348, *349*, 351
Casablanca Conference 362–4, *363*
Casey, Richard 303
cataclysmic collapse, possibility of 236, 357–8
cavalry ethic 295
censorship 47–8, 132
Ceylon (Sri Lanka) 114, 149, 238, 242
Chadwick, Roy 182
Chamberlain, Neville 7, 8, 9, 10, 12, 49, 59
Chang, Robert 110
Channel Dash 79–91, 92, 114, 115, 117, 118
Channel Islands 311
Channon, Henry 'Chips' 57, 71, 88–9, 117, 272, 274, 277
Chelmno 366
Chequers 19–20, 355
Cherbourg 279, 281, 311
Chief of Staffs Committee 145
Child, Pat 175–6
China 66, 96, 124, 147–8
Christmas, wartime 39, 355–6
Churchill, Clementine 74, 301, 309, 355

Churchill, Mary 140–1
Churchill, Randolph 10, 34, 355
Churchill, Winston *11*, *35*, *306*, *363*
  and the Abdication Crisis 12, 58
  ambivalent relationship with the army 287
  American ancestry 33–4
  and America's entry into the war 21–3
  anti-appeasement 9, 12, 59
  and the Arctic convoys 160, 167–8, 173
  and the Asia-Pacific war 242, 243
  and the Battle of the Atlantic 76, 128, 132, 138, 140
  bombing campaigns, enthusiasm for 178–9, 181, 183, 184
  'Cairo purge' 305, *306*
  Casablanca Conference 362–4, *363*
  and the Channel Dash 88, 90–1, 92, 115, 117
  controversial figure 17–18
  defeats censure motions 18, 70–3, *73*, 123, 273–8, 286
  and the defence of Malta 206, 208, 210
  drinking habits 19, 31
  and El Alamein 338, 341, 343, 345, 369
  heart problems 35–6, 37
  on the Holocaust 367
  impatient nature 332, 335
  imperialist 32
  and Indian independence 12, 32, 58, 149–50, 153–4
  leadership style 13–14, 32, 145, 369
  loses 1945 election 369
  low moods 138, 140–1, 154, 286, 336
  meetings with Roosevelt 27–33, 248–9, 257–9, *258*, 268, 269–70
  military career 287
  Minister of Defence 11–12, 111, 114, 115, 123, 273
  and the North African campaign 69–70, 216–17, 220, 221, 223, 224, 227–8, 252–3, 258–9, 267, 271–2, 280, 332
  and Operation Sledgehammer 279–80
  and Operation Torch 332, 348
  oratory 15, 34, 70–1, 72–3, 112–14, 230–2, 276–7, 353–4, 365
  parliamentary career 58
  and planned invasion of France

269, 279–80, 281, 282
political criticisms of 18, 57, 60,
    70–2, 88–90, 114–18, 231, 271,
    272–8, 286
popular criticisms of 88, 90, 111–12,
    230, 231–2, 278
and post-war Britain, failure to
    address 18, 359–60, 369
Prime Minister and Conservative
    Party leader 9–11, 59, 111, 114
racism 17, 64
reflects on the series of failures 356
relationship with the Conservative
    Party 57–8, 59–60
relationship with Roosevelt 30–3,
    259, 278, 282, 364
and Singapore 64–6, 100, 103, 109,
    111, 114–15, 118, 140
and Sir Stafford Cripps 120–1,
    122–3, 334–5, 367
Stalin-Churchill meeting 308–20,
    316
and support for the Soviet Union
    157–9, 173, 183, 190, 308–20
and Tobruk 258–9, 271, 277
on U-boats 76
visits Egypt 285–6, 300–8, 323–4
Washington conference 27–36, 125
'wilderness years' 58
Churchill tanks 326–7
Churchill War Rooms 118
Ciliax, Vice Admiral 79, 81, 82, 85
cinema 2, 3, 42
    audience surveys 52
    documentary film movement 48–9
    drama documentaries 50–1
    feature films 51
    Ministry of Information Films
        Division 48, 49–51
    wartime attendances 50
civilian casualties, British 38, 54
civilian morale 43
    characteristics of 54
    effect of El Alamein victory on 345
    effects of bombing on 4, 16, 180,
        183–4, 186
    information management and 43–7
    low 17, 155, 262–3, 278–9, 334, 356–7
    maintenance, importance of 54
    measuring 54
    Wartime Social Survey 51
Clark, Kenneth 49
Clark, General Mark 270, 347
Clark Kerr, Sir Archibald 310

Cleopatra, HMS 202
Clinton, Bill 31
Clipper flying boat 249, 272
clothes
    rationing 43
    Utility clothing 43
coal shortages 138–9
Coalition Government, formation of
    10, 12, 120
cod liver oil 41
codebreaking 69, 132–7, 156–7, 172,
    244, 245
    see also Bletchley Park; Ultra
        decrypts
Cologne 181, 184–5, 187, 188
Colombo 149, 238, 239
Colville, Jock 113–14
Combined Chiefs of Staff 28
Combined Operations 142, 146, 243,
    325, 326, 327
Combined Raw Materials Board 28
Communist Party 229
Coningham, Air Marshal 303
conscription 291–2
convoy system 128–9
    see also Arctic convoys; merchant
        convoys
Cooper, Alfred Duff 47
Coral Sea 244–5
Corbett, Lieutenant-General Thomas
    303, 304
Cornwall, HMS 239
Corregidor 107
cost of living, rise in 43
Courage brewery 46
Coventry 55, 183, 199, 204
Crete 140, 202, 207, 329
Crimea 234, 235
Cripps, Sir Stafford 118–23, 122, 144,
    152, 155, 157, 158, 334–5
    austere lifestyle 119, 124
    Churchill and 120–1, 122–3, 334–5,
        367
    and the 'Crippery' 121, 150
    and Indian independence 149,
        150–3
    Leader of the House 123–4
    Minister of Aircraft Production
        335, 367
    War Cabinet member 123, 335
Crown Film Unit 49
Crusader tanks 222, 274, 294
Cunningham, General Alan 216, 217,
    306

Curtin, John 64, 66
Cyprus 284
Cyrenaica 68, 140, 216, 218, 219

Daily Express 44, 214, 229, 298
Daily Mail 44, 87, 88, 92, 121
Daily Mirror 44, 73, 88, 120, 121, 297
Daily Telegraph 121
Dam Busters raid 191
Damascus 264
Darlan, Admiral François 348, 350,
    352, 355
Darwin 236
Dauntless bomber 246, 247
Davidson, Major-General Francis 252
death penalty
    for 'desertion'/'cowardice' 260
    for espionage 44
defeatism 16, 263, 278–9, 356–7
    see also civilian morale
Denmark 177
    German occupation of 15
Denmark Strait 77
Department of Information 44
Desert Air Force 69, 217, 223, 254, 265
Desert War see Western Desert
    campaign
Devastator bomber 246
Diego Suarez 243, 244
Dieppe Raid 325–7, 328, 328
Dig for Victory 50
Dill, Field Marshal Sir John 26, 37
dockyards 129–30
domestic labour 6
Dönitz, Admiral Karl 136, 199
Doolittle, Lieutenant Colonel James 242
Dorsetshire, HMS 78, 239
double summer time 42
Dover Straits see Channel Dash
Drake, Sir Francis 88
Driberg, Tom 272
Duke of York, HMS 26–7, 169
Dunkirk 63, 67, 293, 294, 321, 332
Dutch East Indies see Indonesia; Java;
    Sumatra

Eagle, HMS 206, 208, 209
East India Company 61
Eastern Front 208, 220, 232, 318
    see also Soviet Union
Eclipse, HMS 166
Eden, Anthony 25, 57, 60, 67, 111, 123,
    144, 158, 249, 271, 285, 286, 300–1,
    320, 335

Edinburgh, HMS 168
Edward VIII, King 12, 58
Egypt 68, 194, 207, 209, 211, 215, 236,
    264–5, 344
    Churchill visits 285–6, 300–8,
        323–4
    see also Western Desert campaign
        (Desert War)
Eighth Army 199, 211, 216, 222, 223,
    224
    Battle of Gazala 225–8, 296, 304, 330
    command of 216, 217, 262, 304–5,
        307, 321
    composition of 211, 339–40
    desertions 266
    effect of Montgomery's command
        on 323, 324, 337
    fighting strength 211, 323, 337
    First Battle of El Alamein 262–3,
        265, 273, 280, 284, 296
    losses 266–7
    low morale 259–60, 263, 266, 267,
        285, 303, 307, 321, 322, 324, 356
    military reforms 296
    reorganisation of 331–2
    in retreat 199, 201, 219, 250, 251, 262,
        263
    Second Battle of El Alamein 17, 322,
        338, 339–45, 369
    and Tobruk 68, 69–70, 216–18, 251,
        253–7, 349, 350
    Tunisian campaign 355, 364–6
    war materiel 252, 323
Eisenhower, General Dwight D. 270,
    332, 347–8
El Adem 253
El Agheila 218, 351
El Alamein
    First Battle of 262–3, 265, 273, 280,
        284, 296
    Second Battle of 17, 322, 338, 339–
        45, 369
electricity consumption 42
Elizabeth, Queen (The Queen
    Mother) 46
Emergency Powers Act 1
Enigma 80, 133–5, 198
Enterprise, USS 245, 246
Erskine-Hill, Alexander 57
Esmonde, Lieutenant Commander
    Eugene 78, 83, 84, 87
espionage 44
Essen 184, 187
evacuees, child 7, 175, 176

Exeter 175–6, 185
extermination camps 366

fascism 18, 120
Final Solution to the Jewish Question
    see Holocaust
First World War 44, 59, 61, 93, 287–8, 361
Fleming, Ian 134
Focke-Wulf 190 84, 327
food
    dried egg powder 40
    growing your own 4
    imports 129 30, 136, 137–8
    National Loaf 42
    orange juice, cheap/free 41
    prices 42–3
    rationing 1, 3–4, 40–2, 55–6, 130, 209
    Spam 40
France
    Allied bombing raids on 184, 191
    Allied invasion proposals 248,
        269–70, 279–80, 281, 282, 283,
        311, 312
    Dieppe Raid 325–7, 328, 328
    Dunkirk 63, 67, 293, 294, 321, 332
    fall of 14, 63
    Free Zone 347, 350
    navy 351–2
    St Nazaire Raid 325
    Vichy France 215, 243, 244, 332,
        346–7, 348, 350
Fraser, Peter 232
Free French 211, 215, 224, 226, 303,
    352, 355
French Indo-China see Cambodia;
    Laos; Vietnam
French North-West Africa 269, 270,
    279, 281, 282
    see also Operation Torch
Freya radar 141
Frost, Major John 143–4
fuel rationing 138–9
Fulmar fighter 239
Furness, Major Stephen 275

Gallacher, Willie 116–17
Gandhi, Mahatma 107, 151, 152, 152
gas masks 46, 90
Gaulle, General de 303, 347, 352, 355
Gazala 211, 219, 220, 221, 223, 250
'Gazala Gallop' 262, 263
Gee navigational aid 181, 184, 189
George VI, King 10, 33, 52, 117, 204,
    249

Germany
    Allied bombing of 177–85, 186–9,
        190–1, 230–1, 311, 320
    armed forces see Wehrmacht
    declares war on United States 24–5,
        39
    Fifth Panzer Army 364
    invasion of Soviet Union 17, 20,
        38–9, 69, 112, 154–5, 156, 200,
        230, 232, 233–5, 310–11, 317,
        336, 361–2
    Kriegsmarine 75–6, 79, 134
    rearmament 58
    rise of the Nazi Party 58, 62
    see also Afrika Korps; Battle of
        the Atlantic; Middle East
        theatre of war; North African
        campaign
Gibraltar 194, 209, 346
Gilliat, Sidney 51
Giraud, General Henri 347, 348, 352
Gladiator biplane fighter 195, 197
Glasgow 129
Glorious, HMS 8
Gloucester, Duke of 274
Gneisenau (German battlecruiser)
    76–7, 79, 85, 86, 87, 91
Godfrey, Admiral John 128
Goebbels, Joseph 132
Göring, Herman 180, 361
Gott, Lieutenant-General William
    222, 227, 303, 304, 305–6
Government Code and Cypher
    School see Bletchley Park
Gozo 193
Grant tanks 222–3, 226, 252, 294, 322
Greece 68, 140, 209
Greenfield, George 339
Greenwood, Arthur 12, 123
Grigg, Sir James 144, 150
Guadalcanal 353, 357

H$_2$S navigational aid 189
Halifax, Lord 9–10, 12, 59, 232
Halifax bomber 85, 182
Hamburg 127, 187, 191
Hamilton, Rear Admiral 169, 170
Hampden bomber 177
Handley Page 182
Harriman, Averell 20, 21, 159, 167, 303,
    309, 310, 312, 313, 358
Harris, Air Marshal Arthur 182–3,
    184, 187, 188–9, 188, 190
Harris, Sir Percy 116

Harrison, Tom 52
Harvey, Oliver 114, 305, 309
Harwood, Admiral 303
Haw-Haw, Lord 132
Haydon, Brigadier C.W. 225, 226
Headlam, Cuthbert 74
Heath, Lieutenant-General Sir Lewis
    92
Hermes, HMS 239
HF/DF (High Frequency Direction
    Finding) 131
Hill, Commander Roger 210
Hinsley, Harry 134–5
Hirohito, Emperor 106
Hiryu (Japanese carrier) 247
Hitler, Adolf 8, 10, 12, 14, 59, 79, 87, 171
    and assault on Malta 199, 207, 260
    and the Baedeker Raids 185
    declares war on United States 24–5,
        39
    and El Alamein 343
    and invasion of Soviet Union 69,
        200, 230, 233–4, 235, 362
    and North African campaign 68,
        215, 257, 261
    response to Operation Torch 350
    Rommel and 257, 337
Hitler Youth 186, 293
hoarding household goods 1
Hodgson, Vere 186
Hoggart, Richard 300
Holocaust 366–7
home entertainment 6–7
Home Front, impact of war on 17, 43,
    44
    civilian casualties 38
    see also civilian morale
Home Guard 42, 56
'Homes Fit for Heroes' 361
Homma, General 106, 107
Hong Kong 26, 93, 140
Hood, HMS 77
Hopkins, Harry 30, 36, 248, 258, 272,
    278, 281
Hore-Belisha, Leslie 276
Hornet, USS 242, 245
Hornum 177
hotels, government commandeering
    of 3
household goods, scarcity of 7
Hull 55
Hungry Thirties 42
Hurricane fighter 15, 157, 195, 200,
    239

Hutton, Lieutenant-General Sir
    Thomas 147

I-Tanks 294
identity cards 2
income tax 55
Independent Labour Party 73, 272
India
    Bengal famine 154
    British Raj 61, 149, 154
    defence of 66, 125, 147, 148, 149, 154,
        155, 358
    independence 12, 32, 58, 108,
        149–54
    Indian Congress Party 150, 151,
        153, 154
    Indian National Army 105, 107, 154
    Japanese threat to 236, 238
    Muslim League 151, 153
    Quit India campaign 108, 154
India Act 1935 12, 58
Indian Ocean 24, 148–9, 236, 238, 242,
    244
Indian troops
    defence of Singapore 64, 95, 101,
        104, 105
    Malay campaign 94, 95
    North African campaign 68, 211,
        253, 339
Indonesia 63
information management *see*
    Ministry of Information
Inoue, Vice Admiral Shigeyoshi 244
invasion threat 38, 39, 55, 63, 69, 90,
    358
Iraq 215, 236, 264, 305, 307
Ireland 28, 93
Ironside, General Edmund 8
Ismay, Major-General Sir Hastings 13,
    20, 64, 249, 258, 272
Italy
    Allied invasion of 364
    attacks on Malta 68, 195, 196, 208,
        260
    declaration of war 25, 67, 193, 195
    Greek campaign 68
    North African campaign 68, 215,
        217, 218, 251, 253, 257, 331, 340,
        342, 343, 345, 350
    Regia Aeronautica 195, 196, 199
    Regia Marina 67–8, 196, 202

Jacob, Colonel Sir Ian 303, 305, 309,
    312, 313, 317, 365

Japan
  Allied declaration of war 22
  Asia-Pacific war 20, 24, 26, 56, 57,
    63, 64, 65, 74, 92–110, 112–13,
    114, 124, 125, 147–8, 153, 155,
    236–7, 238–45, 238–48, 353, 357
  and Burma 114, 124, 147–8, 153
  First World War 61
  French Indo-China campaign 63
  jungle warfare 94–5
  Malay campaign 60, 64, 94–6, 104,
    109
  naval power 24, 25, 61, 243, 357
  opts out of League of Nations 62
  Pearl Harbor attack 21–2, 28, 39, 60,
    196, 245
  and the Philippines 106–7
  and Singapore 65, 74, 92–106
  US bombing of 242–3
Java 63, 114, 124, 125
Jellicoe, Admiral 61
Jennings, Humphrey 50–1, 52
Jerusalem 264
Jinnah, Muhammad Ali 153
Joint Production Committees 144–5
journalism 44
  press censorship 47–8
  see also specific publications
jungle warfare 94–5, 148

Kaga (Japanese carrier) 246
Kammhuber Line 180
Kasserine Pass 365
Kennedy, Major-General Sir John 252,
  353, 357–8
Kesselring, Field Marshal Albert
  199–200, 203, 207, 208
Keyes, Admiral Sir Roger 274
Kiel 127
Kiev 69
King, Admiral Ernest 270, 279, 281,
  282, 363
King George V, HMS 78, 164
Kirkenes 163, 166
Kitchener, Lord 44
Klopper, Major-General Hendrik 254,
  255, 256
Knickebein 6
Kriegsmarine 75–6, 79, 134
Kuala Lumpur 95

Labour Party 9, 359, 361
Lancaster bomber 182
Lance, HMS 199

Laos 63
Last, Nella 54
Launder, Frank 51
Laval, Pierre 243–4
leaflet campaigns 45–6, 48, 184
League of Nations 62
Lebanon 215
Ledbury, HMS 210
Leningrad 12, 156, 317
Lexington, USS 244
Liberal Party 58
Liberator bomber 301, 309, 319, 334
Libya 25, 68, 89, 201, 202, 207, 211, 216
  Cyrenaica 68, 140, 216, 218, 219
  see also Western Desert campaign
    (Desert War)
Limitation of Supplies Order 7
Lindemann, Frederick (Lord
  Cherwell) 183–4
Littorio (Italian battleship) 202
Lively, HMS 199
Liverpool 55, 129, 136
Lloyd, Air Vice Marshal Hugh Pughe
  197, 207, 329
Lloyd George, David 67
Loch Ewe 160
London
  Blitz 38, 55, 183, 199
  docks 129
  looting 16
Low, David 297
Lübeck 185, 186, 189
Luftwaffe 48, 133–4
  attacks on Arctic convoys 156, 165,
    167, 168, 169, 171–2, 280, 333
  attacks on Malta 196, 197, 198,
    200–1, 202–3, 208, 329
  Battle of Britain 15, 17, 32, 63, 178,
    199, 329
  and the Channel Dash 79, 81, 84, 86
  North African campaign 255, 261,
    265, 337, 351, 352
  see also Blitz
Lumsden, Lieutenant-General
  Herbert 341
Lütjens, Admiral 77, 78
Lützow (German cruiser) 163, 169, 171
Luxembourg 15
Lyttleton, Oliver 123

MacArthur, General Douglas 107
MacDonald, Ramsay 120
Macmillan, Harold 9, 291, 363
Macmillan, Lord Hugh Pattison 46

Madagascar 243–4
Madge, Charles 52
Mafeking 286
Mainwaring, General Hugh 323
Maisky, Ivan 117
Make Do and Mend 50
Malaya 60, 61, 62–4, 66, 93, 94, 95, 140
   see also Singapore
Maldon by-election 272–3
Malta 193–210, 260, 261
   Axis assault on 68, 70, 193–4, 195,
      196–8, 200–1, 202–5, 207, 208,
      218–19, 260, 329
   blockade of 208–9
   civilian morale 201
   George Cross 204–5
   Royal Navy base 194, 198
   strategic value of 194, 196–7, 204,
      216, 329
   supply shortages 197–8, 202, 203,
      209
Manchester bomber 85, 182
Manchester Guardian 88, 261, 298
Mandalay 148
Manhattan Project 268
Manxman, HMS 80
Mareth Line 365
Margesson, David 144
Marrakesh 364
Marshall, General George 27, 29, 33,
      37, 248, 259, 269, 279, 281, 282,
      363, 367
Martin, Sergeant Albert 253
Martin, John 20
mass media war 45
Mass Observation (MO) 39–40, 41,
      52–3, 90, 111–12, 121, 124, 153, 176,
      177, 278–9, 349
   and the Beveridge Report 360–1
   diarists 2–3, 53, 54, 90, 122, 132, 139,
      143, 155, 229, 231–2, 261–2, 345,
      356–7, 367
   studies of working-class life 52–3
Masters, John 290
Matilda tanks 274, 294
Maxton, James 73
Mediterranean theatre of war 282,
      283, 364
mental health, civilian 5
   see also civilian morale
merchant convoys 75, 76, 77, 115,
      128–9, 131–2, 136, 137, 198–9, 202,
      209–10
see also Arctic convoys; Battle of the

   Atlantic
Mersa Matruh 211, 262, 263
Messerschmitt 109 fighter 84, 197, 200
Messina 196
Middle East theatre of war 215, 237,
      263–4, 284, 305
   see also Iraq; Lebanon; Palestine;
      Persia (Iran); Syria; Western
      Desert campaign (Desert War)
Midway 245–8, 357
milk allowance 40
Ministry of Information 44, 45–54,
      124, 132, 297
   Films Division 48, 49–51
   Home Intelligence Unit 51–2, 53–4,
      89, 232
   initial hectoring style 47
   Press and Censorship section 47–8
Minsk 69
Molotov, Vyacheslav 310, 315, 318–19
Montgomery, General Bernard 289,
      307, 321–3, 322, 337–8, 355, 365,
      369
   Battle of Alam Halfa 328–31
   Eighth Army reorganisation 331–2
   El Alamein 17, 322, 338, 339–45, 369
Moorehead, Alan 214, 218, 219, 298
morale
   civilian see civilian morale
   Eighth Army 259–60, 263, 266, 267,
      285, 303, 307, 321, 322, 324, 337,
      344, 356
Morocco 347, 351
Morrison, Herbert 361
Morshead, General 303
Moscow 112, 156, 232, 234
Mountbatten, Lord 142, 143, 145,
      146–7, 243, 325, 326
Murmansk 161, 163, 164, 166
Murrow, Ed 15
Muslim League 151, 153
Mussolini, Benito 25, 67, 193, 215, 260,
      365

Nagumo, Vice Admiral 236, 239,
      245–6, 247
Nanking massacre 102, 105
Naples 196
Napoleon Bonaparte 319
national diet 41, 42
   see also food rationing
National Gallery 49
National Health Service 360
National Loaf 42

national myth-making 15–16
Nehru, Jawaharlal 151–2
Neptunia (Italian troop carrier) 198
Netherlands, German occupation of
 10, 15, 63
New Guinea 105, 108, 236, 244
New Zealand 62
New Zealand troops 104, 211, 217, 218,
 266, 296, 339, 341, 342, 343
News Chronicle 229
Nicolson, Harold 71, 72, 74, 114, 117,
 277
Nimitz, Admiral Chester 244, 245
Noble, Admiral Sir Percy 76
Norden bombsight 190–1
Norfolk, HMS 78
Norrie, Lieutenant-General William
 222, 227
North African campaign 28, 67–70,
 194
  Egypt and Libya *see* Western
   Desert campaign
  Operation Torch 282, 311–12, 319,
   332–3, 336, 346–9
  Tunisian campaign 350, 351, 352,
   353, 355
Northcliffe, Lord 44
Northern Ireland 28
Norway 280, 352
  German occupation of 8, 15, 163
Norwich 176, 177, 185
Nuremberg 181

Oboe navigational aid 189
Observer 44, 261
Oceania (Italian troop carrier) 198
O'Connor, General Richard 68
Odessa 69
Ohio (American tanker) 210
old age pensions 58
Olivier, Laurence 51
Operation Barbarossa 17, 20, 38–9, 69,
 156, 200, 230, 232, 233–5, 310–11,
 317, 336, 361–2
Operation Battleaxe 68–9
Operation Bolero 269, 270
Operation Crusader 69–70, 216–18
Operation Sledgehammer 279, 281
Operation Torch 282, 311–12, 319,
 332–3, 336, 346–52
  Anglo-American operation 346, 348
  political planning 347
  political ramifications 351–2
Oran 346, 348, 351

Orwell, George 124
Oudna 351

Pacific theatre *see* Asia-Pacific war
Pacific War Council 270
Pahlavi, Mohammad Reza (Shah of
 Iran) 215, 309
Pakistan 150, 287
Palermo 196
Palestine 236, 264, 284, 305
Panter-Downes, Mollie 18, 89, 150,
 278, 345, 356
Panzerarmee Afrika *see* Afrika Korps
paratroopers 142–3, 271
Park, Air Vice Marshal 328–9
Paulus, General Friedrich von 234,
 235, 362
Paulus Potter (Dutch merchant ship)
 172
Peace Pledge Union 59
Pearl Harbor 21–2, 28, 39, 60, 196, 245
Peirse, Air Marshal Sir Richard 181
Penang 94
Penelope, HMS 199
'People's War' 16, 17, 43
Percival, Lieutenant-General Arthur
 92, 93, 96, 97–8, 100, 101, 102, 103,
 104, 106, 109
Persia (Iran) 159, 215, 216, 236, 305, 309
Persian Gulf 215, 358
Persian oilfields 159, 215, 284, 305,
 307, 358
Pétain, Marshal 347, 348
petrol rationing 2, 42
Philippines 106–7, 125
Phillips, Admiral Tom 24, 72
Phoney War 8, 10, 53, 332, 356
photo-reconnaissance 76, 77, 79, 127,
 141–2, 195, 196, 198–9, 207
Picture Post 298
pig clubs 4
Pim, Captain 118
Pinewood Studios 49
Pizey, Captain 85
Plymouth 55
Poland
  codebreakers 133
  extermination camps 366
  German occupation of 14
Port Moresby 236, 244, 245
Portal, Air Chief Marshal Sir Charles
 26, 179, 180, 183, *363*
Portsmouth 55
Post Office, GPO Film Unit 49

post-war Britain 18, 359–61, 369
poster campaigns 2, 46, 48, 52
Pound, Admiral Sir Dudley 14, 23–4,
    25–6, 128, 145, 170, 203, 242, 278,
    363
Powell, Michael 297
Pownall, General Henry 299–300
press censorship 47–8
Pressburger, Emeric 297
Priestley, J.B. 121
Prince of Wales, HMS 24, 26, 60, 64,
    72, 88
Prinz Eugen (German cruiser) 77, 79,
    86, 91, 163
propaganda 44
    see also Ministry of Information
pubs 2, 6

Qattara Depression 262–3
Queen Elizabeth, HMS 70

racism 17, 63, 64, 93–4, 96, 97, 357
radar 82, 131, 141–2, 180, 189
radio censorship 48
Raeder, Admiral 79, 163, 164, 169–70,
    171
Raffles, Sir Stamford 61
Ramsay, Admiral 80, 82, 83, 85
Ramsden, General 251, 303
Rangoon 147
Ratcliffe, Christina 196
rationing
    clothes 43
    domestic fuel 138–9
    food 1, 3–4, 40–2, 55–6, 130, 209
    government restrictions,
        acceptance of 42
    petrol 2, 42
    queuing *41*, 42
    ration books 4
Reagan, Ronald 31
Reith, Lord 46–7
Repulse, HMS 24, 60, 64, 72, 88
revisionist interpretation of events 16
Ritchie, Lieutenant-General Neil 217,
    222, 223–4, 225–6, 227, *227*, 250,
    253, 262, 263, 271, 304
road accidents 5, 42
Rodney, HMS 78
Rommel, Field Marshal Erwin 68–9,
    70, 75, 154–5, 196–7, 199, 201, 204,
    207, 208, 210, 215, 216, 219, 221,
    222, 223, 224, 225, 226, 235–6, 251,
    253, 259, 261, 264, 324, 337

Battle of Alam Halfa 329–31
Battle of Gazala 225–8, 296, 304, 330
First Battle of El Alamein 262–3,
    265, 273, 280, 284, 296
'Gazala Gallop' 262, 263
health problems 330, 340, 365
mastery of mobile warfare 221
myth of invincibility 221
popular admiration of 221, 299, 300
Second Battle of El Alamein 17, 322,
    338, 339–45, 340–4, 369
and Tobruk 217–18, 255–7
Tunisian campaign 364–5
see also Afrika Korps
Roosevelt, Eleanor 30, 33
Roosevelt, Franklin D. 13, 20, 24, 107,
    124–5, 154, 158, 167, 173, 206, 242,
    281–3, 308, 338, 353
address to the American people
    333–4
and America's entry into the war
    21, 23
Casablanca Conference 362–4, *363*
and Indian independence 149, 150
meetings with Churchill 27–33,
    248–9, 257–9, *258*, 268, 269–70,
    362–4
and Operation Torch 282, 346, 348
and Pearl Harbor attack 21
reformist politics 32
relationship with Churchill 30–3,
    259, 278, 282, 364
relationship with Stalin 33
Washington conference 27–36, 125
Rorke's Drift 286
Rostock 186, 189
Rotterdam 183
Rouen 191
Royal Air Force (RAF) 12, 292
    Asia-Pacific war 60, 63–4, 101, 147,
        239
    Battle of the Atlantic 76–7
    Battle of Britain 15, 17, 32, 63, 178,
        199, 329
    Bomber Command 79, 81, 85–6, 141,
        178, 179, 180, 181, 182, 184, 186,
        187, 189, 320, 364
    and the Channel Dash 84–6, 87
    Coastal Command 81, 82, 85, 187
    defence of Malta 194, 195, 197,
        200–1, 206–7, 208, 209
    Desert Air Force 69, 217, 223, 254,
        265
    Dieppe Raid 327

Fighter Command 15, 82, 85
North African campaign 265, 330, 337
see also bombing campaigns
Royal Navy 12, 292
Arctic convoy escorts 164, 165, 166, 168, 172–3
Asia-Pacific war 148–9, 238, 239
Battle of the Atlantic 32, 76, 77–8, 81, 136
Battle of Calabria 68
and the Channel Dash 79–91
defence of Malta 194, 199, 203, 204, 210
Eastern Fleet 238, 239, 242
Fleet Air Arm 78, 80, 83, 196, 239
North African theatre 68, 264
Operation Torch 346
St Nazaire Raid 325
Singapore naval base 62, 63, 64
sinking of the *Bismarck* 77–8
Ruhr 8, 181
Ruhr dam 183

Saigon (Ho Chi Minh City) 24
St Nazaire Raid 325
Salisbury, Lord 8
Sandhurst 289
Savoia-Marchetti bomber 195
Sawyers, Frank 21
Scapa Flow 77, 80
Scharnhorst (German battlecruiser) 76, 79, 84, 85, 86, 87, 91, 163
Sealion, HMS 80, 81–2
Sebastopol 234
second front, demand for 229–30, 232, 248, 311, 328
Soviet support for 157–8, 312, 314, 317–18, 346
Secret Intelligence Service 133
Sherman tanks 259, 322, 337
Shoho (Japanese carrier) 244
Shokaku (Japanese carrier) 244
Short, William 166–7
Short Brothers 182
Siam (Thailand) 20, 94
Siberia 233
Sicily 194, 208, 283, 327–8, 364
Allied invasion of 364
Sidi Barrani 211
Sidi Rezegh 253, 255
Sinclair, Sir Archibald 183
Singapore 26, 60–2, 70, 74, 194
British naval base 62, 63, 64

civil administration 96
defensive weaknesses 64–6, 97, 109
fall of 89, 92–106, 108, 114–15, 118, 140, 259, 298
Singapore strategy 61, 64–5, 109
social divisions 63
Singleton, Justice 88, 186
Slim, General Sir William 148
Smolensk 69
Smuts, Jan 304, 306–7, *306*
Socialist League 120
Solomon Islands 244, 353
Somerville, Admiral Sir James 238
Soryu (Japanese carrier) 246–7
South African troops 225, 253, 254, 256, 339
Soviet Union
Allied supplies to *see* Arctic convoys
Anglo-Soviet Friendship Weeks 55
German invasion of 17, 20, 38–9, 69, 112, 154–5, 156, 200, 230, 232, 233–5, 310–11, 317, 336, 361–2
impact of war on 368
Red Army 156, 200, 232, 233, 234–5, 312, 353, 367, 368
SS war crimes in 157, 235
urges opening a second front 157–8, 312, 314, 317–18, 346
war industries 232–3
Spaatz, Major General Carl 190
Spanish Armada 88
Special Operations Executive 352
'special relationship' 29
Speer, Albert 191
Spitfire 15, 82, 83–4, 85, 127, 206–7, 208, 327, 329
sports venues 3
Spruance, Rear Admiral Raymond 245, 247
Stalin, Joseph 13, 25, 120, 157, 158, 159, 173, 183, 190, 234, 236
relationship with Roosevelt 33
Stalin-Churchill meeting 308–20, *316*
'Uncle Joe' 230
Stalin, Svetlana 318
Stalingrad 17, 233, 235, 236, 336, 352, 353, 358
battle for 361–2
Stilwell, General Joseph 148
Stimson, Henry 269
Stirling bomber 85, 182
strikes and absenteeism 16

Stuart tanks 294
Stumme, General Georg 337, 340
Stummel, Captain 136
Suez Canal 70, 130, 215, 260, 263, 279,
     284, 330, 331, 344
Sumatra 63, 114, 124
Swithinbank, Isabel 119
Swordfish torpedo bomber 78, 80, 83,
     84, 87, 238, 239
Sylt 177
Syria 215, 236, 264, 284, 305

tanks 94–5, 222–3, 226, 259, 265, 274,
     287, 294, 322, 326–7, 337
   American 222, 259, 294
   anti-tank guns 223, 274, 293, 294,
        330, 337
   British 222, 294, 295
   German 293, 295, 364
Tanks for Russia Week 159
Taranto 196
Taylor, A.J.P. 16
Taylor, Stephen 54
Tedder, Air Marshal Arthur 205–6,
     303, 306, 309, 312, 317
Telecommunications Research
     Establishment 181
Thatcher, Margaret 31
Thoma, General von 343
Tiger tanks 364
The Times 10, 44, 67, 121
Tirpitz (German battleship) 78–9,
     80–1, 163, 164, 169, 170, 171, 172,
     242
Tobruk 211, 220, 330
   Operation Battleaxe 68–9
   Operation Crusader 69–70, 216–18
   retaken by Eighth Army 349, 350
   sieges of 69–70, 251, 253–7, 258–9,
        261, 271, 272, 277
Tojo, General 98
total war 38, 44, 45
Toulon 351
Tovey, Admiral 167
train travel 2
travel restrictions, civilian 2
Treblinka 366
Tribune 229, 298
Trincomalee 149, 238, 239
Trinidad, HMS 164, 165, 166
Tripoli 211, 265, 351, 365
Tunisian campaign 350, 351, 352, 353,
     355, 364–6

U-boats
   aircraft anti-U-boat patrols 183
   and the Arctic convoys 164, 168,
        169, 171, 172, 333
   and assault on Malta 199
   attacks on US shipping 137
   Battle of the Atlantic 32, 75, 76,
        127–39
   construction 127–8
   losses inflicted by 76, 132, 135, 136,
        137, 164, 199
   'the happy time' 137
   tracking 130–1, 135, 136
   wolfpacks 135, 136
Ukraine 55, 69, 156, 216
Ultra decrypts 134, 198, 208, 324, 333
unemployment benefits 58
United States
   Asia-Pacific war 106–7, 124–5,
        244–8
   Atlantic Charter 24, 112
   atomic bomb 268, 368
   Doolittle raid 242–3
   economic hegemony 368
   elections 334
   entry into the war 18, 21–3
   favours assault on occupied France
        33, 279, 281
   Germany's declaration of war on
        24–5, 39
   'special relationship' 29
   'Victory Program' 30
   war industries 30, 334
United States Armed Forces
   Operation Torch 282, 311–12, 319,
        332–3, 336, 346–9
   Philippines 108, 125
   Tunisian campaign 365
United States Army Air Forces 364
   bombing campaign 190–1
   Philippines 106–7
United States Navy
   Arctic convoy escorts 168
   Battle of the Coral Sea 244–5
   Battle of Midway 245–8
   Operation Torch 346
   Pacific Fleet 21, 22, 242
   Pearl Harbor 21–2, 28, 39, 60, 196,
        245
   Philippines 107
Upham, Captain Charles 296
Upholder, HMS 198, 203
Utility clothing 43
Utility furniture 43

Valentine tanks 222, 274, 294
Valiant, HMS 70
Valletta 193, 194, 196, 197, 201, 204, *205*
Vampire, HMAS 239
Versailles Treaty 58
Vian, Rear Admiral 202
Vichy French 215, 243, 244, 332, 346–7, 348, 350
Victorious, HMS 78, 164, 169, 170
Vietnam 63
Vildebeest biplane 64
Vitamin Welfare Scheme 41
Voroshilov, Marshal Klimenti 310, 315

wages, civilian 55
Wannsee Conference 366
War Cabinet 11, 12–13, 123, 144
    see also individual members
war industries 30, 55, 334
war memorials 59
War Planning Directorate proposal 334–5
Warburton, Adrian 195–6
Wardlaw-Milne, Sir John 71, 273–4
Warsaw 183
Warspite, HMS 238
Wartime Social Survey 51
Washington, USS 168, 169, 172
Washington conference 27–36, 125
Wasp, USS 168, 206, 208
Watt, Harry 50
Waugh, Evelyn 291
Wavell, Field Marshal Archibald 64, 66, 100, 102–3, 109–10, 125, 147, 155, 289, 299, 304, *306*, 309, 310, 312, 315, 317, 336
    Supreme Commander Asia-Pacific theatre 29–30
Waziristan (British merchant ship) 164
Webb, Beatrice 119
Wehrmacht
    organization 296
    re-equipping 294
    superiority of weapons and armour 293, 295
    see also Kriegsmarine; Luftwaffe
welfare state 58, 360–1
Wellington, Duke of 319

Wellington bomber 85, 177, 187, 201, 330
Welshman, HMS 80, 208–9
West Point 289
Western Approaches 76, 128, *129*
Western Desert campaign (Desert War) 211–28, 235–6, 250–67, 271–2, 321–4, 329–33, 336–45
    Battle of Alam Halfa 329–31
    Battle of Gazala 225–8, 296, 304, 330
    First Battle of El Alamein 262–3, 265, 273, 280, 284, 296, 304, 322
    map *213*
    Second Battle of El Alamein 17, 338, 339–45, 369
    specific hardships of 212
    terrain 212
    Tobruk 251, 253–7, 258–9, 261, 271, 272, 277
    warfare, features of 214
    see also Afrika Korps; Eighth Army
Whitley bomber 177
Wilson, Sir Charles 26, 35–6, 138
Wilson, General Maitland 307
Winant, John G. 20
Winterton, Lord 116
women
    war work 44, 55
    Women's Voluntary Service 55
Wood, Sir Kingsley 8, 123
Woolton, Lord 130
Woolwich Academy 289
Worcester, HMS 85, 87
Würzburg radar 141, 143, 180

X-Geraet 6

Yamaguchi, Rear Admiral 247
Yamamoto, Admiral 245
Yamashita, General 94, 98, 99, 102, 103, 105, 106
York 176, 185
Yorktown, USS 244, 245, 246, 247

Zero fighter 238, 239, 246
Zhukov, General 353
Zuckerman, Solly 180